P9-CQV-897

IMPERIAL HUBRIS

Also by Anonymous

Through Our Enemies' Eyes:
Osama bin Laden, Radical Islam, and the Future of America

IMPERIAL HUBRIS

Why the West Is Losing the War on Terror

ANONYMOUS

BRASSEY'S, INC.
WASHINGTON, D.C.

Library of Congress Cataloging-in-Publication Data

Imperial hubris : why the West is losing the war on terror / Anonymous.—1st ed.
    p. cm.
  Includes bibliographical references and index.
  ISBN 1-57488-849-8 (alk. paper)
  1. War on Terrorism, 2001– 2. Jihad. 3. Bin Laden, Osama, 1957– 4. Qaida (Organization) 5. Terrorism—Government policy—United States. 6. United States—Foreign relations—21st century. I. Brassey's (Firm)
  HV6432.I47   2004
  973.931—dc22   2004009951

Printed in the United States of America on acid-free paper that meets the American National Standards Institute Z39-48 Standard.

Brassey's, Inc.
22841 Quicksilver Drive
Dulles, Virginia 20166

First Edition

10 9 8 7 6 5 4

*For the Ladies of the Bay, Older, Smarter, and Still
Indispensable. America is in your debt, as am I.*

*For P.C.S. and for Lindsey, Amelia, and Aubrey, whom he
never met but would have loved beyond measure.*

*Again, for the Inchon-Chungjo duo and ranch
hands Beth and Bernice.*

*For the U.S. Marine Corps and America's clandestine service,
the sword and the shield of the Republic.*

*For Charlie, Harry, Dave, and Joe, and the unrivaled
examples they set of professionalism, integrity, and decency.*

*And for Jack, Jim, John, and the ambassador,
who most certainly do not.*

Contents

☪

Preface

☪

Duty is the sublimest word in our language. Do your duty in all things. You cannot do more. You should never do less.

Robert E. Lee, *Memoirs*.[1]

"Even by the standards of the terrorists involved," Robert Baer wrote in his valuable book, *See No Evil*, "the scale of assault [on 11 September 2001] was unimaginable. The point, though, is that we didn't even try to find out what was headed our way."[2] Mr. Baer's book is the engaging and often suspenseful story of an excellent field intelligence officer. It has the field operative's savvy and swagger, and the comprehensiveness of a world traveler's view. Still, Mr. Baer's above conclusion is incorrect. Not only was the scale of the 11 September attack imaginable, but Mr. Baer and other U.S. intelligence officers—often at the risk of their lives—had spent most of a decade gathering and analyzing the intelligence that, had it been used fully and honestly, would have allowed all U.S. leaders and, indeed, all Americans to know what sort of storm was approaching. Those officers knew a runaway train was coming at the United States, documented that fact, and then watched helplessly—or were banished for speaking out—as their senior leaders delayed action, downplayed intelligence, ignored repeated warnings, and generally behaved as what they so manifestly are, America's greatest generation—of moral cowards.

I am not, like Mr. Baer, a field intelligence officer. I have traveled some but am by training and temperament a career-long "headquarters' officer." I have been an analyst and have managed analytic and operational activities. For the past seventeen years, my career has focused exclusively on terrorism, Islamic insurgencies, militant Islam, and the

ix

affairs of South Asia—Afghanistan and Pakistan. Based on limited travel and Islamic-issues focus, I do not have Mr. Baer's credentials to speak in global terms. My training, career, experiences, and interests are narrow, but they are deep and fairly comprehensive on the issues for which I have been held responsible. For this on-the-job education and the fine career it yielded, I am indebted to the American taxpayer for footing the bill. I hope this book offers some profit on that investment.

This book, then, is written by one who does not know the world whole, or by one who knows in-depth such top-priority issues as North Korea, China, Russia, globalization, the European Union, world trade, or pandemic illnesses. I know even less about how the U.S. intelligence community deals with those important subjects. No, my knowledge is a very small wedge of a very large intelligence pie. But within that wedge, I have earned my keep and am able to speak with some authority and confidence about Osama bin Laden, al Qaeda, the dangers they pose and symbolize for the United States, and the manner in which they were handled by the intelligence community. The most comprehensive analysis of this danger would, naturally, involve a combination of materials, classified intelligence and unclassified writings and research. Needless to say, there is no classified information in what follows. This does not impede this book's analysis of the subject at hand, but it does illuminate a tragedy, because it proves that the genesis, dimensions, and threat of the bin Laden problem—shorthand for the broader U.S.–Muslim world confrontation—is knowable for anyone who takes the time to read and ponder a representative sample of relevant open-source literature. The conclusions a fair-minded individual would draw from this endeavor would, I believe, include the following:

- U.S. leaders refuse to accept the obvious: We are fighting a worldwide Islamic insurgency—not criminality or terrorism—and our policy and procedures have failed to make more than a modest dent in enemy forces.
- The military is now America's only tool and will remain so while current policies are in place. No public diplomacy, presidential praise for Islam, or politically correct debate masking the reality that many of the world's 1.3 billion Muslims hate us for actions not values, will get America out of this war.
- Bin Laden has been precise in telling America the reasons he is waging war on us. None of the reasons have anything to do with our freedom, liberty, and democracy, but have everything to do with U.S. policies and actions in the Muslim world.

- The war bin Laden is waging has everything to do with the tenets of the Islamic religion. He could not have his current—and increasing—level of success if Muslims did not believe their faith, brethren, resources, and lands to be under attack by the United States and, more generally, the West. Indeed, the United States, and its policies and actions, are bin Laden's only indispensable allies.
- Persian Gulf oil and the lack of serious U.S. alternative-energy development are at the core of the bin Laden issue. For cheap, easily accessible oil, Washington and the West have supported the Muslim tyrannies bin Laden and other Islamists seek to destroy. There can be no other reason for backing Saudi Arabia, a regime that, since its founding, has deliberately fostered an Islamic ideology, whose goals—unlike bin Laden's—can be met only by annihilating all non-Muslims.
- This war has the potential to last beyond our children's lifetimes and to be fought mostly on U.S. soil.

Given that these easy-to-reach conclusions can be drawn from materials found in the public library and on the Internet, Americans should wonder why their political, intelligence, military, and media leaders have not made them. The answer, I believe, lies in another point made by Robert Baer. "I knew enough about the way Washington worked to know that when it did not like some piece of information it did everything in its power to discredit the messenger," he wrote in *See No Evil*.[3] Having spent twenty-two years in the U.S. intelligence community, I can confidently say Mr. Baer is absolutely correct, but that the problem is far greater and more pervasive than he suggests. To obscure threats they do not want to act against; to preserve the false facade of "seamless" intelligence-community cooperation and disguise the incompetence and dereliction of some agencies; to avoid national security debates that would need to focus on such politically sensitive issues as religion, Israel, and Saudi perfidy, and—most of all—to avoid taking risks that could limit careers, post-government employment, or political aspirations; many U.S. intelligence community leaders ensured that most officers who recognized the extent of the threat bin Laden posed before 11 September 2001 were banished to language training, jobs entailing no bin Laden–related work, or excluded from meetings that might afford a chance to present intelligence honestly. After 11 September, these leaders likewise failed to systematically identify and employ the scores of experienced officers who would have brought applicable, in-depth knowledge to the war against bin Laden. As always, Ralph Peters caught exactly the impact my generation has had on the intelligence community when he wrote that, "one of the problems we have with our intelligence services, by the way, is that they are run by minor con men, mere bookies. . . . The motto of our vast intelligence establishment is 'Play it safe.' The mindset may protect careers but does little for our country."[4]

I write this book, then, with a pressing certainty that al Qaeda will attack the continental United States again, that its next strike will be more damaging than that of 11 September 2001, and could include use of weapons of mass destruction. After the next attack, misled Americans and their elected representatives will rightly demand the heads of intelligence-community leaders; that heads did not roll after 11 September is perhaps our most grievous post-attack error.

Using unclassified material, I intend in this book to show there is not now, and never has been, a shortage of knowledge about the nature and immediacy of the bin Laden threat, but only a lack of courage to tell the truth about it fully, openly, and with disregard for the career-related consequences of truth telling. Unfortunately, many in my generation of leaders find the task of doing their duty next to impossible. Duty rests upon the word posterity, Kent Gramm wrote in *Gettysburg: A Meditation on War and Values*, "because duty is always a requirement of the future, often without reward for the doer, and often entailing sacrifice. The sacrifice is made for those to come. Today, those to come are sacrificed for our pleasure."[5] The failure of many to perform their duty lies at the heart of why three thousand Americans perished on 11 September 2001.

Acknowledgments

☪

For assistance in preparing this book, I have four specific thank-yous to deliver. First, to my superb editor at Brassey's, Ms. Christina Davidson, who believed in this work from the start, and who labored mightily to delete from the text excess vitriol, as well as allusions that made perfect sense to me but would have been lost on normal people. Ms. Davidson is a stern, smart, but kind taskmaster, and the book is much better for her efforts. I greatly respect her talents and judgment and am proud to have her as a friend.

Next, I would like to salute, as I did in my first book, the officers of the Federal Broadcast Information Service (FBIS). Osama bin Laden is preeminently a man of words, and a man of his word. The men and women of FBIS labor seven days a week to make sure their country's leaders and citizens have immediate and reliable access to bin Laden's words. FBIS provides U.S. leaders with all of bin Laden's statements in their entirety, a service the commercial print and electronic media do not even attempt to deliver. Since 1996, bin Laden publicly has described each action he intended to take against America, and FBIS has supplied his words almost as they were spoken. This is a record in which FBIS officers should be proud. Though intelligence-community leaders have little regard for unclassified information—it cannot be important if it is not secret, after all—FBIS should take comfort in knowing that it provided as much warning about bin Laden's lethal intentions as any other community component. Sadly, FBIS officers, like others in the intelligence community, have found that you can lead jack-asses to water but you cannot make them drink.

Third, I want to thank a small group of officers who have worked against the bin Laden target since 1996. During these years, this group—mostly women—has provided the U.S. government with repeated opportunities to end the problem of bin Laden, and have done so without fail and at the cost of health, marriage, promotion, vacation, and many other of life's good things. These women remain today the core of America's effort to defeat bin Laden. In the spring of 2004, they were ridiculed by a senior intelligence-community officer in an officially sanctioned leak to a Washington journalist. The leak was printed by the journalist and caused unmerited pain to those women. The only word suitable for describing this leak—and those who approved it—is despicable. If I ever write again on the subject of bin Laden, it will be to defend these officers and make sure the words of their abusers are revealed for the lies they are. Most especially, it will be to tell all Americans about a singular group of their fellow citizens who made every effort to defend them, succeeded more times than not, and were betrayed by the moral cowardice of many of their leaders.

Finally, I want to thank Harry, Joe, Charlie, and Dave, who are mentioned in the dedication, for what they have taught me. These men are rare in their integrity, professionalism, fair-mindedness, compassion, and leadership. They are also painful reminders of how few like them today walk an American landscape that was once home to many such individuals. Like my father, these four men would have fit comfortably among those then-average Americans who simply did their duty by suffering at Valley Forge; saving the Union and ending slavery; fighting with Lee to the end at Appomattox; capturing Iwo Jima; and standing and fighting in Vietnam after most of my generation deserted them. I can offer no higher compliment. God bless each of you.

Introduction:
"Hubris Followed by Defeat"

☪

A confident and care free republic—the city on the hill, whose people have always believed that they are immune from history's harms—now has to confront not only an unending imperial destiny but also a remote possibility that seems to haunt the history of empire: hubris followed by defeat.

Michael Ignatieff, 2003.[1]

As I complete this book, U.S., British, and other coalition forces are trying to govern apparently ungovernable postwar states in Afghanistan and Iraq while simultaneously fighting growing Islamist insurgencies in each—a state of affairs our leaders call victory. In conducting these activities, and the conventional military campaigns preceding them, U.S. forces and policies are completing the radicalization of the Islamic world, something Osama bin Laden has been trying to do with substantial but incomplete success since the early 1990s. As a result, I think it fair to conclude that the United States of America remains bin Laden's only indispensable ally.

As usual, U.S. leaders are oblivious to this fact and to the dire threat America faces from bin Laden and have followed policies that are making the United States incrementally less secure. They refuse, as Nicholas Kristof brilliantly wrote in the *New York Times*, to learn the Trojan War's lesson, namely: "[to avoid] the intoxicating pride and overweening ignorance that sometimes clouds the minds of the strong . . . [and] the paramount need to listen to skeptical views."[2] Instead of facing reality, hubris-soaked U.S. leaders, elites, and media, locked behind an impenetrable wall of political correctness and moral cowardice, act as

naive and arrogant cheerleaders for the universal applicability of Western values and feckless overseas military operations omnipotently entitled Resolute Strike, Enduring Freedom, Winter Resolve, Carpathian
Strike, Infinite Justice, Valiant Strike, and Vigilant Guardian. While al
Qaeda-led, anti-U.S. hatred grows among Muslims, U.S. leaders boast
of being able to create democracy anywhere they choose, ignoring history and, as Stanley Kurtz reminded them in *Policy Review*, failing to

> regard Hobbes's warning that nothing is more disruptive to peace
> within a state of nature than vainglory. . . . If the world is a state of
> nature on a grand scale, than surely a foreign policy governed by a
> 'vainglorious' missionizing spirit rather than a calculation of national
> (and civilizational) interest promises dangerous war and strife.[3]

I believe the war in Afghanistan was necessary, but is being lost
because of our hubris. Those who failed to bring peace to Afghanistan
after 1992 are now repeating their failure by scripting government
affairs and constitution-making in Kabul to portray the birth of Western-
style democracy, religious tolerance, and women's rights—all anathema
to Afghan political and tribal culture and none of which has more than
a small, unarmed constituency. We are succeeding only in fooling ourselves. Certain the Afghans want to be like us, and abstaining from
effective military action against growing numbers of anti-U.S. insurgents, we have allowed the Taleban and al Qaeda to regroup and refit.
They are now waging an insurgency that gradually will increase in
intensity, lethality, and popular support, and ultimately force Washington to massively escalate its military presence or evacuate. In reality,
neither we nor our Karzai-led surrogates have built anything political
or economic that will long outlast the withdrawal of U.S. and NATO
forces. Due to our hubris, what we today identify and promote as a
nascent Afghan democracy is a self-made illusion on life-support; it is a
Western-imposed regime that will be swept away if America and its
allies stop propping it up with their bayonets.

On Iraq, I must candidly say that I abhor aggressive wars like the
one we waged there; it is out of character for America in terms of our
history, sense of morality, and basic decency. This is not to argue that
preemption is unneeded against immediate threats. Never in our history
was preemptive action more needed than in the past decade against the
lethal, imminent threat of bin Laden, al Qaeda, and their allies. But the
U.S. invasion of Iraq was not preemption; it was—like our war on Mex-

ico in 1846—an avaricious, premeditated, unprovoked war against a foe who posed no immediate threat but whose defeat did offer economic advantages. "Disclaimers issued by the White House notwithstanding, this war has not been thrust upon us. We have chosen it," Boston University's Andrew J. Bacevich wrote in the *Los Angeles Times*. "The United States no longer views force as something to be used as a last resort. There is a word for this. It's called militarism."[4]

My objective is not to argue the need or morality of the war against Iraq; it is too late for that. That die has been cast, in part because we saw Iraq through lenses tinted by hubris, not reality. My point is, rather, that in terms of America's national security interests—using the old-fashioned and too-much-ignored definition of national interests as matters of life and death—we simply chose the wrong time to wage the Iraq war. Our choice of timing, moreover, shows an abject, even willful failure to recognize the ideological power, lethality, and growth potential of the threat personified by Osama bin Laden, as well as the impetus that threat has been given by the U.S.–led invasion and occupation of Muslim Iraq. I tend to think that in the face of an insurgency that was accelerating in Afghanistan in early 2003, we would have been well guided on Iraq by Mr. Lincoln's spring 1861 advice to his secretary of state, William Henry Seward. When Secretary Seward proposed starting a war against Britain and France as a means to unite North and South against a common enemy, Mr. Lincoln wisely said, "Mr. Seward, one war at a time."[5] And because I am loath to believe—with a few exceptions—that America's current leaders are dunces, or that I am smarter than they, I can only conclude that for some reason they are unwilling or unable to take bin Laden's measure accurately. Believing that I have some hold on what bin Laden is about, I am herein taking a second shot—the first was in a book called *Through Our Enemies' Eyes: Osama bin Laden, Radical Islam, and the Future of America*—at explaining the dangers our country faces from the forces led and inspired by this truly remarkable man, as well as from the remarkable ineffectiveness of the war America is waging against them.

My thesis is like the one that shaped *Through Our Enemies' Eyes*, namely, that ideas are the main drivers of human history and, in the words of Perry Miller, the American historian of Puritanism, are "coherent and powerful imperatives to human behavior."[6] In short, my thesis is that the threat Osama bin Laden poses lies in the coherence and consistency of his ideas, their precise articulation, and the acts of war he takes to implement them. That threat is sharpened by the fact that bin Laden's ideas are grounded in and powered by the tenets of Islam, divine guidelines that are completely familiar to most of the world's billion-plus Muslims and lived by them on a daily basis. The commonality of religious ideas and the lifestyle they shape, I would argue, equip bin Laden and his coreligionists with a shared mechanism for perceiving and reacting to world events. "Islam is not only a matter of faith and practice," Professor Bernard Lewis has explained, "it is also an identity and a loyalty—for many an identity and loyalty that transcends all others."[7] Most important, for this book, the way in which bin Laden perceives the intent of U.S. policies and actions appears to be shared by much of the Islamic world, whether or not the same percentage of Muslims support bin Laden's martial response to those perceived U.S. intentions. "Arabs may deplore this [bin Laden's] violence, but few will not feel some pull of emotions," British journalist Robert Fisk noted in late 2002. "Amid Israel's brutality toward Palestinians and America's threats toward Iraq, at least one Arab is prepared to hit back."[8]

In the context of the ideas bin Laden shares with his brethren, the military actions of al Qaeda and its allies are acts of war, not terrorism; they are part of a defensive jihad sanctioned by the revealed word of God, as contained in the Koran, and the sayings and traditions of the Prophet Mohammed, the Sunnah. These attacks are meant to advance bin Laden's clear, focused, limited, and widely popular foreign policy goals: the end of U.S. aid to Israel and the ultimate elimination of that state; the removal of U.S. and Western forces from the Arabian Peninsula; the removal of U.S. and Western military forces from Iraq, Afghanistan, and other Muslim lands; the end of U.S. support for the oppression of Muslims by Russia, China, and India; the end of U.S. protection for repressive, apostate Muslim regimes in Saudi Arabia, Kuwait, Egypt, Jordan, et cetera; and the conservation of the Muslim world's energy resources and their sale at higher prices. To secure these goals, bin Laden will make stronger attacks in the United States—complemented elsewhere by attacks by al Qaeda and other Islamist groups allied with or unconnected to it—to try to destroy America's resolve to maintain the policies that maintain Israel, apostate Muslim rulers, infidel garrisons in the Prophet's birthplace, and low oil prices for U.S. consumers. Bin Laden is out to drastically alter U.S. and Western policies toward the Islamic world, not necessarily to destroy America, much less its freedoms and liberties. He is a practical warrior, not an apocalyptic terrorist in search of Armageddon. Should U.S. policies not change, the war between America and the Islamists will go on for the foreseeable future. No one can predict how much damage will be caused by America's blind adherence to failed and counterproductive policies, or by the lack of moral courage now visible in the thirty-plus-year failure of U.S. politicians to review Middle East policy and move America to energy self-sufficiency and alternative fuels.

While my thesis is constant, this book differs from my last in its comprehensiveness. As I wrote in *Through Our Enemies' Eyes*, the age of the Internet ensured there were applicable research materials I missed, despite throwing my net as widely as I could. The events of 11 September 2001 and since, however, have caused such an avalanche of new studies and commentaries about bin Laden, al Qaeda, and America's intercourse with the Muslim world that covering the new work in a single volume is not a reasonable expectation for one of my talents. The flood of new material is of mixed quality, some excellent, much of it good or pedestrian, and some that is simply fatuous, such as analyses that attribute the anger and violence of bin Laden and Islamists toward the West to sexual frustrations inherent to males in Islamic culture.

This mass of new and still-proliferating research precludes any claim on my part to have done a complete review of post-11 September writings on bin Laden. As in my first book, I have hewed closely to what bin Laden has said and, in that regard, his words since 11 September are ample. Supplementing this primary source are statements by Ayman al-Zawahiri, bin Laden's number two, Sulayman Abu Gayeth, a respected Kuwaiti Islamic scholar and al Qaeda's official spokesman, and an excellent series of essays, articles, and editorials on three websites that appear closely associated with bin Laden: *Al-Ansar*, *Al-Neda*, and *Al-Islah*. The first two sites appear to be produced or at least heavily influenced by al Qaeda's leaders, and the latter is the site of Sa'ad al-Faqih's UK–based, Saudi oppositionist Movement for Islamic Reform in Arabia (MIRA), which now also broadcasts on satellite radio and television stations when they are not being jammed. The materials published on these sites are available to any Muslim—really to any person—who can access the Internet. They admirably explain and amplify bin Laden's words and are fundamental to understanding al Qaeda's worldview and intentions. The final source materials for this study are drawn from the post-11 September writings of Western and Muslim historians, reporters, editorialists, intellectuals, and political leaders and commentators. I have tried to study a representative selection of writings from this immense corpus but offer no guarantee of my success other than to say that I used what seemed the best of the lot.

This book's format also differs from *Through Our Enemies' Eyes*. Having done my best in that study to follow bin Laden's ideas and career chronologically, I have, this time, taken a more topical approach, with chapters on such issues as the U.S.–led war in Afghanistan, an analysis of the 2001–2004 wins and losses in the war between America and al Qaeda and its allies, the impact of world events on the U.S.–Islam confrontation, and the detrimental impact of America's hubris and political correctness on its understanding of bin Laden and ability to defeat the forces he leads. I also have tried to refine the portrait of bin Laden, his thought, and how others—Westerners and Muslims—perceive him. I also must tell the reader that this book contains more than my first in the way of personal musings based on my reading of the research materials, views of history, and twenty-plus years working in the U.S. intelligence community. My comments are at times angry and accusatory, reflecting my profound belief that the lives of my children and grandchildren are at risk because most of my generation has willfully failed to understand and confront the threat America faces from bin Laden and his Islamist allies.

Finally, I will try to note errors and misjudgments made in *Through Our Enemies' Eyes*. A main fault in that estimate of al Qaeda lies in understating the Internet's importance to the group. The journalist Robert D. Kaplan hit this point in an analogy to the unrest and war that followed the invention of movable type. "The spread of information will not necessarily encourage stability," Kaplan wrote in *Warrior Politics: Why Leadership Demands a Pagan Ethos*. "Johannes Guttenberg's invention of movable type in the mid-fifteenth century led not only to the Reformation but to the wars of religion that followed it, as the sudden proliferation of texts spurred doctrinal controversies and awakened long dormant grievances."[9] I seek below to show how al Qaeda military and religious texts posted on the Internet—today's movable type—are fueling the group's growth and military viability, as well as rallying Muslims to jihad.

I am responsible for any errors herein, but as I do not intend to write again on this issue, others will have to correct any mistakes. Then again, if U.S. leaders keep underestimating al Qaeda, bin Laden may render moot the need for corrections. And I, for one, am not optimistic. "Every major religion warns its adherents of the danger of vanity," Ralph Peters wrote in his fine book *Fighting for the Future: Will America Triumph?*, "decrying the sin of pride or insisting that only humility can lead to enlightenment. In our rush from religion—be that flight good or bad—we have certainly lost this fundamental insight."[10] Sadly, unless the Divinity rids our eyes of hubris, we are lost. There is no sign we can remove it, and, I fear, al Qaeda sees the world clearer than we. "We thank God for appeasing us with the dilemma in Iraq after Afghanistan," Ayman al-Zawahiri said in late 2003. "The Americans are facing a delicate situation in both countries. If they withdraw they will lose everything and if they stay, they will continue to bleed to death."[11]

1

SOME THOUGHTS ON THE POWER OF FOCUSED, PRINCIPLED HATRED

> In a time of intensifying strains, of faltering ideologies, jaded loyalties, and crumbling institutions, an ideology expressed in Islamic terms offered several advantages: an emotionally familiar basis of group identity, solidarity, and exclusions; an acceptable basis of legitimacy and authority; an immediately intelligible formulation of principles for both a critique of the present and a program for the future. By means of these, Islam could provide the most effective symbols for mobilization, whether for or against a cause or regime.
>
> Bernard Lewis, 2002.[1]

> If there is a single power the West underestimates, it is the power of collective hatred.
>
> Ralph Peters, 1999.[2]

In America's confrontation with Osama bin Laden, al Qaeda, their allies, and the Islamic world, there lies a startlingly clear example of how loving something intensely can stimulate an equally intense and purposeful hatred of things by which it is threatened. This hatred shapes and informs Muslim reactions to U.S. policies and their execution, and it is impossible to understand the threat America faces until the intensity and pervasiveness of this hatred is recognized.

To start, I want for now to avoid debate over whether bin Laden

1

preaches and practices an aberrant form of Islam, as well as charges—almost always by non-Muslims—that he is merely a deranged killer using religious rhetoric to justify his attacks. And though I think both accusations wrong, I will not argue against them here. I ask the reader to suspend judgment and look at how bin Laden and other Muslims—those who support and those who reject his martial actions—appear to genuinely love their God, faith, and fellow Muslims in a passionate, intimate way that is foreign to me and, I suspect, to many in America and the West. This is not to say Westerners do not love their faith, God, and brethren; evangelical Christians have a fervor for God and His word similar to the Islamists', though the former have yet to take up arms in His defense. Even they, however, do not live and love their religion with the ferocity and thoroughness of bin Laden and many Muslims, primarily because Christians—evangelical and otherwise—accept the American and European legal divide between church and state. And while evangelical Christians would like the Bible to have more impact on state behavior, no evangelical leader, or any Christian leader for that matter, has called for creating Western theocracies.

Most Muslims—and bin Laden is in the Islamic mainstream—believe separating church and state is apostasy. "You are the nation," bin Laden criticized Americans in a late-2002 letter to them, "rather than ruling by the law of Allah, chose to implement your own inferior rules and regulations, thus following your own vain whims and desires. You run a society contrary to the nature of mankind by separating religion from your politics."[3] For Muslims, God's word—as He revealed it in the Koran—and the Prophet's sayings and traditions (the Sunnah) are meant to guide all aspects of life: personal, familial, societal, political, and international. God makes laws, man does not. As Professor Lewis explained, "The idea that any group of persons, any kind of activities, any part of human life, is in any sense outside the scope of religious law and jurisdiction is alien to Muslim thought."[4] Anything appearing to attack the ability or right of Muslims to perform this divinely ordained duty to run all of life according to God's law is seen as an act of war and, on a personal level, an attack on a faith they love with an intensity unknown to Christians since Pope Urban II sent Crusaders to the Levant, after granting "remission of sins to all Christians fighting Muslims," and since the wars attendant to the Protestant Reformation.

Parenthetically, Muslims' passionate love and reverence for God and His prophet help explain the great importance they attach to negative remarks made by U.S. Protestant clerics about Islam and the

Prophet, especially by clerics publicly associated to serving administrations. Clerical comments most U.S. citizens disregard are taken as threatening by Muslims because their societal frame of reference is one in which there is no separation of church and state. Thus, words of little consequence in U.S. politics and society are heard and remembered in the Islamic world as threats and blasphemy, earning America increased Muslim hatred. When Pat Robertson says "Adolph Hitler is bad, but what the Muslims do to the Jews is worse"[5]; the Reverend Jerry Falwell refers to the Prophet as a "terrorist"[6]; Jimmy Swaggart prays that "God blesses those who bless Israel and damns those who damn it"[7]; and the Reverend Franklin Graham calls Islam a "wicked religion" and says Christianity and Islam are "different as lightness and darkness,"[8] Muslims believe that "[n]ever has Islam faced such a frantic campaign of insult for centuries."[9] They are particularly troubled because the clerics "hold high positions at the church," are close to the U.S. government, and so conclude that "their statements had a significant impact on a large section of American society."[10] As a result, words that are innocuous to Americans are interpreted as Christian-Judeo attacks on the things Muslims love most. "The United States has a special perception and a clear goal it wants to achieve for itself and its ally Israel," wrote Atif Adwan, professor of politics at the Islamic University of Gaza, to explain the significance of the U.S. clerics' words in the context of the March 2003 U.S. invasion of Iraq.

> The perception is based on the partition of the [Middle East] region into small weak states incapable of posing any threat to Israel and on re-drawing the map of the region accordingly. This perception includes the achievement of religious goals. U.S. modern policies, particularly in the era of President George W. Bush, are based on biblical visions. This is not to say that there are no economic interest involved. These economic interests are parallel with Washington's religious goals.
>
> Israel and the Zionist Christian movement have played a major role in steering U.S. policy in the direction they wanted. They have done so by misinterpreting Bible verses and playing on the emotions of U.S. presidents and politicians. They have recruited for this purpose large numbers of Christian extremists who are more loyal to Israel and Judaism than they are to the United States and Christianity.
>
> The anti-Islam campaign has been led by a number of right-wing Christian leaders who are currently controlling the U.S. administration. They also include the spiritual mentors of the right-wing Chris-

tian leaders such as evangelists Pat Robertson, Jimmy Swaggart, Jim Baker, Jerry Falwell, Kevin Copeland, Richard Han, and others. Evangelist Copeland says that, "God has created Israel and He is acting to support it. It is a magnificent thing that we [the United States] should support our government as long as it supports Israel."[11]

That Islamic clerics and fighters listen to and believe the comments of American clerics, who are often ignored at home, again emphasizes the importance of words. In *Through Our Enemies' Eyes*, I stressed the need for the West to listen to bin Laden's words and believe he means them. Similarly, the words spoken by U.S. clerical or political leaders influence Muslims, many of whom still have the quaint idea that Western leaders say what they mean. Heard in a cultural context in which Islamic scholars often have the last, binding word, our Muslim foes accept the words above as the official U.S. position, as validation that America believes it is a "magnificent thing" to allow Israel to do what it wants in Palestine, whether that means killing Palestinians, razing thousands of West Bank homes, building walls through Jerusalem, or assigning hundreds of thousands to a life in refugee camps. Thus, words we dismiss or ridicule, nurture Muslim hatred to an extent we have not begun to recognize.

While my view is certainly open to criticism and correction by the many who are more expert on the Islamic faith and world, I hold it strongly and believe that an understanding of the Muslim's direct and immediate relationship with God is pivotal to understanding the hatred bin Laden has corralled and focused—but not caused—against the United States, and the West more generally. In listening to and reading bin Laden, one cannot help but believe that he is utterly sincere in expressing devotion to God and respect for the Prophet Mohammed. When bin Laden describes himself as "Allah's slave," "poor to his Lord," and "the humble servant of God," he sounds not just sincere but loving. And bin Laden is not alone in using loving tones to speak of God and His prophet; other al Qaeda leaders—Ayman al-Zawahiri, Sulayman Abu Gayeth, Abu Hafs the Mauritanian, and the late Mohammed Atef, for example—all echo bin Laden's words and tones. The tone also is common to other Islamist leaders, be they from Algeria's Salafist Group for Call and Combat, Kashmir's Lashkar-e Tayyiba, Afghanistan's Hisbi Islami, Indonesia's Jemaah Islamiya, or any of the myriad Islamist groups that dot the lands of five continents.

This loving tone also is common to the individuals whom the West commonly describes as "moderate" Islamic leaders—including those who stood by President Bush to denounce the 11 September attacks and annually dine with him during Ramadan—and such "moderate" Islamic proselytizing or missionary organizations as the Muslim Brotherhood and the Tablighi Jamaat, both of which are worldwide groups with enormous memberships. The same tone flows too from the leaders, spokesmen, and geographically dispersed local representatives of such Islamic nongovernmental organizations (NGOs) as al-Haramain, Mercy International, the International Islamic Relief Organization, and the Kuwaiti Society for the Revival of the Islamic Heritage. Most telling, perhaps, the tone is found almost without fail among the Muslim faithful in all walks of life. While my personal travels in the Islamic world are a tiny fraction of those of T.E. Lawrence, Kermit Roosevelt, or Sir Richard Francis Burton, it is my experience that one does not need to spend decades among Muslims to recognize that most share the same love of God that is audible among their prominent leaders. In my own travels, a conversation with a Muslim lasting a few minutes will reveal the consistent manner in which Muslims view life and their dealings with others through an all-encompassing Islamic prism. Such chance encounters were enough to convince me that the belief among Muslims that they are the "slaves of Allah" and "poor to their Lord" is not limited to bin Laden and Islamists, but are rather a shared Muslim mind-set. "It was devotion," Anthony Shadid wrote of this reality in his fine book *The Legacy of the Prophet*, "that struck me again and again in my travels in the Muslim world—faith influencing life, defining it and directing it at a level outsiders would find difficult to comprehend."[12] Indeed, an example of the saying "the exception proves the rule" lies in the loving tone used by the Persian Gulf's debauched and corrupt leaders when they speak of God. Their subjects expect this tone from them because it is expected of all Muslims. So, without fail, these monarchs sound like bin Laden when they speak of God in speeches or airport farewells before flying to gamble in Monaco or gambol in Bangkok's brothels. Indeed, it is no wonder Westerners hear bin Laden's paean for God as cynical. We in the West, after all, usually hear Arab kings and dictators utter the same praise before going to play high-stakes poker or prance about with teenage prostitutes.

My intention here is not to paint America's sworn and lethal Islamist enemies as simple, well-intentioned Muslims who only want to love and serve Allah and obey His prophet's guidance. Their reverentially loving tones toward God do not make our foes less dangerous, it makes them more dangerous, much more. There is in the Muslim's relationship with God a directness lacking in modern Christianity, most obviously in Catholicism, but also to a growing extent in the Protestant sects. The Muslim relationship is marked by an ongoing, almost easygoing, discourse with God, a conversation in which no man plays an intermediary role. In this sense, Islam seems to be the religion of everyman, open to myriad interpretations and not governed by anything like the Vatican, the Southern Baptist Synod, or any religious hierarchy or lay elite. The Muslim religious experience is intensely personal and yet genuinely communal.

The Koran, the five pillars of Islam, and the Sunnah are the same the world over, as is—and here is the rub for contemporary Christendom—each Muslim's responsibility to defend his faith and coreligionists when they or Muslim territory are attacked. Often referred to as the unofficial "sixth pillar of Islam," the act of defending the faith is more commonly known as "jihad," which is written of frequently in the Koran, the Sunnah, and more than fourteen centuries of Islamic scholarship and jurisprudence. And it is almost always written of in a context that yields a martial connotation, and, as Daniel Pipes has noted, that "is the way the jihadists understand the term. . . . In brief, jihad in the raw remains a powerful force in the Muslim world, and this goes far to explain the immense appeal of a figure like Osama bin Laden. . . ."[13] Thus, the doctrine of jihad, and an individual's responsibilities under it, are familiar to all Muslims; it is divided into two categories: the offensive jihad and the defensive jihad. "One of the basic tasks bequeathed to Muslims by the Prophet was jihad," Professor Lewis has explained. "The overwhelming majority of early authorities, citing the relevant passages in the Qu'ran, the commentaries, and the traditions of the Prophet, discuss jihad in military terms. . . . For most of the fourteen centuries of recorded Muslim history, jihad was most commonly interpreted to mean armed struggle for the defense or advancement of Muslim power."[14] Dr. Pipes has said that the military connotation of jihad should not be a surprise: the Prophet Mohammed himself participated in seventy-eight battles. (I am leaving aside in this discussion the other types of jihad Muslims refer to: the jihad of the hands (good works), the jihad of the heart (charitable donations), and the jihad of the mind (self-improvement), because, as Bernard Lewis and Daniel Pipes have shown, the term jihad occurs in the Islamic cannon overwhelmingly in the context of martial situations or activities.)

At this point in history, we need worry little about the threat of an offensive and expansionist jihad meant to conquer new lands for Islam and convert new peoples to the faith. Such a jihad is the collective—not individual—responsibility of Muslims, and must be called by a Caliph, the recognized leader of the world Islamic community, or ummah. There has not been such an individual since the British destroyed the Ottoman Caliphate's rusticating remains in 1924. The threat facing America is the defensive jihad, an Islamic military reaction triggered by an attack by non-Muslims on the Islamic faith, on Muslims, on Muslim territory, or on all three. In this scenario, it is doctrinally incumbent on each Muslim—as an unavoidable personal responsibility—to contribute to the fight against the attacker to the best of his ability. In such a jihad there is no Koranic requirement for a central Muslim leader or leadership to authorize warlike actions. Once Islam is attacked, each Muslim knows his personal duty is to fight. He needs no one else's authority, not even his parents; indeed, he would be guilty of sin if he did not respond to an attack as best he can. "It is generally agreed within Islam," wrote the American scholar of the concept of jihad, James Turner Johnson, "that the jihad of the first sort (collective) is impossible today, as there is no central caliph or imam. This gives new importance to what was originally considered an exceptional case: the idea of jihad as an individual duty in the face of external aggressions."[15]

The reality of individual responsibility in a defensive jihad is entirely congruent with the individual Muslim's direct relationship with God and with Islamic history. "The historical model for such action," Turner explains, "is the medieval hero Saladin, who though only a regional commander (not a caliph) organized and led a successful defense against the armies of the second Crusade."[16] Doctrine and historical practice, therefore, void any claim that bin Laden cannot lead a jihad because he was not educated as an Islamic scholar and has no religious credentials. The fact is that bin Laden believes Islam is being attacked by America and its allies and is simply recognizing his responsibility to fight in a defensive jihad. Further, bin Laden is calling on other Muslims to similarly identify the threat and to do their duty to God and their brethren. It is the attack by infidels on Muslims that triggers the jihad, not the call or directive of a suitably educated leader. Bin Laden is waging a defensive jihad against the United States; he is inciting others to join, not because he orders them to, but because God has ordered them to do so in what He revealed in the Koran. Bin Laden's genius lies not in his call for a defensive jihad, but in constructing and articulating a consistent, convincing case that an attack on Islam is under way and is being led and directed by America. In turn, as his argument is increasingly accepted by Muslims, each individual faces a fateful decision, one that will decide where he or she spends eternity. If bin Laden's argument is accepted, he or she must take up arms or otherwise support the mujahideen, or face eternal damnation for not performing a duty mandated by God.

Having looked at what I have described as the Muslim's loving relationship with his God, and the responsibility of each Muslim to fight those attacking his faith, brethren, and territory, I now want to examine how these factors have combined to yield an enemy who is aflame with hatred and yet carefully and coolly calculating. First, I want to draw a distinction between the things a Muslim would find offensive, and those he would deem an attack of the kind requiring a response under the defensive jihad doctrine. This distinction is important. It delineates the threat posed by bin Laden *et al.* as a focused threat to national security that is calculated, incremental, and designed to achieve victory. It is neither a simple but lethal lashing out against all things non-Islamic, nor an inchoate eagerness to indiscriminately damage the many in an effort to hit the few who offend Muslim sensibilities. One of the greatest dangers for Americans in deciding how to confront the Islamist threat lies in continuing to believe—at the urging of senior U.S. leaders—that Muslims hate and attack us for what we are and think, rather than for what we do. The Islamic world is not so offended by our democratic system of politics, guarantees of personal rights and civil liberties, and separation of church and state that it is willing to wage war against overwhelming odds in order to stop Americans from voting, speaking freely, and praying, or not, as they wish. With due respect for those who have concluded that we are hated for what we are, think, and represent, I beg to disagree and contend that your conclusion is errant and potentially fatal nonsense. As Ronald Spiers, a former U.S. ambassador to Turkey and Pakistan, has said, the "Robotic repetition of 'because they hate freedom' does not do as an explanation."[17]

The world abounds with people, things, activities, and beliefs that offend each of us in one way or another. Rare, I would guess, is the individual who can take in stride all he encounters and not be bothered, disgusted, or angered by some of it. For devout Muslims—as for some evangelical Christians—the contemporary world must be a particularly annoying place because so many of the things most regard as welcome evidence of modernity, diversity, and the uncrusting of old ways are offensive to those who deeply hold the Islamic faith. Coeducational schools, pornographic movies, Jews, alcoholic drinks, man-made laws, gay rights, abortion-on-demand, salsa dancing, the secular state, the denigration and disavowal of moral absolutes, Catholics, Protestants, Hindus, immodest clothing, Buddhists, devil-worshippers, women in universities, the workplace, and politics, atheists, the nation-state, usury, all these things and more are offensive to many Muslims, men and women, across the gamut from Islamic liberals to militants. And yet the world is not subject—except in extraordinarily isolated cases—to Muslims striking out savagely and indiscriminately against the neighborhood Buddhist, the interest-charging banker, the audiences at X-rated movies, or abortion-practicing doctors. Likewise, the non-Muslim world sees on a daily basis, and in the overwhelming number of cases, Muslims living side-by-side in peace with monotheists, polytheists, druids, communists, democrats, snake-charmers, and even National League baseball fans. One does read or hear occasional stories about angry Muslims killing an heir to Martin Luther's theses or slaying a person who goes home after work to worship a blue monkey and the god Shiva. But by and large, Muslims take the world as it comes, and although they may be more offended by some aspects of modernity than the members of other confessions—perhaps even more than me—there is no record of a Muslim leader urging his brethren to wage jihad to destroy participatory democracy, the National Association of Credit Unions, or the coed Ivy League universities. Many Muslims may not particularly like what and who the rest of us are, but those things seldom if ever make them hate us enough to attack us.

What the United States does in formulating and implementing policies affecting the Muslim world, however, is infinitely more inflammatory. While there may be a few militant Muslims out there who would blow up themselves and others because they are offended by McDonald's restaurants, Iowa's early presidential primary, and the seminude, fully pregnant Demi Moore on *Esquire*'s cover, they are exactly that: few, and no threat at all to U.S. national security. The focused and lethal threat posed to U.S. national security arises not from Muslims being offended by what America is, but rather from their plausible perception that the things they most love and value—God, Islam, their brethren, and Muslim lands—are being attacked by America. What we as a nation do, then, is the key causal factor in our confrontation with Islam. It is, I believe, the Muslim perception that the things they love are being intentionally destroyed by America that engenders Islamist hatred toward the United States, and that simultaneously motivates a few

Muslims to act alone and attack U.S. interests; a great many more to join organizations like al Qaeda and its allies; and massive numbers to support those organizations' defensive military actions with prayers, donations, blind eyes, or logistical assistance. Part of bin Laden's genius is that he recognized early on the difference between issues Muslims find offensive about America and the West, and those they find intolerable and life threatening. The difference, that is, that moves large numbers of people from demonstrating with placards to demolishing with plastic explosives. And in the movement-causing category fall, almost exclusively, U.S. political, military, and economic policies toward the Islamic world.

Bin Laden learned much of this lesson in Afghanistan. He and thousands of other non-Afghan Muslims went there to fight the Red Army not because the Soviets were atheists and communists—not because of what they were and thought—but rather because they were atheists and communists who had invaded and occupied a Muslim land, had arbitrarily killed more than a million Muslim men, women, and children, had driven three-plus million more into exile, and clearly sought to eradicate Islam from the country. The Soviets were fought and killed by the Afghan mujahideen and the non-Afghan Muslim fighters for what they did in Afghanistan; the Soviets' presence and behavior, not their beliefs, triggered a victorious defensive jihad, the impact of which still reverberates worldwide. The Soviets were just as much practitioners of atheism and communism at home in the USSR, but Muslims outside the Soviet empire never, in its seventy-plus year history, launched an offensive jihad to destroy the Soviet way of life and conquer the land for Islam, although most Muslims were offended by Moscow's denial of God, routine denigration of the Islamic religion, and abuse of its Muslim population. The Soviets, moreover, never fooled themselves as to why the Muslim world hated and fought them in Afghanistan. They knew the hatred stemmed from the Red Army's actions, and that cold, hard perception of their Islamic enemy's motivation is the only thing we should copy from the Soviet Union.

Though U.S. leaders say truthfully that America neither wants nor is waging a war on Islam, we need to understand how things look from where bin Laden works to align his own forces and incite others. Specifically, how do Islamists, and likely many tens of millions of other Muslims, perceive U.S. policies and their implementation? Is it possible, in the context of the above discussion about the things Muslims most love, that U.S. actions could easily be viewed by Muslims as attacks on

Islam, its peoples, and its lands? That is, is it possible that Muslims perceive U.S. actions in the Islamic world in a manner like that with which they perceived Soviet actions in Afghanistan? Unfortunately, the objective answer must be yes, and following is a series of snapshots of how I think bin Laden and many of his brethren view U.S. policies and actions.

Challenging God's Word

- America has declared that waging jihad against Islam's attackers is a criminal act and has seized and incarcerated—often without trial—hundreds of suspected mujahideen around the world. For a Muslim to refrain from joining a defensive jihad to protect Islam means disobeying God's law and earning damnation. The focus of the United States, wrote Dr. Mohammed Abd al-Halim, a professor at Cairo's al-Azhar University, "is against the concept of Islamic jihad. Jihad in Islam is one of the greatest actions to repulse tyranny and to restore justice and rights."[18] Going further, the historian Malise Ruthven contends that jihad "is as essential to Islamic identity and self-definition as the Mass is to Catholicism."[19]
- America has demanded that Muslim regimes limit, control, and track the donations Muslims make to charitable organizations that serve their poor, refugee, or embattled brethren. Tithing is one of Islam's five pillars, and so America is asking Muslims to abandon God's law for man-made law. "I believe that the [U.S.] siege of welfare work," Shaykh Yusuf al-Qaradawi has told Muslims, "is also intended to separate Muslims from each other, so each group would keep to itself, and not think about the others."[20]
- America has demanded Muslim educational authorities alter their curricula to teach a brand of Islam more in keeping with modernity and, not coincidentally, U.S. interests. Thus, America wants Muslims to abandon the word of God as He revealed it in the Koran—which Muslims consider perfect and unalterable—and the Prophet Mohammed's traditions and sayings for U.S.–dictated and man-made replacements. "The other thing is that no one, no matter who he is, may interfere with our learning material . . . ," declared Mohammed Sayyid Tantawi, the Grand Shaykh of al-Azhar University, in early 2001. "No one may interfere in our religious curricula, which we decide on the prerequisites of our shariah. No one may stick his nose in our affairs, or in the affairs of a country like Saudi Arabia. . . . one who can force specific curricula on us has not been born yet."[21]

Attacking the Islamic Faithful and Their Resources

- U.S. policy supports oppression and often aggression by Hindu India in Kashmir, Catholic Filipinos in Mindanao, Orthodox Christian Russians in Chechnya, Uzbek ex-communists in Uzbekistan, Chinese communists in Xinjiang Province, apostate al-Sauds in the Arabian Peninsula, and Israeli Jews in Palestine. The U.S. military also has sent troops to help governments kill mujahideen in the Philippines, the Caucasus, Yemen, and eastern Africa. "Ironically, too, U.S. efforts to fight terrorism have sometimes fostered rather than diminished anti-U.S. perceptions," said the scholar Daniel Byman in assessing Muslim perceptions of U.S policy for the *National Interest.* "Washington's embrace of sordid governments such as the Karimov regime in Uzbekistan, its silence regarding Russian brutality in Chechnya and other distasteful concessions offered to ensure these governments' cooperation against al Qaeda are bolstering claims that the United States supports the oppression of Muslims and props up brutal governments."[22]

- America supports apostate Islamic governments in Kuwait, the UAE, Egypt, Jordan, Saudi Arabia, and elsewhere. The regimes are corrupt, ruled by man-made not God's law, and oppress Muslims trying to install shariah law. Muslims view these police states as being approved of and protected by the American democracy. "The overwhelming evidence is that the majority of our terrorist enemies come from purportedly friendly countries," Bernard Lewis said in the *Wall Street Journal* in fall 2002, "and their main grievance against us is that, in their eyes, we are responsible for maintaining the tyrannical regimes that rule over them—an accusation that has, to say the very least, some plausibility."[23]

- America, on its own or with the UN, often imposes economic and military sanctions on Muslims, including the peoples of Iraq, Syria, Sudan, Afghanistan, Libya, Pakistan, Iran, and Indonesia. These actions force Muslims to follow U.S. orders, sanctioning Pakistan, for example, for building a nuclear weapon while condoning the possession of such weapons by India and Israel. "Washington has begun an incitement campaign against Damascus," Mohammed Kawash wrote in a Jordanian daily after Congress authorized sanctions on Syria in late 2003, "insinuating that it would impose sanctions against it and threatening military action. . . . The U.S. administration has resorted to escalation and threats and has hardened its position toward Syria because Damascus supports Palestinian factions hostile to Israel and because Damascus has refused to play the role of border guard for the U.S. occupation forces in Iraq."[24]

- The U.S. government and oil companies are seeking control of the Arab Peninsula to make sure its energy resources are sold to the West at below-market prices. The goal of a U.S. war in Iraq, in large part, is to gain "control of the oil wells," asserted Abu-Ubayd al-Qurashi in al Qaeda's journal *Al-Ansar* in August 2002. "If we take into consideration the fact that the Iraqi land contains 112 billion barrels of confirmed oil reserves in addition to 215 billion barrels of presumed oil reserves, Iraq becomes the world's second biggest reservoir of oil reserves after Saudi Arabia. This is one of the major reasons for striking at and occupying the two, even if it is done in stages."[25]

Occupying or Dismembering Muslim Lands

- America helped the UN create a new Christian state in East Timor, taking it from Indonesia, the most populous Muslim state, and ignoring the principle of self-determination. Justifying the August 2003 attack that killed Sergio Viera de Mello, the UN special representative for Iraq, al Qaeda said that, "He was the Crusader who carved up part of the land of Islam (East Timor). In the UN law against Islam, independence is forbidden to Muslims: Independence is permissible for East Timor, but taboo for Kashmir; Independence is permissible for Christian Georgia, but taboo for Chechnya; Independence is permissible for Crusader Croatia, but taboo for Bosnia. . . ."[26]
- America now occupies and effectively rules the Muslim states of Afghanistan, Iraq, and the states of the Arabian Peninsula, the Prophet Mohammed's birthplace. "The shameful fact that we must not overlook," al Qaeda's *Al-Ansar* journal noted during the 2003 U.S.–Iraq war, "is that all the countries of the Gulf Cooperation Council are occupied. The occupation took place without losses in the ranks of the enemy because it was unconditional, complete surrender. Kuwait became an American base without any fighting. A miniature Pentagon established itself in Qatar without any fighting. In the land of the two sanctuaries [Saudi Arabia] there are military settlements that have surrounded Mecca and Medina without any fighting. Therefore, the foreign occupation exists throughout the region. . . ."[27]
- America invariably backs Israel's occupation of Muslim Palestine and invaded Iraq to advance the Jews' goal of creating a "Greater Israel" from the Nile to the Euphrates. Damning this support for Israel, the influential Saudi Shaykh Salman al-Awdah claimed U.S. aid is meant to ready Israel to destroy Islam. "In the state of Israel," al-Awdah explained, "they even train young women. Why do they train them? They train them so that they, in turn, may train their nascent generations for the days to come. The Jews are planning to take over Arab and Islamic countries, wherein they have ambitions and designs. They plan to establish what they term the dream of 'Greater Israel.'"[28]

And perhaps this threat is not all in Muslim minds. "And Israel, despite efforts in secular state schools to present a more balanced view of Arab history," Chris Hedges wrote in his provocative book *War Is a Force That Gives Us Meaning*, "allows state-funded religious schools to preach that Jewish rule should extend from the Nile in Egypt to the Euphrates in Iraq and that the Kingdom of Jordan is occupied Jewish land."[29]

Let me again emphasize that I am not arguing that the foregoing are entirely accurate summaries of U.S. policies, intentions, or actions. However, these descriptions do depict their interpretation by bin Laden and his allies, and by a large percentage of the world's Muslims across the political spectrum from liberals to militants, whether or not they support al Qaeda's military actions. The resulting impression of America is that of a nation determined to eliminate all aspects of Islam it finds unsatisfactory, if not Muslims themselves. If there is doubt on this latter point, a quick review of the coverage of the recent Iraq war, and the budding postwar insurgency there, by Arab satellite radio and television channels, by Muslim newspapers and magazines, and even by such entities as the BBC and Deutsche Welle, will convincingly persuade that the interpretations of U.S. policy outlined above are not far-fetched. Likewise, the ferocious, militaristic, and bin Laden-echoing content of many of the fatwas calling for a defensive jihad against the United States because of its invasion of Iraq shows that Islamic scholars across the theological spectrum share many of bin Laden's perceptions of U.S. policy. "The significance of these Fatwas," wrote Dr. Ahmad al-Khatib in the journal *Al-Sh'ab* after reviewing al-Azhar University's fatwa and a number of others from Shia and Sunni clerics, "is that they have urged people to embark on the path of jihad. . . . The Fatwas also explained that sacrificing one's life to kill a number of enemy men is considered martyrdom."[30] It may well be that bin Laden's perceptions are dominant in the Muslim world. "Al-Azhar's religious decree [fatwa]," the American scholar of Islam John Esposito concluded, "reflects widespread popular opinion that cuts across the political and social spectrum in the Muslim world," and the fine journalist Geneive Abdo added that the fatwas show "[m]ainstream Muslim clerics in the Middle East who had denounced Osama bin Laden are now urging followers to rise up against the United States . . . a sign that some Islamic moderates are finding common cause with the extremists."[31]

Possible universality also is suggested by the failure of the post-11 September U.S. State Department public-diplomacy campaign "Shared

Values." The effort was designed by a talented Madison Avenue advertising executive; she described the task as "almost as though we have to redefine what America is. This is the most sophisticated brand assignment I have ever had."[32] It was to feature public-service ads televised in Muslim countries, as well as CD-ROMs, pamphlets, and a splashy magazine for young Muslims. The materials were apparently conceptually flawed, with the films showing how well Muslims lived and were treated in America, rather than explaining or defending U.S. policies. Worse, the countries asked to run the films—Egypt, Jordan, and Lebanon—refused, saying they would not "run messages on behalf of other governments."[33] While "Shared Values" was ended in early 2003, it is not clear that U.S. leaders recognize that it is far too late for public diplomacy, or talk of any kind, to defuse Muslim hatred, except at the margins. "We in the West, in the United States, cannot wage that war of ideas. For one thing, we would not be trusted," Shibley Telhami argued in *The Middle East Journal*.

> I do not think that U.S. policy right now can be oriented at "winning hearts and minds" of the Middle East in the short term. That is not going to happen. The U.S. has a legacy of decades that is based in part on our policy and in part on impression; it is not going to be able to change the paradigm overnight simply by a charm campaign. . . . People are not going to trust the message if they don't trust the messenger.[34]

Professor Telhami's accurate depiction of America's non-credibility in the Muslim world encapsulates the consequences of a half-century of U.S. Middle Eastern policy that moved America from being the much-admired champion of liberty and self-government to the hated and feared advocate of a new imperial order, one that has much the same characteristics as nineteenth-century European imperialism: military garrisons; economic penetration and control; support for leaders, no matter how brutal and undemocratic, as long as they obey the imperial power; and the exploitation and depletion of natural resources.

Because Muslims have seen this before, America is no longer the nation of Franklin Roosevelt, who destroyed fascism and forced Churchill to begin dismantling the British Empire, nor of Dwight Eisenhower, who stopped the brazen, racist Anglo-French-Israeli land grab at Suez, nor even of Ronald Reagan, who defied the atheistic Soviets, armed the Afghan mujahideen, and freed Eastern Europe. It is, moreover, no longer the nation to which Muslims will give the benefit of the doubt in situations where America claims to be an even-handed, honest broker in dealing with them vis-à-vis Israel or other matters. We have used up all our chits with Muslims. Rather, America is now regarded as a nation that supports and protects Arab tyrants from Rabat to Riyadh, that has abandoned multiple generations of Palestinians to cradle-to-grave life in refugee camps, and that blindly supports Israel, arming and funding her anti-Muslim violence and preventing Muslims from arming sufficiently to defend themselves.

Also catastrophic to U.S. credibility is her new, almost blithely acquired reputation as the restorer—sacrificing that of the killer—of nineteenth- and twentieth-century European colonialism, as the occupation of Afghanistan and Iraq and domination of the Arabian Peninsula ensures a supply of cheap oil to the U.S.–led West. Sadly, al Qaeda's journal *Al-Ansar* best caught the Muslim view of the United States as the world's new, predatory colonial power. With U.S. tanks on the streets of Iraq's capital, Abu-Ubayd al-Qurashi explained to his audience that,

> After the fall of Baghdad, voices of wailing and mourning swelled in many Islamic countries, while total numbness and silence encompassed other circles. While some lamented the capital of al-Rashid, others recalled the fall of al-Andalus. They forgot that the entire Arab world is as good as fallen, as long as Islamic law is abrogated and the people of Islam fill the prisons and detention camps. . . . Yes, direct colonialism has returned again. Another Arab capital has fallen into its hands, as Jerusalem, Beirut (before resistance flared), and Kabul fell.[35]

Confronting the Muslim view of U.S. actions as it is, and not as we think it should be, then, is the starting point for more research and debate, a process that will negate the idea that the United States faces in bin Laden an inchoate threat, offended by secularism, that is indiscriminately and lethally lashing out. In its stead, it will find that we face a precise, thoughtful, and hatred-fueled threat meant to win a decisive victory for Allah in a war being waged because of the fighters' love for Him. Bin Laden *et al.* are and will continue fighting and killing Americans, once again, because of what we have done and are doing in the Islamic world and not because of who we are and how we run our political, economic, and social systems. The brilliant analyst Ralph Peters is simply wrong when he writes that bin Laden "is an apocalyptic terrorist of the worst kind, and his superficial agenda . . . is nothing compared to his compulsion to slaughter and destroy."[36] There is nothing apocalyptic or narcissistic about bin Laden or our Islamist foes. They are not trying to destroy the world in an Armageddon-like battle, and they are not psychologically deranged people prone to and delighting in the murder of innocents. And with the greatest respect for Professor Bernard Lewis, bin Laden and his ilk also are not motivated by the "failure of Muslim society" to modernize and evolve in the successful pattern of the West. When they ask Professor Lewis's question, "What Went Wrong?" the answer comes back: the actions of the United States, as heir to the British Empire in the Muslim world, are what is wrong. As evidence for their claim, they point to specific real-world realities. For these men, the problem is clear—Islam is under attack—and the solution lies in war or, in Islamic terms, a defensive jihad. In October 2002, bin Laden said the war must go on because U.S. leaders and people show no understanding of "the lesson of the New York and Washington raids" and were not changing U.S. policies, or, as he described them, "your previous crimes" against Muslims. "However, those who follow the movement of the criminal gang at the White House, the agents of the Jews," bin Laden said,

> who are preparing to attack and partition the Islamic world, without disapproving of this, realize that you have not understood anything from the message of the two raids. Therefore, I am telling you, and God is my witness, whether America escalates or de-escalates the conflict, we will reply to it in kind, God willing. God is my witness, the youth of Islam are preparing things that will fill your hearts with fear. They will target key sectors of your economy until you stop your injustice and aggression or until the more short-lived of us die."[37]

Bin Laden and most militant Islamists, therefore, can be said to be motivated by their love for Allah and their hatred for a few, specific U.S. policies and actions they believe are damaging—and threatening to destroy—the things they love. Theirs is a war against a specific target and for specific, limited purposes. While they will use whatever weapon comes to hand—including weapons of mass destruction—their goal is not to wipe out our secular democracy, but to deter us by military means from attacking the things they love. Bin Laden *et al.* are not eternal warriors; there is no evidence they are fighting for fighting's sake, or that they would be lost for things to do without a war to wage. There is evidence to the contrary, in fact, showing bin Laden and other Islamist leaders would like to end the war, get back to their families, and live a less martial lifestyle. They share the attitude of the Afghan mujahideen during the Afghan-Soviet war: They are weary of war, but not war weary in a way making them ready to compromise or fight less enthusiastically. In both cases, participating in a defensive jihad was a duty to God and therefore had to be pursued until victory or martyrdom. For the Afghans, their jihad continued until the Soviets were stopped from destroying Islam, killing Muslims, and occupying Afghan land—the three things they loved most and that united the ethnically and linguistically diverse insurgent groups. For bin Laden and the Islamists, jihad against America is the Afghan jihad writ worldwide, and, like that jihad, it is fueled by hatred for the United States based on what they see as American attacks on the things they most love—their faith, brethren, and land.

There is, finally, one more factor that sharpens the edge of the hatred held by America's Muslim enemies. In a world where Muslim leaders are mostly effete kings and princes who preach austere Islam but live in luxuriant debauchery; or murderous family dictatorships, like Iraq's Husseins, Egypt's Mubaraks, Libya's Qadahfis, and Syria's Assads; or coup-installed generals holding countries together after politicians have emptied the till, bin Laden, al Qaeda, Mullah Omar, and "the mujahideen" have won the aura of Robin Hood. This status is part respect for their bravery and piety, part recognition of the Muslim leadership void, and part admiration for the romantic lives Islamist fighters lead. Bin Laden, for example, is the perfect lead for a modern version of David vs. Goliath: a tall, gaunt, often ill merchant prince who renounced a life of ease to live in Afghanistan and, with history-echoing rhetoric, challenged the military might of the USSR and the United States, slaying the first outright and repeatedly wounding the second. Add to this mix bin Laden's combat wounds—the most recent in late 2001—readiness to spend his fortune to fund jihad and care for its Muslim victims, steady optimism and faith in Allah's pledge of victory, and you have stuff Hollywood could use to write a starring role for Errol Flynn.

In a way then, bin Laden and the mujahideen become another reason why Muslims hate the United States. In a society bereft of talented, manly, pious, and dignified leaders, the mujahideen are both legitimate and romantic heroes. And, as in the Robin Hood saga, those whom Robin defended hated even more those who tried to kill him and his band. With no competition for the Muslim world's leadership, and with their battles now seen globally in real-time by proliferating Arab satellite television and radio channels, the mujahideen hold the respect, gratitude, and love of many Muslims. For tens of millions of Muslims, and especially for the young, they are, to use the title of Ayman al-Zawahiri's memoirs, "Knights Under the Banner of the Prophet."

Thus, as bin Laden and his ilk defend the things they love—a love held by most Muslims—they are themselves loved not just for defending the faith, but as symbols of hope in a Muslim world conditioned to massive military defeats, Islamic charlatans as rulers, and U.S.-protected and coddled tyrants. While America's political, military, and media elites portray efforts to kill bin Laden as nothing more than a necessary act to annihilate a deranged gangster, many Muslims see that effort as an attempt to kill a heroic and holy man who lives and works only to protect his brethren and preserve their faith. While Americans are told U.S. forces are hunting an Arab version of Timothy McVeigh, Muslims are praying and working for the survival of a man better characterized for them as a combination of Robin Hood and St. Francis of Assisi, an inspiring, devout leader who is unlikely to be betrayed for $25 million in U.S. reward money. Therefore, the hatred many Muslims nurture for what they see as deliberate U.S. attacks on Islam and Muslims is hardened by America's dedication to killing a man who not only symbolizes the defense of the faith, but who—due to his actions and the lack of Muslim leaders—has become the most respected, loved, romantic, charismatic, and perhaps able figure in the last 150 years of Islamic history. Americans would do well to recall that bin Laden, in Muslim eyes and hearts, is not unlike another man—also, ironically, pious, quiet, and dedicated—who strove for four extremely bloody years to destroy the United States, and, in doing so, evoked unprecedented loyalty and love from millions that endures even today. "Any criticism of Lee is bound to prompt outrage," Kent Gramm writes when discussing the Virginian in his wise and moving book, *Gettysburg: A Meditation on War and Values.*

> What was Lee then? Not a tragic hero, not a tragic figure at all, but a charismatic, gifted soldier. Onto charismatic figures, we put our wishes, and we dress them according to our dreams. They stand in front of our quiet desperation, and the last thing we let them be is what they are.[38]

So, too, stands Osama bin Laden, while millions of Muslims put upon him their wishes and dress him with their dreams.

2

AN UNPREPARED AND IGNORANT LUNGE TO DEFEAT—THE UNITED STATES IN AFGHANISTAN

The art of war is simple enough. Find out where the enemy is. Get at him as soon as you can. Strike him as hard as you can and as often as you can, and keep moving on.

General U.S. Grant.[1]

Today the United States in Afghanistan deludes itself with the vanity of apparent power and imagines that its fate will be better than the fate of earlier invaders. . . . Apparently it has not properly read Afghanistan's history.

Mullah Omar, 13 September 2002.[2]

The Russians, moreover, foolishly did not try to punish rogue Afghans, as [Britain's Lord] Roberts did, but to rule the country. Since Afghanistan is ungovernable, the failure of their effort was predictable. . . . America should not seek to change the regime, but simply to find and kill terrorists.

John Keegan, 24 September 2001.[3]

When entering on duty as an intelligence officer two decades and more ago, one of my first supervisors often said the key to framing and solving intelligence problems was to first "do the checkables." The checkables were those parts of a problem that were knowable, the things on which there were classified archival records, pertinent and available human experience, current human assets to consult, or even the results of media and academic research—the latter then, as now, generally underused because of the false assumption that information is not useful unless classified. This supervisor's recipe was to exploit to exhaustion the "checkables" to learn the problem's history and context, determine precisely what we already knew, establish the range of things we knew little or nothing about, and, thereby, identify the information we needed to acquire before acting to resolve the problem. To the know-it-all new intelligence officer I was then, the supervisor's emphasis on following this procedure seemed self-evident and hardly the product of genius. Yet, two decades on, it is astonishing how often the checkables are ignored, or, at best, partially exploited. I know of no case in post-1945 U.S. foreign and military policy where failure to exploit the checkables has yielded a more complete disaster than in the period before and since the start of the U.S. campaign in Afghanistan— although the jury is still out on Iraq. So bad has been our performance in Afghanistan that one must assume a long list of Afghan checkables lie—like John Brown's body—a' moldering in a locked and dust-covered archive. It is, overall, hard to disagree with al Qaeda's assessment of the U.S. Afghan campaign. "For it is obvious that the U.S. administration, in defining this goal [winning the Afghan war]," the Internet journal *Al-Ansar* commented in August 2002, "did not proceed from a careful and in-depth study of the enemy it was about to face. Instead, it proceeded from a hysterical state that made its position lack the basic scientific rules that ought to be considered when making a decision."[4]

At War's Start: The Cost of Prolonged Failure, 11 September–7 October 2001

In a list of al Qaeda victories, the attacks on New York and the Pentagon on 11 September 2001 are far from the first entries. Before that day, which al Qaeda calls "Victory Tuesday," the date of "blessed strikes against world infidelity," and which historian Malise Ruthven describes as "the perfect icon of destruction, of hubris punished and arrogance brought low,"[5] bin Laden's fighters had stitched to their battle flag six major victories: Aden, Yemen (1992); Mogadishu, Somalia (1993); Riyadh, Saudi Arabia (1995); Dhahran, Saudi Arabia (1996); Nairobi,

Kenya, and Dar es Salaam, Tanzania (1998); and, again, Aden, Yemen (2000). Given these attacks, their increasing lethality, and the fact bin Laden and al Qaeda had been based in Afghanistan since May 1996, one would have expected the U.S. government to have had its military—if not since the 1998 East Africa attacks, then surely since the 2000 Aden strike—ready to respond immediately to the next al Qaeda attack, which anyone listening to bin Laden knew was a sure bet. Even if the Clinton administration's sordid blend of moral cowardice and political calculation prevented America's defense in late 2000, U.S. citizens and al Qaeda's leaders had to believe the world's greatest military power would not let another anti-U.S. attack go quietly by the boards. So as the immobilized destroyer USS *Cole* came home aboard a floating dry dock, and the 2000 presidential election likewise limped to a delayed finale, the commonsense assumption was that when Osama bin Laden next pulled the trigger, his side would be struck by a precise and devastating U.S. military attack on long-identified al Qaeda and Taleban targets. Among these, one would have bet, were training camps, airfields, air defenses, and government facilities in major Afghan cities; vehicle depots, ammunition dumps, and weapons storage areas; the facilities of the heroin-refining industry that helped fund the Taleban and al Qaeda; troop barracks; intelligence headquarters; and cave-and-tunnel complexes identified since the 1980s. Such an immediate, savage attack would come not only because it was deserved, but because U.S. generals knew they had to hit al Qaeda and the Taleban fast and hard before they dispersed into the Afghan mountains and countryside, or across the border into Pakistan, Iran, or Central Asia. An instant U.S. response, moreover, was possible because we knew the enemy could not deter an attack. The Taleban air force and air-defense system consisted of thirty-year-old, Soviet junk: ancient, unmaintained MiG fighters, decrepit past-generation radars, and Vietnam-era antiaircraft weapons. This prewar knowledge was validated by Lieutenant General C. F. Wald, USAF, who said Taleban air defenses and command-and-control were destroyed "in the first fifteen minutes or so" of war. In sum, Mullah Omar was not capable of interfering with a U.S. counterattack on his or al Qaeda's manpower, armaments, or facilities. "In terms of conventional arms," Don Chipman wrote straight-faced in *Air Power History*, "Taleban fortifications were not overly formidable."[6]

Unintimidated by U.S. military power, bin Laden after the *Cole* attack publicly repeated his intention to strike the United States at home and abroad, pledging each attack would be of better quality than the last—meaning more casualties and greater physical and economic damage. For most Americans, bin Laden was courting annihilation; surely the U.S. military had zeroed-in on al Qaeda and Taleban targets in Afghanistan, as well as al Qaeda-related targets in Sudan, Yemen, Somalia, and the Philippines. After all, a nation with reconnaissance satellites, high-altitude aircraft, a $28 billion intelligence community, and the most lethal military ever built surely could target a man and a group such journalists as Peter Bergen, Abd al-Bari Atwan, John Miller, Robert Fisk, Hamid Mir, Jamal Ismail, Peter Arnett, and Rahimullah Yusufzai had found and covered. Even John Walker Lindh, the American Taleban, had met bin Laden several times. With these tools and five years to plan a counterstrike since bin Laden's 1996 declaration of war, Americans confidently assumed al Qaeda's next attack probably would be its last.

And yet, as is often the case in today's America, expectations based on common sense and the tenets of professional behavior proved unfounded when al Qaeda's exquisitely planned and executed attack occurred over two hours on 11 September 2001. As smoke billowed over al Qaeda's massive victories in New York City and Washington, D.C., no savage, preplanned U.S. military response was initiated; none had been planned in the eleven months since the attack on the USS *Cole,* or in the five-plus years since bin Laden declared war. Oddly, the National Security Council and FBI did move with speed to assist the "dead of night exodus" of twenty-plus bin Laden family members from the United States to Saudi Arabia. The FBI did not "verify whether the fleeing bin Ladens were both personally and financially estranged from Osama."[7]

While the 11 September attack was a human-economic calamity, Washington's failure to have its military ready for a crippling, next-day attack on al Qaeda turned it into catastrophe. It cost America its best—perhaps only—chance to deliver what is called a "decapitation" operation, one with a chance to kill at a stroke many al Qaeda and Taleban leaders. Even if the leaders survived, immediate U.S. strikes could have pounded thousands of enemy soldiers into pulp. But no attack came on Tuesday, 11 September, or on Wednesday the 12th, or on Thursday the 13th, and, even later, the scandalous absence of a counterstrike was not only universally ignored, but such scholars as Frederick W. Kagan chided the Bush administration not for paralysis, but for surrendering to a "perceived need to start operations [in Afghanistan] hastily."[8]

In the first postattack days, the only launches were of Clintonite excuses: "We must have a smoking gun"; "Al Qaeda could not have done this, it must have been a state sponsor like Iran or Iraq"; "What about Hizballah?"; and that hoary excuse for supine inaction, "We must consult with our allies and build a coalition." And there were those whose Pavlovian response was to blame America, implicitly suggesting a limited military response. "To a large extent," terrorism expert Brian M. Jenkins absurdly asserted, "Osama bin Laden is our own creation. The United States encouraged and helped him wage a holy war against the Soviet Army in Afghanistan."[9] These cynical and false mantras filled the air and gave the appearance of a sensible, sober, and European-pleasing U.S. desire to avoid counterattacking the wrong target—though since 1996 America had but one foe who had declared war on and attacked it. In hindsight it is clear the mantras were meant to hide the fact that the U.S. military's cupboard was as bare as Mother Hubbard's, no forces in place, no plans on the shelf—not even any to destroy the Afghan heroin factories that have killed more Americans than the 11 September attacks—only negligence and dereliction far and wide. "The U.S. military, which seemed to have contingency plans for the most inconceivable scenarios," Bob Woodward wrote in *Bush at War*, a book that fascinates and terrifies by describing the ill-informed and timid support the president received as he led America to war, "had no plans for Afghanistan, the sanctuary of bin Laden and his network. There was nothing on the shelf that could be pulled down to provide at least an outline."[10] The best that could be done was Secretary of Defense Donald Rumsfeld asking his planners for "credible military options" on 12 September—a stark underscoring of the bare cupboard—and getting a response on 21 September. Rumsfeld sent it back to the planners on 1 October for more detailed "target sets and force requirements," and the plan did not get President Bush's okay until 2 October.[11] As a result, U.S. military action was delayed a month. "Only in America," Professor R.K. Betts has written, "could the nation's armed forces think of direct defense of national territory as a distraction."[12]

This inexcusable delay afforded al Qaeda and Taleban leaders an unexpected lull to further disperse personnel, military stores, and funds within the Texas-size nation of Afghanistan, across its borders with Iran, Pakistan, and Central Asia, and from there to the rest of the world. This process probably was under way before 11 September because al Qaeda had expected a massive U.S. attack since the 1998 East Africa bombings, and especially since the October 2000 strike on the *Cole.* "It is no secret," al Qaeda said in July 2002, "that the crusade against Islam and Afghanistan was planned a long time ago, even before the 11 September incident."[13] In addition, bin Laden had six days warning of the 11 September attacks and presumably took evasive action. Still, a foe susceptible to considerable damage on 11 September was, by the war's start on 7 October, largely out of America's view and capable of continuing its worldwide anti-U.S. insurgency. In this context, America probably lost the war against al Qaeda on 11 September because the U.S. military had been caught completely unprepared. The more than three-week delay denied America the chance, for once, to respond to an al Qaeda attack with a fury and bloodthirstiness that would have cost bin Laden dearly, and that Western governmental and public opinion would have tolerated because visions of the collapsing towers and burning Pentagon were still fresh. By 7 October, however, the window for savagery had shut, and whiners about "collateral damage" and "innocent Afghans" steadily constricted President Bush's ability to, as one of his windier CIA officials said, "take off the gloves." The negative impact caused by the U.S. failure to prepare was well-described by a Harvard scholar in November 2001. The status of the warring sides, Graham Allison wrote in the *Economist,* were different as night from day—the Americans *ad hoc-ing* their way to war, the Islamists steering a long-planned course.

> Yet as the American government scrambles to pursue a war for which it was not prepared, it must, in the idiom, "go with what we've got." Assembling a coalition of very strange bedfellows, acquiring intelligence from sources and by methods it had mostly neglected, and jerry-rigging defenses around the most obvious vulnerabilities, it gallops off in all directions. It does so without a comprehensive assessment of the threats it now faces, and lacking a coherent strategy for combating mega-terrorism.
>
> In contrast, Mr. Bin Ladin and his al Qaeda network have been thinking, planning, and training for this war for most of a decade. September 11th demonstrated a level of imagination, sophistication, and audacity previously thought impossible by the American, or any other, government.[14]

In the next section, an attempt is made to explain why America was willfully unprepared for the New York and Washington attacks and what that lack of preparation has so far cost. The final cost of 11 September's unpreparedness, of course, will be clear only after al Qaeda's next attack in the United States. On that day, America will stand quivering with rage, massively powerful but unable to respond unless willing to destroy areas in Pakistan's North West Frontier Province thought to shelter al Qaeda and Taleban fighters, strikes that would be more likely to destroy Pakistan than our enemy. "Unencumbered by a territorial base that would make a convenient cruise-missile target, and fully dispersed," Jonathan Stevenson wrote in the *Wall Street Journal*, "al Qaeda is now less susceptible to counterterrorism measures than it was before Sept. 11."[15] Change the word "less" to "not" and Stevenson would have it exactly right.

Into Afghanistan: Tragic Country, Absurd Analysis

Afghanistan. It is hard to think of another country on earth that has suffered more in every conceivable way in the last quarter-century. Since being invaded by the Red Army in December 1979, the Afghans have waged war to rid their country of homegrown or foreign atheists and infidels. To date, they have partially succeeded, but at a cost nearly impossible to comprehend—of a prewar invasion population of about fifteen million, more than 1.5 million dead; nearly five million forced into exile in Pakistani or Iranian refugee camps; and several million internally displaced. In addition, centuries-old and indispensable irrigation and agricultural-terracing systems were ruined during the war by natural deterioration after farmers were driven abroad, or, more tellingly, by deliberate destruction by the Soviets in their effort to depopulate areas supporting the insurgency. Afghanistan's limited road system was likewise destroyed, and the penury produced by years of war spurred a lucrative crop-substitution program that saw farmers abandon grains and fruits for poppies to feed the expanding heroin industry. "On a percentage basis," the leading Western analyst of the Red Army's Afghan war has estimated, "the Soviet Union inflicted more suffering on Afghanistan than Germany inflicted on the Soviet Union in World War II."[16] Throughout this horror, the Afghans continued to fight foreigners and their influence—as well as amongst themselves—and clung to a lifestyle in which ethnic and tribal affiliations dominate to a degree unimaginable in the West.

By the end of the day on 11 September 2001, Afghanistan was again the starring act on the world's stage and was soon to be smack at the center of a bull's-eye tardily drawn by the United States. On reflection,

America's political leaders, generals, and military planners should have been overjoyed that Osama bin Laden and al Qaeda were based in Afghanistan. The U.S. intelligence community and, to a lesser extent, the U.S. military had been closely involved in and around Afghanistan even before the 1979 Soviet invasion because of the country's strategic Cold War location on the USSR's southern border. In addition, these institutions—led by the Central Intelligence Agency (CIA)—had run in Afghanistan the largest, most expensive, and most well-publicized covert action program in U.S. history to support the anti-Soviet mujahideen. This thirteen-year program was capped by success when the last Bolshevik general walked out of the country in February 1989, and when the Afghan communist regime was defeated in April 1992.

During the course of this endeavor, multiple hundreds of uniformed military personnel, intelligence officers, analysts, logisticians, military trainers, medics, geographers, imagery analysts, demolition experts, mule skinners, communication specialists, and cartographers developed strong expertise on Afghanistan. As important, they experienced an intimate acquaintance with the patient, brave, devout, brutal, and stubborn men who beat the Soviet and Afghan communists. In addition, hundreds more State Department and Administration for International Development officers participated in implementing the diplomatic, economic, and humanitarian aspects of U.S. Afghan policy. Finally, the interest of members of both houses of Congress in the Afghan covert program was intense; many senators and congressmen demanded regular, detailed briefings on the war, traveled repeatedly to the region, and voted enthusiastically for the war's steadily growing covert action budget. The range of motivations among the politicians ran from an altruistic desire to help the dirt-poor Afghan David against the nuclear-armed Soviet Goliath to a simple, cold-blooded eagerness to pay back Moscow for Vietnam.

On 11 September 2001, the bottom line on Afghanistan was that it was one country in which the usually geographically challenged Americans knew their way around, and one in which their intelligence community had either collected or commissioned an enormous amount of information, much, but not all of it, right up to date. The U.S. government had experts on both the fundamental facts and the esoterica of Afghan society, history, and tribalism; on the country's demography and topography; on the role of the country's multiple ethnic and sectarian groups and their at-times-vicious rivalries; and, most important, the U.S. government had experience in dealing face-to-face with Afghans and in appreciating the obdurate determination and endless patience of these people when it came to resisting with arms foreigners who sought to impose their will on the country. And the thing that these American experts knew best and above all others was that there was no possibility of installing a broad-based, Western-style, democratic, power-sharing central government in Kabul. They knew also that any attempt to do so would inevitably fail and take that much-brutalized country on yet another long and bloody trail that would end, at some point, in the restoration of a Pashtun-dominated Islamist government that would mirror the Taleban in all but name.

In short, the list of "checkables" was immense, the cadre of qualified checkers was large, and yet tragically—for Americans as well as Afghans—almost no checking seems to have been done. Indeed, so uneducated was the U.S. intelligence community's official input to America's Afghan strategy that began to be implemented on 7 October 2001 that it was almost as if the task of advising policy makers and planning covert action had been left to African and Latin American experts. As I will explain, for example, the strategy Bob Woodward describes in *Bush at War* as the "Tenet Plan" was used because it made sense to the U.S. mind—using the power of money and few Americans while having foreigners die for us—not because it had drawn on the U.S. government's vast repository of Afghan knowledge.[17] However, the strategy's subsequent failure shows its planners' complete lack of comprehension of Afghanistan's tribal, ethnic, and religious realities. Using nonexperts to devise strategy when experts were at hand would, of course, be a great disservice by the U.S. intelligence community (IC) to Americans and their elected leaders too serious to contemplate. Then again, soon after the war began the *New York Times* quoted unnamed "senior intelligence officials" who claimed the U.S. government did not "have the people to exploit [information about Afghanistan]." The senior officials and several academic experts led *Times*' journalist Diana Jean Schemo to conclude that, "As the United States takes up a war against terrorism that will demand human intelligence as well as smart bombs, it faces a nationwide shortage of Americans with a deep knowledge of the languages and cultures of Afghanistan and the surrounding region. . . ."[18] While the U.S. was indeed short on fluent speakers of the regional languages, it beggars the imagination that any "senior intelligence official" could utter the bald-faced lie that the U.S. government lacked expertise on South Asia, the region most likely to host the world's first nuclear war. I have found, in my career, that the IC leaks this kind of comment only when senior managers have failed to develop a cadre of substantive experts, when they want to put their "pets" in charge of programs for which they have no substantive expertise, or when they want to prepare the public for failure. As noted, the first motivation is not the case here, and our hubris ensured no thought went to possible failure. And so, it seems, substantive experts were not used, and that we are paying an exorbitant price because we ignored Sun Tzu's advice not to "demand accomplishments of those who have no talent." What follows is a look at the disasters that have befallen America in Afghanistan and speculation about those to come. Past and future, these harvests of pain were predictable but not forecast because no U.S. leader was given the expert analysis that would have allowed him to see beyond the war's easy part—bombing the air-defenseless Taleban from power.

Hey, Did Anyone Know the Red Army Lost a War in Afghanistan?

For those fortunate enough to have assisted the Afghan mujahideen to force the USSR's withdrawal from Afghanistan, the unfolding of U.S. operations there since October 2001 has been horrifying. Although the media in late 2001 lamented the U.S. government's lack of expertise on Afghanistan, few assertions—as noted above—could be more incorrect. As George Crile wrote in his excellent book *Charlie Wilson's War*, U.S. aid to the Afghan mujahideen, as administered by the CIA, was the largest, most successful covert action program in American history.[19] Given the size and diverse nature of this 13-year program—guns, food, vehicles, money, training, uniforms, orange drink, donkeys, you name it—there are hundreds of military, intelligence, diplomatic, and AID officers who gained extensive Afghan experience and knowledge. Many worked on the Afghan program far longer than the two- or three-year tour common in the federal services, a longevity due to the program's unique size, a desire to see the Afghans defeat the Red Army and its barbarity toward civilians, and an itch to pay back Moscow for Vietnam. Many officers also were held by South Asia's intoxicating appeal. Americans in the 1980s were as enthralled as British sahibs in the 1870s by the people, topography, and history of a region that was ancient when Alexander neared the Indus River in the fourth century before Christ. To date, no benefit from this hard and expensively won experience can be seen in America's two-year-old Afghan misadventure.

The debilitating impact of not tapping America's Afghan expertise has been compounded by our failure to learn from the experience of the USSR, the most recent nation to join the list of states that failed to win wars in Afghanistan. Here, too, detailed studies of the Soviets' disastrous Afghan experience are readily available at local libraries and the nearest Borders. Soviet soldiers—conscripts, field-grade officers, and generals—have written a number of excellent memoirs of the war, and the University of Kansas Press has published, in a translation by Lester Grau and Michael A. Gress, the Soviet General Staff's after-action report on the Soviet–Afghan war.[20] This study details what the Soviet armed forces did in Afghanistan—save for atrocities—and assesses which political and military policies and actions succeeded or failed. Generally, the study depicts the frustrations of an arrogant superpower trying to cope with a people and a country it did not understand, as well as with an enemy all but invulnerable to conventional military operations and more than able to deal with special forces (Spetsnaz). The study's conclusions were condensed by a senior Russian official when he met senior CIA officials in mid-September 2001. "With regret," the Russian said, "I have to say that you are going to get the hell kicked out of you." One of the Americans responded in words that will someday be found in a U.S. military study of its failed Afghan war. "We're going to kill them," the U.S. official asserted. "We're going to put their heads on sticks. We're going to rock their world."[21] The occasional substitution of bravado for thought is truly an eternal attribute of senior intelligence and military officers.

Grau's translation of the Soviet study is a must-read for any group of officials responsible for invading Afghanistan—an admittedly small audience—or, more generally, by anyone preparing to use conventional forces against a large and experienced insurgent organization. And beyond this easily acquired public material, one also must assume that the multiple analytic arms of the U.S. intelligence community produced an ocean of classified, electronically retrievable analyses about all aspects of Afghanistan's travails, from coup d'etat, to invasion, to occupation and war, to a victory triggering the USSR's demise, to civil war, to the rise of the Taleban and large-scale heroin trafficking, to Mullah Omar's rule and the return of Osama bin Laden. More especially, the IC had to have produced detailed analyses of why the Red Army failed in Afghanistan and what it might have done to win. Given the wealth of public and classified data that appears to have gone unused, one is tempted to paraphrase Churchill to the effect that never in the history of U.S. foreign policy have so many officials failed to read so much pertinent information to the detriment of so many of their fellow citizens.

Checkables: success rides on how fully they are retrieved, reviewed, and absorbed. Perhaps the most acute observation made about Soviet performance in Afghanistan, sadly, can likewise be made about America's 2001–2004 performance. The comment is in the Soviet General Staff study noted above; it ought to haunt U.S. leaders who did not read it before starting to "rock their world" on 7 October 2001.

> When the highest political leaders of the USSR sent its forces into war, they did not consider historic, religious, and national peculiarities of Afghanistan. After the entry these peculiarities proved the most important factors as they foreordained the long and very difficult nature of the armed conflict. Now it is completely clear that it was an impetuous decision to send Soviet forces into this land. It is now clear that the Afghans, whose history involves many centuries of warfare with various warring groups, could not see these armed strangers as anything but armed invaders. And since these strangers were not Muslims, a religious element was added to the national enmity. Both of these factors were enough to trigger a large mass resistance among the people, which various warriors throughout history have been unable to overcome and which the Soviet forces met when they arrived in Afghanistan.[22]

Interestingly, the Soviet General Staff tries to attribute much of the Red Army's failure to the fact that it had not previously fought this type of war, much as U.S. leaders now say that U.S. forces in Afghanistan are fighting a "new" type of war. Grau and Gress correctly reject the Soviet General Staff's alibis—as Americans might consider doing with new-type-of-war claims—and call attention to the Red Army–run insurgent campaigns of World War II, as well as the mass of material pertinent to fighting Afghan insurgents available long before the 1979 Soviet invasion. "Therefore, the initial inept approach of the [Soviet] 40th Army to fighting guerrillas was not due the lack of historical experience to draw on," Grau and Gress snorted. "Further, British experience on their Indian Northwest Frontier is replete with tactical solutions to fighting the ancestors of the mujahideen. Mujahideen tactics were basically unchanged over the decades, and the British lessons were still valid."[23]

From Day One—A Worse Dance Partner Was Not Available

By 1 September 2001, the Taleban, with important but not indispensable help from al Qaeda, had defeated the multiethnic Northern Alliance. The Alliance, led by Ahmed Shah Masood, held only 10–15 percent of Afghanistan—some estimates are as low as 5 percent—and was a military force, as historian Frederick W. Kagan has written, "that had exhausted its ability to continue fighting [the Taleban]."[24] The Alliance's viability also was, as always, overwhelmingly dependent on its leader's unquestioned brilliance as an insurgent commander, his media-winning charisma, and the weapons, funds, and economic aid coming from Russia, Iran, India, and Uzbekistan. The first three were trying to seal Afghanistan to isolate the Taleban contagion, while India sought an anti-Pakistani regime in Kabul that kept military forces active near Pakistan's western border. France, too, flitted about in this picture, providing lavish rhetorical support for Masood and some clandestine military aid and funding to his fighters. France had no strategic interest in Afghanistan, understood little about it, and was involved mainly due to its self-deluding love affair with Masood's image as a moderately Islamic, long-suffering artist-turned-warrior; an image Masood cynically crafted and that European journalists and politicians eagerly consumed for over twenty years. No doubt the French teared up over the Northern Alliance chief's death and were anguished by the news that on the night before his death Masood and several colleagues had stayed up late, reading Persian poetry aloud until three in the morning.

External support might have enabled Masood's Alliance to survive for several more years and perhaps even add small bits of territory to its enclave in what had been a back-and-forth war with the Taleban, but for all intents and purposes the Taleban stood victorious on 1 September 2001 and had installed a harsh but stable law-and-order regime over most of the country. More important, Mullah Omar's regime was increasingly accepted by Afghans as they started to see the end of pervasive banditry and warlordism and the gradual return of safety for themselves, their children, and their meager amounts of property. Most Afghans seem to have regarded this as a fair exchange for the Taleban's rigorous, unforgiving application of strict Sunni Islam.

The Taleban's victory, of course, was sealed on 9 September 2001 when a patient, sophisticated al Qaeda operation killed Masood as he sat down to be interviewed by two explosives-laden al Qaeda fighters. Exploiting Masood's belief that the Alliance's survival required positive media coverage, and Masood's well-known love for playing reporters like violins, the two al Qaeda fighters used the interview to kill themselves and Masood. The meeting appears to have been arranged by Abdul Rasul Sayyaf, a man who was Masood's partner in the Northern Alliance, the chief of the Islamic Union for the Liberation of Afghanistan, and—perhaps not coincidentally—a longtime friend of Osama bin Laden. The assassins gained an audience with Masood, explained Engineer Arif, a senior Masood lieutenant, because "Sayyaf's imprimatur permitted the Arabs to bypass normal security procedures."[25]

Masood's death ended the Northern Alliance's chances for surviving as a viable political-military force, let alone as one that might serve as the framework for a national government. As Professor Michael Doran wrote in the *Political Science Quarterly*, "bin Laden engineered the decapitation of the Northern Alliance in order to throw it into such disarray that it would be useless to the United States as an instrument of retribution."[26] Indeed, only the fact that the assassination of Masood occurred three weeks later than scheduled prevented the Taleban from crushing Alliance remnants, thereby completely denying the United States an Afghan ally. Masood was the Northern Alliance; he groomed no successor, and while he lived it was clear that the other Alliance "leaders"—Mohammed Fahim, Abdullah Abdullah, Rashid Dostum, Yunus Qanooni, et cetera—were at best second-raters, perhaps able to work effectively under the great man's direction but unable to fill his shoes. They commanded little respect in the Alliance—although Qanooni was feared as Masood's security chief[27]—and each was unknown internationally.

Faced with imminent organizational implosion and final military defeat by the Taleban, the Northern Alliance's leaders found a last-minute life-support system known as the United States when New York and Washington, D.C., were attacked by al Qaeda forty-eight hours after Masood's death. Surprised by the attack, and utterly unprepared to respond with its own military forces, Washington reinvigorated long-established ties to the Northern Alliance, delaying its inevitable demise. Indeed, by using it as indigenous window-dressing for the application of U.S. air power, the Bush administration kept the Northern Alliance alive to an extent that its leaders appear to believe they have defeated the Taleban and won the war. The truth, however, is that America won a single battle using Tajik- and Uzbek-dominated Northern Alliance auxiliaries and is now "politically beholden to its indigenous allies" who have formed an untenable regime.[28] "Under any circumstances," Professor Kagan has said, "it would be difficult to imagine a stable Afghan state in which Pashtuns were ruled over by Tajiks and Uzbeks."[29] Thus, most of the war is still to be fought. It is a war the Alliance cannot win unless America provides a far larger infantry force, defeats the Taleban-and-al Qaeda insurgency, and is ready to occupy Afghanistan indefinitely. This scenario, even for men as lucky as Masood's successors, is a bridge too far.

The mistake America made in the first months of its Afghan war was not that it used the Northern Alliance to drive the Taleban from power, nor even that it portrayed the Alliance as a military force that mattered in the long run. It is clear, in fact, that for immediate U.S. purposes, the Alliance was the only game in town: it was at war with the Taleban, it had a military force in the field, and, most important, it had the cannon fodder that foreclosed—at least in the near term—the need to deploy to Afghanistan large numbers of killable U.S. infantrymen. U.S. military planners accurately gauged the obvious by taking advantage of the Alliance's post-Masood desperation, but took no account of the future. As Ralph Peters has written, "Our enemies play the long game, while we play jailbird chess—never thinking more than one move ahead."[30] In a severe miscalculation, Washington compounded the mistake by failing to see that the Alliance was soon to be a corpse, operating as if it was only damaged and momentarily leaderless. Moreover, Washington did not recognize that the Alliance had no growth potential to serve as the base for a democratic government in a de-Talebanized Afghanistan. This series of mistakes merits further examination, and at this point it is time to look at some of the easily checkable checkables that were obviously not checked.

Did Anyone Do Their Homework?

What did we know about the Northern Alliance on 11 September that should have informed and hedged the way we used, depended, and still depend on it? Well, we knew Masood formed the Alliance to resist the Pashtun mujahideen groups when fighting began in earnest among the Afghan resistance's constituent members after the pro-Soviet Afghan regime in Kabul fell in April 1992. From inception, the Alliance was an overwhelmingly Tajik-dominated organization. It was dominated, moreover, by the leaders of a small subset of the country's Tajik minority, men from the Panjshir Valley. In a sense, the Alliance, born of desperation, never had a chance to be the basis for a national government. Even with Masood's guiding genius, the Alliance's raison d'etre—to force the Pashtuns to share power equally with the minorities—was a forlorn hope. The Pashtuns were not and are not going to abide a political relationship with minority groups they do not dominate. There is something tragically quixotic about Masood. Notwithstanding the confident tone with which he spoke of the future, he was never in a position to do more than hope something would come along to force the Pashtuns to deal equitably with the minorities.

Masood was the most politically important and militarily capable Panjshiri Tajik. He worked tirelessly to bring and keep groups from the country's other ethnic minorities—Uzbeks, northern Pashtuns, Turkmens, Hazara Shias, Ismailis, et cetera—under the Alliance umbrella. His work bore some fruit as General Rashid Dostum's Uzbek forces joined, as did the country's largest Shia group, the Hizbi Wahdat, and some members of the late communist regime. Masood also gave the Alliance a veneer of inclusiveness after the Taleban took power in southern Afghanistan in 1994–1995 by enlisting the tenuous allegiance of the Pashtun groups led by Abdul Rasul Sayyaf and Gulbuddin Hekmatyar, the IULA and the Hisbi Islami (HIG). The Alliance was most cohesive in late 1995 through summer 1996 but weakened after the Taleban took Kabul in September 1996 and its forces slowly retreated north toward the Tajik heartland.

As noted earlier, by 1 September 2001 the Taleban had contained the Alliance in a 10–15 percent slice of Afghan territory adjacent to the borders of Uzbekistan and Tajikistan. In that ethnically favorable enclave, the Alliance had enough fighters but was dependent on financial, military, and other forms of aid from Iran, Russia, and India, and had little chance of keeping the land it held, let alone expanding. Masood, because of his substantive military brilliance and his international renown, was the key to ensuring this support continued and allowed the Alliance's survival, even in a much reduced form. When Masood was killed by al Qaeda, the Alliance died with him. There was simply no one to take his place. Had there been no foreign intervention after Masood's death on 9 September 2001, we would have seen the military defeat of the Northern Alliance, the nationwide consolidation of Taleban power, and the slow emergence of the first chance for relative peace and security in Afghanistan for nearly a quarter century.

All these things were "knowable" on 11 September 2001 as the World Trade Center and the Pentagon were burning. The question is, therefore, why was the information derived from doing the "checkables" not integrated into U.S. military and political planning for Afghanistan?

The Price of Winging It

The answer to the question, obviously and unfortunately, is that available data was not retrieved, collated, and used; given the content of cabinet-level discussions presented in Bob Woodward's book *Bush at War*, it may not have been requested.[31] Like Judy Garland and Mickey Rooney in the 1930s movies, U.S. government agencies got the neighborhood kids together, gave each a role and a script, and expected to produce a professional Broadway musical in the backyard—*Andy Hardy Conquers and Rebuilds Kabul,* perhaps. Sadly, success from "winging it" occurs only in movies, and Washington's attempt to duplicate Hollywood's methods in Afghanistan yielded a full-blown disaster. As Ralph Peters has wisely posited, "If you intervene ignorant of local conditions, you will likely fail—and you will certainly pay in blood."[32]

Of course, no senior U.S. or UK official will admit to winging it. The immediate response from U.S. policy makers and military planners, if asked if they had thoroughly reviewed the checkables, would be something like: "We didn't have time." "We had to work with the material we had on hand." "We had to defend America." Good rhetoric, superficially plausible in days of unthinking high emotion, and self-protectively wrapped in red, white, and blue—and just as clearly factually wrong and deliberately misleading. Once the United States and its allies were unable to strike on the afternoon of 11 September, or the next day, or the next, al Qaeda and the Taleban were well on the way to effective dispersal. As a result, we did have the time to think about what we wanted to do in Afghanistan, line up needed assets, and, most important, identify and accept the things that could not be accomplished there. This was not done, however, and Washington charged ahead to align with a group whose only plausible leaders were second-raters from Masood's Panjshiri mafia—Fahim, Abdullah, and Qanooni—and the Uzbek leader Dostum. The result, journalist Michael Massing has written, is that the "government's top three ministries [defense, foreign affairs, and interior] are controlled by men who belong to a tiny subgroup of an ethnic minority. . . . Even many Tajiks are unsettled by the prominence of the Panjshiris, regarding them as war criminals."[33] In Dostum, the United States befriended the single most hated man in Afghanistan due to his behavior during and since the Soviet-Afghan war. Among Dostum's endearing habits were having tanks run over trussed-up civilians or prisoners of war, and dousing villagers—men, women, and children, and overwhelmingly Pashtuns—with gasoline and then lighting them up. Dostum's status as a top-ten world villain faded only when more murderous monsters emerged in the Balkans and Central Africa.

Overall, the United States took willy-nilly a Northern Alliance in its death throes, kept it alive and united through the work of a few dozen extraordinarily brave, talented, and lucky U.S. intelligence officers, and assured its capture of Kabul with American air power and special forces. The Alliance's leaders played their part well, strutting into Kabul to the enthusiastic applause of a population unrepresentative of the country; Kabul, now and historically, is much less Islamic and more cosmopolitan than the rest of Afghanistan—witness its status as a haven for hippies in the 1960s, and the Kabulis' willingness to tolerate their decidedly un-Islamic presence—a point that I heard no Western journalist, media expert, or government official mention as they analyzed the city's populace rejoicing over the Taleban's defeat. The hopelessly naive reaction in the United States probably is best described by Bob Woodward. "Soon there were [television] pictures of real liberation," Woodward wrote in *Bush at War*, "women in the streets doing all the things that had been forbidden previously. [National Security Adviser Condoleezza] Rice felt that [U.S. leaders] had underestimated the pent-up desire of the Afghan people to take on the Taleban."[34] The Alliance leaders behaved as magnanimous victors before the cameras, while quietly and quickly flooding the capital with fighters and intelligence operatives no more savory than the Taleban fighters they replaced. Rather than the masters of all they surveyed, the Alliance leaders were then—and are now—dead men walking.

Since the United States did no homework on the Northern Alliance, it is not surprising that the Pashtun leaders America welded to the now Fahim-led Alliance to form a "broad-based" interim regime amounted to more dead weight and are, indeed, the kiss of death. In most ways, U.S. officials repeated the same failure they engineered in Afghanistan between 1989 and 1992, when U.S., UN, and other Western diplomats tried to construct a broad-based government—meaning non-

Islamist—to replace the Soviet–Afghan communist regime. The purpose of that attempt was—as is today's—to allow the barest minimum of participation in the new regime by the mujahideen, the uncouth, violent, devout, and bearded men who had won the war. Having banished these unwashed, medieval Islamists to the periphery of politics, the diplomats intended to give the bulk of the new government's posts and power to people more like themselves: secularized Afghans; westernized Afghans who refused to fight for their country and spent a comfortable, self-imposed exile in Europe, India, or the United States; technocrats who had worked for the Soviet and Afghan communists; tribal leaders who had emigrated to preside over refugee camps in Pakistan or Iran and avoid being shot at; the deposed Rome-based Afghan king, his effete, Italianate entourage, and their Gucci-suited "field commanders" who never fired a shot; and even Najibullah, the head butcher of the just-defeated Afghan communist regime. As always for Western diplomats, well-coiffed men who dressed well, spoke a smattering of English or French, and shared an aggressive contempt for religion, were preferable as rulers to the hirsute men wearing funny looking pajama-style clothes who had merely fought and defeated a mass-murdering, superpower enemy in a ten-year war. Style over credibility every time.

Flash ahead a decade and this scenario repeats itself with a new, more ludicrous twist. This time out, the same U.S., Western, and UN diplomats intend to create an interim government from an even less credible crowd, again proving their infallible ability to pick losers. Taking the dimming shadow that is the Northern Alliance—for whom U.S. intelligence officers and soldiers won a battle it could never have won on its own—U.S. officials added the Westernized Pashtun Hamid Karzai as leader of the new government. A genuinely decent, courageous, and intelligent man, Karzai had nonetheless absented himself from the fight against the Soviets, and also from the one against the Taleban, until he jumped in on the side of the Americans and their overwhelmingly powerful military. With no Islamist credentials and minimal tribal support, the India-educated Karzai was and is a man clearly adept and comfortable hobnobbing with U.S. and British elites, but far less so at chewing sinewy goat taken by hand from a common bowl with an assembly of grimy-fingered Islamist insurgent and tribal leaders and their field commanders. Fixing Karzai as chief of the transitional administration via a UN–run and U.S.–manipulated conference held in Bonn, Germany—another sure disqualifier for the xenophobic Afghans—we then liberally salted the new regime with well-educated, detribalized, and minimally Islamic Afghan expatriates who had been waiting in the wings in the West since the early 1990s for a prize they wanted but for which they would not risk life and limb. We then enlisted tribal warlords such as Hazret Ali in Nangarhar Province, Pacha Khan Zadran in Khowst Province, and Mohammed Shirzai in Qandahar Province to provide Karzai with military muscle in regions where the Pashtun tribes were politically and demographically dominant.

This is not a winning lineup. While Karzai and his expatriate assistants shivered in cold, dark, and bankrupt Kabul, the warlords depended on the forces of the U.S.–led coalition for support because their supposed muscle was nowhere to be found. Having ignored the foregoing checkables, the West quickly discovered that these warlords had been in exile or under domestic subordination not because they disagreed with the Taleban, but because they had failed to provide leadership and security when they ruled Afghanistan before the Taleban arose (they then specialized in banditry and heroin trafficking), had little support inside the country, and were afraid of Taleban and al Qaeda forces.

Thus, the government the West installed in Kabul in early 2002 was missing every component that might have given it a slim chance to survive without long-term propping-up by non-Islamic, foreign bayonets. The Northern Alliance formally represented several minority ethnic groups, but it was and is nothing more than the tool of Masood's Panjshiri clique. There is virtually no genuine Pashtun representation in the regime, though Karzai and some returning expatriates were unrepresentative Pashtuns: they had been living in the West or Pakistan, had not fought the Soviets, and were only nominally Islamic. Likewise, the interim government's warlords were military nonentities unless backed by U.S. and UK military forces. Karzai's regime, at day's end, is the perfect example of the unnecessary mess that always ensues when time is not taken to review and digest the "checkables." And on this occasion, to make matters worse, the checkables were available in local public and university libraries, federal government archives, and the memories and experiences of hundreds of serving and retired U.S. government employees. The data were not hiding until they could be clandestinely acquired by the West's intelligence services. On reflection, one again has the strong but surely incorrect impression that responsibility for U.S. political and military planning for Afghanistan was deliberately given to officials who had spent their careers working on African or Russian affairs and not on the Middle East, South Asia, and Islam. But not even my generation of senior civil servants could be that criminally negligent. Could they?

Why Are All the Fighters on the Other Side?

The second half of 2003 and early 2004 saw a substantial increase in Taleban and al Qaeda attacks on the military forces of the Karzai government and the U.S.–led coalition, as well as the discrediting of another group of Western experts on the war in Afghanistan. The rising tempo of combat gave lie to such analyses as *Newsweek*'s early 2003 speculation that al Qaeda's back "may finally have been broken"[35]; Max Boot's conclusion that the defeat of the Taleban in 2001 "should have shattered for all time the mystique of the guerrilla"[36]; and the February 2003 assertion by Steven Simon and Daniel Benjamin that "after the punishment meted out in late 2001, it is unlikely that U.S. forces will again face al Qaeda forces on the battlefield."[37] The current consensus of media reporting and official U.S. announcements is that "remnants" of the Taleban and al Qaeda are "regrouped and reformed" and are waging a guerrilla war against the Kabul regime and its foreign allies. "Regrouped, rearmed, and well-funded," wrote the *Christian Science Monitor*'s Scott Baldauf in May 2003, "they are ready to carry on a guerrilla war as long as it takes to expel U.S. forces from Afghanistan."[38] This conclusion is supported by both empirical evidence and the corpses at hand—although whoever coined the term "remnants" for the unvanquished forces of bin Laden and Mullah Omar will regret it— and was underscored when General John Abizaid, head of the U.S. Central Command, said in mid-November 2003 that daily combat operations in Afghanistan are "every bit as much and every bit as difficult as those that go on in Iraq."[39] The forces that oppose Karzai's regime and its allies, however, go far beyond the Taleban and al Qaeda, and therein lies another example of the cost of not reviewing the checkables before acting.

While sparsely covered in the Western media—save for the *Christian Science Monitor*'s superb reporting, which continues to this day— the Afghan insurgents' war against the Red Army and Afghan communists was among the most vicious, lonely, and lengthy of what are now fashionably called the twentieth century's "small wars." Although over time increasing numbers of non-Afghan Muslims traveled to Afghanistan to fight alongside the Afghan Islamic resistance, the war was fought and won by the Afghans. American and Saudi involvement in the war was important in terms of money—it allowed the mujahideen to fight with AK-47s and RPGs rather than 100-year-old Lee-Enfield rifles—but the war, again, was fought and won by the Afghans. And the most talented, effective, and durable fighters of this war were from the hard-line Islamist guerrilla organizations, those led by Ahmed Shah Masood, Yunis Khalis, Jalaluddin Haqqani, Abdul Rasul Sayyaf, Ismail Khan, and Gulbuddin Hekmatyar. These groups, not coincidentally, also attracted the lion's share of the funds, ordnance, and manpower from governments, individuals, and religious organizations across the Muslim world, including, of course, Osama bin Laden. The Afghan Islamist leaders did not get along because of ethnic differences and political rivalry, and each was the foe of political unity in the Afghan resistance movement. Each, at times, took a break from killing communists to kill each other. The firefights and assassinations between the forces of Masood and Hekmatyar, for example, are legendary.

The Afghan Islamists' power and perseverance, therefore, came not from nationalism or personal affinity for each other, but from their faith, their hatred of communism and atheism as an affront to God and His prophet, and, most of all, the extraordinary pride, stubbornness, tribalism, and xenophobia that are central to the Afghan character, traits making it impossible for Afghans to obey non-Afghans or long tolerate a foreign presence on their soil. The reader need go no further to verify this claim than to read Robert D. Kaplan's outstanding and courageous firsthand account of the mujahideen, *Soldiers of God: With Islamic Warriors in Afghanistan and Pakistan.* Yes, external supplies of weaponry and money were important assets in defeating the Soviets in just ten years, but the external aid bought the foreign donors not an atom of control over the mujahideen, except in that the Afghans agreed to use most of the foreign ordnance and money to kill Soviets. Faith, tribalism, and xenophobia provided enough glue to keep most resistance activity focused on the Soviet and Afghan communists, and it was only after the Red Army's defeat and withdrawal that ethnic and theological clashes led to the final breakup of the resistance. This, in turn, led to a decade-long civil war that the Taleban had largely ended by mid-2001. Notwithstanding the cruel civil war that followed victory over the USSR and led to the Taleban's rise, the above-mentioned Afghan leaders and other Islamist commanders have entered Afghan history's pantheon of military heroes. They are like the Confederate generals of the U.S. Civil War, men such as Joseph Johnston, James

Longstreet, and Edward Porter Alexander who were hated by the North as traitors during the war and yet redeemed as "American heroes" afterward by the men they fought, the populations whose sons they killed, and the government they sought to destroy. The older generation of Afghan commanders remain heroes today for millions of Afghans who experienced the war's horrors firsthand, as well as those tens of thousands who grew from infant to adult to parent in Pakistani and Iranian refugee camps.

The foregoing, again, is all checkable information. The great bulk of it requires no access to signals intelligence, clandestine collection, diplomatic reporting, or satellite imagery. A trip to the local library probably would suffice to show the pivotal importance of these "old" mujahideen; a visit to a university library surely would; and, for the unambitious or sedentary, accessing the Internet from home would fill the bill. And yet there is no sign that Western officials made much if any effort to contact these men and their field commanders with either of the equally worthy goals of securing their help against the Taleban or, if they refused to cooperate, killing them. U.S. leaders seem to have completely ignored these men, apparently agreeing with the tragically ill-informed conclusion of two former senior National Security Council terrorism officials that "the most Islamically radical Afghan commanders, Adbul Rasul Sayyaf and Gulbuddin Hekmatyar . . . [were] men who were both vicious and ineffective leaders."[40] Indeed, the only sign sent to them was the same one now hung in Baghdad: "No Islamists Need Apply."

These veteran guerrilla chiefs and field commanders are the swing force in the Afghan military-political equation. They are mostly Pashtun but fought the Soviets in league with Masood's forces. At the same time, because they are Pashtuns, they have strong ethnic, linguistic, tribal, and cultural affinities with the Taleban, even though differing over what kind of Islam is best for Afghanistan. The nub of the matter for the United States was that while these men could have been engaged or killed, they could not be ignored if Washington was to have a chance for long-term success in Afghanistan in terms of creating a stable government of some sort. These leaders were latently anti-Western, militarily adept, used to defying and defeating Great Powers, extremely xenophobic, and commanded greater or lesser numbers of armed and experienced insurgents. Two of the Soviet-era insurgent leaders were even good enough to remind the United States of the power and potential animosity of this group before the U.S. invasion was launched.

"[W]e give nobody the right to launch a raid on Afghanistan," Hisbi Islami chief Yunis Khalis told the *Afghan Islamic Press News Agency* on 21 September 2001. "Anybody who under any kind of pretext mounts an attack is an aggressor and the Afghans will confront them relying on God's help as they did against the aggressors in the past."[41] Then, on 2 October 2001, Gulbuddin Hekmatyar announced that, "We should defend our country. . . . The Talebans fought against us [the Northern Alliance], but today we will forget all about our disputes with them and fight against our common enemy."[42] Over time—and not much time—Afghan xenophobia and tribalism predictably would move the old mujahideen to aid the Taleban and al Qaeda and fight to rid Afghanistan of another foreign army of occupation, leaving for the post-victory period the visiting of revenge on those who helped the foreigners and the squaring-off to fight for power amongst themselves.

One other easily acquired piece of information would have told U.S. planners that the leaders of the anti-Soviet jihad, to a man, had strong personal ties to another well-known mujahideen from that era, a slender Saudi named Osama bin Laden. Sayyaf, for example, allowed bin Laden to set up his first training camp in an area of eastern Afghanistan controlled by his IULA organization. Hekmatyar had signed the passport permitting bin Laden to reenter Afghanistan from Sudan in May 1996 and then backed the Taleban to the hilt—at a time when his forces were aligned with the Northern Alliance—when Mullah Omar refused to turn bin Laden over to the United States or any other country. Yunis Khalis had cooperated with bin Laden during the Soviet war and detailed one of his leading commanders, Engineer Mahmoud, to help bin Laden get settled in Nangarhar Province on arriving from Khartoum. When Mahmoud was killed soon thereafter, Khalis again stepped in and allowed bin Laden to use two of his organization's remote military bases in Nangarhar, one at Tora Bora, the other at Malawi. Jalaluddin Haqqani—Khalis's senior field commander, *de facto* emir of Paktia Province, and the Gulf Arabs' oldest and closest Afghan colleague—also helped bin Laden get settled, allowed al Qaeda to use his training camps near Khowst, and acceded to bin Laden's request to send some veteran fighters to spur the Taleban's victorious push on Kabul in September 1996. And, ironically, given al Qaeda's role in his death, Masood himself told the Russian media in 2000 that bin Laden played a valuable and truly Islamic role in supplying funds to the Islamist Afghan groups fighting the USSR.[43]

As the pace of the new guerrilla war in Afghanistan picked up in mid-2003, it is not difficult to guess which leaders appeared most often in the media damning the U.S. "occupation" of the country and promising to teach the Americans the jihad lesson already administered to Britain and the USSR. Coming off the sidelines to support the Taleban and al Qaeda in attacking Karzai's forces and their U.S. and Western protectors were, among others, the just-mentioned Khalis, Haqqani, and Hekmatyar, Hekmatyar being the most vocal and militarily active. Masood is too dead to be heard from, and Sayyaf—who helped Masood get dead—has so far kept quiet in his mountainous strongholds in Paghman—from where his militia reaches into western Kabul[44]—and Maidan Shahr, west and southwest of Kabul. When the time comes, however, Sayyaf and his fighters will attack the Karzai regime along with the forces of Mullah Omar, bin Laden, and other Soviet jihad-era leaders. The position of the "old mujahideen" was summed up in the call for jihad against "U.S.-led foreign forces" made by Yunis Khalis in October 2003. "The U.S.-led invasion of Afghanistan is unjustified and unprincipled and is no less than the Soviet aggression against our homeland," Khalis instructed "all mujahideen and common Afghans" in his fatwa. "If they fail to withdraw from Afghanistan, the foreign forces will be responsible for the consequences."[45] The U.S. failure to co-opt or destroy the leaders and forces of the older generation of Afghan mujahideen ensured it would face a formidable enemy; indeed, the same enemy that negated U.S.-led efforts to establish peace in Afghanistan between 1992 and 1996.

In short, the West is out of time in Afghanistan, the decisive swing votes have been cast by Hekmatyar, Haqqani, Khalis, *et al.* in favor of the Taleban and al Qaeda, and this, in turn, has ensured the demise of the Karzai-led Afghan Transitional Administration (ATA). Karzai's defeat may not come tomorrow, the day after, or even next year—I have been wrong too many times predicting the timing of events in Afghanistan to try again—but come it will, and the Prophet's banner will again be unfurled over Kabul. Further sealing the ATA's doom, the West will soon find that parts of the coalition now backing Karzai—especially Masood's rank-and-file fighters—will begin working against the ATA and seeking a *modus vivendi* with Taleban-led opposition. There is no great wisdom or predictive power in this observation, only a willingness to review the checkables and to keep up with al Qaeda's electronic journals. The Northern Alliance forces have most in common with Russia and Iran, not the U.S., *Al-Neda* explained in September 2002, ". . . and these will not be loyal to Karzai, but to the leaders of their parties, and they would fight in the ranks of their parties, whenever the need arose."[46] Masood's men, like all who oppose Karzai, fought the Red Army to rid their country of an anti-Islamic military occupation. For the most part, Masood's men see America as less brutal, less brave, and less determined than the Soviets, but just as anti-Islamic; on the latter point, they have seen Karzai's nebulously Islamic government and have heard Secretary of Defense Rumsfeld define "self-determination" as the creation of any government as long as it is not Islamic. Most important, Masood's fighters are Afghans and, although not Pashtuns, they share the Afghan character's xenophobia, devotion to Allah, and resolve to never give an inch no matter how powerful the foe. They will not trade a Soviet master for a U.S. ambassador with proconsul ambitions, nor will they trade what the West calls their harsh and medieval Islamic theology for the Pillsbury Doughboy–version of Christianity now on offer from the Vatican and Canterbury. The gentle refrain of "kumbaya" will never replace the full-throated "Allahu Akhbar"—"God Is Greatest"—in the land of the Hindu Kush.

This gradual, fatal shifting of allegiances is again something that could have been readily forecast if the checkables had been checked. A short visit to the local library would document this sort of defection among the Afghans allied to the Soviets and the British—it happened twice to Britain—and would confirm that those Afghans who stood to the end with the foreigners expected and met, as did Sergeant Billy Fish in *The Man Who Would Be King*—Kipling's timeless tale of foreigners coming to grief in Afghanistan—no mercy at the hands of the country's liberators. Neither before nor after Masood's death were he or his fighters pro-Western, pro-American, or Islamic moderates. They were and are as anti-Western, radically Islamic, and militantly xenophobic as the forces led by Khalis, Haqqani, and Hekmatyar. We in the West were able to cultivate our delusion about Masood and what he represented only because of Masood's indisputable genius for media manipulation, and the Western media's own desperate search for a major Afghan commander their words could shape into a man who seemed somewhat like "us." Regret over Masood's demise and lingering memories of that heroic man have so far blocked the West from seeing his successors as the treacherous, isolated, second-rate lot they are. This worm will eventually turn with a vengeance, however, and we will again suffer for ignoring the checkables.

The Fatal Seven

The list of ignored Afghan checkables that might have saved the United States from the now unfolding nightmare and ultimate ignominy is too lengthy for comprehensive examination here. I therefore have selected, with apologies to T.E. Lawrence, what can be called the "Seven Pillars of Truth about Afghanistan." Ignoring any of these pillars would have endangered U.S. chances for success in Afghanistan; being on the wrong side of all seven—while a negative accomplishment of Homeric proportion—ensures a self-inflicted, and so, thoroughly merited disaster. For those interested in a detailed, painful, but at times hilarious account of the near-complete ignorance of these pillars among U.S. leaders—and apparently among the intelligence-community analysts who wrote for them—see Bob Woodward's *Bush at War*.

Pillar I: Minorities Can Rule in Kabul, but Not for Long

For more than three centuries, Afghanistan's Pashtun tribes, their tribal codes and traditions, and the tenets of a strongly conservative Islam have dominated the country's usually monarchical central government. There have been three exceptions to this rule: the Tajik Habibullah Ghazi—a.k.a. Bacho-i-Saqo or "son of the water carrier"—who overthrew a westernizing Pashtun king and was Islamic but not Pashtun; the Afghan communist regime, which was overwhelmingly Pashtun but not Islamic; and Karzai's Tajik-dominated government, which is neither Pashtun nor more than nominally Islamic. The first two experiments in minority rule ended when they were violently overthrown by Pashtun forces, Habibullah—until recently the only case in Afghan history of rule passing to the Tajiks—after nine months (December 1928–September 1929) and the Afghan communists after fifteen Red Army–backed years (1978–1992). The same fate seems likely for Karzai's minority-dominated administration. "The Pashtuns, who have ruled Afghanistan for 250 years," explained Pakistan's former chief of army staff, General Mirza Aslam Beg, "have been pushed into a corner and are brooding over the [mis]treatment of fellow Pashtuns" by the Karzai regime.[47] Unless U.S.–led foreign forces are massively increased and are prepared to kill liberally and remain in Afghanistan permanently, the current Afghan regime cannot survive.

Pillar II: The Afghans Who Matter Are Muslim Tribal Xenophobes

In 1989 or 1990, I was assigned to accompany a senior intelligence-community official to give a briefing on Afghanistan to the Senate Select Committee on Intelligence. My small role was to provide a concise but detailed sketch of the current political-military situation in the country. The plan was to finish this presentation quickly, so most of the session could be devoted to the senators' questions for my boss. All went according to plan, but as I finished, a clearly agitated senator asked me a question. Having caught my attention, this distinguished gentleman—who represented one of what Mr. Lincoln called the "border states"—cleared his throat and drawled: "Sir, do I understand you correctly? Do you mean that after the United States has spent ten years and billions of dollars to support the Afghan resistance, we are soon going to have anti-American Muslims running the government in Kabul? Are you saying that we have helped to create an Islamic regime in Afghanistan?" Standing nonplussed and suppressing a grin, I was providentially rescued by the senior official, who soothingly told the senator that the Afghan Islamists did have the whip hand at the moment, but the composition of the next regime in Kabul was still not set.

I recount this incident because quite a few current U.S. officials share that border-state senator's surprise that Afghans are Muslims, tribal, and xenophobic. Besides the Red Army's presence and depredations, these were the only forces that maintained the tenuous alliance of the ethnically diverse resistance groups during the Soviet–Afghan war. They are as powerful as they were twenty years ago; Islam, in fact, is far stronger and more conservative. Today, the few pro-Western Afghans in Kabul are clustered around Karzai and the returned expatriates in the transitional regime created by the UN in the Bonn Accords and installed by U.S. air power and bayonets. In most ways, Karzai and the returnees are Afghans in name only. In their opposition to tribalism; support for secular political and liberal religious views; and faith in the quick growth of democracy, they are more Westerners. They in no way are regarded by Afghans as leaders. "We do not know what sort of human being with sound wisdom and conscience," Gulbuddin Hekmatyar wrote in a letter to the U.S. Democratic Party explaining the Afghans' disdain for Karzai and his lieutenants,

> would consider people rulers of a country whose personal security is also maintained by foreigners—who cannot trust any of their compa-

triots in the entire country and cannot find any force inside the country to keep them safe inside their own palace; those who go to their own province and to their own countrymen under the protection of American commandos, and even then they are attacked.[48]

In a short time—much of it now elapsed—the Afghans' revulsion at the infidels' installation and management of the regime, occupation of the land, and their ingrained tribal pride, localism, and xenophobia, will yield a violently anti-U.S. attitude among most Pashtuns and some of the minorities who helped put Karzai in power. As of January 2004, U.S. forces in Afghanistan face a slowly accelerating shift that will end in Afghans of all ethnic groups fighting to evict U.S.–led forces. As this eventuality nears, there will be wailing and complaining by Afghans that the United States, the West, and Japan have failed to provide enough food, money, technology, expertise, peacekeepers, computers, and whatever to "rebuild the Afghan nation" and have thereby reneged on their promises and—as in 1989–1992—abandoned Afghanistan. Nonsense. The amount of foreign aid flowing to Afghanistan is relevant only in that higher amounts may give Karzai a limited stay of execution; it will not allow his survival. In Afghanistan, above all other places, familiarity with foreigners breeds not just contempt, but war to the death.

Pillar III: Afghans Cannot Be Bought

Perhaps the hardiest myth about Afghanistan is that money can buy anyone and anything in the country. This myth was trumpeted as gospel before and after the U.S. invasion began in October 2001. The media quoted tens of "unnamed" U.S. officials who told of stories of U.S. intelligence officers and soldiers moving about the Afghan countryside with boxes of cash, cleverly buying the loyalty of Afghans to ensure the Taleban's fall, limit U.S. casualties, and make way for democracy. "I always found," a former CIA station chief swaggered forward to say, "that a few million here and there worked wonders [in Afghanistan]. Loyalties are complex there but money will still work."[49] The truth about this often-told tale is that nothing could be more untrue. That said, the myth is so sturdy that people hold it even when simultaneously faced with irrefutably definitive evidence to the contrary. Again we return to *Bush at War*. First, Woodward recounts several senior U.S. government officials explaining how they had bought control of the Northern Alliance; one such episode described CIA officers giving a senior Alliance leader $500,000 in ten one-foot stacks of hundred-dollar bills and a promise that "there was more money available—much more."[50] Next, Woodward quotes the U.S. secretary of state as saying, "no one wants the Northern Alliance in Kabul, not even the Northern Alliance" because, Woodward explains, "the Southern tribes would go bonkers seeing their rivals in the capital."[51] This being the case, one would be excused for assuming several one-foot stacks of hundred-dollar bills would have been used to keep the Northern Alliance out of Kabul. The Alliance entered Kabul with utter disdain for U.S. concerns on 13 December 2003.

Afghans will always take your money, but afterwards they will do what you want only if they were going to do it anyway. So stubbornly contrary are the Afghans, moreover, that they may well take your money and then decide not to do what they had intended just to avoid appearing to do your bidding. America, Saudi Arabia, and other states sent billions of dollars in cash, weapons, bribes, salaries, and supplies to the Afghan resistance in the course of its ten-year jihad against the Soviets, and many U.S. officials and politicians spoke as if the Afghans therefore had been under our command. In truth, the Afghan jihadists took all the swag we and others could deliver and then did what they would have done without it—they killed Russians. The Afghans consistently refused to attack, move, or speak as we directed, asked, suggested, or pleaded, no matter how much financial support we provided. Ironically, no organization was more eager to take our money and less willing to do what was asked than Masood and his Jamiat Islami fighters, those whom Washington's desk-bound chest beaters crowed about buying lock, stock, and barrel in late 2001. An excellent example of the Afghans' determination to go their own way is made in the following anecdote, which may even be true. In the late 1980s, it is said, a senior U.S. diplomat—speaking for a government that was donating billions of dollars to the mujahideen—met Hisbi Islami chief Yunis Khalis, a recipient of American largesse, and told him that because Soviet leader Mikhail Gorbachev was seriously considering the withdrawal of Soviet forces from Afghanistan, the insurgents should encourage Moscow by slowing combat activity. Khalis is said to have quietly responded: "No, we will kill them until they go." Taken aback, the diplomat revised his argument, this time stressing that U.S. and Western diplomatic activities were key to forcing a Soviet withdrawal, and that this pressure would be greater if the Afghans reduced attacks on the Red Army. Khalis, as he walked away, quietly said: "No, they will leave because we are killing them and we will kill them until they leave. If we keep killing them, they will go."

Despite the claims of "unnamed" senior U.S. officials, our profligate distribution of boxes and suitcases of cash between 7 October 2001 and the conclusion of the March 2002 battle of Shahi Kowt bought us two things: auxiliaries who created a permissive environment in which Taleban and al Qaeda forces returned to their natural state as insurgents, and the chance to install a new but already-dead government of hated minorities in Kabul. All major al Qaeda and Taleban leaders—except the former's Mohammed Atef and the latter's intelligence chief Qari Amadullah, who were killed by U.S. air power—were allowed to escape by our Afghan hirelings. Most of the groups' rank-and-file fighters also eluded our just-purchased allies to fight another day—a study by the UK–based International Institute of Strategic Studies estimates "ninety percent of bin Laden's forces survived"[52]—and the battles of Tora Bora and Shahi Kowt were only the most egregious examples of our allies neglecting to dog the escape hatches. "Anyone who follows the news from Afghanistan," al Qaeda's Abu-Ubayd al-Qurashi wrote just after the end of the Shahi Kowt battle, "will see how the different factions are playing with the Americans in order to prolong the flow of dollars as much as possible and are trying to strengthen their own interests without participating seriously in the American crusade."[53]

Finally, if more proof of the Afghans' refusal to be bought is needed, we can note that no Afghan has provided information yielding the capture of what are called "high value targets" (HVTs). Despite living in the planet's poorest state, and the bait of $100 million of U.S. reward money that is widely advertised on radio, matchbooks, newspapers, and posters, not one Afghan—you know, the breed that does anything for money—has been willing to betray Islam and his tribal code to help capture Messrs. Omar, bin Laden, and al-Zawahiri and make himself rich. "The astronomical figures of the rewards, in millions of dollars, failed to move Muslims in Afghanistan an inch from their principles," al Qaeda's *Al-Ansar* journal said in an essay entitled "The Illusions of America," which derided U.S. ignorance of its enemy. "America did not receive any significant information that could enable it to win the war. This was an example of sincerity that is unknown in modern history, one that has upset the calculations of America, which has started its countdown for defeat in America."[54] As the saying goes, *caveat emptor*.

Pillar IV: Strong Governments in Kabul Cause War

This truism so far seems to have escaped President Karzai and his U.S. and Western advisers. The U.S. State Department, for example, wants a strong central government in Kabul to prevent a situation where "interested parties would try to carve out territory or spheres of interest," and Karzai himself, according to the UN's political adviser in Afghanistan in the 1990s, "has attempted to impose the kind of centralized rule [the Taleban] envisioned—if not its religious principles."[55] This is yet another strong indicator that Karzai is not a representative Afghan and that his foreign advisers have not bothered to read a survey or two of Afghan history. Afghanistan preeminently is a country of regions, subregions within regions, and subdivisions within subregions based on ethnic, tribal, and linguistic differences. In this complex web of interrelationships, the central government in Kabul historically played a limited role, one primarily focused on foreign affairs and running a national military organization of sorts. Since 1945, Kabul also has served as the conduit through which aid from foreign governments, international institutions, and nongovernmental organizations is received and dispersed to the regions. Even when ruled by a monarchy—until 1973—the central government was weak. The king was greatly respected as an individual, but, in terms of direct rule, his government's power did not extend much beyond Kabul—thus Karzai's current moniker, "the mayor of Kabul." The last Kabul government that tried to impose direct rule and uniform laws and regulations on the country's regions, ethnic groups, and tribes was the Peoples' Democratic Party of Afghanistan, the Afghan communists. Even a casual reader of the media will recall that this attempt at centralized rule from Kabul, in the name of modernization, Marx, and secularism, sparked uprisings across the country, nearly overthrew the regime in the late 1970s, and led to the 1979 Soviet invasion and all the horrors that followed. After twenty years of war and ineffective or alien government in Kabul, the regions, subregions, and tribes have never been more autonomously minded and jealous of their prerogatives. In this environment, even mild direction from Karzai's Kabul is likely to be interpreted as dictatorial and resisted, leaving Karzai in a lose-lose situation: abandon his centralizing policies or bloodily enforce them with the infidels' soldiers.

Pillar V: An International Cockpit Not Insular Backwater

"Russia is arming one warlord, Iran another," the hard-nosed Pakistani journalist Ahmed Rashid told the West in early 2003. "Wealthy Saudis have resumed funding Islamic extremists and some Central Asian Republics are backing their ethnic allies. India and Pakistan are playing out an intense rivalry as they secretly back opposing forces." Far too often, the West ignores the reality occurring on what Rashid termed the "playing fields of Afghanistan" and believes that if only a stable government ruled in Afghanistan, the country would fade into a brooding insularity in which the Afghans would torment themselves but stop bothering the rest of the world. This is what the historian Thucydides referred to as "hope, which is the prop of the desperate."

While each of Afghanistan's neighbors publicly speak of a desire and support for a united, stable Afghanistan, none of them share the same definition of unity and stability, and none will tolerate a stable Afghanistan unless it protects their interests. Pakistan wants a stable Islamist and Pashtun-dominated government in Kabul, one that hates India and aspires to Islamicize Central Asia, this last to keep the Islamist Afghans focused northward and not east toward Pakistan. Russia, Uzbekistan, Turkey, and Tajikistan want a state dominated by mildly Islamic Tajik and Uzbek Afghans, which will create a buffer in the country's northern tier to stem the flow of Sunni militancy to Central Asia from southern Afghanistan and the Persian Gulf. Toward this end, Moscow and Turkey have been directing much of their aid to, respectively, the senior Tajik leader Field Marshall Fahim and Uzbek general Dostum, rather than to Karzai's regime as a whole. Iran, as always, is aiming for an Afghan regime that protects the lives and interests of the country's historically persecuted Shia minority, greatly reduces the production and export of heroin, and allows for the expansion of Iranian Shi'ism into Central Asia. Saudi Arabia and the other Gulf states, conversely, still require what they required during the anti-Soviet jihad: a Sunni Islamic, Taleban-like regime that will block the expansion of Shi'-ism through Afghanistan to Central Asia and will instead spur the growth of Sunni militancy there. India, needless to say, dreams of a near-to-secular government in Kabul, that is friendly to New Delhi, promotes the growth of neither Sunnism nor Shi'ism in Afghanistan and Central Asia, and works with India's military and intelligence services to spy on and conduct subversion in Pakistan, thereby making sure that

Islamabad always has to worry about the security and stability of its western border. The United States, the West, and the UN want to believe that the just-named governments' often-voiced support for Afghan unity and stability under Karzai's ATA is genuine; therefore, they will be sorely disappointed.

Pillar VI: Pakistan Must Have an Islamist, Pashtun-dominated Afghan Regime

Although akin to Pillar V, this reality merits separate treatment because it is always ignored by Westerners and because it involves the stability and even survival of a nuclear power. Since the subcontinent was partitioned in 1947, Pakistan has had three paramount and nonnegotiable security concerns: most important, deterring its giant Hindu neighbor India; acquiring and then protecting a nuclear weapons capability; and ensuring to the greatest extent possible that a friendly, Pashtun-dominated government rules in Kabul. Actually, deterring India is Pakistan's overriding national security concern, and the other two issues enable and support that deterrent. Only once in Pakistan's history—between 1998 and 2001—were all three of these national interests adequately and simultaneously addressed. In May 1998, Pakistan successfully tested a nuclear weapon—matching India's long-ago-acquired bomb—and, at the same time, the Taleban held about three-quarters of Afghanistan, ensuring amity along the Durand line that demarcated the Pakistan–Afghanistan border. For a golden moment, Islamabad found that Allah had perfectly aligned the planets.

Today, the Afghan leg of Pakistan's national security triumvirate lies shattered in a thousand and more pieces—and matters are growing worse. The Taleban was routed in the first major battle of the U.S.–Afghan war and has reverted to an insurgent government-in-waiting—it will return to power; it is only a question of when and under what name. Also troubling for Islamabad—not because it might succeed, but because it destabilizes Afghanistan—is the U.S.–backed ATA, which is trying to lay the groundwork for what would be a nominally Islamic state, and one that is demonstrably non-Pashtun, pro-Russia, and pro-India. Always eager to get a lick in on Pakistan, New Delhi has worked closely with Karzai's regime, sending military observers to Afghanistan and resuming training Afghan officers in India's military academies; reopening its Kabul embassy with the anti-Pakistani Vivek Katju as ambassador; and has established an extensive diplomatic presence, with consulates in Herat, Mazar-e Sharif, Jalalabad, and Qandahar.

In addition, Washington and U.S. military commanders—the latter always willing to fight to the last drop of the other guy's blood—are pushing Pakistan to move its regular military forces into the country's border regions adjacent to Afghanistan. This is an area where Islamabad's writ is seldom observed and where a destabilizing revolt against Pakistan by the border's autonomous Pashtun tribes—and their Afghan Pashtun brothers—is the most likely result of the endeavor so cavalierly urged by America. "A recent visit to the tribal area," David Rohde reported for the *New York Times* in December 2002, "confirmed that opposition to the United States is vehement and growing. . . . As a result, a year after the Taleban's fall, the tribal areas are emerging as a newly emboldened stronghold of Islamic militancy."[56] Given Pakistan's overriding concern with the threat from India, the current Afghan situation, from Islamabad's perspective, is simply and dangerously intolerable. While doing what it can to appear helpful to the United States and rhetorically supportive of the ATA, Pakistan's national survival depends on reinstalling a Taleban-like regime in Kabul and avoiding actions that would trigger warfare—civil war, really—between the Pakistan's well-armed Pashtun tribes and the Pakistani military. President Musharraf will move army units into the tribal areas to placate Washington—as he did in the fall of 2003 and early 2004—but odds are they consistently will be just a bit tardy when opportunities arise to capture or destroy major al Qaeda or Taleban targets. Stability and peace in the tribal belt must be Islamabad's top priority, whatever the wishes of the Americans.

At day's end, Islamabad cannot endlessly play America's game vis-à-vis Afghanistan and count on the survival of the government and Pakistani sovereignty. Whether under President Musharraf or his successor, Islamabad will support the Taleban's effort to retake Afghanistan. While the West will decry this as the work of "rogue elements" in the Pakistani military or intelligence service, they will be wrong. As it has been since the 1979 Soviet invasion, support for the Taleban will be a government-wide, if covert, effort to ensure a Pakistan-friendly Kabul regime. Indeed, it may be that Pakistani assistance never has stopped doing so. Pakistani border units, for example, offered no opposition to al Qaeda escapees after the Tora Bora and Shahi Kowt battles, and now appear to be letting Taleban and al Qaeda forces cross the border to attack U.S. and ATA targets and then return to Pakistan. There are reports, moreover, that Pakistani intelligence moved al Qaeda

fighters to safety in Pakistani Kashmir; that post-invasion help was provided al Qaeda by Pakistan's surrogate Kashmiri insurgent groups,
Lashkar-e Tayyiba and Jaish-e-Mohammed; and that the Islamist-
dominated government of the North West Frontier Province will not
allow serious actions by Pakistan's army against the Taleban and al
Qaeda in the border areas, though it has clearly agreed to Islamabad
stationing additional army units in the area. These units will stage
enough operations and spill enough blood to satisfy U.S. demands for
"action"—and thereby avoid giving U.S. leaders a basis for unilateral
action inside Pakistan—but they will not take actions that risk capturing bin Laden or Mullah Omar, events that would offend Pakistan's
Gulf benefactors and foment armed conflict with the Pashtun tribes.
Faced with an eroding economy; rising Islamist power in Pakistan's
society, politics, military, and security services; and India's growing
conventional military strength, Pakistan's rulers cannot afford to
blithely increase threats to national security by letting an anti-Pakistani
Kabul regime take root or by taking coercive, bloody anti-Taleban and
anti-al Qaeda military action in the Pakistan–Afghanistan border area
that could spark civil war or drive the Afghan and Pakistani Pashtun
tribes to secede and form their own nation.

Pillar VII: There Will Be an Islamist Regime in Kabul

To state the obvious, Afghanistan is a country of truly conservative
Islamic temperament. This was true in the British Raj, when the Afghan
communists took power in the 1970s, when Moscow invaded in 1979,
and it remains so today. And the trend is toward an ever more conservative brand of Islam. Why so? First, because of the thirteen-year war
(1979–1992) against the Soviets and the Afghan communists fought in
God's name and fueled by unwavering faith. Second, because a two-
year civil war (1992–1994) was fought to a draw because the United
States, the West, and the UN—in an early version of the doctrine now
seen in Iraq—prevented the Afghan Islamist insurgents, who beat the
Soviets, from taking power and implementing Islamic law. As in Iraq,
self-determination was defined as a U.S.–approved government that is
not an Islamic regime. Third, because of the seven-year armed struggle
(1994–2001) it took to end this deadlock, begin the formation of a
national regime, and nearly establish countrywide law and order.
Fourth, because the Afghans are now waging a war that, though of the
Taleban's making, has taken their xenophobic and tribally dominated

country into a new era of foreign domination, one characterized by armed resistance to Western occupation and the bayonet-point installation of a regime with no Islamic credentials. "I do not find a convincing reason for their [U.S. and NATO troops] continued presence," IULA leader and nominal Karzai ally Abdul Rasul Sayyaf told *al-Sharq al-Awsat*. "We did not get rid of the Soviets to get the Americans in the end."[57]

As always, the Afghans themselves said it best prior to the 2001 U.S. invasion. "We thank God," said the Taleban radio service, in words that could have been said about invading infidels by any ethnic group, Sunni or Shia, today or any time in two millennia of Afghan history,

> that the Afghans with such small power and such poverty are confronted by America, which is a powerful force. It is coming with all its force to confront the Afghans from the East to the West. In response, we, Afghans, also thank God that [the United States] is standing against us. . . . If America make[s] aggression on our country, we are ready with all our resources. Our children, praise be to God, are also ready. We, with love, want from Almighty God that America comes to our territory.[58]

As seen from an Afghan-centric perspective, the Afghan Islamists have twice been denied the fruit of their military victories; they are certain to try for them again. Beyond their strong faith and traditional xenophobia, three other factors will aid the Islamists' drive to power. First, since 1979 nearly six million Afghans have, at one or another time, lived as refugees in camps in Pakistan and Iran. The education for children raised, or born and raised, in the camps featured a militant curriculum taught by Iranian clerics, Saudi clerics, clerics from other Gulf countries, Pakistani clerics who were trained in Saudi universities or by Saudi clerics, and Afghan clerics—like Taleban chief Mullah Omar—who were trained by Saudi, Pakistani, Iranian, or Gulf clerics. The refugees' return to Afghanistan, therefore, must inevitably enhance the militant Islamists'—Sunni and Shia—dominance of Afghan society, and move the once-isolated Islam of Afghanistan further into the Muslim's world mainstream. Second, Sunni Islamic NGOs—many of them from Saudi Arabia—have been at work in Afghanistan for a quarter century, educating young Afghans with the same Salafi Islamic curriculum taught in the refugee camps in Pakistan, and that was taught to

Osama bin Laden in Saudi Arabia. Along with potable water, prenatal care, and cottage-industry skills, the NGOs have provided another stimulus to the deepening conservatism of Afghan Islam. Third, most Afghans realize that only three entities consistently stood by them in the years since the Soviet invasion: Allah, the Islamic NGOs, and Osama bin Laden. Mullah Omar has told Afghans, "Usama helped us in the war against the Russians. He is not going to leave us now. . . . Usama will live with us and die with us."[59] These three realities taught them that Islam was the key to survival and ultimate victory and that little or no non-Islamic help was coming to them, a reality that added another stimulus to faith. The reestablishment of an Islamic regime in Kabul is as close to an inevitability as exists. One hopes that Karzai and the rest of the Westernized, secular, and followerless Afghan expatriates we installed in Kabul are able to get out with their lives.

3

NOT DOWN, NOT OUT: AL QAEDA'S RESILIENCY, EXPANSION, AND MOMENTUM

With a rank and file vastly inferior to our own, intellectually and physically, [the Army of Northern Virginia] had, by discipline alone, acquired a character for steadiness and efficiency unsurpassed, in my judgment, in ancient or modern times.

Major General Joseph Hooker, c. 1863.[1]

[A] more sinewy, tawny, formidable-looking set of men could not be. In education they are certainly inferior to our native-born people, but they are usually very quick-witted within their own sphere of comprehension; and they know how to handle weapons with terrible effect. Their great characteristic is their stoical manliness; they never beg, whimper, or complain; but look you straight in the face, with as little animosity as if they have never heard a gun.

Colonel Theodore Draper, 1922.[2]

General Robert E. Lee's Army of Northern Virginia. There is no military organization in American history that is more—or more justly—famous and admired, even revered. I chose the epigrams above because they come from the throats of Hooker and Draper, senior U.S. military

59

officers who represented, understood, and applied the overwhelming military, economic, and manpower advantages the Union held over the Confederacy, and yet recognized that these immense advantages did not guarantee the rebels' defeat and the Union's restoration. Before that desired end could be attained, the men of the Army of Northern Virginia—underfed, dirty, unkempt, poorly supported logistically, unpaid, and armed with a variety of old and new weapons—had to be fought and broken, militarily and psychologically. The rebels had to be made to both see and believe that further resistance was pointless. Messrs. Hooker and Draper—as well as Grant, Sherman, Thomas, Sheridan, Stanton, Mr. Lincoln, and hundreds of others—knew the rebels' looks deceived and that, no matter how they appeared, the rebels were at least their equals in determination, audacity, endurance, loyalty to their cause, religious zealousness, optimism, and just plain pluck. Hooker, Draper, and the rest knew that, to save the Union, the Army of Northern Virginia would have to be all but annihilated, which was its condition when Lee surrendered to Grant at Appomattox Court House.

The Hookers and Drapers of today's Union are confronting another nation's—the Muslim ummah's—rebels or, more properly, mujahideen. Like Lee's boys, the mujahideen are often dirty, unkempt, bearded, armed with a variety of weapons, rarely paid, and haphazardly supplied. And like Lee's boys, they are aflame with courage, audaciousness, commitment to their cause, optimism, and religious zeal. As did Hooker, Draper, and their colleagues, the political and military officers of today's Union understand its overwhelming economic and conventional military advantage. Unlike those men, however, today's Union leaders appear deceived by the looks of their foes. And so, we are, as a country, a long way from Appomattox.

First, Survive

The first job of an insurgent organization like al Qaeda is neither to stand and fight nor to be able to hit its foe with a single, fatal blow. Its first responsibility always is to be positioned to prevent its annihilation by a single, comprehensive military strike or campaign by its always more powerful enemy. "Turn the mujahedin military force into small units with good administrative capabilities; [this] will spare us big losses," al Qaeda's chief of military operations Sayf al-Adil advised the nascent Iraqi Islamist resistance in March 2003. "Large military units pose management problems. They occupy large areas which are difficult to conceal from air reconnaissance and air attack"[3] As al-Adil noted, the historical *modus operandi* of successful insurgent groups is, first, to avoid concentrating forces and thereby prevent catastrophic defeat; second, to protect senior leaders to the greatest extent possible while expecting significant leadership losses and having succession arrangements in place; and, third, to use whatever weapons come to hand to wear down the enemy in military, economic, political, and morale terms. Al Qaeda has followed historical precedent since its inception in the late 1980s, and in doing so remains, after seven years of war with the United States, so effective an organization that senior U.S. officials repeatedly warn the citizenry that bin Laden's fighters are as dangerous now as on 11 September 2001. "Even catastrophic attacks on the scale of 11 September," said the director of central intelligence in early 2004, "remain within al Qaeda's reach"[4] Indeed, senior U.S. officials suggest al Qaeda may be more dangerous, warning that it aspires to detonate a weapon of mass destruction in the continental United States. "I have consistently warned this committee," the director of central intelligence told U.S. senators in February 2004, "of al Qaeda's interest in chemical, biological, radiological (CBRN) weapons. Over the last year we have also seen an increase in the threat of more sophisticated CBRN [attacks.]"[5]

How did al Qaeda survive the onslaught of the United States, the world's strongest and most lethal military power? In the first instance, al Qaeda owes much to the decision of U.S. officials to define it as a terrorist group, and its Taleban hosts as a traditional nation-state. The consensus supporting these inaccurate decisions yielded what I referred to in Chapter 1 as the "deadly delay." If America's assumptions about its enemies had been valid, the Taleban might have been sitting and waiting to be annihilated when we attacked on 7 October 2001, and the relatively small numbers of al Qaeda terrorists—terrorist groups, by definition, must have small numbers—might have been rounded up after Mullah Omar's lads were dished. Tragically, neither assumption was correct, and, to make matters worse, they had been proven demonstrably wrong long before 11 September 2001.

Saving as Much as Possible in Afghanistan

While the Taleban controlled at least 85 percent of Afghanistan's territory when Masood was killed, it was far from a national government in the Western sense. The Taleban kept its headquarters in Qandahar—never moving its main offices to Kabul—and from there gradually won control of the countryside and cities, gradually imposing order and harsh justice based on Islamic law across the country. Notwithstanding these actions, the Taleban remained what it always has been: a rural-based, Islamist insurgency that ruled by force, ethnic domination, and application of the shariah. Given this status, the Taleban could be—and was—quickly driven from Afghan cities in late 2001, but this loss was not a defeat in the way a traditional nation-state would be defeated if it lost its major urban centers. After losing the battle of the cities, Mullah Omar and his forces simply returned to their state of nature as a rural insurgent organization. In many ways, the Taleban became stronger and more focused after losing the cities because it was relieved of the burden of delivering water, electricity, sanitation and police services, food, medicine, and education to urban populations. It also deftly stepped off America's bull's-eye by dispersing—fully armed—to the countryside to resume living in the multitude of villages from which it came, there shielded by sympathetic tribes, clans, and families. This reality, wrote the U.S. Army War College's Stephen Biddle, was bad for U.S.–led coalition forces because it placed "thousands of still-hostile observers in villages across the country."[6]

All told, the defense-issues website *Stratfor.com* in November 2001 concluded that the Taleban "are now stripped to their ethnic and ideological core, intact, with most of their arms and equipment. . . . The Taleban are now prepared to adopt a strategy that is more amenable to their tactical strength and resources."[7] It must also be noted that the U.S. commanders did their part to preserve the Taleban by their complete unwillingness to root the group out of mountainous, rural Afghanistan because that process promised high Afghan civilian or U.S. military casualties. While it is crazy to argue the Taleban wanted to lose the cities—they clearly did not—it would be madness to assume they were defeated because the cities fell in the first battle of what is destined to be a long and ultimately losing war for the United States.

Al Qaeda also benefited from the fact that the Taleban, despite losing a battle, remained functional and, even better, had become more geographically dispersed and therefore able to hide bin Laden's fighters in broader areas of the country. Contrary to Washington's operative assumption, al Qaeda had far more personnel in Afghanistan than would have been found on a terrorist group's manning table. This is because al Qaeda is an insurgent, vice terrorist, organization and has two primary, manpower-intensive missions: to provide quality insurgent training to Muslims from around the world, and to build an ample cadre of veteran fighters who can be sent foreign legion–like to serve as combat leaders, trainers, engineers, logisticians, financial advisers, or administrators wherever militant Islam needs them. In September 2001, al Qaeda's Afghan camps were training insurgents as they had since the late 1980s. Some terrorists or urban warfare specialists—the two have much in common—were surely being trained, but at a ratio any less than fifteen to one would be surprising.

As noted in Chapter 2 (and as will be discussed in detail in Chapter 6), the documents recovered from the Afghan camps, the intelligence gained from prisoners of war, and, especially, the superb combat performance of al Qaeda and al Qaeda-trained units against U.S.–led forces show that the West has been wrong about the camps' main purpose for more than a decade. Al Qaeda's camps were staffed by veteran fighters who trained insurgents who fought, and trained others to fight, not only against the Northern Alliance in Afghanistan, but also against national armies in Indian Kashmir, Chechnya, Uzbekistan, Eritrea, Yemen, Saudi Arabia, Algeria, Tajikistan, Egypt, Bosnia, western China, Indonesia, Malaysia, Macedonia, Kosovo, and the Philippines. Again, this is not to say the camps did not train terrorists; quite the contrary, given the 11 September attacks, they obviously trained the world's most-talented terrorists. It is to say, however, that terrorist or urban warfare training was a small subset of the camps' primary training regimen; the men who got such training are, in effect, the special forces of al Qaeda, the Taleban, and the foreign Islamist groups that send men to the camps. Most men attending al Qaeda camps are trained as "irregular ground combatants," explained U.S. soldiers after exploiting al Qaeda manuals captured in Kabul. But the group's system is "a sort of two-tiered university for waging Islamic war," and only a small fraction of men go to the second tier to train for "terrorist assignments abroad."[8] Just as U.S. Marines are first riflemen, men trained by al Qaeda are first insurgents. And like some Marines, some al Qaeda cadre take subsequent training that adds a specialty to their basic skills, in this case urban warfare or, more commonly, terrorist skills.

Thus, al Qaeda had large numbers of fighters to disperse and protect before the U.S. invasion. While full documentation is lacking, it is safe to assume al Qaeda's leaders began the dispersal process before the 11 September attacks; as noted earlier, bin Laden knew the attack date six days in advance, and had long wanted exactly the U.S. response the attacks generated. Because he wanted and expected U.S. ground forces to invade Afghanistan, bin Laden naturally would have spread his forces thin, sticking to the first rule of insurgency: never give the enemy a target that lets him defeat you in one campaign. Dispersal also allowed bin Laden and his lieutenants to place combat units in areas of Afghanistan where they and the Taleban wanted to fight, while keeping them away from places of no consequence. For al Qaeda, Washington's nearly three-week delay before attacking was heaven sent, and perhaps the most important reason why al Qaeda emerged damaged but not broken from the first round of battles in Afghanistan.

When combat began on 7 October, bin Laden and al Qaeda were substantially reducing their Afghanistan-based manpower to deprive the U.S.–led coalition of targets and because the war they intended to wage would not be ready to initiate for many months; until then, a smaller number of fighters would suffice. "[A]l-Qaeda quickly dismantled itself and did not keep large numbers of Arabs inside Afghanistan," Adb-al-Rahman al-Rashid, a spokesman for the organization told London's *al-Majallah*. "[Al Qaeda leaders] kept the military cadres and numbers needed for managing the military action with the Afghan mujahideen for one year or one year and a half."[9] Having made this decision, al Qaeda moved fighters into the Afghan countryside and mountains, as well as to Pakistan and Iran; while not easy to quantify, it seems certain that far more al Qaeda and non-Afghan Islamic fighters exited to Pakistan rather than to Iran. Other fighters were sent to Central Asia or to their home countries. Few of the fighters wanted to leave. Senior al Qaeda field commander Abd al-Hadi has explained that "we had a great difficulty persuading many of them to leave Afghanistan. . . . I swear some of them wept when they were told to leave."[10]

Al Qaeda also used its long-established ties to the Pashtun tribes in the eastern and southeastern Afghan provinces—many also allies of the mainly Pashtun Taleban—to keep open exit and entry routes along the Afghanistan–Pakistan border. Likewise, the cooperative ties al Qaeda and the Taleban had with the chiefs of the southern Afghan heroin-trafficking networks allowed them to move fighters across the Afghanistan–Iran and Afghanistan–Pakistan borders, and to use the cities of Mashad, Zahedan Chaman, Quetta, and Karachi for transit and safe haven. Via the traffickers' well-established routes through Iran, moreover, al Qaeda was able to move fighters to the Persian Gulf states, Turkey, and, through Turkey, to Europe.

When the out-of-South-Asia-bound fighters reached the ill-defined

Afghanistan–Pakistan border, their onward travel was assisted by Pakistan's Pashtun tribes, sympathetic or corrupt Pakistani bureaucrats—the frontier's "political officers" of whom Kipling wrote—and a large number of Islamists in Pakistan's military, intelligence, security, and border forces. Help also came from Islamic NGOs operating near the border, the vast overt and covert organizations of Pakistan's major Islamic political parties—such as Qazi Hussein Ahmed's Jamaat Islami—and the networks run by such Kashmiri insurgent groups as Jaish-e-Mohammed, Lashkar-e Tayyiba, and Hizbul Mujahideen.[11] Indeed, the pivotal part played by the Kashmiri organizations in helping al Qaeda fighters escape is one of the more ominous post-11 September developments. This collaboration deepened a long but never before so operationally oriented relationship. Overall, al Qaeda moved fighters to safety in Pakistan and beyond by using an informal but extraordinarily broad and effective support system, most of which had been operating for decades or, in the case of the tribes, for centuries. "The al Qaeda expresses its profound thanks and gratitude," the journal *Al-Neda* wrote in thanks for this network of assistance,

> to all those who have cooperated with it and facilitated its course, whether by sacrifice of soul, money, or prayer. We would like to mention in particular the Afghan and Pakistani tribes, which opened their arms and houses, and gave us priority over their sons and relatives in food, drink, dress, and shelter. . . . Why not, after all it was the lofty mountains of these tribes on which the British Empire was smashed.[12]

As noted in Chapter 2, the insurgents al Qaeda kept behind to fight U.S. forces and their Afghan auxiliaries picked their spots and fought uniformly well. "The non-Afghan al Qaeda . . . have proven resolute and capable fighters," Professor Stephen Biddle wrote after debriefing dozens of U.S. military officers who fought in Afghanistan, ". . . against hard-core al Qaeda opposition, outcomes were in doubt [for U.S. forces] even with the benefit of 21st century U.S. air power and American commandos to direct it."[13] The two major battles fought by al Qaeda at Tora Bora and Shahi Kowt, moreover, may also have been delaying actions meant to let other fighters leave Afghanistan. The Tora Bora fighting, for example, gave insurgents south of Nangarhar Province about three weeks to cross unmolested into Pakistan, while the March 2002 Shahi Kowt battle—also about three weeks—let fighters along almost all of Afghanistan's border with Pakistan to scoot unmolested and undetected.

Since the end of the Shahi Kowt battle, U.S.-led coalition forces have conducted what might be termed a "bombing pause" with no sustained, destructive campaigns on the ground or from the air. One Western pundit disgustedly wrote that "some of us would like a pause in the bombing pause," while al Qaeda itself taunted U.S. forces in April 2002: "[T]o the Americans we say, Here we are in the battlefields again, where are you?"[14] Aside from sporadic, short-term ground operations meant to capture, not kill, al Qaeda and Taleban leaders, and infrequent air strikes—which have hit several weddings or social occasions instead of terrorists—al Qaeda and the Taleban have been under almost no military pressure in Afghanistan since March 2002. "But a [U.S.] military campaign that began with a flourish," David Zucchino wrote in the *Los Angeles Times* on the last day of 2002, "has evolved into a sometimes intrusive police action . . ."[15] Claims by Western leaders that U.S.-led forces are eliminating the "last remnants" of al Qaeda and the Taleban are wrong, the result of severe misunderstanding or deliberate dissembling. Only in summer 2003 did a new round of fighting start in the U.S.–Afghan war as the Taleban and al Qaeda—in league with the forces of the "old" mujahideen—increased attacks on U.S. bases, as well as the convoys and patrols of U.S. forces and their Afghan allies. Al Qaeda also began using remotely detonated mines and improvised explosive devices, while the Taleban began killing Afghans working for the coalition. As events of recent months show, al Qaeda and its allies not only survived the wretchedly ill-conceived U.S. military campaign waged against them, but have retained a strong presence in Afghanistan and seized the initiative. Left with lemons, al Qaeda and the Taleban made a lethal brew that is now being served to their foes.

The Fatal Mistake of Defining Insurgents as Terrorists

One must admire and applaud the numerous and significant successes U.S. intelligence has scored against al Qaeda's terrorist/urban warfare arm since 11 September 2001. These victories have continued and expanded the record of steady pre-11 September U.S. intelligence victories documented in *Through Our Enemies' Eyes*.[16] America's clandestine service, acting unilaterally or with foreign services, has scored telling successes against senior leaders of al Qaeda's terrorist wing, although, oddly, only one senior Taleban leader has been killed, the group's former intelligence chief, Qari Amadullah. While a fuller balance of the wins and losses accruing to al Qaeda and the United States will appear later in this chapter, it must be said the capture of Abu Zubaydah, Khalid Sheikh Mohammed, Khalid bin Attash, Nurjaman Ridwan Isamuddin (a.k.a. Hambali), Ramzi bin al-Shibh and the death of Yusif bin Salih al-Iyari are solid victories; taken together, they suggest U.S. intelligence may have had a significant debilitating though short-term impact on the leadership and planning capabilities of al Qaeda's terrorist force.

I say "may have" had a debilitating impact because I have yet to find—or hear U.S. officials refer to—an order-of-battle study for the al Qaeda insurgent organization. Without this basic reference point it is impossible to objectively determine how badly or permanently al Qaeda has been damaged. As Professor Daniel Byman recently wrote in *The National Interest*, without an accurate al Qaeda order-of-battle, U.S. claims of impact have much more in common with Vietnam-like body counts rather than verified, fact-based analysis. "A body count can be misleading," Byman argued, "because the size of the terrorist cadre is unknown, and many of those killed or captured are low-level recruits who can be easily replaced. More importantly, it fails to reflect the impact on the adversary's morale, recruitment, fund-raising, and residual ability to conduct sophisticated attacks."[17] The defense-issues website *Stratfor.com* put the point more harshly in September 2002. "Al Qaeda is a globally distributed irregular army waging a low-grade unconventional war," wrote the authors of an article entitled "Al Qaeda One Year Later." "Washington has no clear initial order-of-battle for al Qaeda, no measure of disruption caused by U.S. countermeasures since Sept. 11, no gauge of the group's regeneration rate, and no reliable count of its casualties."[18] The validity of the argument by Professor Byman and *Stratfor.com* is underscored by the wild discrepancies in the al Qaeda manpower numbers that have appeared in the literature.

- In March 2003, al Qaeda leader Sayf al-Adil said in *Al-Neda* that al Qaeda had nineteen hundred Arab mujahideen, of whom 350 were killed and 180 wounded.[19]
- In April 2002, an unsigned article in the *Al-Neda* said that during the Afghan war the group deployed sixteen hundred Arabs, of whom 350 were killed and 150 captured.[20]
- In June 2003, unnamed U.S. intelligence officials told *U.S. News and World Report* that al Qaeda's "sworn membership" was down to 180 men.[21]

- In July 2003, the UK–based International Institute for Strategic Studies estimated "at least 20,000 jihadists" were trained in al Qaeda's Afghan camps, of which "over 18,000 potential [al Qaeda] terrorists [are] still at large."[22]
- In August 2003, the UK Parliament's Foreign Affairs Committee published a report that claimed there are seventeen thousand al Qaeda fighters dispersed around the world. Professor Paul Wilkinson of the University of Glasgow, who conducted the study, said seventeen thousand was a "conservative estimate."[23]
- In August 2003, the al Qaeda scholar Rohan Gunaratna said that al Qaeda had four thousand fighters on 1 October 2001 but now "no more than 800 remain."[24]

Al Qaeda also supported Byman's point about the lack of an order-of-battle, arguing in mid-2002 "that the U.S. [military] command was completely in the dark due to the lack of any information on its enemy. Even now the U.S. command does not know the actual number of the [al Qaeda] mujahideen, their combat units, their locations, or the exact type of weapons they have."[25] This ignorance was attributed to U.S. officials still looking at al Qaeda as a traditional Islamist terrorist group. "God willing, the enemy will be taken by surprise every now and then because it knows very little about its enemy/the mujahid,"Abu-Ubayd al-Hilali wrote in *Al-Ansar*.com. "The reason for this is that the enemy's old traditional culture about the jihad groups will not help it to understand this new generation, the generation of victory and liberation, God willing."[26] The lack of basic order-of-battle information, al Qaeda ridiculed, forced U.S. commanders to hide their ignorance by claiming each fight with the mujahideen was the last.

> The deception episode continued to unfold as the United States entered into a direct war with the mujahideen in Afghanistan and tried to present itself to the world as a winner. It was a farcical performance featuring paper tigers as the main characters. All [U.S.] actions were portrayed as "eliminating the last remnants of al-Qaeda and the Taleban", "carrying out the last operation", "destroying the last cave", and "controlling the last position." So much so that the "last" became endless.[27]

Regrettably, Mr. Hilali is exactly right; America and the West have no means to measure success against al Qaeda. The old standby U.S. intelligence-community measure—the chance of attack decreases as time elapsed since the last attack increases—has been shattered beyond recall by al Qaeda. Since declaring war, al Qaeda has amply demonstrated that just because it has not mounted an attack for some period of time does not mean that it cannot. Likewise, the long-held U.S. belief that "[t]he war on terrorism was always going to be principally an intelligence and law enforcement effort and not a military one" is also dead wrong.[28] The U.S. clandestine service performed heroically before and since the 11 September attacks and America is still losing the war, and a large part of why this is so lies in the law-enforcement mentality that infects U.S. conduct in the war on terror. "Since the long-comfortable lines between military and law enforcement missions are collapsing in our fractured world," Ralph Peters said in *Fighting for the Future: Will America Triumph?*, "we must treat the most murderous foreign criminals who attack our citizens as military targets."[29] So, as Americans rejoice over U.S. intelligence victories, they ought also pray that Washington puts away the badge and warrant, and that the so-far lame U.S. and Western analytic corps and militaries begin to pull their weight against al Qaeda by deciding that this is a military, not a criminal, foe who, for the moment, requires a much more sustained and vigorous application of military power. The hard reality is that the U.S. clandestine service has been fighting al Qaeda alone since 1995, was never going to do more than buy time for Washington to rally its forces and allies, and is now just about played out.

As just noted, the impact of intelligence-service accomplishments is lessened by knowing al Qaeda can never be beaten while the U.S. attack is conceived and executed as an international version of the saga of the American West, where U.S. intelligence officers and soldiers are sent out, like the storied Texas Rangers, and expected to always get their man. Sending out the posse has not worked to destroy any terrorist group in the past quarter century—Hizballah, the Tamil Tigers, myriad Palestinian groups, the Basque ETA, and Sendero Luminoso are still operating—and it will never work against a large and talented insurgent organization like al Qaeda. The procedure neither kills nor captures fast enough to outpace al Qaeda's astounding ability to replicate. As London's *Spectator* said in June 2003, "The trouble is that every time a seemingly 'essential' al Qaeda leader has been arrested, he has been replaced with no effect at all on the organization."[30] Further, if the chase-capture-incarcerate method is to work, there must be a baseline of how many people there are to chase and catch/kill if progress is to be measured and victory claims taken seriously. As noted above, I know of no such baseline.

Second, the Old West *modus operandi* is tremendously resource intensive, so much so that you end up focused on a relatively limited geographical area to the near exclusion of other regions. America's successes against al Qaeda's senior terrorist leaders, for example, have been scored overwhelmingly in the narrow geographic corridor between Islamabad, Pakistan, and Amman, Jordan. There have been major arrests and cell takedowns as far afield as Morocco, Thailand, and Buffalo, New York, but the bulk of al Qaeda's defeats have occurred between Islamabad and Amman. (See below for details of al Qaeda's 2001–2003 defeats.) Thus, while we value intelligence victories over al Qaeda, their geographic concentration contradicts claims by U.S. leaders and experts that al Qaeda is being defeated—the noted strategist Edward Lutwack said in September 2003 that al Qaeda "no longer exists as a functioning group"[31]—given their concurrent warning that al Qaeda has a presence in ninety or more countries. Perhaps al Qaeda is on the run in the Islamabad–Amman corridor—with clear exceptions in Afghanistan and Iraq—but limited U.S. success against al Qaeda elsewhere suggests many of its cells remain where and as they were on 11 September 2001, and may have grown stronger while U.S. intelligence toiled valiantly, successfully, and versus long odds between Pakistan and Jordan.

When the post-11 September period is examined, then, an unbalanced picture is found: strong, relentless, and effective attacks against al Qaeda in a relatively small portion of the world, offset by much more limited success elsewhere, all of which is punctuated by the steady pace of al Qaeda military operations. The lack of success in other regions is especially notable in the United States. Given bin Laden's near-obsessive focus on attacking America at home, this fact must be seen as worrying and a scandal-in-waiting for U.S. law-enforcement agencies. Based on this worldwide picture, America would be well served if its leaders took time to review the chase-capture-incarcerate method of attacking al Qaeda and decide if it should remain, as it long has been, the dominant process used by the U.S. government to fight al Qaeda. "America has been fortunate in capturing some high-ranking terrorists," Steven Simon and Daniel Benjamin warned in the *New York Times*, "but we still lack a comprehensive program to cope with a growing global insurgency and the long-term threat of radical Islam, for which intelligence and law enforcement will not suffice."[32] Indeed, as will be seen, the current process does not even stop al Qaeda's ability to grow in areas where it has had a presence or to expand into new ground.

Steady as She Goes in Familiar Locales . . .

Notwithstanding effective U.S. efforts in the Islamabad–Amman corridor, bin Laden's organization continues to exist in areas where it was established before the 11 September attacks, such as (to name a few): Somalia, Kenya, and the East Coast of Africa; the Pacific countries of Indonesia, Malaysia, and the Philippines; Chechnya, Kashmir, and the new Central Asian states; the countries of Western Europe; and Yemen, Saudi Arabia, the United States, and Canada. In these locales, al Qaeda and its allies have used the two years since 11 September to nurture their presence; increase the tempo and lethality of ongoing Islamic insurgencies in the Philippines, Aceh, Kashmir, and Chechnya; and to launch attacks in such places as Kenya, Yemen, Saudi Arabia, Indonesia, Iraq, and Morocco. Indeed, it is possible that the important victories scored by U.S. intelligence between Amman and Islamabad do not outweigh the advances al Qaeda and its allies have made elsewhere. At a minimum, it is true that the U.S.-led coalition has failed to eliminate al Qaeda's presence from even one country where it was established on 11 September 2001. Two good, recent studies of al Qaeda's continued worldwide breadth are Jason Burke's *Al Qaeda: Casting a Shadow of Terror* (2003), and Rohan Gunaratna's *Inside al Qaeda: Global Network of Terror* (2002).[33] Two other measures of the continued viability of al Qaeda's pre-11 September geographical base are found in the constant listings of al Qaeda-infected countries by Western experts—the midsummer 2003 total was sixty, per the UK's International Institute of Strategic Studies[34]—and below in the section detailing the group's 2001–2004 victories.

Saudi Arabia, perhaps, is the most important location to take note of increased al Qaeda activity. The difficulty in analyzing this development, however, lies in determining if al Qaeda is increasing its presence in the kingdom or if its long-established organization there grew more active between 2001 and 2004. There is no doubt that bin Laden is immensely popular in the kingdom. "The majority of the Saudi people," Abd al-Bari Atwan, a critic of the al-Sauds, wrote in *Al-Quds Al-Arabi* in August 2002, "support Shaykh Osama bin Laden and regard him as a popular hero who succeeded in delivering a strong blow to the United States, the primary supporter of Israeli aggression against the Palestinian people."[35] Atwan's opinion seemed to be supported by a poll referred to by Adam Garfinckle in the spring 2002 issue of *National Interest.* "[I]n a recent poll conducted by Saudi intelligence and shared with the U.S. government," Garfinckle wrote, "more than 95 percent of Saudis between 25 and 41 expressed sympathy with Osama bin Laden."[36] Similar views were voiced by an al-Saud supporter, Qenan al-Ghamdi, former editor-in-chief of the daily *Al-Watan.* "Al Qaeda has infiltrated Saudi Arabia more than we had imagined because extremist ideas, like those of bin Laden, have roots here," al-Ghamdi told an interviewer. "When bin Laden calls for jihad or recruits, his ideas find many takers here. . . . We need to admit this. These are not unique cases."[37]

It also seems likely that al Qaeda has penetrated the Saudi security establishment. Just after Kabul fell in late 2001, for example, an al Qaeda computer was recovered that "contained a selection of secret [Saudi] government documents apparently pilfered by al Qaeda sympathizers in the Saudi bureaucracy. These included scanned copies of the handwritten notes of a Saudi secret police agent who had been assigned to monitor the activities of radical Islamic preachers and their followers."[38] In June 2002, Sa'd al-Faqih, leader of the UK–based Movement for Islamic Reform in Arabia, also told *Al-Jazirah* television that his well-informed sources in the kingdom have reported that "Saudi authorities have information that there is in the security agencies themselves huge support and an unprecedented sympathy for bin Laden. . . ."[39] Rohan Gunaratna, an expert on al Qaeda, also has claimed that in Saudi Arabia and other Arab states the organization is "running agents into the political establishments, security forces, or security and intelligence apparatus. . . ."[40] In addition, journalistic and academic reporting on the Soviet–Afghan war over the past decade has shown that Saudis may have been the largest non-Afghan and non-Pakistani Muslim group to have participated in that war. Thus, we know bin Laden is revered in the kingdom, and we must assume a large cadre of veteran insurgent fighters has resettled in Saudi Arabia and may have been training young Saudis in paramilitary skills since their return. In mid-2003, for example, Minister of Interior Prince Nayef said he knew that "a small number [of fighters] perhaps were trained on farms and the like inside the country."[41]

Whether or not al Qaeda's presence has grown or just become

active, the frequency of violent activity and political events by Islamists in Saudi Arabia during 2003 was unprecedented. European and American expatriate workers were shot and killed; anti-regime demonstrations have been staged in several cities; senior Saudi government officials were assassinated; and two car bombings occurred at residential compounds in Riyadh on 12 May and 8 November. While only the 12 May 2003 bombings can be directly attributed to al Qaeda, the other attacks may have been associated with the group or at least conducted by groups cut from roughly the same cloth. Since May 2003, the Saudi domestic security service has conducted frequent raids of Islamist residences and safe houses in Riyadh, Mecca, and other cities and has arrested hundreds of people, killed or captured a handful of men thought to be al Qaeda's top operatives in the kingdom, and seized large quantities of weapons. The Saudi service has suffered at least a dozen officers killed and wounded, and also has recovered plastic explosives, gas masks, and large sums of cash. Notwithstanding these successes, the Saudis are fighting an uphill battle, given the number of al Qaeda supporters in the kingdom, the populace's general antipathy for the al-Saud tyranny, and indications that arms and ammunition are being supplied to the militants from contacts in the Saudi National Guard. Additional weaponry, moreover, is now flowing into the kingdom from the huge ordnance stocks that became available in Iraq after the fall of Saddam. *Newsweek* reported in mid-November 2003, for example, that more and more Iraqi AK-47s and RPGs were turning up in Saudi Arabia, and that AK-47s could be purchased for five or six U.S. dollars.[42]

Thus, in early 2004 the two countries with the world's largest oil reserves—Iraq and Saudi Arabia—found themselves beset by domestic Islamist violence. While Iraq is far worse off and will continue to grow increasingly violent, there is every chance that the al-Saud regime has quietly climbed on its deathbed. Osama bin Laden, after all, is not an aberrant product of Saudi society—he is its poster boy. The kingdom is loaded with bin Laden types, and, as Abd al-Bari Atwan has written, the al-Sauds are now confronting the depth of al Qaeda's "penetration of their social and security fabrics and their inability to uproot it despite their repressive measures and haphazard arrests. . . ."[43] In addition, al Qaeda has begun a campaign that taunts and threatens the al-Sauds, attempting to create fear in the regime and its Western protectors and oil purchasers. Al Qaeda has "large quantities of weapons and explosives in Gulf cities that have been prepared for carrying out these operations," al Qaeda commander Abu Mohammed al-Ablaj said after the May 2003 Riyadh bombing. "We will make the atmosphere so tense so as to confuse the security organs and then carry out qualitative operations and deliver lethal blows at the core."[44] Thus, the Saudi regime is left with few choices other than moving from a brutal but inefficient tyranny to a more brutal and methodical tyranny, a transformation likely to yield short-term order at the cost of steadily increasing support for bin Laden and armed resistance.

. . . and Setting Course for New Climes . . .

Question: What do Iraq, Lebanon, and the Internet have in common? Answer: All are new fields of vigorous endeavor by al Qaeda and bin Laden. In an atmosphere filled with U.S. claims that the last "remnants" of al Qaeda and the Taleban are being mopped up, bin Laden's boys have opened up new areas of physical endeavor across Iraq since April 2003, and in Lebanon, as well as an aggressive ethereal presence on the World Wide Web.

Al Qaeda's ties to and presence in northern Iraq existed before 11 September 2001 but took on greater momentum and importance thereafter. While it was long known that Kurdistan was home to multiple, largely secular Sunni Kurdish groups opposed to Saddam Hussein's regime, the presence there of an assortment of militant Sunni Kurdish groups opposed to Saddam, secular Sunni Kurds, and the West was less clear. What Western observers for the most part missed, however, was not overlooked by al Qaeda and the Taleban. The *New York Times* has reported, for example, that documents from an al Qaeda computer captured by U.S. forces in Kabul show that bin Laden hosted the leaders of several Kurdish Islamist groups in Afghanistan in 2000 and 2001, meetings in which Taleban representatives were included.[45] The message delivered to the Iraqis appears to have been threefold: unite the disparate Sunni Islamist factions in northern Iraq; propagate the teachings of the Salafi sect of Islam among the Sunni population there and try to create a Taleban-style regime in Iraq; and train and prepare fighters for war against U.S. forces if Washington again invades Iraq. In addition, the Iraqi Kurds received $350,000 in funding, weapons, Land Cruisers, and instruction in administration, logistics, and military-training methods, as well as an offer—which was accepted—to provide al Qaeda cadre to assist in putting the administrative and military sides of their house in order. Finally, it appears that the Ansar al-Islam group asked for and received from al Qaeda training in the fabrication and use of toxic weapons; manuals for producing toxins found in 2002 in Ansar camps in Iraq are identical to those taken from al Qaeda in Afghanistan. By late summer 2002, Ansar al-Islam had built a toxin-producing facility near Khurma, Iraq, and was testing ricin and other poisons on farm animals—perhaps with the guidance of senior al Qaeda ally Abu Musab al-Zarqawi. The British media have reported that the Khurma camp may have been involved in training and supplying the poison ricin to Islamists who were arrested in London in late 2002 and found to have traces of it in their possession. Based on documents recovered in Kabul in 2001 and Iraq in 2003, *New York Times'* correspondent C.J. Chivers has concluded,

> Al Qaeda seeded Ansar [al-Islam] with experienced fighters who helped organize the group's training, administration, and ambitions . . . [and] documents [recovered in Iraq] also included passports, driver's licenses, identification cards, or university transcripts from young men from Algeria, Sudan, Syria, Morocco, Tunisia, Qatar, Saudi Arabia, Germany, Spain, Italy, and Canada. . . . [M]ethodical cooperation had gone far beyond helping Ansar get its start and demonstrates that al Qaeda has the ability to export its training lessons from place to place.[46]

The militant Sunni Kurds seem to have been eager learners and in summer 2001 the Ansar al-Islam organization—led then by Norway-based Mullah Krekar, and now by Abu Abdallah al-Shafi'i—undertook efforts to unite the large Jund al-Islam group and several other Sunni groups under Ansar's banner. The efforts succeeded and Ansar al-Islam's manpower rose from six hundred to more than two thousand by January 2003; these numbers do not include the "scores" of Arab Afghan insurgents who entered Iraq after the fall of the Taleban. Based in the mountains near Halabja, the newly united group began in summer 2001 to stage guerrilla-style attacks on the U.S.–allied secular Kurdish groups—including assassinations, car bombs, and ambushes. In doing so, Ansar al-Islam showed an unexpected military competence, an inventory of modern weaponry, and an ability to conduct suicide attacks. These operations again showed the qualitative edge given to a Sunni militant group by a small number of al Qaeda trainers and combat veterans. In every country where an Islamic insurgency is under way, al Qaeda trainers have improved the military skills and enhanced the religious zeal of local fighters. Al Qaeda's trainers are proving the truth of bin Laden's late mentor Shaykh Abdullah Azzam's assertion that the Koran and the AK-47, together, yield the levels of lethality needed for Islam to triumph.

> History does not write its lines except in blood. Glory does not build its lofty edifice except with skulls. Honour and respect cannot be established except on a foundation of cripples and corpses. . . . Indeed those who think they can change reality, or change societies, without blood sacrifices and wounds, without pure innocent souls, do not understand the essence of our religion.[47]

Al Qaeda also has expanded its presence in Lebanon. That country has long been home to the Shia insurgent group Hizballah, which is still ranked as the most dangerous such organization—ahead of al Qaeda—by some U.S. officials, politicians, and academics; a senior U.S. senator, for example, continues to assert that "Hizballah of course is the A-team of terrorists . . .,"[48] while a respected Harvard academician concludes that the Lebanese group "is the most sophisticated terrorist group in the world."[49] These assertions are seconded by a seemingly endless stream of media "experts" who are, as a group, stuck in a time warp where state sponsors and their surrogates are deemed most dangerous to U.S. interests. Indeed, these officials, politicians, and experts have concocted a piece of analysis by assertion that subordinates al Qaeda as a junior partner in an alliance with Hizballah, one that is directed by Iran toward the goal of destroying the United States and Israel. Even in March 2004, for example, Ralph de Toledano argued in *Insight Magazine* that Deputy Secretary of State Richard Armitage's claim that "Hizballah may well be the A-team of international terrorism" is an "understatement" based on "evidence [that] is incontrovertible."[50] This view has been put forth so many times, by so many "in-the-know" people, that it is now unthinkingly accepted when heard. It is, however, a piece of common wisdom that is uncommonly wrong. Al Qaeda and Hizballah share two things: each nurtures a burning hatred for the United States, and each has a set of insurgent training camps that has been ignored for decades by the United States and its allies. While there are surely contacts between the groups, and perhaps some sharing of data and expertise, the only operational cooperation and joint attacks occurring are in the muddled minds of U.S. and Western officials and analysts—and a former director of central intelligence—who cannot escape the antiquated state-sponsor-of-terrorism paradigm.

Al Qaeda came to Lebanon for the more prosaic reason of acquiring an operating base closer to the Israel–Palestine and Iraq theaters of war. A position in Lebanon gives bin Laden, for the first time, contiguous territory from which to try to kill Israelis, thereby satisfying a goal al Qaeda has established for itself. "[I]f we want to help [the Intifadah] completely," Abu-Ubayd al-Qurashi wrote in *Al-Ansar* in October 2002, "our duty is greater [than just rhetorical support]. Studies of the mujahedin in Palestine show that they need more support. For example, rear bases for the mujahedin need to be established in all countries. An attempt must be made to penetrate the borders with Palestine and bring in weapons. Military operations must be carried out against the Zionists, their sponsors, and their domesticated clients."[51] A base in Lebanon also allows al Qaeda to move fighters into Iraq through Syria or Jordan. The Lebanese Sunni Islamists appear to have welcomed al Qaeda, and fighters from al-Zawahiri's Egyptian Islamic Jihad (EIJ) appear to have been the first contingent sent; London's *Al-Majallah* reported in February 2003 that "al Qaeda's principles and ideology" are entering "Palestinian refugee camps on a small-scale."[52] At this time, al Qaeda is based in one or more of Lebanon's Palestinian refugee camps—its presence seems strongest in the Ayn al-Hilwah camp[53]—and in the Sunni areas of northern Lebanon; there is no evidence that it has yet staged an attack from Lebanon into Israel. That Israel perceives al Qaeda's physical and ideological presence as a threat, however, was shown by the March 2003 car-bomb assassination of EIJ leader Abd-al-Sattar al-Masri in the Ayn al-Hilwah refugee camp by Mossad or an element from its large corps of Palestinian turncoats.

Iraq and Lebanon, then, provide additional examples of how little al Qaeda has been hurt by the war on terrorism outside the Islamabad–Amman corridor, and how it remains able not only to attack, but also to establish itself in places where it had little if any pre-11 September presence. Beginning in 1999, al Qaeda worked rapidly to unite the Iraqi Sunni groups, squared away some of their organizational and administrative problems, and inserted a few of their own training cadre and fighters into the region. Bin Laden thereby made sure that al Qaeda would be established in and around Iraq when many of the most important Sunni clerics around the world called—as he knew they would—for Muslims to wage a defensive jihad against the U.S. and British "occupiers" of Iraq. Likewise, the U.S. invasion of Iraq found al Qaeda positioned in Lebanon to reinforce its forces in Iraq that are participating in the insurgency against the U.S.-led coalition. Bin Laden also has veteran al Qaeda administrators and logisticians in Iraq who can—as they did in the Soviet–Afghan war—greet, shelter, feed, arm, and train Muslim volunteers flowing to Iraq from around the Islamic world.

. . . and Forging into a New Domain

Al Qaeda's most important growth since the 11 September attacks has not been physical but has been, rather, its expansion into the Internet. Bin Laden's fighters had used the Internet for propaganda and communication purposes before the attacks, but their use of the medium expanded quickly thereafter. Part of this expansion is due to necessity; Afghanistan has somewhat less utility than previously as a safe haven, and the consequent dispersal of fighters has forced the organization to become more "virtual," or "al Qaeda 2.0," as CNN's Peter Bergen insightfully has described its current status.[54] Al Qaeda's reach into the Internet also is due to the rapid development of both the medium and the computers, cell and satellite phones, and Inmarsat radios with which it can be accessed. The World Wide Web continues to evolve toward greater sophistication; computers keep getting faster, smaller, cheaper, and more powerful; and commercial encryption is making communications increasingly immune to interception. The rapid worldwide proliferation of "Internet cafes" also provides ready and cheap Internet access to al Qaeda operatives, their allies, and other militant Islamists who do not have their own computers. It is difficult to know how al Qaeda's operational communications are divided among the Internet, land-line telephones, cell and satellite telephones, Inmarsat radios, obsolete but reliable HF/VHF radios, and couriers. The latter "primitive" means of communication is used by al Qaeda in Afghanistan "to carry notes or memorized messages" to defeat U.S. electronic intercept capabilities, the *Independent*'s Robert Fisk has reported.[55] That al Qaeda uses the Internet for substantive communications is clear, however, based on common sense and repeated leaks by senior U.S. officials citing an ability to read other peoples' electronic mail. The latter activity, of course, alerts the enemy to U.S. eavesdropping and thus makes it a wasting asset.

Al Qaeda also uses the Internet for propaganda and educational purposes. Since January 2002, al Qaeda has been using two Internet websites, *Al-Neda* and *Al-Ansar*. The former also is known as the "Center for Islamic Studies and Research" and has been described by Internet expert Paul Eedle as a "professionally produced database-driven site with an imaginative webmaster."[56] Al Qaeda has not claimed ownership of the sites, but senior al Qaeda commander Abu-al-Layth al-Libi recommended *Al-Neda* to *Islamic Jihad On Line* readers, saying it is a "website run by reliable brothers . . . and financed by brothers that you know. It is a good website and we hope that God will accept its actions. . . . [W]e will not spare any effort or withhold anything we can offer to this website."[57] *Al-Neda* and *Al-Ansar* publish, among other things, biweekly electronic journals containing analyses of the wars in Afghanistan and Iraq; evaluations and explanations by Islamic scholars and clerics of what al Qaeda has done, is planning to do, and has urged others to do; and erudite, well-researched essays describing al Qaeda's war aims and assessing how achieving these goals would benefit the Muslim ummah by defeating the United States and, in their turn, Israel and the world's apostate Muslim governments. In a post-11 September environment in which bin Laden has deliberately refrained from frequent media appearances—to avoid the enemy fixing his position and because he knows silence induces fear—these Internet sites provide his followers and those he tries to incite to jihad with a regular, easily accessible flow of information and comment carrying al Qaeda's imprimatur. "As a result of the al Qaeda viewpoint," Eedle has written about the impact of the websites, "it now takes great courage to speak out against the jihadi view. . . . [and] public debate in the Muslim world is now very radical."[58]

Ironically, the United States and its allies have increased the appeal and presumed importance of the websites by repeatedly staging "information warfare attacks" on them, thereby forcing them off-line and making their producers hunt for new host servers. The UK–based Arabic daily *Al-Hayat*, for example, has reported that *Al-Neda* has been the target of twenty U.S. attacks.[59] These attacks have proven the viability of the U.S. military's information-warfare capability and certainly have made the websites more difficult to find for Muslim readers. In the end, however, the attacks are interpreted by Islamists as evidence of U.S. fear of what al Qaeda is saying, validation for bin Laden's claim that freedom of speech is not for Muslims, and have probably boosted readership. "Every time you [the United States] close a site," *Al-Neda* noted in October 2002, "you only further expose yourself to the world and the truth about the democracy you brag about. It is a democracy that is tailored to your measurements only. And when people oppose you, your democracy turns into the ugliest forms of domination, tyranny, and despotism on earth."[60] The attacks also deny U.S. intelligence analysts easy access to what al Qaeda is thinking and telling its followers. "The 'real arguments' among Muslims about the future of Islam and its confrontation with the West," Professor Eedle has written, "take place on websites, bulletin boards, e-mail lists, and [chat rooms]."[61] At the same time, those commanding the info-warriors merrily leak information about the U.S. ability to make such attacks. In essence, the attacks inflict a lose-lose situation on America: we look the gift horse of the websites in the mouth by closing them, while telling our foe that we intercept their communications.

Rueven Paz, the doyen of Israel's terrorism analysts and one of the few who does not seem a government shill, has drawn attention to the importance of the "Internet interpreters" of bin Laden and al Qaeda, stressing that the authors offer the West an excellent education in the as-yet-underestimated dimensions of the threat Islamists pose. An "interesting phenomenon" since the 11 September attacks, Paz wrote in early 2003, has been

> the emergence of a group of interpreters of Usama Bin Ladin, Tanzim Qa'idat al-Jihad [al Qaeda], and the nature of the war between radical Islam and the West. These interpreters, primarily Saudi, Yemeni, and Egyptian scholars and intellectuals, have published throughout the last year, dozens of articles on Islamist websites and in on-line magazines. Their articles are widely distributed and circulated throughout numerous Internet forums. The numerous responses to them provide ample evidence of their popularity. . . .
>
> [T]he importance of the "interpreters" lies in spreading the political messages of the global jihad throughout the Arab and Muslim world and in promoting and encouraging radical Muslim youths onward towards further struggle and more anti-Western and anti-Jewish sentiments. Part of their articles could be viewed in the West as disinformation and psychological warfare. Yet, serious research of the phenomenon of global jihad and their radical Jihadi Salafist doctrines, as well as [al Qaeda's] policies, should not be ignored. . . . Even if their final targets are vague, their view of the struggle is vivid and their persistence is clear.[62]

Another Internet-related development that helps bin Laden is the increasing number of Islamist groups and individuals that post articles, exchange information, voice opinions, and debate ideas on the websites and chat rooms they have established. The Internet today allows militant Muslims from every country to meet, talk, and get to know each other electronically, a familiarization and bonding process that in the 1980s and early 1990s required a trip to Sudan, Yemen, Afghanistan, or Pakistan. The Islamic community or ummah, David Martin Jones noted in the *National Interest,* "is no longer a geographical concept; the 'virtual' world of the potential cybercaliphate knows no conventional boundaries."[63] Many of the websites are explicitly pro-bin Laden, praising him as today's only Muslim hero and applauding al Qaeda's announcements and attacks. This sort of thing, of course, is free advertising for al Qaeda's cause, but for bin Laden the more important facet of this development is the number of Muslim groups and individuals who become aware of jihad-related activities and the religious justifications for them. New websites appear frequently, chat rooms have lists of applicants awaiting admission, and most sites are technically able to include audio, video, and links to other sites. All of this adds up to a tremendous contribution to what bin Laden always has said is his and al Qaeda's first priority: the instigation to jihad of as many Muslims in as many locales as possible. Al Qaeda does not fund, manage, or provide articles for most of these sites, but they are a valuable and ubiquitous force-multiplier for its program of propagation and incitement. Recognizing this benefit, al Qaeda has assured its "Internet brothers" that "the media war with the oppressive crusader enemy takes a common effort and can use a lot of ideas. We are prepared to help out with these ideas."[64]

On a narrower, more utilitarian front, the non-al Qaeda websites and chat rooms are playing a major part in providing on-demand military, security, and intelligence training to interested Muslims; indeed, to interested browsers of all confessions, and to America's other unconventional enemies—organized crime, drug traffickers, narco-terrorists, et cetera. Especially since the Afghan war started in October 2001, there has been an expansion in the availability of online military training: small-unit tactics; the use and manufacture of explosives; weapons instructions; formulas for manufacturing toxins and poisons; trade craft for intelligence activities; martial arts manuals; textbooks, or sections thereof, dealing with the theory and construction of weapons of mass destruction; al Qaeda's now-famous *Encyclopedia of Jihad;* and, of course, religious instruction pertinent to waging a defensive jihad. While most training manuals are in English or Arabic, translations are appearing that will increase the ease with which the materials can be used.

The availability of this wide-ranging material begins to make good al Qaeda's temporary loss of training camps in Afghanistan. While the *Wall Street Journal* may be a bit premature in arguing that "[t]hanks to technology . . . the Afghanistan training camps are unnecessary,"[65] al Qaeda members and trainers can access the manuals anywhere in the world and then conduct training at local camps, houses, and secluded sites—cellars are as appropriate as camps for training on explosives, toxins, intelligence-gathering, and martial arts—or at facilities of allied Islamist groups in Pakistan, Yemen, Chechnya, Uzbekistan, Tajikistan, Sudan, Malaysia, Indonesia, the Philippines, and a host of other places. As Colonel Hackworth has written, "[T]oday's international terrorists don't need either sanctuaries or much outside help to outfit, train, and hide soldiers."[66] In addition, this Internet library of war lets Muslim individuals and groups unaffiliated with al Qaeda or its allies train at their leisure at home and then conduct the attacks they concoct, operations that are planned and executed with almost no chance of being detected or interdicted. Obviously, at-home training also greatly reduces the need for would-be mujahideen to travel, thereby partially neutralizing the ability of governments to capture fighters via the traditional methods of watch-listing names, examining travel documents, and matching photos, fingerprints, or eye patterns. In short, the Internet's jihad library facilitates the kind of unstoppable attacks that are the stuff of bin Laden's dreams while degrading the ability of governments to use immigration, customs, and police services to apprehend traveling militants.

The Internet sites also play an important instructional role in regard to the worldwide diffusion of religious studies supporting bin Laden's call for defensive jihad. It has been particularly important for disseminating tracts by Sunni Islam's Salafi sect, which is the most martial and fastest-growing Sunni sect. The Internet has served the jihadists' cause, Sa'd al-Faqih's *Al-Islah* website explained, by "facilitating access to legal religious texts."

> A youth can now push a button and obtain information, which was until recently exclusive to the scholars of al-Hadith. Therefore, it is a paradox that information technology has served the growth of Salafist thought and that the challenges of globalization are now at the service of a project to return to legal religious texts and their hegemony over Islamic thought.[67]

As al Qaeda provides services to Islamists on the Internet, so would-be mujahideen provide important data to al Qaeda via the same medium. In al Qaeda operations, intelligence collection, surveillance, and photographic reconnaissance—doing the checkables—are essential elements of pre-attack planning. The Internet has allowed the group to post data requirements and ask Muslims to help meet them; most respondents are not al Qaeda members, may have done nothing to attract police attention, and remain anonymous. In November 2002, for example, al Qaeda issued an "appeal to our brother workers" in the Arabian Peninsula to support the jihad by providing information about facilities used by the United States. "You might ask: what can we do when we are far from the fields of jihad?" the al Qaeda author wrote,

> We say to you that you are in the midst of these fields. The enemies we are seeking to destroy are the infidels you are serving and bolstering against us. You know their positions, movements, and capabilities. You know their military soft spots and weaknesses. With this knowledge you can be a source of strength to us. This advantage will give you a decisive role, God willing, in serving the religion of your Lord and serving your nation.

Al Qaeda's posting went on to define the kinds of information needed. "Pass [to us] reports about important economic and military targets . . . of the American infidel crusaders," the author requested, and then listed such things as the locations of the offices and pipelines of U.S. oil companies; U.S. ammunition storage areas; living quarters and recreational areas for U.S. military personnel; air corridors and refueling sites used by U.S. military aircraft; and the docks used by U.S. military and commercial ships. The author also requested the names and addresses of senior U.S. military and intelligence officers. "You can post these reports through these sites openly," the anonymous author said.

> It would be better if they were supported by photographs or if the location is pinpointed on a scanned commercial map and attached to the report. If the reports are top secret, they can be sent to the poster and we hope that, through him, they will reach those who can greatly benefit from them. . . . From your positions you must carry out what your nation expects of you in such important times in its history. By God, you will be achieving one of two good things: victory or martyr-

dom. You know very well how to hurt the infidels most, because you know them and know their weak points.[68]

Finally, the existence of the al Qaeda-related websites, and the ongoing proliferation of Islamist websites and chat rooms, naturally yields a bountiful harvest of loose talk, exaggeration, and attack plans that often exist only in the minds of posters and chatters. The ether, therefore, is filled with anti-U.S. threats that run the gamut from kidnapping to nuclear strikes. And some must be taken seriously, especially those posted on the al Qaeda websites. Although generally unspecific, they are often focused and pertinent enough to give U.S. intelligence analysts pause and U.S. policy makers worries. "American officials are even more fearful," Abu-Ubayd al-Qurashi wrote in *Al-Ansar* in early 2002, "when it comes to the opportunities that globalization provides those who want to bring such weapons [nuclear or radiological] into America. In 1996, 254 million persons, 75 million automobiles, and 3.5 million trucks entered America from Mexico. At the 38 official border crossings, only 5 percent of this huge total is inspected." After planting this seed, al-Qurashi went on for a few sentences and then concluded, "These are figures that really call for contemplation."[69] Alarm bells surely rang on that one.

Nonetheless, the average adult normally would look at the slate of threats, assess most as remote possibilities, and focus further work on what appear to be the most plausible. In regard to evaluating risks, however, post-11 September U.S. officialdom is anything but adult. Fixed on protecting their posteriors, U.S. officials are determined to warn every American about every threat they can lay their hands on. The so-called threat matrix briefed to the president each morning—and now a weekly television program on a channel near you—has become nearly as famous as the Department of Homeland Security's multicolored, streetlight-of-death warning system, surely the ultimate example of what Mark Helprin described as "a series of bureaucratic absurdities that attempt little, achieve nothing, and protect no one."[70] Inherent in this particular victory for moral-cowardice-driven careerism over common sense are two more signs showing that bin Laden and al Qaeda are winning. The first is the ruinous impact of chasing down each and every threat. This dire lack of discernment—few senior bureaucrats will discount a threat if there is a one-in-a-billion chance it might occur and cost a promotion—results in a massive misapplication of manpower, computer time, and national-level intelligence collection systems against a mass of threats, most of which are palpably absurd. As a result, like a fire department plagued by false alarms, analysts, spies, equipment, and police at all levels are worn out chasing nonexistent threats. In doing so, moreover, an atmosphere is created where the constant crying of wolf dulls our analytic edge and increases the risk of the career-ruining oversight senior bureaucrats fear. When America is next hit at home by a surprise al Qaeda attack—which it will be—the cause may lie in the exhaustion and cynicism of its government's human resources, especially its best officers, those who too frequently have been told to pull on their boots, slide down the pole, and go forth into rainy, cold nights—at the cost of health, family, and marriage—to chase threats they and their superiors know are patently false.

The obsession with threats again underscores the fundamental reason bin Laden is still winning. The laser focus of U.S. officials on threats translates, *ipso facto*, into an obsession with defense. By treating each threat as a real possibility, we try to protect everything and end up protecting little. We have forgotten that a wise Chinese philosopher once said, "And when he prepares everywhere, he will be weak everywhere." That U.S. leaders continue to cling to this *modus operandi* indicates that official America does not genuinely believe we are at war, and that, instead, the 11 September attacks were simply one-off events. If U.S. leaders truly believed the country is at war with bin Laden and the Islamists, they would dump the terminally adolescent bureaucrats and their threat matrix, accept and tell the voters that war brings repeated and at times grievous defeats as well as victories, and proceed with relentless, brutal, and, yes, blood-soaked offensive military actions until we have annihilated the Islamists who threaten us, or so mutilate their forces, supporting populations, and physical infrastructure that they recognize continued war-making on their part is futile. The severe human cost to Muslims and Americans of such action could be lessened by changes in U.S. foreign policy toward the Islamic world—new policies would cut the Islamists' support—but because frank debate on the changes needed is unlikely, America will literally have to stick to its guns. A policy *status quo*, in essence, leaves America no choice but a war of annihilation. War is hell, as William Tecumseh Sherman famously said, but, with static foreign policies, America's current option was better defined by General Curtis Lemay during World War II. "I'll tell you what war is about," Lemay once said. "You have got to kill people, and when you have killed enough of them they stop fighting."[71] Unless General Lemay's advice is followed, or U.S. policies are changed, bin Laden wins.

Toting Up the Score: 12 September 2001–12 September 2003

The following is an attempt to produce a balance sheet of 2001–2004 wins and losses in the war between bin Laden's forces writ large and the coalitions led by the United States. As in *Through Our Enemies' Eyes*, the balance sheet is not comprehensive and so cannot be definitive; it is meant only to document the war's major events to the greatest extent possible. Unlike the balance sheet in the earlier book, however, this one includes political and economic actions of a kind America and others had not taken before 11 September 2001. While not a scientific measure of the war's progress, it does provide a baseline for speculations on the war's course.

A word of explanation before proceeding: The reader will note that in the following material no effort is made to track five of the seven main Islamic insurgencies now being waged in the world. The omitted wars are those in Kashmir, the Philippines, Algeria, Palestine, and Aceh in Indonesia; they were excluded because they are wide-ranging wars, and recording their major events would require a full book. Needless to say, these omissions cause a significant underestimate of the pace and lethality of overall Islamist violence. The two other major Islamist insurgencies—Afghanistan and Chechnya—are included for specific reasons. Afghanistan is covered to show U.S. claims of victory there are premature. Chechnya is included to warn those in the West who believe the Islamist threat would dissipate if bin Laden is captured or killed. The reader will see that the pace and lethality of Chechen Islamist attacks on Moscow's forces increased after the Russians poisoned Ibn al-Khattab in March 2002. Khattab was the senior Arab military leader in Chechnya, had unrivaled combat experience in the Afghan and Tajik jihads, and—after bin Laden—was the most well known and beloved Arab mujahideen chief in the Muslim world. Again, his death was followed by more—not fewer—sophisticated and deadly attacks.

Finally, I must again emphasize that I am not attributing to bin Laden and al Qaeda command-and-control over attacks by Chechen, Kashmiri, Indonesian, or other groups. Such command-and-control by al Qaeda does not exist. Attacks by these groups do, however, suggest that bin Laden's call for a worldwide jihad may be catching fire. The attacks also enhance the stature of bin Laden and al Qaeda because the media tends to designate bin Laden as their leader, manager, financier, or inspirer.

Victories for the United States and Its Allies, 2001–2004

The victories scored against al Qaeda in the 2001–2004 period by the United States and its allies are impressive. They are also almost entirely tactical in nature and offer startling testimony to how dominated the U.S.-led war effort is by a law-enforcement mentality—chase-capture-jail—and how much America and the West owe to the U.S. clandestine service's operations. While numerous, U.S. victories have not, as noted above, stopped or slowed the shift in strategic advantage toward al Qaeda that began on 11 September 2001. Indeed, this unchanged and unimaginative U.S. government *modus operandi* suggests U.S. official-dom has not an inkling that it must attack the threat bin Laden speaks for and personifies in a comprehensive manner before America impoverishes herself and/or bleeds to death while celebrating worthwhile but strategically inconsequential tactical victories.

- 9–24 December 2001: Singaporean police break up a Jamaah Islamiya (JI) cell and arrest fifteen Islamists, fourteen Singaporeans, and one Malaysian. Thirteen of fifteen were JI members, and eight of those received physical and religious training in Malaysia and military training in Afghanistan. The cell was formed in 1997 and had planned six truck-bomb attacks against U.S., UK, Israeli, and Australian diplomatic and military targets, as well as against U.S.–owned businesses.
- 14 December 2001: U.S. Marines enter the Qandahar airport to establish the U.S.-led coalition's control of the Taleban's capital. The action ends the Afghan war's first battle, one that evicted the Taleban and al Qaeda from Afghan cities.
- 20–21 December 2001: Egyptian Islamic Jihad faction leaders Ahmad Husayn Aghiza and Mohammed Sulayman al-Dharri are extradited from Sweden to Egypt. Aghiza took part in the 1995 bombing of Egypt's embassy in Pakistan.
- 19 March 2002: Ibn al-Khattab, leader of the Arab Afghans fighting in Chechnya, is killed by a letter contaminated with poison. The letter was made by Russian authorities and delivered to Khattab by a Chechen suborned by them. Khattab also had fought in Tajik and Afghan jihads

and was a folk hero among Islamists. A Saudi national, his true name was Salim Suwaylin.

- 28 March 2002: Al Qaeda ally Abu Zubaydah was captured in Faisalbad, Pakistan. A thirty-year-old Palestinian with Saudi citizenship, Zubaydah was a chief recruiter and ran an Afghan training camp. He was under a Jordanian death sentence for his part in al Qaeda's millennium plot to attack U.S. and Israeli targets.
- Late-May 2002: Moroccan security arrests five al Qaeda fighters of Saudi nationality in Rabat and Casablanca for planning attacks on U.S. and UK warships in the Straits of Gibraltar. The Saudis had come to Morocco from Afghanistan after transiting Iran and Syria.
- 10 September 2002: Ramzi bin al-Shibh is arrested in Karachi. He was to be a pilot in the 11 September attacks but failed to get a U.S. visa.
- 12 September 2002: Al Qaeda's chief for northern and western Africa, a thirty-seven-year-old Yemeni named Emad Abdelwahid Ahmed Alwan is killed by Algerian police in eastern Algeria. Alwan was al Qaeda's liaison to the Salafist Group for Call and Combat, an Algerian Islamist insurgent group.
- 13–15 September 2002: The FBI arrests seven Yemen-born men in a suburb of Buffalo, New York, saying they are an al Qaeda "sleeper cell" and had received religious training in Pakistan and military training in Afghanistan.
- Late October 2002: United Arab Emirates (UAE) authorities arrest al Qaeda's Persian Gulf operations chief, Abdel-Rahim al-Nashiri. A Yemen-born Saudi citizen, Nashiri is charged with planning to destroy "vital economic targets" in the UAE. He also helped plan attacks on U.S. and UK warships in the Straits of Gibraltar, and ships of the U.S. Fifth Fleet in Bahrain. Al-Nashiri was an explosives specialist, fought in Afghanistan with bin Laden, and fought in Bosnia. He took part in al Qaeda's 1998 East Africa attacks, the attacks on the U.S. destroyers *The Sullivans* and *Cole,* and the attack on the French super tanker *Limburg.*
- 3 November 2002: CIA's unmanned "Predator" aircraft destroys a vehicle, killing six al Qaeda members. Among the dead are al Qaeda's chief in Yemen, al-Qaed Sinan al-Harithi, and U.S. citizen/al Qaeda member Ahmed Hijazi. Afterwards al Qaeda deputy leader al-Zawahiri said: "When Abu al-Harithi was killed by U.S. missiles in Yemen, it was a warning to us that the Israeli method of killing the mujahideen in Palestine has come to the Arab world."[72]
- 5–23 January 2003: British police arrest eight men—six Algerians, an Ethiopian, and a Moroccan—and one woman in London. They find equipment for a chemical laboratory and traces of the toxin ricin in one of the raided apartments. The British suspect the group may be tied to Algerian Islamists in France and the Islamist leader Abu Musab al-Zarqawi, who is allied with al Qaeda.

- 12–15 February 2003: Bahrain's National Security Agency arrests five al Qaeda associated Bahrainis for plotting terrorist attacks. It also recovers four AK-47s, two handguns, ammunition, chemical "powders," and a bomb-making manual on a CD-ROM.
- 13 February 2003: Police in Quetta arrest Mohammed Abdel Rahman, son of jailed Gama'a al-Islamiyya's spiritual leader Shaykh Omar Abdel Rahman. Bin Laden had cared for him after his father's arrest in the United States.
- 24 February 2003: Kuwaiti police arrest threee Kuwaiti nationals who were planning to attack U.S. military convoys in Kuwait. One had been in Afghanistan in 2001, and all three expressed support for bin Laden after their arrest.
- 1 March 2003: A car bomb kills EIJ leader Abd-al-Sattar al-Masri in Ayn al-Hilwah refugee camp in Lebanon. Al-Masri—true name Mohammed Abdel-Hamid Shanouha—was an explosives expert and an Afghan veteran. He was al Qaeda's leader in the camp and was killed by the Israelis or their proxies.
- 1 March 2003: Pakistani police arrest al Qaeda operations chief Khalid Sheikh Mohammed in an upscale section of Rawalpindi. They also seize his computer, cell phones, and documents. Mohammed designed the 11 September attacks, was involved in the East Africa and *Cole* bombings, and participated in Ramzi Ahmed Yousef's 1995 plot to destroy U.S. airliners flying Pacific routes.
- 1 March 2003: Pakistani police arrest al Qaeda financial officer Mustafa Ahmed al-Hisawai. Hisawai funded the 11 September attackers via wire transfers.
- 15 March 2003: Pakistani authorities arrest Moroccan national Yasser al-Jazeri, who, according to U.S. officials, was a "trusted subordinate of Osama bin Laden." He was responsible for facilitating communications among al Qaeda leaders and was captured in a "posh" neighborhood in Lahore.
- 29 April 2003: In Karachi, Pakistani police arrest Tawfiq bin Attash and Amar al-Baluchi, Khalid Sheikh Mohammed's nephew. A Saudi citizen of Yemeni origin, bin Attash was a close friend of bin Laden, had fought with him in Afghanistan—where he lost a leg—and had run the attack on the U.S. destroyer *Cole*. Al-Baluchi was an al Qaeda financial officer and had sent nearly $120,000 to Mohammed Atta, the leader of the 11 September attacks.
- 6 May 2003: Saudi security raids an al Qaeda safe house in Riyadh near an expatriate housing compound. The Saudis capture no one but recover more than eight hundred pounds of explosives, fifty-five hand grenades, dozens of assault rifles, other weapons, disguises, twenty-five hundred rounds of ammunition, and eighty-thousand dollars in cash. Some of the weapons are traced to stocks owned by the Saudi National Guard.

- 31 May 2003: Saudi police kill Yusuf bin Salih al-Ayiri, al Qaeda's senior propagandist, and capture his deputy Abdullah ibn Ibrahim Abdullah al-Shabrani. The shootout occurred near the town of Ha'il; two Saudi officers were killed and three wounded. Al-Ayiri ran al Qaeda's *Al-Neda* website and was said to be the group's "unknown soldier." The UK–based EIJ exile and specialist on Islamism Hani al-Saba'i said al-Ayiri provided Islamic guidance "for al Qaeda inside the Gulf region." Al-Ayiri was a close friend of bin Laden and traveled on the same plane when al Qaeda's chief flew from Afghanistan to Sudan in 1991.[73]
- 12 June 2003: U.S. forces raid and destroy a base for non-Iraqi mujahideen at Rawah, Iraq, about thirty miles from the Syrian border. The attack kills more than eighty foreign Muslims in Iraq to fight the U.S.-led occupation. Among the dead were Saudis, Yemenis, Syrians, Afghans, and Sudanese.
- 12 August 2003: Thai police arrest JI operations chief Nurjaman Ridwan Isamuddin—a.k.a. Hambali—in Ayutthaya, north of Bangkok. U.S. officials say he played an "important role" in the October 2002 Bali attack and was al Qaeda's "top strategist" in Southeast Asia. Before Thailand, Hambali lived in the Muslim community of Phnom Phenn, Cambodia, from September 2002 to March 2003. Hambali fought the Soviets in Afghanistan, worked in the 1990s with Khalid Sheikh Mohammed and Ramzi Yousef, and was one of the few non-Arabs in al Qaeda authorized to make independent decisions.
- 20 September 2003: Pakistani security arrests fifteen Asian Islamic seminary students in Karachi—two Malaysians, thirteen Indonesians—and charges them with being linked to the Jemaah Islamiya, the Indonesian militant group allied with al Qaeda.
- 25 November 2003: Yemeni authorities announce the arrest of Abu-Asim al-Makki, a leading member of the al Qaeda organization in Yemen. The Yemenis also announce the earlier arrest of al Qaeda leader Hadi Dalqam.
- 15 and 23 January 2004: In Iraq, U.S. authorities capture al Qaeda operatives Husam al-Yemeni and Hasan Ghul. Ghul is known to have been a senior aide to 11 September planner Khalid Sheikh Mohammed.
- 15 March 2004: Saudi security forces kill two senior al Qaeda operatives—Khaled Ali Ali Haj and Ibrahim al-Mezeini—in Riyadh when they try to run a roadblock. The dead Yemeni nationals had six grenades, two AK-47s, three 9mm pistols, and $137,000 in cash in their car.
- 31 March–2 April 2004: Ten Islamist fighters are arrested in Canada and Britain after a long police investigation; all are Pakistanis and naturalized Canadians or Britons. British police also seize eleven hundred pounds of fertilizer suitable for making a bomb. UK intelligence sources tell the media that the eight men arrested in London were tied to al Qaeda members in Pakistan.

- 4 April 2004: Spanish police corner six members of the al Qaeda cell that conducted the 11 March 2004 railway bombings in Madrid. The six fighters blew themselves up rather than be captured. The leader of the railway attack—the Tunisian Sarhane Abdelmajid Fakhet—was one of the dead. Police recover twenty-two pounds of explosives identical to those used in the railway bombing.

Al Qaeda Victories, 2001–2003

The pace and lethality of attacks by al Qaeda and its allies between 11 September 2001 and early 2004 are substantially greater than those during the period 1994–2001, which were covered in *Through Our Enemies' Eyes*.[74] In addition, there are a number of "victories" in the list below that are actions taken by others, but redound to al Qaeda's advantage. Among these are the U.S. invasion and occupation of Afghanistan and Iraq; the decision by some Western scientific journals to censor articles that might be useful to the Islamists; Washington's repeated public support for Russia, China, and India in suppressing domestic Islamist insurgents; and the attacks staged on the interests and citizens of the United States and its allies by Muslim groups and individuals entirely unconnected to al Qaeda, except in their admiration for bin Laden.

What is visible in the below recounting of al Qaeda's victories is a post-11 September shift of the strategic environment in favor of bin Laden's organization and goals. Al Qaeda has survived the U.S. military onslaught and—at least by measure of operational tempo—is thriving militarily. More important, bin Laden has made long strides—via al Qaeda attacks, propaganda, and his own statements—in focusing general anti-Western sentiments of Muslims specifically on the United States. This marks success for bin Laden's incitement activities and is most apparent in the attacks by Islamist individuals or groups without known ties to al Qaeda. In an ironic twist, moreover, actions by the United States and its allies have increased the effectiveness and impact of al Qaeda's efforts, leaving Washington confronted by a lose-lose situation almost every time it needs to make a decision vis-à-vis what it inaccurately describes as "the global war on terrorism."

- 7 October 2001: U.S. and UK air forces bomb Taleban bases in Afghanistan, starting the U.S.-led invasion and guerrilla war bin Laden long wanted.

- 1–15 December 2001: After two weeks of U.S. air bombardment of al Qaeda forces in the Tora Bora Mountains, the Northern Alliance fails to fully engage al Qaeda; bin Laden, al-Zawahiri, and most of their fighters escape to Pakistan. Of this victory, bin Laden says, "If all the forces of world evil could not achieve their goals on a one square mile area against a small number of mujahideen . . . how can these evil forces triumph over the Muslim world?"[75]
- 23 January 2002: *Wall Street Journal* reporter Daniel Pearl is abducted in Karachi while going to interview Shaykh Sayyid Giliani, leader of Jamaat al-Fuqra, a group based in Pakistan and North America and tied to al Qaeda and Kashmiri guerrillas. Pearl is beheaded. His remains are found in May 2002.
- 27 February–2 March 2002: After Muslims burn cars of a passenger train in Godhra, in India's Gujarat State—killing fifty-eight Hindus, wounding forty—Hindu mobs riot in Ahmedabad, killing more than two thousand, mostly Muslims. Reports claim the Hindu government "turned a blind eye" to the killings and property destruction. Satellite television coverage of the riots again validate for Muslims bin Laden's contention that the West will not intervene to stop the killing of Muslims.
- 3–18 March 2002: A U.S. military offensive into the Shahi Kowt area of eastern Afghanistan ends in failure when most of al Qaeda's force escape into Pakistan. The U.S. military's Afghan auxiliaries are again reluctant to fight. U.S. forces suffer eight killed and about one hundred wounded; many casualties come from an undetected al Qaeda ambush in the helicopter landing zone. Initial U.S. estimates claim seven hundred to one thousand al Qaeda fighters are killed, but only a few dozen bodies are recovered.
- 17 March 2002: An attack on the Protestant International Church in Islamabad's diplomatic enclave kills five and wounds forty-six; two dead and nine wounded are Americans. The church was attended by foreign diplomats, their families, and other expatriates.
- 5 April 2002: Four thousand men in Sakaka in al-Jawf Province demonstrate against Riyadh's support for Israel and the United States. Five hundred Saudi riot police are sent to control the area.
- 11 April 2002: An al Qaeda fighter detonates a truck bomb at a synagogue on Tunisia's Djerba Island, killing fourteen German tourists and seven others. Al Qaeda's postattack statement said, "The Jewish synagogue in Djerba village was targeted by one single person, the hero Nizar (Sayf-al-Din al-Tunisi). . . . It followed the same pattern and course of the blessed jihad in defense of our Islam's sacred places and in support for the jihad of our Muslim brothers in all parts of the world."[76]
- 17–18 April 2002: On 17 April, Chechen guerrillas kill six Russian sol-

diers in Noviye Atagi, a village ten miles southeast of Grozny. On 18 April, guerrillas detonate a mine in a roadway in Grozny, killing seventeen Russian servicemen.

- 8 May 2002: In Karachi, a car bomb is driven into a minibus carrying French naval technicians who were working for Pakistan's navy. Eleven French workers are killed, twelve wounded; two Pakistanis are killed and twelve wounded. Al Qaeda said that "the armed operation that targeted the French military technicians has come to show the weakness of this regime [Pakistan's] and prove that what the regime had built [has] started to crumble like a deck of cards."[77]
- 17 June 2002: A car bomb explodes outside the U.S. consulate in Karachi, killing eleven and wounding more than forty.
- 4 July 2002: Egyptian Hesham Mohamed Ali Hadayet kills two U.S. citizens at the El Al counter in Los Angeles airport. He is killed by El Al security.
- 13 July 2002: Grenades are thrown at an archaeological site near Manshera, Pakistan, wounding twelve, including seven Germans, one Austrian, and one Slovak.
- 5 August 2002: Islamists raid a Christian school for the children of foreign aid workers northwest of Islamabad. Six staff members are killed.
- 10 August 2002: A Christian church in Taxila, Pakistan, is bombed. Five people are killed, including three nurses, and twenty-five are wounded.
- 19 August 2002: Chechen guerrillas shoot down a Russian MI-26 helicopter using a STRELA surface-to-air missile, killing 118 and wounding twenty-nine.
- 27 August 2002: In Beijing, U.S. Deputy Secretary of State Richard Armitage announces U.S. support for Chinese military actions against Uighur separatists in western China, saying the United States agreed that the Uighurs have "committed acts of terrorism." In Washington, the State Department adds the East Turkistan Islamic Movement to its list of proscribed terrorist organizations.
- 6 October 2002: An al Qaeda suicide bomber sails an explosives-laden boat into the 290,000 ton, French-owned tanker *Limburg* off Aden, Yemen. The tanker was carrying 397,000 barrels of Saudi crude to Malaysia. The attack was a warning to France, said al Qaeda's claim for the bombing, as well as to "the regime of treason and treachery in Yemen [that] did all it could . . . to hunt down, pursue, and arrest the Muslim mujahid youths in Yemen." The attack was the second success in al Qaeda's maritime jihad and was meant to "stop the theft of the Muslims' wealth [i.e., oil] for which nothing worth mentioning is paid."[78]
- 8 October 2002: Two Islamists kill a U.S. Marine and wound another on Kuwait's Faylaka Island. Both Islamists are killed. Al Qaeda claims

the attack, saying it was "the correct, on-target attack at this stage," praises "the mujahedin Anas al-Kandari and Jasim Hajiri," and tells "the Americans: your road to Iraq and the other countries of the Muslims will not be as easy as you imagine and hope."[79]

- 12 October 2002: Indonesia's al Qaeda-tied Jemaah Islamiya (JI) detonates a suicide car bomb at a Bali nightclub, killing more than two hundred, about half Australians. A JI fighter named Amorzi, who ran the attack, later said, "There's some pride in my heart. For the white people it serves them right. They know how to destroy religion by the most subtle ways through bars and gambling dens."[80]

- 23–26 October 2002: Chechen Islamists seize a theater in Moscow and hold more than eight hundred people for fifty-eight hours before Russian forces retake the theater. More than forty Chechen guerrillas are killed, including several female fighters. At least 129 in the audience die from gas used by the security units before they stormed the theater. "As a goal it was an extremely daring operation," al Qaeda said in congratulating the Chechens, ". . . the mujahideen have clearly demonstrated that they can strike at the enemy on its own turf whenever they want."[81]

- 28 October 2002: Two attackers—a Libyan and a Jordanian—kill U.S. diplomat Laurence Foley at his home in Amman, Jordan. Foley worked in the U.S. embassy. The attackers probably were from Jordanian Abu Musab al-Zarqawi's group, which is tied to al Qaeda and Iraq's Ansar al-Islam.

- 20 November 2002: President Bush supports Russia's handling of the October 2002 Chechen raid on a Moscow theater, stating Chechnya "is Russia's internal affair . . ." He equates Chechens with "the killers who came to America," says President Putin should "do what it takes to protect his people," and rejects those who "tried to blame Vladimir. They ought to blame the terrorists. They're the ones who caused the situation, not President Putin." Al Qaeda damns Washington and its allies for letting Russia "liquidate the Chechen issue through brutality."[82]

- 20 November 2002: American nurse Bonnie Penner Wetherall is killed at a Christian church in Sidon, Lebanon. Penner was an active proselytizer bent on converting young Muslims to Christianity. Penner had been warned to stop, and Shaykh Maher Mammoud of Sidon said that "the murder occurred within the context of widespread anger at America . . . we do not condemn [it]."[83]

- 20–23 November 2002: Muslims rioting in Kaduna, Nigeria, leave 220 dead, fifteen hundred wounded, six thousand families homeless, and sixteen churches and nine mosques destroyed. Rioting was sparked by a reporter's "blasphemous" claim that, if alive, the Prophet might have wanted a wife from the women in the Miss World contest to be held in Kaduna. The event was moved to the United Kingdom. Muslim leaders called it a "parade of nudity" and criticized the government for agreeing to host the Miss World contest during Ramadan.

- 21 November 2002: A Kuwaiti policeman wounds two U.S. soldiers after he stops their car. The policeman flees to Saudi Arabia but is returned.
- 28 November 2002: Al Qaeda attacks Israeli interests in Mombasa, Kenya, using a suicide car bomb against the Israeli-owned Paradise Hotel and firing a surface-to-air missile at a Boeing 757 owned by an Israeli charter company. Twelve Kenyans and three Israelis are killed at the hotel, forty others were wounded. The missile misses the aircraft, which was carrying 261 Israelis. "The message here," *Al-Ansar* explained, "is to pursue the Zionist targets all over the world. . . ."[84]
- 27 December 2002: Ahmed Ali Jarallah kills Yemen's Socialist Party chief. When captured, Jarallah says he killed the man because he was a "secularist" and says: "I do not regret what I did because I am seeking paradise. I wish I had an atomic bomb that explodes and incinerates every secularist and renegade."[85]
- 27 December 2002: In Grozny, Chechen fighters drive car bombs into the headquarters of the Russian-backed regime and a communications center. More than sixty people are killed and more than a hundred are wounded.
- 30 December 2002: Islamist fighters from a group linked to al Qaeda attack the Jiblah Hospital in southern Yemen, killing three American medical workers and wounding another. The hospital had been run for thirty-five years by Southern Baptist missionaries from the United States. Yemeni officials later said the facility was attacked because it was converting Muslims to Christianity.
- 21 January 2003: A U.S. military civilian contractor is killed and another wounded when their car is ambushed on a Kuwaiti highway near Qatar. The attacker is a Kuwaiti civil servant, Sami Mutairi. He flees to Saudi Arabia but is captured and returned by Saudi authorities. Mutairi tells Kuwaiti officials the attack was meant as a "gift for Osama bin Laden."
- 16 February 2003: A group of thirty-two editors, representing the world's leading scientific journals, say they will delete details from studies they publish if they might help terrorists build biological weapons. The editors said they would "censor scientific data" and admitted this could slow breakthroughs in basic science and engineering. Among the to-be-censored journals are *Science*, *Nature*, *The Lancet*, *The New England Journal of Medicine*, and the *Proceedings of the National Academy of Sciences*.
- 17 February 2003: Islamists ambush and kill Dr. Hamid bin-Abd-al-Rhaman al-Wardi, the U.S. educated, deputy governor of Saudi Arabia's

al-Jawf Province. Al-Wardi had been involving Saudi politicians in women's gatherings, and in doing so, according to the Islamist website *Ilaf*, had "angered the people of al-Jawf who are known for their hard-line attitude on matters of honor."[86]

- 20 February 2003: Robert Dent, a thirty-seven-year-old British Aerospace employee, is shot to death at a traffic light in Riyadh. Saudi police arrest Yemen-born Saudi national Saud ibn Ali ibn Nasser and suggest he is tied to al Qaeda.

- 21 February 2003: Envelopes containing cyanide are received to the U.S. embassy and the Australian and British high commissions in Wellington, New Zealand. The letter said: "Our purpose is to challenge the actions of the great Satan America and resist its imperialist ambitions in the Islamic world."[87]

- 28 February 2003: Islamists attack Pakistani police guarding the U.S. consulate in Karachi, leaving two dead and five wounded. Pakistani officials claim that "[t]he policemen were hate-targets because they were protecting Americans."[88]

- 18 March 2003: A Yemeni Islamist shoots four Hunt Oil Company employees in the Al-Safir area of northern Yemen, killing an American, a Yemeni, and a Canadian. Another Canadian is wounded. The attacker then kills himself.

- 20 March 2003: The U.S.-led coalition invades Iraq. "Bin Laden must be laughing in his grave or cave," Professor Gerges Fawaz wrote in the *Los Angeles Times*. ". . . [W]hat was unthinkable 18 months ago has happened. The U.S. has alienated those in the Islamic world who were its best hope." Al Qaeda applauded the war, rejoicing that with U.S. forces in Afghanistan, the Arabian Peninsula, and Iraq, "The enemy is now spread out, close at hand, and easy to target."[89]

- 25 March 2003: Two Saudi security officers are shot by drive-by gunmen at a roadblock in Sakaka, al-Jawf Province. One is killed, the other wounded.

- 11 April 2003: Ten al Qaeda fighters escape a Yemeni high-security prison. All are suspects in the October 2000 bombing of the U.S. destroyer *Cole;* two of them are thought to have run the attack: Jamal al-Badawi and Fahd al-Qasa.

- 1 May–1 June 2003: Chechen insurgents attack Russian forces using ambushes, land mines, and remotely detonated mines. In this period, thirty-two Russian military and security personnel are killed, eight wounded, and twenty-nine trucks, cars, and armored vehicles are destroyed. Russian sappers, in addition, defused 120 explosive devices— including twenty-four land mines—between 26 May and 1 June.

- 12 May 2003: A two-story building housing officials of the Russian-backed Chechen government and of the Russian security services is destroyed in the town of Znamenskoye. The town is in an area of northern Chechnya that had been largely untouched by war. The insurgents drove a suicide truck bomb containing about a ton of TNT into the compound, killing fifty-nine and wounding 197.

- 12 May 2003: Al Qaeda suicide car bombs hit three expatriate compounds in Riyadh; bin Laden hinted at the attacks in late 2002, warning, "[The] people of the Peninsula . . . are facing difficult days ahead and very dangerous ordeals that Allah will test you with. . . ." Nearly simultaneous, the attacks kill thirty-four people—nine U.S. citizens—and wound two hundred. The cars drove far into two compounds, suggesting that the guards helped. For Muslims, the attacks had anti-Christian salience; the compounds were named by the Saudis—with their usual contempt for the West—for three Christian-occupied cities of Islamic Anadalusia, today's Spain.

- 16 May 2003: Fourteen Islamists in five teams attack targets in Casablanca, Morocco, including a Spanish restaurant, a Jewish-owned Italian restaurant, a Jewish cemetery, a Kuwaiti-owned hotel, and a Jewish community center. The attacks are roughly simultaneous and use homemade explosives strapped to the attackers; fourteen of the fifteen fighters are killed. The attacks kill forty-six and wound about one hundred. Moroccan police said the fighters belonged to local Islamist groups and had received fifty thousand dollars from al Qaeda to fund the operations.

- 5 June 2003: A female Chechen suicide bomber stops and destroys a bus near Russia's military airfield at Mozdok, North Ossetia. The attack kills twenty Russian air force personnel and wounds fifteen. Mozdok is the main north Causasus air base for fixed- and rotary-wing aircraft flying combat missions in Chechnya.

- 7 June 2003: In Kabul, a taxi explodes next to a bus of German troops from the International Stabilization and Assistance Force. Four die; twenty-nine are wounded.

- 5 July 2003: Two female Chechen suicide bombers detonate themselves at a concert at Moscow's Tushino airfield. Sixteen are killed and twenty wounded.

- 1 August 2003: Chechens detonate a suicide truck bomb at Russia's military hospital in Mozdok, killing fifty, wounding sixty-four, and destroying the hospital.

- 5 August 2003: A JI suicide bomber attacks the Marriott Hotel in Jakarta—a popular meeting place for Americans—killing ten and wounding 152. Indonesian police said casualties would have been worse, but the driver detonated the bomb prematurely. Imam Samudra, on trial for the 2002 Bali bombing, said: "I'm happy . . . Thanks to Allah . . . [The Marriott attack] was part of the war against America. The revenge on the suppressors of Muslims will continue."[90]

- 7 August 2003: A car bomb is detonated at the perimeter wall of Jordan's embassy compound in Baghdad, blowing a thirty-foot hole in the wall and damaging several buildings. The attack kills nineteen and wounds sixty-five. The al Qaeda-related group Ansar al-Islam is among the suspected perpetrators.
- 20 August 2003: A suicide truck bomb is driven into the UN's Baghdad headquarters in the Canal Hotel. The UN special representative for Iraq, Sergio Vieira de Mello, and twenty-two others are killed; more than a hundred are wounded. "This criminal, Sergio Vieira de Mello," al Qaeda wrote in claiming the attack, ". . . was the Crusader who carved up part of the land of Islam (East Timor)."[91]
- 25 August 2003: Two taxis packed with the military explosive RDX are detonated fifteen minutes apart in the Indian city of Mumbai, killing fifty-three and wounding more than 190. Indian police arrest four men they say belong to the Kashmiri Lashkar-e Tayyiba—an ally of al Qaeda—and are tied to India's Student Islamic Movement. The Indians say the groups also detonated bombs in Mumbai in December 2002, killing seventeen and wounding 189, and speculate that both attacks were retaliation for anti-Muslim riots in Gujarat state in March 2002.
- September–October 2003: Egypt and Yemen release, respectively, 113 and one thousand Islamists from prison, the former group reportedly at the end of their sentences, the latter because they repented. Many of the Yemenis are tied to al Qaeda; all the Egyptians belong to the Islamic Group. The releases mimic the way some Arab regimes freed jailed Islamists early in the Afghan jihad if they would go to Afghanistan and join the mujahideen. If past is prologue, as Victor Hanson Davis wrote, the regimes might use the same device to "export them all to Iraq."[92]
- September–October 2003: Events undercut Pakistan president Musharraf's pro-U.S. policy. Israeli prime minister Sharon made an official visit to India, supported India on Kashmir, and sold India three Phalcon radar systems. The Phalcons will allow India to see far into Pakistan and, said *Jane's Defense Weekly*, "give India a big strategic advantage over Pakistan." The visit coincided with U.S. criticism of Musharraf for letting Kashmiri fighters enter India, and a joint U.S.–Indian Special Forces exercise in Indian Kashmir. Al Qaeda's al-Zawahiri cited the events, warning the arms deal and "[t]he visit by criminal Sharon . . . are only the tip of the iceberg. This U.S.–Jewish–Indian alliance is against Muslims."[93]
- 11 September 2003: The Salafist Group for Call and Combat (GSPC)—Algeria's main Islamist insurgents—declares allegiance to "the direction of Mullah Omar and the [al Qaeda] organization of Shaykh Usama Bin Ladin," as well an intention to attack U.S. interests. The GSPC was long stubbornly Algeria-centric, and its decision to take al Qaeda's lead and give priority to anti-U.S. attacks is a major accomplishment for bin Laden.

- 11–13 September 2003: Two elderly Moroccan Jews are killed in Casablanca and Meknes, respectively. The police tie the attacks to the Salafia Jihadia group, which was linked to the 16 May 2003 Casablanca bombings.
- 7 October 2003: NATO announces it will deploy more troops to Afghanistan, and for the first time deploy them outside Kabul. The action appears to Afghans as the spreading and lengthening of the Western occupation of their country.
- 26–27 October 2003: On 26 October, rockets hit Baghdad's Al-Rashid Hotel—headquarters of the U.S. occupation authority—killing one U.S. soldier and wounding seventeen people. On 27 October, the headquarters of the International Committee of the Red Cross and four Baghdad police stations are car-bombed in a period of forty-five minutes. A fifth police station is spared when the driver of another vehicle is shot. The attacks, which kill thirty-five and wound 224, are attributed to foreign mujahideen.
- 9 November 2003: Al-Muhaya residential compound in Riyadh is bombed; eighteen are killed and more than two hundred wounded. Nearly all casualties are expatriate Muslims. Al Qaeda issues a statement denying responsibility for the attack.
- 12 November 2003: The headquarters of the Italian military police in al-Nasariyah, Iraq, is attacked with a truck bomb. Eighteen Italian military personnel and eleven Iraqis are killed. More than a hundred people are wounded.
- 15 November 2003: Two Jewish synagogues in Istanbul are attacked by suicide car bombs; twenty-three people are killed and 303 are wounded.
- 20 November 2003: The UK Consulate and HSBC Bank building in Istanbul are attacked with suicide car bombs, killing twenty-seven people and wounding at least 450. In Iraq, a remotely detonated bomb destroys a Polish military vehicle but causes no casualties; earlier, on 6 November, a Polish officer was killed by insurgents.
- 30 November 2003: Insurgents kill seven Spanish intelligence officers near Baghdad and two Japanese diplomats in Tikrit. Another Spanish intelligence officer was killed in Baghdad on 9 October 2003. In March 2003, an al Qaeda associate had warned Spain not to go to Iraq. "The wound of the occupation of Andalusia [Spain] has not healed," Ahmed Rafat wrote, "and the decision of your government, which represents the old crusaders, to support the new crusade of U.S. Protestants is a real threat to the safety of every Spaniard. . . ."[94]
- 5 December 2003: A female Chechen suicide bomber detonates herself on an intercity commuter train in Russia's Stavropol region near Chechnya. At least forty-two people are killed, and more than one hundred are wounded.

- 14 and 25 December 2003: Pakistan president Musharraf survives two attempted assassinations near Islamabad. On 14 December a mine is detonated along his travel route; on 25 December his convoy is hit by two suicide car bombs.
- 27 December 2003: In Karbala, Iraq, Islamist fighters kill four Bulgarian soldiers and two Thai soldiers.
- 27 and 28 January 2004: Suicide car bombs in Kabul on successive days kill a Canadian and a UK soldier; three Canadian and four UK soldiers are wounded.
- 1 February 2004: In Iraq, Islamist insurgents detonate themselves in the Irbil headquarters of the two main Kurdish political parties, killing 110 and wounding almost 250.
- 6 February 2004: A Chechen suicide bomber detonates himself on the Moscow subway, killing thirty-nine people and wounding 134.
- 11 March 2004: In Madrid, al Qaeda detonates ten nearly simultaneous bombs in four packed commuter trains, killing 191 people and wounding more than twelve hundred. When claiming responsibility for the attack, al Qaeda described the operation as "part of a settlement of old accounts with Crusade[r] Spain, the ally of the United States in its war against Islam." Several days later, the conservative Spanish government is defeated in a general election, and the new socialist prime minister announces he will withdraw Spanish troops from Iraq.
- 15 March 2004: Iraqi mujahideen kill four Southern Baptist missionaries near Mosul, in northern Iraq. The attack brought to eight the number of Southern Baptist missionaries killed by Islamists around the world since 2003.
- 22 March 2004: Israel assassinates wheelchair-bound Hamas leader Shaykh Ahmed Yasin as he leaves the mosque after prayers. Yasin is a loss to Hamas and the Islamist movement generally, but his status as martyr will increase recruits for Islamist groups worldwide. The United States enhances the benefit derived by Islamists from Yasin's murder by vetoing a UN resolution censuring the Israeli attack and reasserting Israel's "right to defend herself from terror."
- 28–31 March 2004: Multiple bombs are detonated by Islamist fighters in the Uzbek capital Tashkent over three days. The bombings and subsequent gunfights result in the death of thirty-three Islamists, seven of whom are women. Fourteen Uzbeks—including ten policemen—are killed and thirty-five are wounded. The Uzbek government suspects that the Islamic Movement of Uzbekistan was responsible for the attacks.

And Finally, a Quiet, Steady, Unnoticed Bleeding

Just under the noise, death, and rhetoric yielded by the foregoing episodes of war lies a largely ignored factor that may constitute al Qaeda's main war effort—the steady bleeding of the U.S. economy. In late 2002, Abu-Ubayd al-Qurashi wrote an essay in *Al-Ansar* called "A Lesson in War" wherein he described al Qaeda's intention to follow Clausewitz's principle of attacking its foe's "center of gravity."[95] He said al Qaeda would unrelentingly focus on identifying that point and make "sure to direct all available force against the center of gravity during the great offensive."[96] Al-Qurashi wrote that al Qaeda had studied North Vietnam's victory over the United States, and found that Hanoi had "fully understood that America's center of gravity lay in the American people," and by killing America's "dearest ones . . . the war ended with victory on the Vietnamese side."[97] Al Qaeda took this lesson to heart, Qurashi wrote, but believes that America's current center of gravity is its economy.

> On the other hand, we find that God has graciously enabled the mujahedin to understand the [American] enemy's essence and nature, and indeed his center of gravity. A conviction has formed among the mujahedin that American public opinion is not the center of gravity in America. The Zionist lobbies, and with them the security agencies, have long been able to bridle all the media that control the formation of public opinion in America. This time it is clearly apparent that the American economy is the American center of gravity. This is what Shaykh Usama Bin Ladin has said quite explicitly. Supporting this penetrating strategic view is that the Disunited States of America are a mixture of nationalities, ethnic groups, and races united only by the "American Dream," or, to put it more correctly, worship of the dollar, which they openly call "the Almighty Dollar." May God be exalted greatly above what they say! Furthermore, the entire American war effort is based on pumping enormous wealth at all times, money being, as has been said, the sinew of war.[98]

Leaving aside jargon about Zionists and conspiracies, al-Qurashi's depiction of al Qaeda's intent seems to mesh with reality. The 11 September attacks, of course, devastated the U.S. economy; it is only now, in early 2004, recovering. But beyond the immediate impact lie massive expenditures—at all levels of American government—that will add permanently to the size and cost of government. In addition to the cost of hiring thousands of federal employees for homeland security purposes; acquiring buildings, equipment, and training to make them effective; and requiring proportionate upgrading at state, municipal, and local levels; there lie what must be substantial amounts of unpredictable expenditures for overtime wages—in government and business alike—whenever Washington raises the threat level, or when high levels of security are provided at public places or functions heretofore not seen as serious security risks. Likewise, al Qaeda is at the core of massive increases in defense spending, costs that are likely to accelerate as U.S. officials find the military is not organized, manned, trained, or equipped to fight the kind of wars being waged in Afghanistan and Iraq. Finally, economic planning by government and business must be experiencing significant difficulty in projecting expenditures, given threats of a weapons of mass destruction (WMD) attack in the United States; the enormous monetary, materiel, and manpower costs of running several worsening wars; the steady diet of shocks thrown into business by steady call-ups of reserve-soldier employees; and—especially in the transport and tourist sectors—by such events as the "emergency" cancellation of flights from Western Europe to the United States in late 2003 and early 2004. Beyond the sound of bombs, then, al Qaeda's attack has continued since 11 September on its notion of the U.S. "center of gravity." Without a second 11 September-like attack, al Qaeda has stimulated immense unanticipated spending, much of which will become fixed in budgets at all levels of government. "Aborting the American economy is not an unattainable dream," al-Qurashi wrote in *Al-Ansar*.[99] Perhaps he is correct.

4

THE WORLD'S VIEW OF BIN LADEN: A MUSLIM LEADER AND HERO COMING INTO FOCUS?

Until this day, Saladin remains a preeminent hero of the Islamic world. It was he who united the Arabs, who defeated the Crusaders in epic battles, who recaptured Jerusalem, and who threw the European invaders out of Arab lands. In the seemingly endless struggle of modern-day Arabs to reassert the essentially Arab nature of Palestine, Saladin lives, vibrantly, as a symbol of hope and as the stuff of myth. In Damascus or Cairo, Amman or East Jerusalem, one can easily fall into lengthy conversations about Saladin, for these ancient memories are central to Arab sensibility and their ideology of liberation.

James R. Reston Jr., 2001.[1]

If you wish to conduct offensive war you must know the men employed by the enemy. Are they wise or stupid, clever of clumsy? Having assessed their qualities, you prepare appropriate measures.

Sun Tzu.[2]

Viewed from any angle, Osama bin Laden is a great man, one who smashed the expected unfolding of universal post–Cold War peace. The New York and Washington attacks, Andrew Bacevich and Sebastian

103

Malleby wrote in the *Wilson Quarterly*, "revealed that the pilgrimage to perfection was far from over," though "not for a moment did they cause American political leaders to question the project's feasibility."[3] Post-11 September, Dr. Bruce Hoffman also offered an acute judgment of bin Laden's impact. "Whatever else," Hoffman wrote, "bin Laden is one of the few persons who can argue that they changed the course of history."

> Indeed, in an age arguably devoid of ideological leadership, when these impersonal forces [globalization and economic determinism] are thought to have erased the ability of a single man to affect the course of history, bin Laden—despite all efforts—managed to taunt and strike at the United States even before September 11. His effective melding of the strands of religious fervor, Muslim piety, and a profound sense of grievance into a powerful ideological force stands—however invidious and repugnant—as a towering achievement. In his own inimitable way, bin Laden cast this struggle as precisely the "clash of civilization" that America and its coalition partners have labored so hard to negate.[4]

Now, before everyone gets irate, "great" in this instance, at least in my view, does not mean good, positive, valuable, or any other such accolade. That, however, is just one guy's view, and it is clear that there are literally tens and tens of millions of Muslims who regard bin Laden as both a great man and a man who merits all the positive connotations of the adjective "great." In contrast to Saddam Hussein, whom Muslims hated for his brutality and non-Islamic behavior but applauded for spitting in America's eye, bin Laden is seen by millions of his coreligionists—because of his defense of Islam, personal piety, physical bravery, integrity, and generosity—as an Islamic hero, as that faith's ideal type, and almost as a modern-day Saladin, determined to defend Islam and protect Muslims. It also is fair to speculate that there are some millions of non-Muslims who are opposed to the United States for foreign policy, environmental, financial, or antiglobalization reasons who silently applaud bin Laden simply because he rhetorically defies the United States and physically attacks its citizens and interests

All told, bin Laden certainly is the most popular anti-American leader in the world today. His name is legend from Houston to Zanzibar to Jakarta, and his face and sayings are emblazoned on T-shirts, CDs, audio and videotapes, posters, photographs, cigarette lighters, and stationery across the earth. "Afghanistan's children," Daniel Bergener wrote in the *New York Times Magazine* in July 2003, "suck on bin Laden candies, sugary balls in wrappers showing the leader's face, his pointed finger and the tip of a rocket."[5] So too with his name. "One of the most common names for new born males is Osama," James Kitfield reported in the *National Journal* in November 2002. "Even among those who publicly denounce his terrorist methods, the namings indicate the nearly mythical status the Islamic world has bestowed on Osama bin Laden."[6] Thanks to the Internet, his words also are available to anyone on the planet with access to a computer, or via the largest Arabic satellite television channels, *Al-Jazirah* and *Al-Arabiyah*. For a man often said to be on the run, suffering from multiple fatal diseases, and living in dank caves, bin Laden remains well and safe enough to pretty well call the tune to which the United States and much of the West dances, at least when al Qaeda's video technicians give him and his sidekick al-Zawahiri a break from hiking in the Hindu Kush. This chapter will look at how the world—Western and Muslim—has come to view bin Laden in the time since 11 September 2001. The importance of this issue is obvious. The closer the Western media comes to accurately portraying bin Laden, the better the United States and its allies will understand the threat, and the better they can plan and execute its destruction. On the Muslim side, the portrayal of bin Laden continues to play a role in the amount of support he receives and, more important, how effective he is in inciting his brethren to take part in a defensive jihad against the United States.

What Is Being Said about Bin Laden? The Stubborn Naysayers

The amount of writing about Osama bin Laden since 11 September 2001 is staggering. Muslim and Western journalists, historians, "experts," editorialists, pundits, politicians, and government officials the world over have weighed in on the man's character, abilities, and potential. There are those—as before 11 September 2001—who continue to portray bin Laden as a merely more-lethal-than-usual gangster, to denigrate the threat he poses, or to assess him as basically a bloodthirsty and depraved nonentity controlled by others, a role most often assigned to Ayman al-Zawahiri, al Qaeda's deputy chief. Bin Laden is described, alternately, as a "stateless psychopath"; a man of "mad ambitions"; the leader of "a new breed of savage and suicidal terrorists

. . . [who follow a] fanatical warping of Islam"; a "mass murderer" who, with al Qaeda, produces "mumbo-jumbo to justify their various atrocities"; or the leader of the "avatars of fanatic intolerance."[7] "What a vile and despicable excuse for a man," journalist Mona Charen wrote in a February 2003 assessment of bin Laden. "He delights in the image of burning men and women hurling themselves from the top floors of skyscrapers and of orphans mourning the loss of parents. And he seems to enjoy the infliction of fear just as much."[8] These writers were wrong before 11 September and are wrong now, although their stubborn resistance to post-11 September reality is remarkable. Bin Laden is not a "man of destiny," Don D. Chipman recently wrote in *Studies in Conflict and Terrorism,* and finds support only in "isolated cauldrons of hatred."[9] Joining Chipman was the scholar Fareed Zakaria, who wrote in *Newsweek,* "Today's Islamic terrorism is motivated not by a specific policy but a nihilistic rage against the modern world"[10]—again proving that Westernized Muslim scholars are among the least reliable guides in the war on al Qaeda. Though incorrect, the work of these writers is worth examining because it is useful to leaders and others intent on claiming victory over, or at least downplaying, the national security threat posed by bin Laden, al Qaeda, and the forces they lead or incite. These writers also provide the grist that allows senior U.S. government leaders to offer their countrymen such gems of ignorance as saying bin Laden and Stalin are two peas in a pod, and those Muslims who follow bin Laden are "the fringe of the fringe of the Muslim world. . . ."[11]

Then, there are some writers who seem to have given up on trying to understand bin Laden and al Qaeda as human phenomena. "You behave with them in the same manner you would deal with a fatal disease," Lee Harris wrote in an otherwise useful and provocative essay in *Policy Review,* "so perhaps it is time to retire the war scenario to deploy one that is more fitting: the struggle to eradicate disease."[12] The analogy to disease, of course, dehumanizes bin Laden and al Qaeda, ensuring—notwithstanding Mr. Harris's desire to "retire the war scenario"—that U.S. policies will be unchanged and war remains America's only option, the idea being, I gather, to feel no more qualms about killing Muslims than we feel about killing bacteria. And it is true that a disease cannot be influenced or defeated by policy. From disease we go to Ivy League jargon, finding there a description of what bin Laden stands for that helps no one but guarantees arcane and irrelevant debate among the tenured of academe for years to come. To wit: "Totalitarian Islamist revivalism has become the ideology of the dystopian new world order."[13] In all bin Laden literature there is not a more interesting sentence.

Despite the professional design and execution of the 11 September attacks, there also remain denigrators of bin Laden's character, abilities, and record. In the *New York Times Magazine*, for example, James Traub said bin Laden is America's "great idee fixe" because "he is evil personified,"[14] while the *Wall Street Journal*'s G.F. Seib suggested bin Laden resembles "Lord Voldemort of the Harry Potter books: an evil but invisible force so fearful that none dare mention him directly."[15] Also advocating the evil-criminal view of bin Laden is al Qaeda scholar Rohan Gunaratna, who writes of "Osama's exceedingly duplicitous nature. . . . Openly, he is kind, compassionate and evinces love for all Muslims whereas in private he is utterly ruthless, single-minded, never doubting that what he wants to happen will become a reality."[16]

The line of argument is expanded by the odd pairing of a Saudi commentator and a noted American classicist and military historian. The combination yields a bin Laden who is not only a criminal, but a media-hungry, megalomaniac sorcerer who seduces and manipulates Muslims. In one of the few pieces by a Saudi directly criticizing bin Laden, the writer Mansur Ibrahim al-Nuqadyan described the al Qaeda chief's baleful influence over Muslims. Young Muslims, the Taleban, and the Afghan people, al-Nuqadyan wrote, "are the fodder of his publicity stunt and the fuel for his lust for stardom that reverberated in the far corners, villages, and dales of the world to make the myth of bin Laden."[17] The eminent American scholar Victor Davis Hanson reduces bin Laden to something akin to an evil hypnotist, sort of the Pied Piper of the Hijaz.

> Rather than looking to itself . . . the Islamic world has more often cursed others. And, consequently, a musician [bin Laden] has been welcomed into town—one not conversant with the true tune of salvation, but arriving as a sinister player, whose narcotic of resentment has captivated the Muslim world and so tragically led it, singing as it went, right over the precipice of disaster.[18]

Playing a variation on the theme of bin Laden's limited mental and leadership abilities have been a number of Saudi officials and writers. Their intent seems simple enough: to prove that bin Laden is intellectually incapable of managing al Qaeda and designing its operations. These statements—all surely vetted by the Saudi media censors—range from the abusive to the condescending to the gently dismissive, with most falling into the latter category. "When I first met bin Laden in the 1980s," said Saudi ambassador to the United States Prince Bandar bin Sultan, "I thought he couldn't lead eight ducks across the street."[19] Less harsh, but clearly denigrating, Saudi prince Mamdouh bin Abdel-Aziz told the *New York Times* that he recalled

> that night a decade ago when Osama bin Laden attended an evening salon to describe his exploits fighting in Afghanistan. . . . He [the prince] remembers young Osama floundering when guests questioned him about the interpretation of religious texts. "Finally, I had to signal with my hands for them to stop it," said the prince. "He really is quite a simple man."[20]

The most common form of the Saudis' defamation of bin Laden is done by having his friends in the kingdom describe him as a gentle, amiable, and relatively unintelligent man. This seems to be an effort to suggest to the world that bin Laden is not capable of the 11 September attacks, while sparing the regime the anger and resentment that too harsh a critique of bin Laden would produce in the politically powerful bin Laden family—a pillar of the Saudi establishment—and the majority of the Saudi populace that polls show admire bin Laden. Most recently, the Saudis have had two longtime bin Laden friends discuss him with the domestic and international media. The men were Khalid Batarfi, managing editor of the Saudi newspaper *Al-Madina*, and bin Laden's brother-in-law Mohammed Jamal Khalifah, a known militant Islamist turned Jeddah restaurateur. Each gave an identical portrait of the naive, gentle, and pliable bin Laden.

> *Batarfi*: He struck me as a nice considerate guy. He went out of his way to help others. He wouldn't hurt a bird, as we say. He was religious from the beginning. He was not an extremist but he was very decent. He watched television but preferred cowboy films because the women were always clothed. He was so shy. He would use any means to avoid trouble. If two friends were at odds, he was the one who tried to make peace. He had a very nice attitude. . . . He was a leader but in a very low-profile way. You would follow him without him shouting. If someone else was in charge, say the captain of the [soccer] team, he would follow orders so he would have modesty about him.[21]
>
> *Khalifah*: Osama [is] one of the best persons I have ever met. . . . Osama was a very normal person, very humble, and a very simple per-

son. Osama also is a very polite, quiet person. He forces you to respect him from his attitudes. He's not a person who is aggressive. He is not a person who is even thinking to hate any person, even by words. . . . I am very surprised to hear about what Osama is doing now because it is not in his personality [to lead]. He doesn't have the capacity to organize something as simple as a 15-minute trip. Even at prayer time he would say: "You lead the prayers."[22]

A final side to the effort in the Muslim and Western worlds to denigrate bin Laden's brains and talents lies in the studied attempt to depict bin Laden as a simpleton who is directed by that evil terrorist genius Ayman al-Zawahiri, former chief of the Egyptian Islamic Jihad and now bin Laden's deputy in al Qaeda. "My knowledge of bin Ladin makes me unable to conceive what is happening now," said Dr. Abdullah al-Mu'ayyad, a former director general of the Saudi finance ministry who worked with bin Laden during the Afghan jihad. "Usama is a gentle, reasonable, and very peaceful person. . . . I believe that he changed dramatically after meeting the [Egyptian] al-Jihad and Takfir wa al-Hijra. [The Egyptians] wanted to control him from the start. Shaykh Abdullah Azzam advised him to stay away from them."[23] Khalid Batarfi picks up this theme, describing bin Laden as lost, alone, and helpless in Afghanistan after being booted out of Sudan when "the Egyptians came and told him the Americans were behind all this [his own and the Muslim world's troubles]. They filled his brain with hate and he became angry and desperate. . . . They filled his head with things that were not Islamic and convinced him it was Islam."[24] Khalifah, bin Laden's other much-quoted friend, follows suit, explaining that the leaders of the Egyptian Islamic Jihad "had observed Usama well, and knew that, had they asked him to head thousands of youth in holy war in the name of Allah, he would not have refused. He was too keen on religion."[25] In the West, Stephen Simon and Daniel Benjamin—former National Security Council senior terrorism officials who wrote the useful book *The Age of Sacred Terror*—asserted that al-Zawahiri "always has been a clearer thinker" than bin Laden.[26] Rohan Gunaratna has concluded that al-Zawahiri is bin Laden's eminence gris. Having met the older Egyptian at a young age, Gunaratna explains, "Osama was too mature under the guidance [of al-Zawahiri]. . . . What is undeniable is the influence that al-Zawahiri wields over Osama."[27]

The foregoing are carryovers from assessments of bin Laden current before the 11 September attacks. As I said, they were off the mark then, they are more so now, but because there are fewer of them, they do not greatly distract the debate over the threat bin Laden poses. The one distractive theme that has emerged with a vengeance since the 11 September attacks, however, is dangerous to national security because it is wrong but plausible, and because it is comforting to American elites still refusing to see that U.S. government actions in the Islamic world are causing Muslims to attack the United States. The argument's gist is that bin Laden, his allies, and their goals have been spawned by a "failed civilization"—one hostile to democratization, capitalism, and modernity, save for the tools of war—and that they are driven by both the realization that Islamic society is dying and a maniacal desire to destroy other civilizations that are successful and causing the demise of Islam. These men, the argument goes, recognize this failure, blame it on the West, and are lashing out with indiscriminate violence to spark an Armageddon-like battle with Western civilization. This line of analysis takes a brilliant, calculating, and patient foe like bin Laden and reduces him to the status of a madman, bloodthirsty and irrational.

It is with some trepidation that I disagree with this line of analysis. First, it is held by writers for whom I have profound respect, especially Bernard Lewis, Ralph Peters[28], Malise Ruthven[29], and Victor Davis Hanson[30]. Second, I believe that in a general sense there is much truth in this analysis. There is no avoiding that fact that there is a systemic breakdown across much of the Muslim world that is most evident in rampant illiteracy, technological backwardness, poor educational systems, decrepit public services, rudimentary health care, discrimination against women, tyrannical governments, and a host of other problems. And there indeed are many Muslims who blame other civilizations—Western, Modern, Christian, secular, call it what you will—for each of these misfortunes. "Meanwhile the blame game—the Turks, the Mongols, the imperialists, the Jews, the Americans—continues, and shows little sign of abating," wrote Bernard Lewis in the book *What Went Wrong? Western Impact and Middle Eastern Response*, in which he presents the failed-civilization thesis.

> If the peoples of the Middle East continue on their present path, the suicide bomber may become a metaphor for the entire region, and there will be no escape from the downward spiral of hate and spite, rage and self-pity, poverty and oppression, culminating sooner or later in another alien domination; perhaps from a new Europe reverting to old ways, perhaps from a resurgent Russia, perhaps from some new,

expanding superpower in the East. If they abandon grievance and victimhood, settle their differences, and join their talents, energies, and resources in a common creative endeavor, then they can once again make the Middle East, in modern times as it was in antiquity and the Middle Ages, a major center of civilization. For the time being, the choice is their own.[31]

The question for me, however, is whether this is a failure of Islamic civilization, or the result of a transition from the era of European colonialism—which planted the seeds of modernization in the Middle East—to one of unrelenting tyranny by the states and regimes made from Europe's former colonies. Arguably, many Muslims have fewer personal freedoms and modern amenities—potable water, quality schools, adequate electricity, et cetera—than they did during the age of European imperialism. Does the situation today result from Muslims turning their backs on modernization, or from having entered the post-colonial era under a system of absolutist monarchies and dictator-run regimes that represent a retrograde step from what might, astoundingly, be seen as the more enlightened age of colonialism? I am certainly not arguing here for a return to colonialism, although, as noted, al Qaeda heralds the invasion and occupation of Iraq as the return of direct colonial rule. I am only suggesting that the postcolonial governing arrangements—which, for reasons of economic self-interest, the West has defended as sacrosanct—have further enslaved Muslims rather than freeing them.

The failed-civilization analysis, unfortunately, allows U.S. elites, policy makers, and voters to take refuge in the idea that the Islamic world has gone mad, and that nothing the United States has done has caused al Qaeda's attacks, or generated the widely held anti-U.S. sentiment in the Islamic world. This analysis can be used to buttress a belief that such attacks are the irrational, almost-crazed Muslim response to the death throes of a once glorious and worldwide Islamic civilization, and that the violence is meant only to destroy the "others" who are blamed for Islam's demise. In July 2002, the journalist James Klurfield wrote an article providing a good summary of the erroneous conclusions that flow from the failed-civilization thesis. The attacks of 11 September 2001, Klurfield argued in tones nearly identical to those of Bernard Lewis, Ralph Peters, and others,

> came from a religious sect lashing out at modernity and the leading exponent of modernity, the United States. Osama bin Laden is the

product of failure, a failed culture that is being left behind by the rest of the world. He and his followers are lashing out because they cannot cope with the modern world. . . . Bin Ladenism and other forms of Islamic fundamentalism are attempts to deal with the Arab world's inability to cope with modernity. . . . Fundamentalism is a dead-end road."[32]

With the problem framed in this context, the other lines of analysis that accompany the thesis—ones that deal with the Islamists' war aims and bin Laden's personal goals—move the reader further down the road toward believing that the Islamists and bin Laden have no specific complaints about the policies and actions of the United States and its Western allies, and are attacking because they do not like us and resent our affluence and way of life. "For Osama bin Laden," wrote the eminent historian Bernard Lewis,

> his declaration of war against the United States marks the resumption of the struggle for religious dominance that began in the seventh century. For him and his followers, this is a moment of opportunity. Today, America exemplifies the civilization and embodies the leadership of the House of War, and like Rome and Byzantium, it has become degenerate and demoralized, ready to be overthrown. But despite its weakness, it is also dangerous. . . . for members of al Qaeda it is the seduction of America and its profligate dissolute way of life that represents the greatest threat to the kind of Islam they want to impose on their fellow Muslims.[33]

At this point, we are again faced with the chance to incorrectly answer the question "Why do Muslims hate us?" Do they hate us for what we think and how we live, or do they hate us because of what we do in the Muslim world? The answer, per Professor Lewis, would be mostly the former, amounting to the same kind of ill-defined threat posed by America and the West to Islam that Ayatollah Khomeini railed so shrilly against for more than a decade. Khomeini's rhetoric about the threat posed to Islam by evil, degenerate, and irreligious Americans fueled some sporadic acts of anti-U.S. violence but never stimulated anything resembling a jihad. Indeed, the most destructive anti-U.S. act of the Khomeini era—the bombing of the U.S. Marine barracks in Beirut in 1983—was conducted by Hizballah using Khomeini's rhetoric to cover its simple goal of preventing the U.S. military from establishing a long-term presence in Lebanon. Notwithstanding Khomeini, Hizballah

attacked because of what the United States did—intervened in Lebanon—not because of what it is or thought. Given the similarity between
the failed-civilization thesis and the ayatollah's indictment, the brilliant
analyst Ralph Peters creates a portrait of bin Laden as a Sunni Khomeini, violently lashing out hither and yon in an effort to destroy an
evil civilization and its lifestyle. "Consider a minor player on the world
stage who has been hyped into international stardom," Peters wrote
late in 2000,

> Osama bin Laden is not waging a war against the West's realities. He
> doesn't know them. He struggles against a riveting, overwhelming,
> wildly skewed personal vision of the West, exemplified by an America
> that he has conjured from shreds of information and his own deepest
> fears. . . . Mr. bin Laden's acolytes know little—often nothing—of the
> mundane West, but are galvanized by the psychologically rewarding
> opportunity to hate. Men of few earthly prospects, they imagine a
> divine mission for themselves. It is the summit of self-gratification.[34]

So, by this point, we have progressed from the ramifications of a
failed civilization and the anger it engenders, to a Khomeini-like hatred
of America because of its "dissolute way of life" that seduces Muslims,
to a group of ignorant young men with few "earthly prospects" who
sustain themselves psychologically by hating and killing what they hate.
The payoff, naturally, is Osama bin Laden the madman. Again, Ralph
Peters paints the scene, this time from his excellent book, *Beyond Terror: Strategy in a Changing World.*

> Osama bin Laden is willing to die—but he wants a commensurate
> effect when he goes. . . . In terms of religion, he imagines himself
> Allah's humble servant but is, in fact, an extreme egomaniac, "leading
> God from below."
> But [bin Laden] cannot be dealt with as a rational actor, since,
> under the cunning surface, he is irrational in the extreme. His methods
> make cruel sense, but his goals are far beyond the demise of a particu-
> lar regime or the recognition of a Palestinian state. He wants to
> destroy, at the very least, a civilization he has cast as satanic. He does
> not want to defeat the West—he wants to annihilate us. If he had the
> technology today, he would use it.[35]

This line of analysis, as already noted, comes from excellent and
learned writers, and I am loath to challenge and criticize those from

whom I have learned so much. Still, I think these analyses miss the mark regarding Osama bin Laden. For nearly a decade now, bin Laden has demonstrated patience, brilliant planning, managerial expertise, sound strategic and tactical sense, admirable character traits, eloquence, and focused, limited war aims. He has never, to my knowledge, behaved or spoken in a way that could be described as "irrational in the extreme." The term "irrational," it seems to me, is better applied to Americans who have forgotten, or never learned, Nathan Bedford Forrest's lesson that "war means fighting and fighting means killing," and are horrified by the modest—compared to what is coming—casualties bin Laden has so far exacted.

There has been no similar reporting from those who know, fought alongside, served under, fought against, or interviewed him. To the contrary, bin Laden is much more frank—about al Qaeda's successes and, especially, its defeats—and much less prone to hyperbole than many of the Western leaders who thunder denunciations of him. Professor Lewis and Mr. Peters may well be correct that contemporary Islam is a failed civilization; Peters argues the "Arab homelands of Islam" should be written off as "incapable of constructive change."[36] There also probably are many millions of Muslims who blame the West for that failure and are eager to use indiscriminate violence in seeking revenge. Bin Laden, however, is not one of those individuals. "In the same way," bin Laden wrote in February 2003, "I inform you of the good news that our ummah has been promised victory by Allah, but if this victory has become delayed, then it is due to our sins and our sitting back from helping the religion of Allah."[37]

Bin Laden consistently has put the blame for the decrepit condition of Islamic civilization squarely on Muslims themselves. He certainly damns the West for attacking Islam and accuses it of stealing Islam's natural resources and trying to eliminate all Muslims, but he gives credit for the Crusaders' success to the fact that many Muslims have strayed from the path set down by Allah and His prophet and failed to join a defensive jihad to defeat the West's attacks and then work to restore the greatness of Islam. The enemies of Muslims—be they Americans, Christians, Jews, apostates, or polytheists—are dominating the Islamic world, according to bin Laden, because an insufficient number of Muslims have stood up and fought for their faith. Rather than taking the negative road of blaming non-Muslims for the plight of Islam, bin Laden has stuck resolutely to the positive message that the Islamic world cannot be defeated because Allah promised it victory if Muslims obeyed His words and His prophet's guidance. Yes, bin Laden does blame others—especially the U.S.-led Crusaders—for attacking Islam, Muslims, and Muslim territory, but he claims that Muslims, if they return to Islam, have it in their power, and need help from no one but God, to annihilate the attackers. Bin Laden, at the end of the day, is a happy warrior, a brilliant hunter-killer waging war to achieve precise, devastating, but limited goals. There simply is no evidence to support the idea that he is vaingloriously trying to lead the world—Muslim, Christian, and other—to Armageddon. And it is for this reason that I, with respect, strongly disagree with those who apply the failed-civilization theory to bin Laden and al Qaeda. An armed, patient, and positive predator always is more dangerous and less prone to errors than the bomb-throwing madman crazy for revenge.

What Is Being Said about Bin Laden? Some Are Catching On

There is an increasing number of Western journalists and scholars who are coming to view bin Laden as much more than a terrorist and al Qaeda as much more than a terrorist group. This is all to the good because it facilitates a more informed assessment of the national security threat America is facing. Still, Western writers—including myself—have a ways to go in mastering the subject. The catching-on writers have captured bin Laden's talents and strength of will, the manpower, depth, and resiliency of his organization, the wide range of like-minded Islamist leaders and organizations, and the innovations bin Laden and al Qaeda have brought to the concept of asymmetric warfare. While the recognition of these realities is a major post-11 September intellectual advance, these writers—and, to be fair, most of the Western world—have not fully factored in the role Islam plays in the thinking, plans, flexibility, patience, and endurance of bin Laden and his allies. This situation exists because some in the West discount the power of religion, know little about the religion of Islam, or recognize Islam's motivating role but are afraid to raise the issue in debate for fear of being labeled a racist or bigot. The latter concern is the deadly enemy of an effective American debate to formulate a strategy to destroy the Islamists' threat. In reviewing *The Age of Sacred Terror* for *Foreign Affairs*, for example, Ellen Laipson, the incisive scholar and former deputy chief of the National Intelligence Council, wrote that the "book's most important and lasting contribution is its exploration of the relationship between al Qaeda's toxic message and the Muslim mainstream."[38] This, she continued, is an area of debate and intellectual exploration largely closed to the U.S. government's analytic corps.

> U.S. government officials face many constraints, formal and informal, in addressing religion as a threat. Norms of tolerance and multi-culturalism discourage the analysis of religion or cultural beliefs. . . . But the burden runs deeper than that. Many good civil servants, fearing political incorrectness, are uncomfortable openly assessing foreign cultures on the basis of religious or cultural beliefs.[39]

In the Muslim world, on the other hand, journalists, commentators, and scholars have long recognized the primacy of Islam in bin Laden's thinking and behavior, as well as in providing much of al Qaeda's appeal, cohesion, and durability. Since the 11 September attacks, they have focused on the increasingly prominent leadership position bin Laden holds in the Islamic world. In their writings, Muslim authors have begun to discuss and assess bin Laden in terms of his resemblance to the major leaders and heroes in Islamic history. In a culture where historic figures and events a millennium and more old are revered and still discussed or alluded to in public and private discourse, this sort of pan-Islamic conversation about bin Laden's place in history increases his popularity and the esteem in which he and al Qaeda are held. It also makes bin Laden the leader on whom untold numbers of Muslims pin their hopes and aspirations for the future.

Western writers have made substantial strides toward a better understanding of bin Laden, although this is true for some more than others. Thomas Friedman, for example, has concluded that bin Laden "is not a mere terrorist," but he still tends to view bin Laden as an irrational actor, "a super-empowered angry man who has all the geopolitical objectives and instincts of a nation-state."[40] Other analysts share Friedman's conclusion that bin Laden is more than a terrorist but depart from him in depicting the al Qaeda leader as a coldly calculating individual, a man who is rational, logical, amoral, businesslike, and "the quintessential product of the 1990s and globalism."[41] For these writers, two main lines of analysis have emerged: bin Laden as an innovative military man, and bin Laden as a combination of the warrior and the chief executive officer (CEO) whose dual talents allowed him to design a "business continuity plan" to protect al Qaeda's "leaders and finances" from U.S. arms.[42] In the first incarnation, Christopher Bellamy has written in *The Independent* that because of "the scale and audacity of the attacks on New York and Washington . . . [bin Laden] will join the ranks of history's most infamous men, a notorious politico-military-religious leader who changed the world."

> . . . Mr. bin Laden's genius has not only created terrorist attacks of unprecedented scale, but introduced a new element—synergy. . . . [H]e has shown a military genius's instinct for exploiting the disproportionate effect of attacks on several targets at once, confusing the defenders and paralyzing the response. . . . As an innovator and practitioner of asymmetric warfare, Mr. Bin Laden follows in the tradition of Mao Zedung. Mao traded space for time, and in facing a conventional army also looked to the intangible element of will.[43]

Taking Bellamy's conclusion a step further, defense analyst Larry Seaquist and RAND's Bruce Hoffman define bin Laden more as a warrior–chief executive officer; instead of looking back in history for analogous figures like Mao, these authors see bin Laden as having meshed the warrior's skills with the model of the aggressive, flexible, risk-taking, out-of-the-box thinking, and hugely successful CEO prominent in the 1990s. Writing in the *Christian Science Monitor*, Seaquist credited bin Laden with CEO-like attributes and termed him an "executive terrorist" and a "first-rate innovator." Bin Laden, Seaquist argued, had "thought big" by assimilating local causes into a global campaign; had known his consumers and cleverly shaped his anti-U.S. message to "resonate with Muslims of all stripes and cultures . . . including many of the well-educated and prosperous"; and had stayed on message by keeping al Qaeda's major attacks focused on the United States. Al Qaeda under bin Laden, Seaquist concluded, "has a capacity for what a business executive would term strategic control—for tailoring itself, its work force, and its 'products' to the changing 'marketplace'."[44]

RAND's Dr. Hoffman makes this warrior–CEO analogy even more strongly. In a short, brilliant essay in the April 2002 *Atlantic Monthly*—entitled "The Leadership Secrets of Osama bin Laden: The Terrorist as CEO"—Hoffman explained bin Laden's innovative use of business principles to transform al Qaeda from a regionally based organization to one that is transnational and ready, at the dawn of the twenty-first century, to compete globally with the United States in a war.

> In the 1990s, [bin Laden] did what executives of transnational companies did throughout much of the industrialized world—namely, design

and implement a flexible new organizational framework and strategy incorporating multiple levels and both top-down and bottom-up approaches. In his top-down mode, bin Laden has defined specific goals, issued orders, and ensured that they are carried out. . . . But he has also operated as a venture capitalist, soliciting ideas from below, encouraging creative approaches, and funding proposals he finds promising.[45]

What Is Being Said about Bin Laden? The Missing Piece for Those Catching On

The portraits of bin Laden as an innovative military man and warrior–CEO move us closer to an accurate, useable estimate of the man. Both are too dispassionate, mechanistic, and measurable, however. They do not make an assessment of the religious piety and faith that drive bin Laden, and by missing this factor they miss the key element that makes him much more than just an intelligent soldier and a formidable CEO. The last puzzle piece is provided—with two prominent exceptions—by Muslim writers and commentators who focus on bin Laden's personal character and behavior, and how these factors slowly are raising him in the esteem of the world's Muslims, whether or not they support al Qaeda's military actions. These writers claim that before our eyes bin Laden has become a heroic figure, not only in the present, but as a man who is marked with the same attributes as the heroes of Islamic history. It is the combination of bin Laden's admirable and self-effacing character—as seen through Muslim eyes—and his resonance with Muslims familiar with fourteen-plus centuries of Islamic history that add the necessary and unquantifiable human dimension to fill out the portrait of bin Laden as the warrior–CEO.

A pair of excellent American analysts offer good brief explanations of how bin Laden's character traits fit with those of the heroic figures of Islamic history, and how his and al Qaeda's behavior strike, to paraphrase Mr. Lincoln, the mystic chords of Muslim memory. "In the Middle East as well as in Europe," Professor Bernard Lewis explained in the *Wall Street Journal*,

> there is a strong tradition of bandit heroes, challenging authority and eluding capture. . . . The role of the Middle Eastern Robin Hood, unlike his Western prototype, is not to rob the rich and give to the poor, though some such expectation may lurk in the background; it is

rather to defy the strong and to protect—and ultimately avenge—the weak. For Osama bin Laden and his merry men, The Sheriff of Nottingham is their local potentate, which ever that may be. The ultimate enemy, King John, lives far away, as he always has done—in Constantinople and Vienna, London and Paris, and now in Washington and New York.[46]

Addressing this same issue, the Lebanese-American journalist Geneive Abdo, author of *No God But God: Egypt and the Triumph of Islam*,[47] the finest book in print on the quiet but pervasive power of Islamism, argues that it is a disastrous mistake for Americans to believe that bin Laden lies on the Muslim world's lunatic fringe. Ms. Abdo contends that bin Laden and al Qaeda are mortal threats not just because they have declared war on the United States and proven themselves militarily potent, but also because they already have become part of the continuum of Islamic history. "We are told by U.S. leaders," Ms. Abdo warned in September 2003,

> that [bin Laden] is out to destroy our way of life and to crush our notions of freedom and pursuit of happiness.
>
> But to cast bin Laden in such narrow terms is to dismiss his profound standing among some of the world's 1.2 billion Muslims and to overlook his rightful place in Islamic history. Where the West sees him as a mad-dog terrorist, many of his Muslim partisans regard him as the latest in a long tradition of radical Islamic thinkers and revolutionary leaders, all of whom advocated violence in pursuit of their own vision of a united, worldwide ummah, or community of believers.[48]

In the context of the welcoming historical memory of Muslims, Professor Lewis points out that bin Laden's personality and character traits are an exceptionally good fit with those of Islamic heroes of the past, and that, because of this reality, "he remains an enormously popular figure, not only with extremists and radicals . . . but in much wider circles in the Muslim and particularly the Arab world."[49] Lewis notes that bin Laden follows the historic Islamic model of the well-spoken, austere, brave, and self-effacing hero. "The first and most obvious reason for [bin Laden's] popularity is his eloquence," Lewis writes, "a skill much appreciated and admired in the Arab world since ancient times . . . [and] in the modern Arab world there is little sign of eloquence. In his use of language, bin Laden brings a return to the traditional virtues. Modern devices, notably satellite television, can bring his eloquence all over the Arab world."[50] This point is emphasized in many discussions of bin Laden, and bin Laden himself apparently pays close attention to word choice and phrasing when preparing his public words. The Islamist website *Al-Sha'b*, for example, has reported that bin Laden "likes to be precise when using Arabic at a media event, or whenever he writes a statement or a letter"[51], and his brother-in-law Mohammed Jamal Khalifah has said that throughout his life bin Laden could be found "selecting his words very carefully when he's talking."[52] Professor Lewis further explains that bin Laden uses Arabic in a way that reminds Muslims of "traditional virtues," and that this style, in turn, keeps his listeners focused on his character, lifestyle, and common touch.

> Bin Laden is not a ruler, and therefore not tainted with tyranny and corruption. . . . Even more striking is the contrast demonstrated in his personal life between himself and the present-day rulers of most of the Arab lands. . . . Osama bin Laden presents the inspiring spectacle of one who, by his own free choice, has forsaken a life of riches and comfort for one of hardship and danger.[53]

The qualities of the Islamic hero these American scholars describe—eloquence, a strong but self-effacing personality, and the courage to defy the mighty in word and deed—have been amply documented by Muslim writers since 11 September. Even in the denigrating, Saudi-regime-coaxed words of bin Laden's friends Batarfi and Khalifah, bin Laden is still a quiet, amiable, and pious man. Prince Turki al-Faisal, the Saudi ambassador in the United Kingdom and ex-chief of the Saudi intelligence service that is said to have tried to kill bin Laden more than once, has said that in meeting bin Laden "four or five times over ten years" he found him to be "a handsome, well-mannered, and nice, cultured person. This is what I noticed about him."[54] Even bin Laden's sworn enemies, it seems, find it hard to dislike him or doubt his religious sincerity.

Muslims neutral about bin Laden and those prone to support him seem to find clear evidence that he is, or is becoming, an important Islamic leader and hero in that religion's classic mold. Professor Lewis's point about the importance of eloquence for a Muslim leader is expressed repeatedly in the Muslim media. On the first anniversary of the attacks on Washington and New York, for example, Abd al-Bari Atwan, editor-in-chief of the prestigious, UK-based Arabic daily *Al-Quds Al-Arabi*, remarked on the history-tinged eloquence of bin Laden's words about the nineteen martyrs. "[H]e spoke of them," Atwan told *Al-Jazirah*, "as if they were commanders of jihad squads in early Islam, when Islamic conquests were underway. He introduced them very beautifully and impressively to address the young Muslim generation and say the following: Here are the new role models for Islam. . . ."[55] Another explanation of how bin Laden's speaking style is heard by Muslims was provided by the London-based Egyptian dissident and Islamic lawyer Hani al-Siba'i. Speaking to *Al-Jazirah* about a late-2002 broadcast of bin Laden's statement regarding Iraq, al-Siba'i drew attention to bin Laden's eloquence and historical resonance.

> I believe Shaykh Osama's talk reminds me of Jarir [a classical Arab poet] who says: "I continue to emerge against the wishes of my enemies." The man, Shaykh Osama, has accustomed us to such pleasant talk. The message is addressed to the whole world, not to a specific person. The message proves beyond any doubt . . . that the man is alive. This is not speculation. This is his voice, this is his hoarseness, and this is his speech. This is a wise, calm, and rational message, in which he explains his grievances. He explains them to the whole world with extreme fairness to the effect that he is not a man of aggression, but through this approach he is defending the [Islamic] nation.[56]

Beyond rhetoric lies the personal example set by bin Laden over the course of his life and insurgent career, the latter now approaching a quarter century. All of the traditional attributes of the Islamic hero described by Professor Lewis and others likewise have been cited by people who have known or encountered bin Laden for both short periods and long. The best way, I think, to depict the power and influence of bin Laden's personal example on Muslims is to let several people who have known or dealt with him since the mid-1980s speak for themselves. This especially is the case because the authenticity of bin Laden's renunciation of wealth and luxury to live and fight in Afghanistan is one of the things about him most often doubted in the West.

> The truth is that Usama bin Ladin does not care about, and does not attach much importance to, his death. . . . Usama bin Laden believes strongly in his religion. He admits that he gets nervous sometimes and that he makes mistakes. But he is a magnanimous, good, and brave man. He is an educated and struggling man.[57]

> I met bin Laden, or Abu al-Qaqa as he was called on the frontline whenever the Arab Afghans mentioned his name in their communica-

tions. I found him to be a calm young man to a great degree and [he] possessed a certain "charisma" when dealing with others. I was captivated by the simple life he led. . . . I lived with him for four years, some of them in the Tora Bora caves and tunnels near Jalalabad. Daily life was extremely difficult and I faced death many times.[58]

[Bin Laden] was a tall, thin, and gracious man. Engineer Mahmoud [an Afghan commander of the Yunis Khalis group] asked me and all the tribal leaders from the Tora Bora area to meet his new guest at Malawi [near Jalalabad]. Bin Laden shook each of our hands and said a few words. He had a young boy with him and about ten Arab bodyguards.[59]

The other thing is that what has made the Saudis admire bin Laden the most is his renunciation of the pleasure of worldly things. For example, the Saudis compare him to the most distinguished people and see that bin Laden has left the life of luxury and luxury of hotels to the trenches, the trenches of jihad. But they see others compete for the worldly life and its vanities and palaces and ranches, etc.[60]

They said [bin Laden] was a kind and humble man who led a very simple life [in Khartoum]. They said he did not talk much and used to visit his Sudanese neighbors on religious holidays and special occasions.[61]

Usama was very kind to us. He even built the road that runs from Tora Bora back to Jalalabad so that we could get to market more easily. His men were always very polite and gave us wheat and flour.[62]

[Bin Laden] was a very normal man. He had no bodyguards, would go out shopping at the bazaars, and conversed lightheartedly with friends. Within the society of 10,000 Arabic people [in Peshawar, Pakistan], he was a well-known person, but he kept his lifestyle simple so as not to be conspicuous relative to the average Arabian.[63]

I was once with [bin Laden] in Afghanistan during the war with the Soviet Union. He is a struggler and a pious scholar. He is a man with tender emotions. We have all respected him. We have never felt any harshness or unfairness on his part.[64]

Well-spoken, kind, considerate, pious, and humble, bin Laden also killed more than three thousand Americans on 11 September 2001, and with that act—defying the mighty in deed as well as word—completed the composite picture of a classical Islamic hero. As Larry Seaquist noted in the *Christian Science Monitor*, "The ultimate measure of a fighter is the size of his foe,"[65] and bin Laden decided to fight the United States, the entity that many Muslims perceive as the biggest threat to Islam since the Crusades, and perhaps even since the Mongol invasion. And in picking on the United States and escaping capture, bin Laden also, as the *Economist* emphasized, "bolstered his reputation for cocking a mighty snook at America, and [this] helped to make him a powerful totem of Islamic 'resistance.' "[66] In addition, bin Laden has lived by his own definition of a pious Muslim as one who "understood the worth of [religious] knowledge depends on how you work according to it."[67] The work he did, of course, was to attack the United States. "Thus the victory of religion cannot occur merely by the giving of lectures," bin Laden said in February 2003, "without sacrificing our time and our wealth as the commodity of Allah (paradise) is expensive. When Jihad becomes compulsory, there is a massive difference between sitting and giving lectures, and sacrificing lives and heads for the victory of religion."[68] And for all the denouncing of the attacks by America's Muslim allies—those corrupt, effete, and despotic princelings and dictators—and the clerics in their pay and under their thumb, the reaction of the average Muslim may well have been that expressed by a crippled Saudi cleric late in 2001. "You have given us weapons," the cleric told bin Laden, "you have given us hope and we thank Allah for you. . . . People are now supporting us more, even those who did not support us in the past . . . [E]verybody praises what you did, the great action you did, which was first and foremost by the Grace of Allah. This is the guidance of Allah, and the blessed fruit of jihad."[69]

So what is bin Laden today in terms of a public figure? Is he a mad and evil sorcerer smack out of the pages of *Harry Potter*? A gangster of singular genius? A simpleton directed by the Egyptian Dr. Moriarity? The nearly best answer, it seems to me, is found in a combination of the portraits presented by the Western writers I have described as "catching on," and the words and analyses of the Muslims who have known bin Laden, listened to him, and have tried to put him into the context of the sweep of Islamic history. These individuals variously describe bin Laden as a soldier, a CEO, a pious scholar, a warrior, one with the common people, and even a product of globalization. There are parts of all of these in bin Laden, but I believe that there is one more element to be recognized, one that completes the picture. And that element is love.

Love not so much for Osama bin Laden the person—although there is much of that—but love for his defense of the faith, the life he lives, the heroic example he sets, and the similarity of that example to other heroes in the pantheon of Islamic history. Three passages written by Muslims capture, I think, this love for bin Laden's efforts, a factor that makes him a threat to the United States now and long after his death. The first passage is from a Pakistani political commentator who describes the emotional bond that has developed between bin Laden and Muslims, and the second is from a Pakistani scholar who addresses the resonance bin Laden has on the historical memory and imagination of Muslims.

> Usama bin Ladin is a liberator of the downtrodden people. They do not only respect Usama bin Ladin, they love him. They consider it a great achievement, if their lives are lost working for Usama bin Ladin. Usama bin Ladin has become a larger than life figure. Where is he and how is he taking care of himself are the most important questions in the world nowadays. He is a symbol of love. Usama bin Ladin is a person in whom the entire world sees their hopes and wishes. Usama bin Ladin is a symbol of the peoples' hatred of the United States. Usama bin Ladin has become as dangerous as a nuclear bomb. The United States can never catch Usama bin Ladin because he lives in the heart of every Muslim.[70]

> Islam's splendid history is replete with characters who through their deeds taught Muslims not to bow down to Satanism and to fight the forces of evil. While these people have proved to be a beacon for Muslims, by the dint of their courage, steadfastness and bravery, they became a horror for the forces of evil and proved to be nerve-wracking. In the present era, Shaykh Usama Bin Ladin is one of these millions of characters who sacrificed for Allah Almighty. When he arrived at the arena, a bolt of lightning struck the forces of evil and infidelity. The entire world with its huge armies and most modern weaponry was bent on killing this one person. But those who try to extinguish the sun themselves die, and therefore, these forces have failed and Usama has been successful in his sacred mission.[71]

While the emotional and historical responses to bin Laden are important in terms of the dimensions and durability of his popular support, a third passage pertains more explicitly to the allegiance he inspires among those men who intend to take up arms against the United States and the West. This passage comes from a fellow warrior of bin Laden's, the Taleban leader Mullah Mohammed Omar. Mullah Omar, as is usual for him, has no time for emotion and speaks in terse declarative sentences. He describes bin Laden as something of an Islamic Oliver Cromwell or Thomas Jackson, an implacable Ironsides of a believer, unyielding in his views and goals, and steadfast in striving to achieve what he believes God has demanded. In regard to those men who will seek to attack America, Mullah Omar's words amount to a mission statement for them and bin Laden. "Osama is my brother," Mullah Omar told the daily *Pakistan* in April 2002.

> He is still living in tents in Afghanistan with us, with the Afghan nation. He is a great son of the ummah who did not waste his wealth on luxuries. He is a man of principle and possesses religious valor. He is a custodian of Muslim honor. He is a staunch supporter of jihad. He spreads the message of God Almighty in the world. He has demonstrated great courage in the battlefield where not the Generals of glass but only iron men can stay.
>
> He has been fighting all satanic forces in the world by risking his life. He does not like an easy life, instead he prefers to work hard. He strikes the enemy effectively and that is why the United States is scared of him. The infidels are worried whether the ummah may not get united under his leadership. Imperialist forces want to kill him but we believe that death is the savior of life. Everybody has his own scales of victory and defeat. Sometimes an apparent winner is a loser, and sometimes the one who seems defeated actually wins with the help of God Almighty.[72]

None of these statements describe the man the West views as a criminal and mass murderer. That said, even those still resisting Dr. Huntington's clash-of-civilizations paradigm can, I think, see a clash between each civilization's perception of bin Laden, a wide divergence pitting the West's madman against Islam's hero. An appreciation of the Muslim perspective—this does not mean acceptance—allows the West to gauge bin Laden's appeal and staying power. As well, it helps explain the hatred stirred in Muslims by the West's pursuit of bin Laden, jailing of hundreds of mujahideen, and public denigration of the man and, implicitly, the religious principles he champions. I turn again to Kent Gramm's powerful book on Gettysburg to build an analogy, one that will anger some because its juxtaposes Mr. Lincoln and bin Laden. Gramm argues that much of Lincoln's thought would be alien to today's America because its law and culture are "becoming abjectly secular," and because "we now have a society increasingly uncivilized and more pervasively without conscience. . . ."[73] Gramm says Lincoln believed in the existence of a moral universe in which men could know right from wrong and act accordingly. I would argue bin Laden believes in the same universe, and that Muslims love, respect, and support him because he speaks of and defends that reality. In understanding bin Laden's impact on Muslims, Gramm's description of Lincoln's moral sense and behavior—which Americans still revere, if not apply—is a useful insight for trying to analyze bin Laden's stature in the Islamic world. "Lincoln's assumptions are not modern," Professor Gramm wrote in 1994,

> To him, the universe if not random, is not morally neutral, is not masterless; and humankind has to answer for its actions in a cosmos that is not only physical but moral. The difference between good and evil can sometimes be known. There are such things as duty and responsibility toward others. We are not the ultimate judges. And, as in the Old Testament, nations are held accountable as if they were individuals."[74]

5

BIN LADEN VIEWS THE WORLD: SOME OLD, SOME NEW, AND A TWIST

War is about thoughts and words. . . . It is especially difficult for Americans to consider the connection, for the country as a whole does not seem to believe words and thoughts are very important. But how the world's fundamentalists read their holy books during the next one hundred years will be a matter of life and death for millions.

Kent Gramm, 1999.[1]

The portrait of bin Laden that emerges is richer, more complex and more accurate than the simple caricature of a hate-filled, mindless fanatic. "All men dream; but not equally," T.E. Lawrence, the legendary Lawrence of Arabia, wrote. "Those who dream by night in the dusty recesses of their minds wake in the day to find it was vanity: but the dreamers of the day are dangerous men, for they may act their dreams with open eyes, to make it possible." Bin Laden is indeed one of the dangerous men Lawrence described.

Bruce Hoffman, 2001.[2]

A quiver of excitement and anxiety pulses through U.S. officialdom each time rumors spread that another Osama bin Laden video or audio-tape has been passed to *Al-Jazirah*, *Al-Arabiyah*, or another television news outlet. It is as if the mere words of the man have become a threat to the "Homeland"—an odd, unnerving word to use to refer to America, reminiscent, as it is, of phrases used by Hitler and Stalin in World War II. Anyway, the tape is soon played and almost before bin Laden's statement ends a blast of official U.S. indignation is launched and a blitz of forensic experts attack al Qaeda's latest media production. The U.S. State Department condemns this or that Arabic satellite channel for "irresponsibly" broadcasting a message from a terrorist, and this statement is soon seconded by other U.S. officials and pundits. As this public huffing and pouting proceeds, government and media experts are unleashed on the tape, assigned to answer questions that are meant, I suppose, to make the United States more secure. To wit: Is his beard longer? Is it greyer? Look, he is not moving his left shoulder! Has he been wounded? Is he dying? Is that his voice? Doesn't it sound more hoarse than usual? Is he drinking more water than last time? Does that mean his kidneys are failing? Aha, he is using a stick to walk down the mountainside! Is his back hurt? And what about those rocks? Igneous or sedimentary? Call the geologists! Can we locate those rocks in Afghanistan? Are those spring flowers or Arctic lichens? Wait! What about that fir tree on the third mountain from the left? Can imagery locate it? Does he look paler than usual? Is he wearing Arab or Afghan clothes? Are those birds singing in the background? Send for an ornithologist! Look at that hat! Has he ever worn that type before? Is that a dagger in his belt? Why is there no dagger in his belt? Look, he is blinking his eyes! Could he be blinking attack orders? Call the eye-blink decoder! What about . . .

In this blizzard of blather, bin Laden's words are the most overlooked part of the tape under review. (See the select bibliography at the end of the book for the websites bin Laden has used most.) Indeed, major U.S. or Western media have made no consistent effort to publish bin Laden's statements, thereby failing to give their audience the words that put his thoughts and actions in cultural and historical context, and which would increase the West's awareness of the mortal threat he poses. Spoken quietly and precisely, bin Laden's statements slowly build on each other, repeating and refining long-established themes, and taking account of recent world events and U.S. actions. In the two-plus years since the 11 September attacks, bin Laden has spoken with less frequency, in part because of the exigencies of war and in part because he recognizes the significant power of silence, a bit of knowledge long lost in the West, especially in Washington. When he has spoken, bin

Laden has used old themes and new. Continuity is most evident in his descriptions of attacks on Islam that require Muslim unity and defensive jihad; of the major role for himself and al Qaeda being to incite jihad; of Allah's command that each Muslim assist the jihad to the best of his or her ability, and that young males lead the way; of the vital importance of keeping the United States as the jihad's priority military target; and of the Islamic world's duty to assist Mullah Omar and the Taleban retake Afghanistan. Bin Laden's new rhetorical themes include warnings to America's allies to stop supporting U.S. actions in the Muslim world; approval for limited Islamist attacks on "apostate" Muslim regimes; withering condemnations of Islamic clerics and scholars for supporting the Muslim regimes aiding America; and direct addresses and requests to U.S. citizens. Finally, bin Laden's post-11 September rhetoric again shows he knows us, and how we will react, far better than we know him.

Staying the Course on Main Themes

For bin Laden, the Crusaders' offensive attacks on Islam are the main thing. The theological credibility of his call for a defensive jihad depends on Muslims being convinced that Islam is under attack by non-Muslim forces, those bin Laden identifies as the U.S.-led Crusader Christians and Jews. Unfortunately for America, U.S. policies and actions in the Muslim world provide Muslim eyes' with incontrovertible proof of what bin Laden describes as "an ocean of oppression, injustice, slaughter, and plunder carried out by you against our Islamic ummah. It is therefore commanded by our religion that we must fight back. We are defending ourselves against the United States. This is a 'defensive jihad' as we want to protect our land and people." And what does bin Laden say constitutes this "ocean" of disasters to which the U.S.-led crusaders are subjecting Muslims? Well, I am afraid he has got us there—at least in the way his brethren's eyes see and assimilate U.S. activities in the Islamic world. "We say that the brutal enemy does not need documents or excuses for continuing the war he has started against Islam and Muslims many decades ago," bin Laden said in response to critics who said the last wills of the 11 September attackers allowed the U.S. government to justify its war on terrorism.

> For God's sake, what are the documents that incriminate the Palestinian people that warrant the massacres against them, which have been

going on for more than five decades at the hands of the Crusaders and the Jews. What is the evidence against the people of Iraq to warrant their blockade and being killed in a way that is unprecedented in history. What documents incriminated the Muslims of Bosnia-Herzegovina and warranted the Western Crusaders, with the United States at their head, to unleash their Serb ally to annihilate and displace the Muslim people in the region under UN cover. What is the crime of the Kashmiri people and what documents do the worshipers of cows possess to make them sanction their blood for more than fifty years. What have Muslims in Chechnya, Afghanistan, and the Central Asian republics committed to warrant being invaded by the brutal Soviet military regime and after it communism's killing, annihilating, and displacing tens of millions of them. What evidence did the United States have the day it destroyed Afghanistan and killed and displaced the Muslims there. It even launched prior to that the unfair blockade of [the Afghans] under UN cover. Under the same cover Indonesia was ripped apart; Muslims were forced to leave Timor. . . . Under the UN cover too, it intervened in Somalia, killing and desecrating the land of Islam there. It is even the first to urge the Crusade ruler in the Philippines to annihilate our Muslim brothers there. There are many other countless issues. We say that all the Muslims that the international Crusader–Zionist machine is annihilating have not committed any crime other than to say God is our Allah.[3]

Bin Laden's indictment is pretty much factual, although colored by his conviction of the West's malevolence toward Muslims. All the conflicts noted have occurred or are in progress—and, more important, his portrayal of them as attacks on Islam and Muslims are completely plausible to Muslims worldwide. Faced with what he describes as the Crusader "onslaught," bin Laden is doctrinally correct in claiming that the proper Koran-based response for such attacks is a defensive jihad. "Muslims are not instructed to turn the other cheek," Bernard Lewis reminded the West in his excellent book *The Crisis of Islam*, "nor do they expect to beat their swords into ploughshares and their spears into pruning hooks."[4] The U.S. scholar of the Islamic way of war, James Turner Johnson, has written that although there are several ways to wage jihad, ". . . the [Islamic] jurists regarded the jihad of the sword as necessary, first because the dar-al-harb [the House of War, in this case the U.S.-led West], the source of all strife, forces itself upon the dar-al-Islam. . . ."[5] In his 2002 letter to the American people, bin Laden put it as did Professor Johnson. Posing the rhetorical question "Why are we waging jihad against you?" bin Laden responded: "The answer to that question is very simple. Because you attacked us and continue to attack us."[6]

Inciting the Faithful

Having defined the threat to Islam as the U.S.-led crusaders' attacks and prescribing a defensive jihad as the only appropriate response, bin Laden regards al Qaeda as having an important role to play—"the vanguard of a Muslim nation," as al-Zawahiri described it, "that decided to fight you to the last breath and not surrender to your crimes and vices."[7] For bin Laden, al Qaeda is most important not for his personal contribution or the group's military capabilities; he always emphasizes that he and al Qaeda alone cannot produce a Muslim victory. Instead, bin Laden sees al Qaeda's primary responsibility as inciting Muslims to join a defensive jihad and to help train and lead those who come forward. Al Qaeda, bin Laden says, took incitement as its duty on the basis of the example set by Islamic leaders early in the religion's history, noting that "Allah asked it from the best of humans, the Prophet."[8] Following this model, bin Laden stresses how important it is to "provide our ummah with the inspiration it requires" to resist the crusaders.[9] "I must say that my duty is just to awaken Muslims," he explained just after the 11 September attacks,

> to tell them as to what is good for them and what is not. . . . Al Qaeda was set up to wage jihad against infidelity, particularly to encounter the onslaught of the infidel countries against the Islamic states. Jihad is the sixth undeclared element of Islam. Every anti-Islamic element is afraid of it, Al Qaeda wants to keep this element alive and active and make it part of the daily lives of Muslims. It wants to give it the status of worship.[10]

Bin Laden always stresses that each Muslim must play a part in the defensive jihad because it is "Fard-Ain [obligatory] upon each and every Muslim," rather than "Fard Kifayah" [a collective duty].[11] "Our nation is rich with many resources and capabilities," bin Laden says, "and the absolutely most important resource is the Muslim person who is the battle's fuel and the conflict's motor."[12] And nowhere does this responsibility weigh more heavily, bin Laden argues, than on the true leaders of jihad, the "honest scholars, propagators, and reformers."[13] Bin

Laden consistently argues that he took the lead in fighting the United States only because the most important Islamic clerics were imprisoned in Saudi Arabia, other Middle Eastern nations, and the United States. In normal circumstances, he says, Muslim scholars, jurists, and clerics "should be at the head of the ranks [of jihad], lead the action, and direct the march."[14] He believes that if these learned scholars were able to speak freely there would be much less trouble prompting Muslims to participate in the nonmilitary fields of the jihad. Unable to affect their release, and angered by the words of clerics paid by the al-Sauds, Mubarak, and their kind, bin Laden reminds the clerics of their duty. "So, Jihad today is compulsory on the entire ummah," bin Laden wrote,

> and she [the ummah] will remain in sin until she produces her sons, her wealth, and her power to the extent of being able to wage jihad and defend against the evil of the disbelievers upon all the Muslims in Palestine and elsewhere.
>
> Your first duty is to tell the truth to the nation and to declare it in the face of darkness without equivocation or fear. This is the requirement of the covenant Allah took from you, "And remember Allah took a covenant from the People of the Book, to make it known and clear to mankind, and not to hide [Koranic verse]."
>
> The importance of your task stems from the dangerous act of deception and misguidance practiced by the authority's scholars and the ruler's clerics who are trading with religion, who were put in charge of it before the nation, and who have sold their faith for temporal gain.[15]

Turning to the great majority of Muslims destined to be neither clerics nor soldiers, bin Laden warns those who cannot fight or provide guidance that "there is no place to claim that if everyone went to Jihad it could not take them all."[16] Every Muslim has a role assigned by a "commandment" from God. "This means," Abu-Ayman al-Hilali wrote in *Al-Ansar* in March 2002, "that every member of the Islamic nation could take part . . . in his position and within his own capabilities, using all methods that are available (bombing, boycotting, inciting, capturing, financing, enlightening, praying, assassinating. . . .)."[17] Citing the Western media's "vicious campaign" against Islam, for example, bin Laden calls on the Muslim publishers and broadcasters to take "[their] rightful position and play [their] required role in confronting . . . [the West's] visual, audio, and written organs."[18] The wealthy too are called to join the jihad because "[s]pending in the cause of Allah is a religious duty" and as necessary as firing guns. "There is a group of merchants and financiers who are as important as others in propelling this battle toward its desired aim," bin Laden explained. "The money you will spend, even if little, will stop a sweeping torrent that wants to destroy us all. . . . Jihad with wealth is more obligatory today upon wealthy Muslims than on those who are not as wealthy as them."[19] Being catholic in his incitement of Muslims to join the jihad, bin Laden also appeals to Muslim women "whose role [in the jihad] is by no means less than that of men." After comparing contemporary Muslim women to the early Islamic heroines, bin Laden salutes what women have done in the fight and says more is expected of them.

> O sister who is following in the footsteps of the virtuous ones by sending her brothers to the arenas of heroism with firmness and determination.
>
> You are the ones who have incited and motivated and before then reared all the men who fight the jihad in Palestine, Lebanon, Afghanistan, and Chechnya. You are the ones who brought forth the band of heroes in the New York and Washington conquests.
>
> If we do forget [some things], we will not forget the heroism of the Muslim Palestinian woman in the sacred land and her great stands that many men could not equal. She has not spared a husband or a son in her support for the blessed al-Aqsa [mosque]. She has even offered and sacrificed herself to join the convoy of martyrs so as to find sustenance in the presence of her Lord, thus ignoring all the world's temptations and attractions.
>
> O Muslim women we are expecting too [sic: "very"?] much from you today. You do not lack any means for supporting your religion, nation, and the sunnah of your Prophet when you are true to Allah.[20]

As always, bin Laden also maintains his decade-long dialogue with young Muslim men, stressing that while the defensive jihad is obligatory for all Muslims, "it is even more obligatory upon the youths in the prime of their lives than upon the old."[21] Since 11 September 2001, the tone of bin Laden's rhetoric toward young males has changed; where it was once critical and meant to shame young men into action, it is now supportive and complimentary. The change probably is due to the steady flow of young men to the dozen or so Islamist insurgencies now being fought in the world. Certainly for al Qaeda, manpower does not appear to be a problem. As noted above, in late 2001 the organization sent fighters home from Afghanistan because they were not needed in that phase of the war, and it was only in mid-2003 that they began returning to the country. Finally, Washington's maintenance of a policy *status quo* toward the Muslim world and its more-or-less constant green light for Israel's actions against the Palestinians would have resulted in more young men volunteering for jihad even if bin Laden did not exist and Iraq was not invaded. For bin Laden, the most effective recruiting tool imaginable is for the United States to keep doing what it has been doing in the Islamic world for the past thirty years. The invasion of Iraq and the subsequent insurgency there is icing on the cake for al Qaeda.

Bin Laden's decision to change the tone of his statements for young men from critical to nurturing also seems a deliberate attempt to institutionalize the tradition of young Muslims going off to fight in the jihad, to make it as much a part of each man's maturing process as being drafted on or about your eighteenth birthday once was for post-1945 American males. In an attempt to write history as well as make it, bin Laden's message is that young Muslim men can now be counted on as steadfast and reliable defenders of the ummah—like the youth of ancient Islamic history—and that succeeding generations will follow their example. "We have been struggling right from our youth," bin Laden told young Muslims after the 11 September attacks,

> we sacrificed our homes, families and all the luxuries of the worldly life in the path of Allah. In our youth we fought with and defeated the USSR (with the help of Allah), a world superpower at the time, and now we are fighting the USA. We have never let the Muslim ummah down. . . .
>
> We men of mature age have laid down guideposts for the young people of the ummah on the way of jihad and have mapped the path for them. Young people, you need not but follow this path. Transmit these experiences to the generations that come after you. We have communicated them to you from those who were before us; you transmit them to those who come after you. . . .[22]

Bin Laden uses not only the idea of being part of Islamic history to encourage young men to join the fight, but he also makes much of the example set by the 11 September attackers. The West, I believe, completely underestimates the degree of admiration, respect, and even love accorded to the 11 September attackers, especially by young Muslims. For years, we in the West have watched the actions of Palestinian suicide bombers and concluded that the young men and, now, women are tragic figures, victims of poverty, poor education, joblessness, despair, and brainwashing by cynical political and religious leaders. The formula is simple: suicide in the West is thought to be caused by despair, hopelessness, panic, and mental illness, and so we assume that such must be the case among Muslims. We judge suicide bombers and their work as negative phenomena; based on our experience, we could see them in no other way. To date, we have been unable to see the issue through any but Western eyes, and so have missed recognizing that the young Palestinian bombers are seen by large numbers of Muslims as heroes who are willing to sacrifice their lives—in martyrdom, not suicide attacks—for a cause that is greater than themselves and sanctioned by their God. What the West sees as tragic brutality practiced by despairing or deviant individuals is perceived in much of the Muslim world as a heroic act of self-sacrifice, patriotism, and worship, an act to be greeted not with condemnation and revulsion, but with awe, respect, and a determination to emulate. Moreover, it is an act Muslims deem a just military response to Israel's fifty-plus-year occupation of Palestine and its relegation of three generations of Palestinians to refugee camps.

The 11 September attacks took—and were intended to take—suicide operations to a higher level, one at which they focused the Muslim world on the raging battle between the Christian crusaders, their Zionist allies, and God's defending mujahideen. "Those young men said in deed, in New York and Washington," bin Laden said, "speeches that overshadowed all other speeches made elsewhere in the world. The speeches were understood by Arabs and non-Arabs—even Chinese."[23] Keeping faith with its view of suicide, the West reviled the attackers as evil, brutal killers who only wanted to kill innocents, and, again, the act was judged by many to be the product of despair and brainwashing. When a captured video of bin Laden not meant for public broadcast was shown on television, for example, Western officials, analysts, and journalists agreed almost unanimously that his description of the 11 September attackers was cynical and smug and that he was laughing at the naiveté that allowed them to board the aircraft before learning they were to die that day. Western analysis of the tape made the nineteen men appear as hapless pawns in a monstrous game bin Laden manipulated, and it meshed perfectly with our preconceived notions of how and why suicide bombers are produced.

If for a moment, however, the events of 11 September are examined through the eyes and ears of a Muslim who believes the defense of the

Islamic world and his faith at times requires one to sacrifice his life for his brethren and God's glory, the tape of bin Laden takes on a much different perspective. "The brothers, who conducted the operation," bin Laden explained in the tape to the individuals assembled with him, "all they knew was that they have a martyrdom operation and we asked each of them to go to America but they didn't know anything about the operation not even one letter. But they were trained and we did not reveal the operation to them until they are there [in the United States] and just before they boarded the planes."[24] What the West heard in bin Laden's voice as cynicism and cruel manipulation, was heard by Muslims for what it was, a quietly and proudly spoken elegy by a man overcome by awe and admiration for the unquestioning young men who willingly defended Islam with their lives. In later statements, bin Laden described what probably is a widely held Muslim view of the nineteen attackers.

> These men understood that jihad for the sake of God is the way to establish right and defeat falsehood. They understood that jihad for the sake of God is the way to deter the tyranny of the infidels. . . . These men sought to prepare a response for the Day of Reckoning. Faith in God and the Hereafter and emulating the traditions of Mohammed, may God's peace be upon him, is what prompted them to leave their homes. . . .[25]

Thus, America's evil suicide bombers can also be seen as Islam's martyr-heroes, men and women following in the steps and under the guidance of their prophet and according to the revealed word of their God. The latter view of the attackers is evident in the audience *Al-Jazirah* television draws, and the media commentary it spurs, when it shows the last wills and testaments that were videotaped by the attackers. The West discounts too quickly the fact that the Muslim suicide bombers of Palestine and 11 September have become role models for many of their young coreligionists. While most suicide attacks since 11 September 2001 continue to be perpetrated by Arabs in the Arab heartland, Muslim eyes have seen exactly the same kind of heroic self-sacrifice in such far-afield places as Grozny, Tunisia, Jakarta, Moscow, Kashmir, India, and Bali. Bin Laden has reason to be awed by their performance and encouraged by their numbers. Again alluding to history, bin Laden in October 2002 compared current young Muslim male and female fighters to the young heroes of Islam's past, rejoicing that the young who always have been "the driving force of change throughout the [Islamic] nation's history" remain so today. "O youths of Islam," bin Laden wrote, "[y]ou are the ones over whose bridge of sacrifices this nation will cross to the stage of glory and the arena of dignity and the vault that will bring happiness to mankind and mercy to humanity. You are the knights of the fight and the heroes of the battle."[26]

Among bin Laden's statements, the only detectable note of frustration—and perhaps anger and almost a touch of despair—is found in his efforts to incite more support among Muslims for the nonmilitary aspects of the jihad. Frustrated, bin Laden continues to remind Muslims that al Qaeda cannot defeat the infidels alone. "If the particular groups [like al Qaeda] have their role to play that others do not undertake," bin Laden said in October 2002 to Muslims who could but were not supporting the jihad in nonmilitary ways, "then the general groups are the real fuel of the battle and the explosive material."[27] Al Qaeda's role, he said, can be only "that of the detonator and the motor that detonates the material" because "repelling the aggressive enemy is done by means of a very small portion of the nation."[28] As noted, recruitment among all Muslim social classes for Islamist insurgencies appears to be no problem, and will remain satisfactory as long as bin Laden and other Islamists have current U.S. policies and Israeli actions as their foil. Bin Laden's frustration is directed to the older members of Muslim middle and upper-middle classes—Islamic scholars and jurists, the wealthy, university professors, the media, et cetera—which he believes should support the mujahideen more fully than they have to date. "The common people have understood the issue [of the need for jihad]," bin Laden said in November 2001. The problem lies with "those who continue to flatter those [Muslim regimes] who colluded with the unbelievers to anaesthetize [the better-off Muslims] to prevent it [sic: 'them'?] from carrying out the duty of jihad so that the word of God be above all other words."[29] Due to the unresponsiveness of these classes and their support for apostate regimes, bin Laden said, "[W]e must admit that the enemy's dominance over us is partially the result of what our hands wrought."[30]

Al Qaeda's media unit addresses Muslims primarily with audio and videotapes, Internet articles and essays, and statements by the group's leaders. These products are meant not only to provide information, but to produce enthusiasm and participation among the "common people," and to induce shame and embarrassment among the affluent for not doing what God requires to support the mujahideen and defend their faith. The latter is an excellent tactic because the motivating power of shame and embarrassment in Islamic culture remains as potent, and perhaps more so, than it was in Western society many decades ago. In June 2002, for example, bin Laden wrote and published a poem that expressed his own frustration and attempted to make Muslim slackers feel shame. The poem was written as a response to one written by his son Hamzah.

> What can I say if we are living in a world of laziness and discontent?
> What can I say to a world that is blind in both sight and perception?
> Nations are sold and bought like hooves.
>
> Pardon me, my son, but I can only see a very steep path ahead.
> A decade has gone by in vagrancy and travel.
> What are you asking me about?
> About people who are sedated?
>
> Here we are in our tragedy.
> Security has gone but danger remains.
> It is a world of crimes in which children are slaughtered like cows.
> Zion is killing our brothers, and the Arabs are holding a conference.[31]

In addition to frustration, the poem shows bin Laden's resourcefulness in using a variety of ways to get his message across. Today, poetry is much more widely admired and used in public discourse in the Islamic world—and especially in Arab society—than it is in the West. Through poetry, explains Issa Boullata, professor of Arabic literature at McGill University in Montreal, bin Laden follows a long tradition of Muslim leaders using poetry, or allusions to other literature or historical events, in public speaking, and he also demonstrates a knowledge of the culture's literature, which the educated would expect of their leader. "The function of poetry in the Arab world is much broader and wider that it is in Western culture," Professor Boullata explained. "[Bin Laden] wants to show he is a leader and knows the culture, and he is using the medium the traditional society accepts. Even those who are not literate people, who cannot read, when this kind of Arabic is read to them understand it because they recite the Koran everyday."[32]

Target America

In working to direct Muslim ire toward the United States, bin Laden is engaged in one of his most difficult struggles, and one he has yet to decisively win. One of the last resilient vestiges of nineteenth-century European colonialism in the Muslim world is that Islamic resistance movements tend to focus on the governing regimes of their own individual nation-states. This leftover, moreover, is supported by the Prophet Mohammed's injunction to wage jihad against the "near" enemy first before turning to the "far" enemy. As a result, Egyptians traditionally fight the Cairo regime, Algerians the Algerian regime, Yemenis the Yemen regime, and so on. While the Afghans' anti-Soviet jihad brought Muslims from around the world together to fight the Red Army, most returned home after the war to fight their national governments. Until bin Laden appeared on the international scene at the end of the Afghan war, few Islamic leaders put much of a dent in the national orientation of Islamic resistance groups. Bin Laden has labored hard to shift the focus of attack from Muslim nation-states to the United States, arguing that the nation-states survive only because of U.S. protection and support, and on a practical level, as the authors of *The Age of Sacred Terror* noted, "[T]he jihadists were overmatched by the security apparatus of the state."[33] For each victory bin Laden has scored in this regard—Egypt being the most prominent—others remain domestically focused, as if a European power was still in control.

In the military sphere, this is bin Laden's main unfinished project, and the aspect of the al Qaeda movement most likely to regress if he is killed or captured. The multinational, multiethnic al Qaeda organization is a tremendous accomplishment—indeed, in the modern Islamic world, an unprecedented one—and it is attributable in large part to bin Laden's leadership and ability to keep the hatred of al Qaeda's members fixed on the United States. While the jury is out on whether the group would survive in its present form and cohesion without bin Laden, Dr. Abdullah al-Nafisi, director of the Ibn Rashid Studies Center in London, has argued that bin Laden's focus on America has been a key to al Qaeda's unity. "The simplicity of the direct proposition [of focusing military action on the United States]," Dr. al-Nafisi told an *Al-Jazirah* interviewer in February 2002, "might be a source of strength. There are no controversial issues within the [al Qaeda] organization while you would always find controversial issues within any Islamic organization."[34]

For now, however, bin Laden appears to be steadily carrying the day in focusing the Muslim world's wrath on the United States. The most prominent recent example of bin Laden's success is the decision of Algeria's most effective insurgent group to pledge loyalty to bin Laden.

The Salafist Group for Call and Combat's leaders said on 11 September 2003 that it would follow bin Laden's "direction" and henceforth focus attacks on U.S. interests. In a field where objective, scientific data are hard to come by, the polling work of Gallup and the Pew Trust and the BBC also has provided a rare insight into how U.S. words and deeds, and those of bin Laden, have combined to yield a result greatly favorable to al Qaeda's goal of focusing Muslim anger on America. A Gallup poll in February 2002, for example, found 53 percent of Muslims worldwide had an "unfavorable" view of America, and among the most frequently chosen words to describe Americans were "ruthless, aggressive, conceited, arrogant, easily provoked, [and] biased."[35] Then, in March 2002, Gallup found that 80 percent of Pakistanis thought U.S. military action against al Qaeda and the Taleban was "largely or totally unjustifiable." Gallup also reported that the Pakistanis' response was mirrored by 86 percent of Moroccans, 89 percent of Indonesians, and 60 percent of Kuwaitis.[36] Finally, in June 2003, the Pew Global Attitudes Project found that majorities in seven of eight Muslim countries feared a U.S. invasion; that anti-U.S. sentiment had "drastically deepened" in Nigeria and Indonesia; and, overall, "the bottom has fallen out of support for America in most of the Muslim world."[37] Given this scientific snapshot of reality, we can only conclude that—for now—the following guidance from bin Laden is being followed. "The priority in this fight and at this stage," he advised in fall 2002,

> should be given to the pagans' leaders, the Americans and Jews who will not end their aggression and stop their domination over us except with jihad. . . . Take care not to be pushed into fragmenting your efforts and squandering your resources in marginal battles with the lackeys and parties but concentrate the blows on the head of the unfaith[ful] until it collapses. Once it collapses, all the other parts will collapse, vanish and be defeated.[38]

The Importance of Afghanistan

While Afghanistan has long since fallen off the screen of U.S. officialdom and the media—save for the *Christian Science Monitor*—it remains at the center of bin Laden's concerns and priorities. The West has largely missed the affection with which bin Laden regards Afghanistan, and the debt of personal honor and religious duty he feels toward Mullah Omar and the Taleban for hosting al Qaeda and refusing U.S.

demands to surrender him. How many men and organizations, after all, are willing to give up the reins of power and control of a country for the sake of one man and religious principle? The West also looked too cynically on bin Laden's late-1990s decision to formally pledge his loyalty to Mullah Omar as the "Commander of the Faithful," concluding that he was showing less-than-sincere respect for the Taleban chief in return for the Taleban's protection. To date, however, there is no evidence that bin Laden regards Mullah Omar as anything other than the world's primary Muslim leader. "My relationship with Mullah Omar," bin Laden said in late 2001, "is one of faith. He is the greatest, most valiant and most content Muslim of this age. He is not afraid of anyone but God."[39]

Beyond the personal debt to the Taleban, bin Laden and other Islamist leaders view Afghanistan as "the only Islamic country" in the world, and that the battle going on there against the United States will decide the Muslim world's future and therefore "is one of Islam's immortal battles."[40] "A core tenet of al Qaeda's strategy is that radical Islamists must gain control of a nation," Steven Simon and Daniel Benjamin wrote in *The Age of Sacred Terror* in a generally accurate explanation that applies in most Islamist circles. "Holding a state, in their view, is a prelude to knocking over the dominoes of the world's secular Muslim regimes. . . . The craving for territory is one reason al Qaeda carries out its own terrorist attacks and supports so many national insurgencies."[41] The other point to be made here, of course, is that the Islamic insurgencies al Qaeda supports are fighting—without exception—to reacquire land once ruled by Muslims and so fit the definition of a defensive jihad. So far as I have found, al Qaeda supports no Islamic insurgency that seeks to conquer new lands, notwithstanding the unsupported but media-pleasing claim of many in the West that bin Laden "makes very clear . . . [his] ultimate goal is to undermine Western civilization in its entirety. . . ."[42] Even Western political leaders are not immune to such hyping. UK foreign secretary Jack Straw, for example, described al Qaeda's November 2002 attack on two British facilities in Istanbul "as an attack on our entire civilization."[43]

But why, one might ask, is one of the poorest countries on earth and a one-eyed, battle-scarred, and not superbly educated mullah pivotal in the Islamists' eyes? The answer, once again, is found in the annals of Islamic history. Since the British completed destruction of the Ottoman Caliphate in 1924, no country has replaced Turkey as the Muslim world's center. In other words, Islam has needed a site from which to launch a new Caliphate, a state that would be governed by the shariah, God's law. "The beauty of the new Islamic system," wrote the Sunni scholar Sayyid Qutb, an Egyptian executed by Nasser and whom bin Laden and most Islamists view as both hero and mentor, "cannot be appreciated until it takes concrete form. To bring it about, there must first be a revival in one Muslim country, enabling it to attain the status of world leadership." Writing in 1997, Professor Samuel P. Huntington, like Qutb, noted that Islam has lacked what he called a "core state" since the Ottomans' demise. "A core state," Huntington contends, "can perform its ordering function because member states perceive it as cultural kin. A civilization is an extended family and, like older members of a family, core states provide their relatives with both support and discipline."[44] While several states have tried to play this role—Saudi Arabia, Iran, Pakistan, and Turkey—none became the "dominant center," which meant "no one of them is in a strong position to mediate conflicts within Islam; no one of them is able to act authoritatively on behalf of Islam in dealing with conflicts between Muslim and non-Muslim groups."[45] Suddenly, when the Taleban captured Kabul in 1996, Afghanistan became an official Islamic state—or emirate—ruled by shariah principles, and so the Islamists found themselves having the long-sought basics: a state ruled by an Islamic scholar from which to revive the Caliphate. On this latter point, much has been written about Mullah Omar's less-than-stellar academic credentials, that they prevent him from being accepted as an international leader of Islam. Clearly, Omar is less well educated than many scholars in Pakistan, Saudi Arabia, Egypt, and elsewhere, but the reality is that Afghanistan is an Islamic state, it was ruled by the shariah, and its leader was a Muslim cleric who fought in a victorious jihad. Given these factors, Mullah Omar may not be the best-educated cleric, but—since only God is perfect—he will do in a pinch. This reality was marked in a January 2002 communiqué sent to the Taleban by several senior Saudi Islamic scholars. Sent via the Internet to "the Commander of the Believers . . . Muhammad Omar and those Mujahedin with him," they congratulated Omar for the Taleban's victory of having "separated the world into two trenches. . . ."

> We—the collective scholars—are honored to have the likes of you attributed to our ummah, because you have affirmed, in reality, the supremacy and honor of the believers.
> And we will bear witness that you were alone the ones who raised

your heads to America; the country of disbelief and the Cross, when Muslims were not honored by a single man who would say, "No!" and again, "No!" to what America sought from him, in this time. Only you did so. So congratulations to the Muslims because of you.[46]

Finally, Afghanistan is important to bin Laden and Islamists worldwide simply because it is Afghanistan, the site of the only Muslim victory over the West in almost eight centuries. The defeat of the Red Army had, and still has, enormous symbolic and emotive power in the Islamic world; it remains a potent motivator for recruiting fighters for al Qaeda and other Islamist insurgent groups. The Western media coverage of the anti-Soviet Afghan jihad was spotty at best, and its coverage post-1989—the year of the Soviet withdrawal—focused mainly on narcotics, the interethnic civil war, and the failure of Taleban leaders to prove themselves radical feminists. As a consequence, the West, in essence, missed the war's importance as one of the major catalysts for what is now called the Islamic awakening. More than any other event, the shock of the Afghans' victorious jihad restored the belief of Sunni Muslims that, if God is willing, anything is possible.

Not surprisingly, bin Laden did not miss the point. He welcomed the U.S. invasion of Afghanistan not only because it made targets of U.S. soldiers, but because it put the infidels on the soil of the only country that has been successfully defended by Muslims in modern memory, and defended against odds reminiscent of the Prophet's come-from-behind military victories in the early years of Islam, such as in the battles of Badr and The Trench. Here again history comes into play because the Prophet's victories—fourteen centuries on—are still topics of regular reference and comment in contemporary public discourse in the Muslim world. "The early period of the ummah remains alive to all Muslims, because it represents a sacred drama," the journalist Stephen Schwartz wrote in his book, *The Two Faces of Islam: The House of Sa'ud from Tradition to Terror*, "and in this sense Islamic history has never been drained of its holy significance. Muslims feel that they participate collectively and individually in the consequences of past events, in a way largely absent from Christianity (but more present in Judaism)."[47] Welcoming the arrival of U.S. troops, bin Laden calmly outlined his confidence that history would repeat itself, God willing. "[The] one who prolonged us with one of His helping hands and stabilized us to defeat the Soviet Empire," bin Laden said, "is capable of prolonging us again to defeat America on the same land, and with the same sayings, and that is the Grace of God."[48] Picturing the war as a new instance of Christendom's Richard the Lion Heart—this time clad in red, white, and blue—trying to crush the Muslim Saladin, bin Laden asserts Afghanistan and its people are standing almost alone: "The entire West, with the exception of a few countries, supports this unfair, barbaric campaign."[49] Appealing to the Afghans' religion, tribal pride, and xenophobia, and simultaneously trying to shame Muslims who have not aided the Afghans, bin Laden identified the Afghans as the vanguard and shield of Islam against the United States, just as they were against the Soviet Union.

> O Afghan people, God has granted you the honor of carrying out jihad in His cause and of sacrificing all that is dear for upholding His great word. . . .
>
> O Afghan people, I am saying this while confident that you will understand this talk more than anyone else, because Afghanistan is the land where invaders never settled throughout history and because its people enjoy strength, resolve, pride, and patience in fighting. It had never opened its doors to anything but Islam. This is because Muslims did not come to it as colonialists nor had they been after earthly ambitions. Rather, they came to spread and call for the worship of God.[50]

The important place Afghanistan holds in bin Laden's affections, as well as in the strategic plans of al Qaeda and other Islamists, ensures that the fight with the United States for control of that country has yet to begin in earnest.

Expanding and Refining Themes

For nearly a decade, bin Laden has been meticulous in focusing his rhetoric on a few clear themes and avoiding major addenda that would cloud the message or sanction actions that would spread thin his military forces. Bin Laden has stuck closely to this practice since the 11 September attacks but has, by the force of circumstances, been forced to refine and expand several of his main themes. These alterations have been made in a way that preserves the core and clarity of his message, while accommodating the demands of war. Al Qaeda also has informed Muslims that they may see a few military operations that do not mesh with the group's stated priorities, presumably meaning attacks not directly or exclusively focused on the United States. "The security, military, and political necessities," Abu-Ayman al-Hilali wrote in *Al-Ansar* in March 2002,

> require that the mujahedin undertake some actions that might seem negative to absorb the power of the enemy, exhaust it more, involve it in a war of attrition, protect the positions and the mujahedin, and keep the cause alive. Such behavior I considered part of the interim tasks and it aims to deter the aggression as part of maintaining a realistic and strategic balance.[51]

Slightly Loosening the Military Reins

The two years after September 2001 saw bin Laden slightly relax the rule of only attacking the United States. This relaxation served two purposes. First, it allowed some of al Qaeda's fighters to remain militarily active while bin Laden and his lieutenants prepared the next major strike in the United States. Second, the resulting attacks were meant by bin Laden to warn U.S. allies—especially those in Europe—that he did not appreciate their involvement in the wars in Afghanistan or Iraq, and that al Qaeda had the ability to hurt them if it chose to do so. This said, the last thing bin Laden wants in the military sphere is to prompt a situation in which several European powers fully join the U.S. war against al Qaeda. This is the main reason why there has been only one large-scale al Qaeda attack in Western Europe, the railway bombings in Madrid in March 2004. That attack, of course, was meant not only to damage Spain because of its participation in Iraq, but as a warning to all West European governments that al Qaeda can and will play havoc with their electoral politics. In many ways, the Madrid attack should be seen as bin Ladin's attempt to deter the West Europeans from supporting the United States. Overall, one of the true tests of bin Laden's brilliance will be his ability to keep Europe as much on the sidelines as possible. Thus, he has walked a narrow line since 11 September. Faced with initial enthusiastic European support for the U.S. invasion of Afghanistan to destroy the Taleban and al Qaeda, bin Laden publicly responded with anger but held his military fire until an Afghan stalemate was reached—circa late-March 2002. He then ordered a series of attacks as warnings to America's allies that would fall short of drawing them further into the war. "So any nation that joins the Jewish trenches has only itself to blame," bin Laden told U.S. allies in late-September 2001, and as [al Qaeda's official spokesman] Shaykh Sulayman Abu Gayeth has declared in some of his previous statements, concerning America and Britain, so that they should not be surprised, but indeed he gave some other nations a chance to review its [sic: "their"?] calculations. What is Japan's concerns? What is making Japan join this hard, strong and ferocious war? It is a blatant violation of our children in Palestine, and Japan didn't predict it would be at war with us, so it should review where it stands. What is the concern of Australia in the farthest south with the case of those weak Afghans? And those weak in Palestine. What is Germany's concern with this war? Besides disbelief and crusade, it is a war which is repeating (bringing back) the Crusades, similarly to the previous wars. Richard the Lion Heart, and Barbarossa from Germany, and Louis from France. . . . similarly is the case today, when they all went immediately forward on the day Bush lifted the cross. The Crusader nations went forward.[52]

Bin Laden's cautionary words went unheeded, as he probably expected. He delayed acting until the situation stabilized for al Qaeda and Taleban forces in Afghanistan but then struck countries supporting the United States in Afghanistan. As described in Chapter 3, the French citizens and interests of today's Louis were hit in Karachi, Pakistan (May 2002) and off the coast of Aden, Yemen (October 2002); Barbarossa's German interests were struck in Djerba, Tunisia (April 2002)—which counts as a lick against Israel because the tourists killed were German Jews—Manshera, Pakistan (July 2002), and Kabul, Afghanistan (June 2003); the troops of today's rather pale version of Richard were killed in combat in Afghanistan and blown up in Istanbul (November 2003); and nearly two hundred Australian citizens, and some British, were killed in Bali, Indonesia (October 2002). These attacks are intended, al Qaeda explained in October 2002, to carry "a strong political message to Washington's allies in its war on and aggression against the Islamic nation, namely, that they will not remain forever safe from Allah's hand of revenge and then that of the mujahedin. If they persist with this alliance, then they must be ready to pay a heavy price from their blood and interests."[53] The statement concluded by appealing to the self-interest of U.S. allies. "There is still a chance," al Qaeda said, "to anyone who wants to reconsider his position before it is too late."[54] Bin Laden and al Qaeda twice more warned states aiding the United States. In February 2003 they recapped the states named to date, and after the Iraq war they issued a list specific to that conflict. Al Qaeda has worked through much of each list. A fuller discussion of bin Laden's fidelity to making good his threats is below in Chapter 6.

For now, bin Laden is unlikely to go beyond warning attacks to more destructive, 11 September-type attacks on America's non-Muslim allies because world events since 2001 have occurred in a way that has driven the United States and Europe apart. The divisive UN debate before the U.S.-led invasion of Iraq, European ire over the treatment of Afghan-war prisoners at Guantanamo Bay, and the heated post-Iraq-war debate between Washington and the Europeans over events in Iraq have combined to put a wide, bin Laden-friendly space between America and Europe. In addition, the Europeans have surely noted that the United States, not Europe, is the main al Qaeda target—a message that al Qaeda's March 2004 attack in Madrid , and bin Laden's subsequent offer of a cease fire to the Europeans, will reemphasize. Currently, Michael Ignatieff has written, this last point has especially widened the gap between the United States and Europe.

> Its allies wept with America after Sept. 11 and then swiftly concluded that only America was under attack. The idea that Western Civilization had been the target was not convincing. While America and its allies stood shoulder to shoulder when they faced a common Soviet foe, Islamic terrorism seemed to have America alone in its sights. Why cozy up to a primary target, America's allies asked themselves, when it will only make you a secondary one?[55]

Given this reality, bin Laden will not stage many near-term, major attacks in Europe to avoid having al Qaeda play the absurd role of prompting transatlantic reconciliation. That said, al Qaeda already has struck Britain, Italy, and Spain—in Turkey, al-Nasiriyah, Iraq, and Madrid, respectively—and probably will continue warning attacks against states that assisted the U.S. military in Iraq, specifically Australia, Japan, and Poland. Attacks against the citizens and interests of those countries—like the paybacks for Afghanistan—are likely to continue to occur primarily in the Middle East and the Pacific, not in Western Europe. Moreover, while al Qaeda will not stage indiscriminate attacks against Muslims in the Gulf states whose bases, airfields, and harbors facilitated the U.S. war in Iraq—Kuwait, the Emirates, and Saudi Arabia—it would not be surprising to see the group assassinate senior military, security, and government officials on the Arabian Peninsula.

Before moving on, it is important to state that bin Laden has given one hostage to fortune that could thwart his goal of keeping other major powers on the sidelines. This potential vulnerability results from bin Laden's passion for trying to incite individual Muslims to attack American crusaders and Jews wherever they can be reached. "So know," bin Laden wrote in February 2003, "that targeting the Americans and Jews by killing them in any corner of the earth, is the greatest of obligations and the most excellent of ways to gain [the] nearness of Allah. Furthermore, I advise the youths to use their intelligence in killing them secretly."[56] Now, while such attacks by individuals or *ad-hoc* groups are unpredictable and almost impossible to preempt, they also pose a latent threat to bin Laden's goal of keeping the West European powers on the bench. If one of the sad-sack, ramshackle groups that have been rounded up in Europe—say, the amateurish Algerians who were holding the toxin ricin when arrested in the UK in early 2003— ever manage to strike it rich and cause devastating damage in Europe, it is a near certainty that al Qaeda will be blamed for the attack. In that case, bin Laden would find himself faced with a level of U.S.–European anti-al Qaeda cooperation similar to, or stronger than, that which existed after 11 September. There is evidence that this situation worries bin Laden. Writing in *Al-Ansar*, for example, al Qaeda essayist Sayf al-Ansari advised Muslims that the "feeling of individual responsibility regarding the issue of jihad should not give rise to a kind of improvised behavior that translates jihad into some kind of spontaneous activity and makes the issue an undisciplined current in which everyone weaves on his own loom."[57] Bin Laden is too far down the road of incitement to turn back, however, and this is one potential problem that always will be lurking over the horizon.

Attacking Apostate Regimes More Directly

As noted earlier, bin Laden has long struggled to shift the orientation of Islamist resistance groups from individual Muslim states to the United States. As also noted, he has not been completely successful in this effort. It would, in fact, be generous to say that bin Laden has accomplished 60 percent of the task he set for himself, although the September 2003 decision of Algeria's heretofore stalwartly nationalist GSPC to ally with al Qaeda is a huge accomplishment for bin Laden. For this reason, it hits a slightly discordant note to hear the steady increase in the rhetorical attention he has focused on apostate Middle Eastern regimes since 2001. The increase, however, is not a sign of resurgent nationalist Islamist movements, but rather evidence of the flexibility of al Qaeda and bin Laden in taking advantage of opportunities created by changing international events. In this case, the supine response of Muslim governments to Israeli military attacks and targeted murders in Palestine, and their quiet but indispensable support for the U.S. invasion of Iraq, have allowed al Qaeda to cast the apostate regimes as lackeys of Washington and Israel, attack them as such and, in the process, not sacrifice too much of al Qaeda's tight military focus on the United States.

The prize for which bin Laden is playing by attacking the Muslim regimes is nothing less than the leadership of the Islamic world. Bin Laden would reject this notion of what he is up to—he truly believes he is just one soldier fighting in God's cause—but it remains true. What bin Laden would agree with is that his contest with the regimes is about making the word of God and His prophet, rather than the word of the Muslim leaders, the rightful source of leadership in the Islamic world. Even with this definition, however, the picture is the same: bin Laden is vying with the al-Sauds, the UAE and Kuwaiti royals, and the likes of Hosni Mubarak, Bashir al-Assad, and King Abdullah II for the leadership of the Islamic world, and to decide whether that world will be governed by God's law or man's law. Since 11 September 2001, bin Laden and God's word have been winning hands down among Muslims because he manifestly obeys God's injunction to oppose evil, protect Muslims, and act as well as speak in defense of Islam. On almost every issue of consequence in the Islamic world today, bin Laden is the only major Muslim leader who is on the side of the angels. Why? Because he speaks in specifics and matches words with deeds.

"Put a glance all around," bin Laden remarked in late September 2001, "and you will see that the slaves of the United States are either rulers or enemies [of Islam]."[58] These "rulers" bin Laden argues are liars whose empty words have taught sincere Muslims that they will never be effective leaders: "They have learned that the deluge of apologies advanced by Arab apologetics will not avail them."[59] So where do Muslims turn for truthful leadership? Bin Laden says Muslims must seek those who know how to attack the apostates and the infidels, "[the] actions carried out by the ardent sons of Islam to defend their religion and in response to the order of their Allah and their Prophet, may peace and blessings be with him."[60] Leadership, bin Laden says, comes from those who both speak and act on God's word.

These great events [the Palestinians' Intifadah and the 11 September attacks] are all a manifestation of the blessed jihad that has stayed its course toward the ultimate objective and Allah's promised end. This jihad came to expose the weak and unsupported statements made by the rulers, such as "What can we do? It is out of our hands!! We have no control over the issue!!" These type of statements no longer have a place in anyone's heart or mind in the light of the bloody attacks perpetrated against our nation.[61]

In Muslim eyes, the two years since 11 September have witnessed an unrivaled display of masterful fecklessness by the leaders of Muslim regimes, or, as bin Laden describes them, "these traitors who want to solve our Islamic causes. . . ."[62] The Israelis have done as they wished in Jenin, Bethlehem, and Rafah, constructed more settlements, and begun building a barrier wall that annexes more Palestinian land. The United States remains in Afghanistan as an occupying power, has invaded and occupied Iraq, has identified Israeli prime minister Sharon as a man of peace, and has repeatedly professed its "understanding and support" for Israel's right to defend itself. In response, Muslim leaders have held Arab League summits, expressed angry indignation over this or that Israeli or U.S. action in well-publicized telephone calls, and, in the end, provided the bases, airfields, and harbors that made possible the U.S.-led invasion and occupation of the Muslim states of Afghanistan and Iraq. It is difficult to identify a shred of leadership in any of these actions—at least from the Islamists' eyes—and easy to appreciate the resonant chord bin Laden strikes across the Muslim world when he describes "how great [the Muslims'] humiliation and disgrace have become since we stopped following [the Prophet Mohammed and his companions] and came under the rule of the disgraceful leaders."[63]

> These leaders destroyed the statement ["There is no god but Allah"] and ignored it by allying themselves with disbelievers, ruling by their own man-made laws, and supporting and agreeing with the Atheist United Nations. Therefore it is prohibited by Shariah to pledge allegiance to them and follow them. . . .
>
> After all this, we ask that is it possible for a Muslim [leader] to say to the Muslims to pledge their hands in the hands of [Afghan president Hamid] Karzai and cooperate with him to establish Islam, lift oppression, and cease the plans of America in their tracks?!! This is impossible because Karzai is an American agent and supporting him against the Muslims takes a person outside the fold of Islam. Here we have to ask ourselves: what is the difference between Karzai the non-Arab and Karzai the Arab? Who are the ones who implanted and established the

rulers of the Arabian Gulf? They are none other than the Crusaders, who appointed the Karzai of Kabul, established the Karzai of Pakistan, implanted the Karzai of Kuwait and the Karzai of Bahrain and the Karzai of Qatar and others. And who are the ones who appointed the Karzai of Riyadh and brought him after he used to be a bandit in Kuwait a long time ago in order to fight with them against the Ottoman Empire and its leader Ibn Rashid? They are none other than the Crusaders and they are continuing to enslave us up [to] this very day!![64]

The utterly eunuch-like appearance of the Middle Eastern regimes also has allowed bin Laden to broaden and intensify his attacks on the Islamic scholars and jurists he refers to as the "scholars of the authorities," those who are in the pay of the al-Sauds, the Kuwaitis, and other Muslim rulers, and whose religious rulings—miraculously—always seem to mirror and sanction the rulers' decisions and desires. Prefacing his critique, bin Laden claims it is the "honest scholars, propagators, and reformers" who are the most important jihad leaders; they are the ones "who should be at the head of the ranks, lead the action, and direct the march. This is the requisite for inheriting the prophets."[65] It is the duty of these men, bin Laden argues, "to tell the truth to the nation and to declare it in the face of darkness without equivocation or fear."[66] But most of these men are in prison; Islam's most important leaders, like Egyptian Shaykh Omar Abd-al-Rahman, are in "the U.S. prison" or in the jails of "the Arabian Peninsula or other countries."[67]

With the rightful leaders unavailable, bin Laden says that it is up to individuals like himself to take leadership roles, identify corrupt scholars who are free because they preach the rulers' desire and not God's word, and persuade or shame those scholars to return to God's path. Bin Laden points out that whereas in most of Islamic history the religious scholars and jurists took the lead in calling and waging jihad against apostates, polytheists, or infidels threatening Islam, today "many bear false witness morning and evening and lead the nation astray."[68] This, bin Laden claims, is a new phenomenon in Islam; Muslims expect such behavior from civil servants—"people know they are lying to them and deceiving them"[69]—but not from clerics.

Great evil is spreading throughout the Islamic world: the imams calling the people to hell are those who appear more than others at the side of the rulers of the region, the rulers of the Arab and Islamic world. . . . from morning to evening they call the people to the gates of hell.

[The clerics] all, except those upon whom Allah had mercy, are busy handing out praise and words of glory to the despotic [rulers] who disbelieved Allah and His Prophet.

The [ummah] has never been damaged by a catastrophe like the one that damages them today. In the past, there was imperfection, but it was partial. Today, however, the imperfection touches the entire public because of the communications revolution and because the media enter every home.

The clerics are the prisoners and hostages of the tyrants. . . . The regime appropriates a huge budget for these bodies [i.e., the authorities' scholars] whose role it is to grant legitimacy to the regime.[70]

While bin Laden long has been critical of these clerics, the events of the Crusaders' war against Islam since 11 September 2001 have given bin Laden far greater scope to attack the scholars whose rulings have supported their employers' failure to protect Muslims.

Targeting America: Justifying Mass Casualties

While keeping the United States on the rhetorical bull's-eye since 11 September 2001, bin Laden has focused equally on making sure that the Muslim world is ready to accept an attack that causes mass American casualties. The effort directed at the Muslim world, in fact, may be the reason there has not been a major attack in the United States since 2001. Toward the goal of preparing Muslims, bin Laden has repeatedly warned Americans that another al Qaeda attack on the United States is in the offing and that it will be worse than that of 11 September. He also offered U.S. leaders and the American people the chance to convert to Islam, volunteering himself to be their teacher and guide on the path to God's truth. It appears, moreover, that al Qaeda prompted a well-known and respected Saudi Islamic scholar to write and publish a treatise that, in religious terms, justifies the use of weapons of mass destruction in the United States. Finally, bin Laden has appealed directly to the American people to use their democratic system of government to force U.S. leaders to abrogate policies that are harming the Muslim world, in essence saying that U.S. citizens have it in their power to end the war between America and Islam and if they do not use it, they merit any tragedy that befalls them. At the end of the day, these actions are made more to address and satisfy the concerns of Muslim critics of the 11

September attacks than with any expectation that America will change its policies and end the war.

"We are defending ourselves against the United States," bin Laden said on behalf of the Islamic world in November 2001. "This is why I used to say that if [the Muslims] do not have security, the Americans also will not have it. This is a very simple formula. . . . This is the formula of live and let live."[71] Declared at the start of the U.S.–Afghan war, bin Laden's warning to the United States has been on his lips ever since. A year after the statement, for example, bin Laden reminded Americans that "[t]he road to safety begins by lifting oppression,"[72] and that their government and its allies had yet to heed this advice. "This is an unfair division. The time has come for us to be equal," bin Laden warned. "Just as you kill, you are killed. Just as you bombard, you are bombarded. Rejoice at the harm coming to you."[73] At times, bin Laden even has sounded frustrated that his message is being ignored.

> So the case is easy, America will not be able to leave this ordeal unless it leaves the Arabian Peninsula, and stops its involvement in Palestine, and in all the Islamic world. If we give this equation to any child in an American school, he will easily solve it within a second. But, according to [President] Bush's actions the equation won't be solved until the swords fall on their heads, with the permission of Allah. . . .
>
> We renew our pledge to Allah, our promise to the nation, and our threat to the Americans and Jews that they shall remain restless, shall not feel at ease, and shall not dream of security until they take their hands off our nation and stop their aggression against us and their support for our enemies. And soon will the unjust assailants know what vicissitudes their affairs will take.[74]

Bin Laden has accompanied his warnings with specific appeals to the U.S. president and American people to convert to Islam, each time offering to serve as their guide and teacher. He made the appeals in October and November 2002, and thereby addressed the concerns of Muslim critics of the 11 September attacks who criticized al Qaeda for not offering Americans a chance to convert before the assaults, thereby violating God's ruling: "We never punish until we have sent a messenger."[75] In so doing, bin Laden cleared the decks in Islamic terms; he has warned and invited before attacking. "All enemies," the religious scholar James Turner Johnson has written, "by their refusal of the invitation to accept Islam and by their resistance to the Islamic mission, are by definition in a state of rebellion against God and God's Prophet, and hence may be killed. . . ."[76] Another U.S. scholar also has detailed the steps preceding war in Islam; they are the ones bin Laden has completed. "[The classical Islamic scholar] al-Shaybani," Dr. John Kelsay wrote in the *Journal of Religious Ethics*, "cites a prophetic saying that Muslim forces may go to war against non-Muslims after a declaration of an intent to fight and an invitation to acknowledge Islam. Al-Shaybani goes on to state his preference that the declaration be made a second time before forces are engaged, though he indicates this is not obligatory."[77] Thus, having met al-Shaybani's requirement of stating intent to attack, bin Laden said to Americans in October 2002, "In the name of God, the merciful, the compassionate,"

A message to the American people: Peace be upon those who follow the right path. I am an honest adviser to you. I urge you to seek the joy of life and the after life and to rid yourself of your dry, miserable, and spiritless materialistic existence. I urge you to become Muslims, for Islam calls for the principle of "there is no God but Allah," and for justice and forbids injustice and criminality. I call on you to understand the lesson of the New York and Washington raids, which came in response to some of your previous crimes. The aggressor deserves punishment.

We call you to Islam; the last religion that has replaced all previous religions; the religion of good manners, sincerity, mercy, fear of Allah, kindness to others, justice between people, giving the rights to the people who deserve them, protection of people from oppressors and unjust acts; the religion which calls upon its followers to amr bi maroof (enjoin the good) and nahi an al-munkar (forbid the evil) with hand, tongue, and heart. This is the religion of Jihad in the way of Allah so that Allah's Word and religion are made Supreme. This is the religion of obligation to Allah, demanding its followers to act with justice and equality between people without differentiating between their language, sex, or color.[78]

Warning Americans of more and bigger attacks, and calling them to embrace Islam, were actions that bin Laden could take himself. But another required step in preparing the Muslim world for an attack on the United States with a weapon of mass destruction (WMD) fell outside his bailiwick and required the assistance of an established, well-qualified, and respected Islamic scholar. Until May 2003, al Qaeda did not have sufficient Islamic grounding on which to convincingly justify a WMD attack. In that month, however, a young Saudi cleric named

Shaykh Nasir bin Hamid al-Fahd published "A Treatise on the Legal Status of Using Weapons of Mass Destruction Against Infidels."[79] The treatise is exactly what al Qaeda needed, and it may have even asked Shaykh al-Fahd to prepare the work. The study is a lucidly written, comprehensive, and well-documented justification and authorization for using weapons of mass destruction against infidels—in this case, against the United States. Perhaps the most important service rendered by Shaykh al-Fahd to bin Laden was in moving discussion about the use of WMD from the arena of Muslim politicians, commentators, academics, generals, and intellectuals and placing it in what he, bin Laden, and other Islamists believe is its proper sphere, that of God. Without question, Shaykh al-Fahd wrote, the "Proscription [of weapons of mass destruction] Belongs to God Almighty, and to None Other Than He, Such as Humans."[80]

Shaykh al-Fahd begins by describing the term "weapons of mass destruction" as an "inexact term," claiming that chemical, biological, or nuclear weapons that killed a thousand people would be called by the West "internationally banned weapons," whereas the use of "high explosive bombs weighing seven tons apiece and [that] killed three thousand or more" would be called "internationally permissible weapons."[81] On that basis, he dismisses the WMD-armed West's treaties and regulations banning WMD proliferation as mere attempts to scare others and protect itself. "Thus it is evident," he wrote, "that [the Western nations] do not wish to protect humanity by these terms, as they assert; rather, they want to protect themselves and monopolize such weapons on the pretext of banning them internationally."[82] After noting this hypocrisy, Shaykh al-Fahd rejects both terms. "All these terms have no standing in Islamic law, because God Almighty has reserved judgment and legislation to Himself. . . . This is a matter so obvious to Muslims that it needs no demonstration. . . . In judging these weapons one looks only to the Koran, the Sunnah [i.e., the sayings and traditions of the Prophet], and the statements of Muslim scholars."[83] Shaykh al-Fahd carries this discussion for twenty-five closely reasoned, scripturally documented pages. Al-Fahd's conclusions, summarized below, satisfactorily justify bin Laden's intention to stage a WMD attack in the United States.

- Shaykh al-Fahd first cites three examples from the Koran in which God says that Muslims may respond reciprocally for attacks made on them. "Anyone who considers America's aggressions against Muslims and their lands during the past decades," al-Fahd wrote, "will conclude that striking her is permissible merely on the rule of treating as one has been treated. Some brothers have totaled the number of Muslims killed directly or indirectly by their weapons and come up with a figure of nearly 10 million."[84]

- Shaykh al-Fahd next argues that large civilian casualties are acceptable if they result from an attack meant to defeat an enemy, and not an attack aimed only at killing the innocent. "The messenger of God [the Prophet Mohammed]," al-Fahd wrote, "commanded an attack on the enemy. In many traditions, he attacked others. . . . He was not prevented from this by what we know, namely that he knew that women and children would not be safe from harm. He allowed the attack because the intent of the attackers was not to harm them. . . . Thus the situation in this regard is that if those engaged in jihad establish that the evil of the infidels can be repelled only by attacking them at night with weapons of mass destruction, they may be used even if they annihilate all the infidels."[85]

- Shaykh al-Fahd concludes by addressing the issue of whether Muslims can kill other Muslims in pursuing jihad in God's name. He says that, indeed, the lives of Muslims are considered sacred and there is no permission from God to wantonly kill another Muslim. But, al-Fahd maintains, "If we accept the argument unrestrictedly, we should entirely suspend jihad, for no infidel land is devoid of Muslims. As long as jihad has been commanded . . . and it can be carried out only in this way [i.e.,, with Muslims being killed in attacks by Muslims], it is permitted." God allows this, al-Fahd explains, "so that the enemy cannot force us to abandon jihad by imprisoning a Muslim among them."[86]

With the requirements for warnings, offers of conversion, and Islamic justification completed, bin Laden went the extra mile in preparing Muslims for a WMD attack on the United States by turning America's democracy back on its own citizenry. "Many people in the West are good and gentle people," bin Laden said.[87] "I have already said that we are not hostile to the United States. We are against the system [i.e., U.S. foreign policy] which makes nations slaves of the United States, or forces them to mortgage their political and economic freedom."[88] Turning the absurd personalized war-making formula so beloved in the West—"We are at war with bin Laden not Muslims," for example, or, "We are at war with Saddam not Iraqis"—against the United States, bin Laden assures Americans that Islam is at war against their government and not them, and he explains that because he understands that America is a democracy, he also understands that Americans have the electoral power to change the leaders who are prosecuting an anti-Islam foreign policy. U.S. citizens, he argues, have the ability to end those policies, remove the cause of the U.S. war with Islam, and end the risk of a WMD attack causing mass American casualties. Because Americans hold this power in their hands, bin Laden argues, they cannot argue that al Qaeda is attacking and killing civilians.

> Well this argument contradicts your claim that America is the land of freedom and democracy, in which every American irrespective of gender, color, age, or intellectual ability has a vote. It is a fundamental principle of any democracy that the people choose their leaders, and as such, approve and are party to the actions of their leaders. So "in the land of freedom" each American is "free" to select their [sic] leader because they have the right to do so and as such they give consent to the policies their elected Government adopts. This includes the support of Israel manifesting itself in many ways including billions of dollars in military aid. By electing these leaders, the American people have given their consent to the incarceration of the Palestinian people, the demolition of Palestinian homes and the slaughter of the children of Iraq. The American people have the ability and choice to refuse the policies of their Government, yet time and again, polls show the American people support the policies of the elected Government. . . . This is why the American people are not innocent. The American people are active members in all these crimes.[89]

Faced with this reality, bin Laden beseeches the American people to use their democratic system to end policies that have earned the United States the hatred and jihad of Muslims. "I will ask the American people to check the anti-Muslim policies of their government," bin Laden explained to Pakistani journalist Hamid Mir in mid-November 2001. "They had described their government's policy against Vietnam as wrong. They should play the same role now that they played during the Vietnam war. The American people should prevent the killing of Muslims at the hands of their government."[90]

While bin Laden would welcome the end of these policies, and any dissent his words might provoke in the United States, he probably expects neither. Rather, he has employed this argument as yet another way of proving to Muslims that he has exhausted every available means to prevent the necessity of using a weapon of mass destruction against Americans. He had warned, offered conversion, sought religious guidance, and—as a last ditch effort—tried to persuade Americans to protect themselves in the best American tradition of using the ballot box.

Nothing has worked for bin Laden, Muslims are still being attacked and killed, and so, as Shaykh al-Fahd wrote, "If people of authority engaged in jihad determine that the evil of the infidels can only be repelled by their means [i.e., by weapons of mass destruction], they may be used."

> Scholars have agreed that it is permissible to bombard an enemy with a catapult and similar things.
> As everyone knows, a catapult stone does not distinguish between women, children, and others; it destroys anything that it hits, buildings or otherwise.
> This proves that the principle of destroying the infidels' lands and killing them if the jihad requires it and those in authority over the jihad decide so is legitimate; for the Muslims bombarded these countries until they were conquered. No one [i.e., the Prophet, his companions, scholars, or historians] reports that they ceased for fear of annihilating the infidels or for fear of destroying their territory. God alone knows best.[91]

It is clear that bin Laden is one of those "in authority over the jihad" who has decided the "jihad requires" the use of weapons of mass destruction against the United States and believes that their use is religiously "legitimate." No one should be surprised when bin Laden and al Qaeda detonate a weapon of mass destruction in the United States.

A New Twist: Bin Laden Anticipates America's Response

A final point to note in bin Laden's post-11 September rhetoric is his anticipation of the widespread unease and fear among Americans that emerged after the attacks on New York and Washington. This is not meant to make bin Laden appear clairvoyant, but rather to offer for consideration a counterpoint to those Western officials and analysts who have assessed him as motivated only by ignorance and hatred, and as unknowledgeable about the United States, the West, and the workings of modern societies. "There is no point in addressing the so-called root causes of [bin Laden's] terrorism," wrote L. Paul Bremmer, now U.S. proconsul in Iraq. "We are the root cause of his terrorism. He doesn't like America. He doesn't like our society. He doesn't like what we stand for. He doesn't like our values."[92] Now, bin Laden may and probably does dislike all the things Bremmer lists, but his hatred and war-making have nothing to do with our society, values, and ideas. Bin Laden hates us—and forgive this repetition—because of our policies and actions in the Muslim world. His hate is neither blind nor ignorant, and he has taken America's measure far more thoroughly than we have taken his—so much so, in fact, that he is able to craft statements that ease Muslim fears and support their beliefs while also stoking American unease and fear about where the war on al Qaeda is leading the country.

The following two passages are from statements bin Laden made within six weeks of the 11 September attacks, before the final course of the U.S. domestic response to the events was set. The passages are chockablock with shibboleths and exaggerations of the type both sides use in the U.S.-Islamic war, but beneath that verbiage there is a sophisticated argument that both reinforces Muslim beliefs and raises doubt in American minds. The first assures Muslims that while the war will make bin Laden's public appearances fewer, he will be safe; at the same time, it suggests to Americans that he will be planning their demise even if they do not hear from him regularly, and that he will have help from their own media. In the second, bin Laden reminds Muslims of U.S. hypocrisy and Zionist perfidy, and feeds the fears of Americans about the growth of the federal government's police powers. While yielding to the reader's judgment, they seem to demonstrate a solid knowledge of the wartime mind in contemporary America.

America's Inability to Endure the Pain of a War with Islam, 28 September 2001

> Our silence is our real propaganda. Rejections, expectations, or corrigendum [on al Qaeda's part] only waste your time, and through them the enemy wants you to engage in things that are not of use to you. These things are pulling you away from your cause. The Western media is unleashing such a baseless propaganda, which makes us surprise[d] but it reflects on what is in their hearts and gradually they themselves become captives of this propaganda. They become afraid of it and begin to cause harm to themselves. Terror is the most dreaded weapon in the modern age and the Western media is [sic] mercilessly using it against their own people. It can add fear and helplessness to the psyche of the people of Europe and the United States. It means what the enemies of the United States cannot do, its media is doing that. You can understand as to what will be the performance of the nation in a war, which suffers from fear and helplessness.[93]

U.S. Hypocrisy about Freedom and Liberty, 21 October 2001

But I mention that there also are other events that took place, greater and more dangerous than the collapse of the towers. It is that this Western Civilization, which is backed by America, has lost its values and appeal. The immense materialistic towers were destroyed, which preach [sic: "symbolize"?] Freedom, and Human Rights and Equality. It became a total mockery and that clearly appeared when the U.S. Government interfered and banned the media outlets from airing our words which don't exceed a few minutes, because they felt the truth started to appear to the American people, and that we truly aren't terrorists by the definition they want, but because we are being violated in Palestine, in Iraq, in Lebanon, in Sudan, in Somalia, in Kashmir, in the Philippines, and in every place. . . . Therefore, they declared what they declared and ordered what they ordered, and they forgot everything they mentioned about Free Speech, and Unbiased Opinion and all those matters. So I say that Freedom and Rights in America, and Human Rights, have been sent forward to the guillotine with no return unless they are quickly reinstated. The [U.S.] Government will take the American people and the West in general will enter into a choking life, into an unsupportable hell, because of the fact that those governments have very strong ties, and are under the payroll, of the Zionist lobby, which serves the needs of Israel who kills our sons and children without right so they can keep on ruling with total control.[94]

And Still, the Words Are Not Heard

To paraphrase the foregoing: I will be mostly quiet. I will attack those who help you. I will wage war on you in Iraq, Afghanistan, and elsewhere. I will incite all Muslims against you. I will strike you again in the United States, if possible with a weapon of mass destruction. I will try to destroy your economy. Though you are evil, I care nothing for you, your beliefs, or your ways, but I will force you to end several of your policies toward Muslims. I will not grow weary, weak, or irresolute. I will not compromise. You will, God willing, be defeated.

Serious words from bin Laden, just like those he uttered before 11 September and then made good. Americans—particularly the elites—refuse to grasp their meaning, which is simply that their country is engaged in war to the death with an enemy who has warned us of his every move and intention. Bin Laden's words leave us without excuses. Whatever comes next, whatever disaster befalls us, our children, and our country, we were warned and chose not to fight to our utmost. For more than two years—really for nearly ten—we have ignored Machiavelli's warning that "you ought never suffer for your designs to be crossed in order to avoid war, since war is not so to be avoided, but is only deferred to your disadvantage." Whether in the area of defense spending, travel, foreign policy, fiscal responsibility, domestic security, or citizen safety, we have supinely allowed our "designs to be crossed" to avoid the sacrifices required to fight the war bin Laden has launched. He will hit us again, more strongly, and we will then be forced to fight the war we have so far "deferred." As we rise from the floor to do so, we should pray that another of Machiavelli's warnings is incorrect. "Hence it comes," Machiavelli advised his prince, "that all armed Prophets have been victorious, and all unarmed Prophets have been destroyed."[95]

6

BLINDING HUBRIS ABOUNDING: INFLICTING DEFEAT ON OURSELVES—NON-WARS, LEAKS, AND MISSIONARY DEMOCRACY

This is a very suggestive age . . . but it will always be found in the end that the only way to whip an army is to go out and fight it.

General U.S. Grant, c. 1865.[1]

In the North the press was free to the point of open treason.

General U.S. Grant, 1885.[2]

Bush does not seem to understand that he is not only the president of the United States, he is president of the free world. . . . He cannot give up the role without causing chaos.

Andrew Greeley, 2003.[3]

The West is deluged daily by newsmakers and the conveyors and interpreters of their words and actions. Since 11 September, the average reader of newspapers, magazines, and the Internet; listener to government officials, media experts, and academics; and watcher of television could judge that the West is winning the war that intensified on that day. An imagined but plausible synopsis of this news could be gisted in the following breathless, headlinelike manner:

Victory in Afghanistan, Taleban destroyed. Bin Laden and al-Zawahiri cowering in Afghan caves. Al Qaeda remnants soon to be captured. Pro-Western, democratic regime rules in Kabul. Enthusiasm for Islamism and jihad waning, becoming, per director of central intelligence, the "fringe of the Muslim lunatic fringe." Israeli prime minister Sharon—"Man of Peace." War on al Qaeda not war on Islam. Anti-terror war has nothing to do with religion. Bin Laden hates United States for its freedom, not its policies. Islamists hate America for what it is, not what it does. Pakistan, Saudi Arabia support U.S. war on al Qaeda. West dries up funds for bin Laden. Road Map for Israel, Palestine working. Victory in Iraq, no Islamist insurgency. Iraq nears secular government, democracy, sovereignty.

Comfortable with the default conclusion that a U.S. victory over bin Laden and his cause is as inevitable as the universal installation of democracy, the Western reader-listener-watcher nevertheless still occasionally finds sharp disconnects in his news about the U.S.-led war on terrorism. In early 2004, amidst loud triumphalism, we still hear the director of central intelligence and the FBI director warning audiences—most often in joint, set piece, we-love-each-other-too-much briefings to Congress—that al Qaeda is as dangerous now as in 2001. Then, if you dig deep into the newspapers, you will find stories claiming these gentlemen are incorrect, that al Qaeda actually is more dangerous than it was before what bin Laden calls the "blessed attacks" of 11 September. As discordant notes linger, we are periodically riled by "breaking news" that the U.S. Department of Homeland Security (DHS) has raised the threat-warning indicator from yellow to amber—or is it amber to yellow?—on a tacky traffic-light-looking device. Adjusting the street-light-of-death is meant to portray DHS's judgment that the threat to U.S. interests from someone, somewhere in the world has increased. As the threat level wanders between "don't worry" and "prepare to die," we also hear experts warning audiences watching CNN, C-SPAN, or Oprah that the next al Qaeda attack on our country will involve WMD. The warnings are then complemented by more otherworldly DHS advice urging citizens to quickly buy a "disaster supply kit" that includes duct tape and plastic sheeting to wrap their homes and make them airtight, WMD-proof fortresses. Though not providing much protection, duct tape and other parts of the kit saw a surge in sales, proving again that when faced with vague threats Washington "does what it always does . . . It scared the hell out of everyone."[4]

To say the least, Americans are getting mixed and confusing messages from their leaders. Are we headed for a victory parade, Cold War bomb shelters, or simply straight to the graveyard? Do repeated warnings of an al Qaeda-produced disaster mark a genuine threat, or have federal bureaucrats learned to cover their butts so they will not have another "failed-to-warn" incident a la 11 September; after all, is there a better definition of useless, and therefore expendable, than a bureaucrat who cannot manage this sort of self-protection? Are bin Laden–related dangers downplayed to nurse the on-again, off-again economic recovery and the presidential prospects of both U.S. political parties? Is there a national security strategy vis-à-vis bin Laden, or are our leaders just winging it? In short, are we to reach for champagne or for a rosary?

This chapter's intent, notwithstanding the above, is to be neither facetious nor flip. It is likewise not to provide final answers to the just-posed questions, although by now the reader will know I think the quantity and quality of bad news is greater than the good. Rather, the goal is to examine a limited number of issues suggesting, I believe, that the way we see and interpret people and events outside North America is heavily clouded by arrogance and self-centeredness amounting to what I called "imperial hubris" in *Through Our Enemies' Eyes*.[5] This is not a genetic flaw in Americans that has been present since the Pilgrims splashed ashore at Plymouth Rock, but rather a way of thinking America's elites have acquired since the end of World War II. It is a process of interpreting the world so it makes sense to us, a process yielding a world in which few events seems alien because we Americanize their components. "When confronted by a culturally exotic enemy," Lee Harris explained in the August/September 2002 issue of *Policy Review*, "our first instinct is to understand such conduct in terms that are familiar to us—terms that make sense to us in light of our own fund of experience. We assume that if our enemy is doing X, it must be for reasons comprehensible in terms of our universe."[6] Thus, for example, bin Laden is a criminal whose activities are fueled by money—not a devout Muslim soldier fueled by faith—because Americans know how to beat well-heeled gangsters. We assume, moreover, that bin Laden and the Islamists hate us for our liberty, freedoms, and democracy—not because they and many millions of Muslims believe U.S. foreign policy is an attack on Islam or because the U.S. military now has a ten-year record of smashing people and things in the Islamic world. Even the fine historian Victor Davis Hanson got it wrong when he wrote on 20 September 2001, "These terrorists hate us for who we are, not what we have done."[7]

Our political leaders contend that America's astoundingly low approval ratings in polls taken in major Muslim countries do not reflect our unquestioning support for Israel and its lethal hijinks under the banner of "targeted killings." As thoughtful a commentator as Steven Simon, in fact, suggests that the United States adopt Israel's targeted-killing practice, apparently believing this does not contradict his advice that Washington "move more boldly to establish contacts . . . [with] moderates" in Egypt and Saudi Arabia.[8] Nor, they say, are the ratings due to our relentless support for tyrannical and corrupt Muslim regimes that are systematically dissipating the Muslim world's energy resources for family fun and profit while imprisoning, torturing, and executing domestic dissenters. Likewise, we are confident that the single-digit approval ratings have nothing to do with our refusal to apply nuclear nonproliferation rules with anything close to an even hand, a situation that makes Israeli and Indian nuclear weapons acceptable—each is a democracy, after all—while Pakistan's weapons are intolerable (perhaps because they are held by Muslims?). Finally, say our elites, the movement bin Laden symbolizes has nothing to do with the Islamic religion because here in America all religions get along amiably and so the rest of the world can work the same way. To make this so, we send forth U.S. diplomats, politicians, officials, and preachers to coercively persuade Muslims to Westernize the Koran and the Prophet's traditions and sayings, especially the parts of the Islamic canon dealing with education, charitable giving, the non-separation of church and state, and that pesky idea of jihad. Surely, we have concluded, if we drive and manage an Islamic Reformation that makes Muslims secular like us, all this unfortunate, nonsensical talk about religious war will end and Muslims will be eager to keep God in the same kind of narrow locker in which the West is slowly asphyxiating Him.

Thus, because of the pervasive imperial hubris that dominates the minds of our political, academic, social, media, and military elites, America is able and content to believe the Islamic world fails to understand the benign intent of U.S. foreign policy and its implementation. Moreover, as noted in the epigram at the head of this chapter by priest-novelist Andrew Greeley, our elites have found that the U.S. Constitution sanctions the election of the "president of the world" instead of the chief magistrate of the American republic. These two lines of thought yield a mind-set that holds that America does not need to reevaluate its policies, let alone change them; it merely needs to better explain the wholesomeness of its views and the purity of its purposes to the uncomprehending Muslim world. What could be more American in the early twenty-first century, after all, then to re-identify a *casus belli* as a communication problem, and then call on Madison Avenue to package and hawk a remedy called "Democracy, Secularism, and Capitalism Are Good for Muslims" to an Islamic world that has, to date, violently refused to purchase.

The foregoing is meant neither to ridicule my countrymen's intellectual abilities nor be supportive of bin Laden and his interpretation of Islam. It is rather to say that most of the world outside North America is not, does not want to be, and probably will never be just like us. Indeed, there probably are people other than Muslims who would take up arms to avoid being forced to become like us. And let me be clear, I am not talking about America's political freedoms, personal liberties, or respect for education and human rights; the same polls showing Muslims hate Americans for their actions find broad support for the ideas and beliefs that make us who we are. Pew Trust polls in 2003, for example, found that while Muslims believed it is "necessary to believe in God to be moral," they also favored what were termed "democratic values." The Pew poll found, overall, that "hostility is toward American policies, not American values."[9] When Americans—leaders and led—process incoming information to make it intelligible in American terms, many not only fail to clearly understand what is going on abroad but, more ominous, fail to accurately gauge the severity of the danger these foreign events, organizations, attitudes, and personalities pose to U.S. national security and our society's welfare and lifestyle. The urgent need to eliminate this perceptual shortcoming is purely to ensure that America is prepared to defend itself, not to increase its empathy for the complaints and troubles of non-Americans. Even less is it meant to imply that Americans should feel more debilitating guilt about events outside North America. Looking just at our attitude toward Israel, for example, it is clear Americans already feel far too much guilt, for no good reason, at far too high a cost. Decisions about America's future security must, as always, remain solely in its own hands.

In sum, this chapter argues that to make the decisions and allocate the resources needed to ensure U.S. security, Americans must understand the world as it is, not as we want—or worse yet, hope—it will be. While I believe this contention is true for all of America's dealings with the world, I am not smart or arrogant enough to formulate an all-inclusive approach to U.S. foreign policy. I do, however, have long experience analyzing and attacking bin Laden and Islamists. I believe they are a growing threat to the United States—there is no greater threat—and that we are being defeated not because the evidence of the threat is unavailable, but because we refuse to accept it at face value and without Americanizing the data that comes easily and voluminously to hand. This must change or our way of life will be unrecognizably changed.

Bin Laden: The Enemy We Want, Not the One We Face

In no other area of America's confrontation with militant Islam have we striven harder to understand an issue on our own terms than in regard to the person and character of Osama bin Laden. And, as shown in Chapter 4, there is no reason, based on the information at hand, to believe bin Laden is anything other than what he appears: a pious, charismatic, gentle, generous, talented, and personally courageous Muslim who is blessed with sound strategic and tactical judgment, able lieutenants, a reluctant but indispensable bloody-mindedness, and extraordinary patience. We have more than seven years of reporting about bin Laden. Some of it is secondhand or anecdotal, but most comes from Muslim and Western journalists who met or interviewed him, or Muslims who have fought and worked alongside him. Buttressing and, in a strong sense, validating this reporting—as documented in Chapter 4 and *Through Our Enemies' Eyes*—is the close correlation between bin Laden's words and deeds for most of a decade.

The preponderance of reporting—90 percent is a fair estimate—supports the judgment just made about bin Laden's talents and character. The other 10 percent is almost entirely from non-Muslim journalists, academics, and current or retired U.S. and Western government officials, or Muslim regimes bin Laden has called apostate and pledged to destroy. The 10-percenters' goal is either to display a profound, willful ignorance—if so, theirs is a bravura performance—or to portray bin Laden as an unintelligent, ruthless gangster with a deviant, other-directed personality. The "other" directing is always Dr. Ayman al-Zawahiri, who, in this odd take on reality, plays an Arab version of Conan Doyle's Napoleon of Crime, Dr. Moriarity. In neither characterization is religion identified as a source of bin Laden's appeal; rather, it is contended that bin Laden is followed due to the money he disperses, without which he would be only a homicidal nuisance. The 10-percenters give us the bin Laden we would prefer to face, and, unfortunately, many of the Western elites subscribe to their contentions.

One way to refute the 10-percenters and the threat they pose to our understanding of the bin Laden phenomenon is to cite bin Laden's fidelity to his threats and the ability of al Qaeda and its allies to make good on them. Since 11 September 2001, bin Laden has not only stated his intention to again attack the United States but has issued three lists of states to be attacked either for assisting Washington in Afghanistan and Iraq or for helping U.S. intelligence to capture and incarcerate al Qaeda fighters. In all cases, bin Laden indicated that these attacks would be designed to make the countries rethink their support for America. The first was issued on 28 September 2001,[10] the second on 11 February 2003,[11] and the third on 18 October 2003.[12] In addition, al-Zawahiri cited as targets those countries "handing over Muslim prisoners to their crusader enemies"[13] and added Turkey and Norway to the list on 11 February 2003; he attributed the first designation to "the ruling regime impudently [announcing] that it is fighting Islam and Muslims" and the latter presumably for its participation in the Afghan war.[14] Of the twenty nations al Qaeda threatened, eighteen have been attacked, a 90-percent correlation. Brief descriptions of the attacks can be found in Chapter 3.

While not all the attacks can be definitively attributed to al Qaeda, all confidently can be ascribed to al Qaeda or groups or individuals bin Laden has targeted via his inciting rhetoric. Although some scholars and journalists have said these attacks show al Qaeda has been so badly hurt that it can hit only "soft targets"—one argued in the London *Times* that the attacks are "a symptom of weakness . . . [a] last desperate stage before U.S. bailiffs arrive"—the group's public dual rationale for the attacks has a more plausible ring. First, wrote Abu-Ayman al-Hilali in *Al-Ansar*, the attacks are "to oppose by a carefully thought-out plan American and Zionist interests and all the enemies that make war throughout the world." Second, Salim al-Makki explained in *Al-Neda*, the attacks are designed to exhaust America—that is, to make the "U.S. security services and media . . . set out on a marathon prepared by the mujahideen. They have been gasping for breath, having run in one week from Mukalla in Yemen, to Faylaka in Kuwait, to Bali in Indonesia in a hunt for the shadowy mujahideen. . . ." In addition, while each attack damaged the United States indirectly by hurting its allies, many attacks hit two or more of the listed countries. The April 2003 al Qaeda attack on German-Jewish tourists in Tunisia, for example, hit the interests of Germany and Israel. The attacks also seem designed to impact the international economy's tourism sector—in which U.S. interests play a large part—such as those occurring in Kenya, Turkey, Kuwait, Tunisia, Jordan, and Indonesia. Al Qaeda stated its goal in this regard in late 2002, noting that "the enemy's tourist industry . . . includes easy targets with major economic, political, and security importance. This is because the impact of an attack on a tourist facility that cannot be protected equals, and sometimes surpasses, the impact of an attack against an enemy warship."[15] All told, bin Laden clearly keeps his word, and that reality ought to be taken at face value by U.S. leaders and elites. Just because he has not attacked inside the United States since 11 September 2001 means neither that al Qaeda is defeated nor that it has changed targets.

War Reporting or Reporting Non-Wars?

It is hard to understand how Americans believe their country has fought any wars since 1990. In the period, we surely have mobilized some, most, or all of our military; called up large numbers of reservists and national guardsmen; bombarded foreign, usually Muslim, lands with ferocious air power from land bases and aircraft carriers; and deployed troops abroad who have fought with skill and courage. We have waged what was called war to free Kuwait, save the starving in Somalia, defeat tyranny in Haiti, stop strife in the Balkans, save Kosovo from Serbia, rid Afghanistan of the Taleban and al Qaeda, and liberate Iraq from Saddam and his now-dead progeny. After each exercise, U.S. leaders declared victory and—until recent months—quickly brought home most troops and equipment. Quite a record, as we so often say so ourselves.

And yet, across thirteen years of frequent military actions, we have not once definitively and finally defeated the force—military, paramilitary, or armed rabble—we defined as the foe, be it Haitian gangsters, Somali warlords, Saddam's fedayeen, or a one-eyed Afghan mullah and his skinny Saudi sidekick. We have seen no huge body counts, no stacking of arms, no formal surrenders, no masses of prisoners of war, and no tangible evidence of victory, save the combination of our leaders' claims thereof and highly staged, melodramatic homecomings more appropriate for America's traditional conscript armies than for her reputedly hard-as-nails professional killers. U.S. officials and political leaders no longer define victory in precise quantitative or qualitative terms, but by whatever can be gained by the military in a tight time frame set by domestic political strategists who estimate how long and costly a war American voters will tolerate. As the strategists' clock ticks out, it seems, we declare victory and bring the boys home.

All told, it is a very neat and tidy process, but does it really defeat the enemy, or does it merely ensure the U.S. military's men and women will have the opportunity to do the job over and, perhaps, over again? Was Ulysses S. Grant wrong to order W.T. Sherman's army in 1864 "to move against [Joseph] Johnston's [rebel] army, to break it up and to get into the interior of the enemy's country as far as you can. . . ."?, or to tell Lincoln that the Army of the Potomac would fight in Virginia in the summer of 1864 until it was beaten or Marse Robert's army was on the path to destruction? Was Grant wrong to devise a strategy that ordered his commanders "to feel that hostile armies, and not cities, are to be their objectives"?[16] I think Grant was correct. He and Sherman produced bloody but complete victories—not occupied cities surrounded by ongoing war, as in Afghanistan and Iraq—that were objectively clear, indisputable, quantifiable, and, most important, recognized as total defeats by the Confederates. "To the extent that one says the Civil War 'settled once and for all' the question of whether or not states may secede from the Union," Tod Linberg wrote in the *Weekly Standard* in emphasizing the importance of the psychological as well as physical dimension of victory, "one refers not only to bloody conflict with a particular outcome but also to a successful exercise in conveying your message. One might say that, in a sense, war is the ultimate means of making your point."[17] In this context, what has the U.S. military produced since 1990? Victories that are asserted, subjective, arguable, and unrecognized by the enemy—none of which had even a second-rate military—as anything more than the loss of round one in a multi-round war. We have forgotten or chosen to ignore the real object of war—it is an open question if the failure originates with the politicians, the generals, or both—which is, in Philip Henry Sheridan's stark words, to "deal as hard blows to the enemies' soldiers as possible, and then cause so much suffering to the inhabitants of the country that they will long for peace and press their government to make it. . . . Nothing," Sheridan concluded, "should be left to the people but eyes to lament the war."[18]

Our hubris in regard to Afghanistan, to take one example, was and is breathtaking. While the UN and the U.S.-led coalition have made strides toward improving everyday life for a portion of the Afghan population—in terms of health services, potable water, schools, and ordnance disposal—these undeniable, even heroic gains have not changed the status quo in the country. Afghanistan's tribal-based society remains ethnically riven, plagued by foreign intervention, and in a state of war; it is a state, moreover, in which the tide of war is rising, not ebbing. Notwithstanding an assortment of direly needed humanitarian and economic advances, the on-the-ground political-military reality in Afghanistan remains starkly disturbing for U.S. interests. Western and U.S. media on the ground, as well as the Muslim reporters on the scene and commentators in their editorial chairs, clearly see the coming disaster for America. The *Christian Science Monitor*'s Scott Baldauf, for example, reminded readers that a "significant number of Afghans—especially the conservative Pashtun majority—are finding that they have more in common with the radical Islamic message of al Qaeda and the Taleban than they do with the pro-Western statements of new Afghan President Hamid Karzai."[19] The brilliant Pakistani journalist Rahimullah Yusufzai, who has excellent access to Pakistan's political and military elites and the country's Islamic militants, warned in early 2003 that "more and more Taleban are volunteering to join the resistance movement building-up in the Pashtun-dominated areas of the war-ravaged country."[20] Even a simple recollection of history and application of common sense by another Pakistani journalist caught the dangers ahead for the United States. "But I am afraid," warned Muzzafar Iqbal in the popular daily *The News*, "Afghans are rather notorious for their tenacity. There is little hope that what the Soviet Union could not achieve with 140,000 men, we can achieve without large-scale disasters soon erupting all over this unruly land."[21] Most ominous, however, was the advice of Sir John Keegan, the doyen of Western military historians, ten days after the attacks on Washington and New York. In a brilliant *Daily Telegraph* article entitled "If America Decides to Take on the Afghans, This is How to Do It," Keegan provided a clear and courteously understated explanation to U.S. leaders of what history promised America if it chose to ignore lessons drawn from nearly two centuries of Western military experience in Afghanistan.

> Efforts to occupy and rule [Afghanistan] usually ended in disaster. But straightforward punitive expeditions, for limited objectives or to bring about a change in Afghan government policy, were successful on more than one occasion. . . . The success achieved by Indian and British troops in the last days of the Raj depended on the avoidance of general war and of policies designed to change society or government in Afghanistan. The Raj accepted that Afghanistan was unstable, frac-

tious, and ultimately ungovernable and thought merely to check its mountain warriors' irrepressible love of raiding and fighting. . . . Russia, in 1979, made the mistake the East India Company had in 1839. It tried to impose a government in Kabul. Putting its own man in place was easy. Keeping him there proved the difficulty. . . . Limited campaigns aimed at penetration, aimed simply at inflicting punishment, can succeed, as long as the punitive forces remain mobile, keep control of the high ground and are skillful at tactical disengagement.[22]

Sadly, firsthand experience and sage advice were ignored. In the face of this reality, U.S. government leaders, generals, media, and experts nonetheless have spoken as if our endeavors had brought forth a budding mini-America in Afghanistan. Visiting Kabul physically but without ever mentally leaving Washington, for example, then-Treasury Secretary Paul O'Neill told reporters of his discussions with Karzai and his cabinet about the economic opportunities emerging in Afghanistan. "We also talked," O'Neill said, "about the important elements which are necessary for economic growth—developing the rule of law, enforceable contracts, and the [everyday] fight against corruption." Just as in America, O'Neill inferred, if these measures are taken the "money that actually belongs to Afghans will come out of the mattresses and out of other countries and will help fuel the development of the private sector." Before skipping town, O'Neill also confided to the press that he told the Afghans they should build a "five-star hotel in Kabul, which would be a useful addition to the economy"—presumably for the rush of well-off European tourists eager to be targets for rounds from a 122mm rocket launcher.[23]

With O'Neill having created capitalism in the country, a former U.S. proconsul in South Asia gushed about the glory of incipient Afghan democracy. Robert Oakley, U.S. ambassador to Pakistan late in the Soviet–Afghan war, greeted the new year of 2003 by asserting that "there is considerable grounds for optimism. . . . The achievements of the first year augur well for the long-term future of Afghanistan." As befits a public servant who always saw the makings of a U.S.-like democracy where no basis for such belief existed, Oakley concluded that "Karzai has achieved many attributes of responsible government."[24] Then the U.S. general in charge was heard from. "Have you thought about the work that was done for the day after the Taleban was no longer in power, and how magnificent that job was?" a breathless General Tommy Franks asked reporters in early 2003. "We have experienced the beginning of a democratic process."[25] With a free market and a democracy in hand, an end to the war was required, and, needless to say, peace miraculously arrived in May 2003 in the person of Secretary of Defense Rumsfeld. "We are at a point," Rumsfeld declared during a visit to Kabul, "where we have clearly moved from combat activities to a period of stability and stabilization and reconstruction activities."[26]

> The bulk of this country today is permissive and secure. It's clear that is the case by the fact we see people returning from across the globe in large numbers, voting with their feet saying the circumstance here is something they want to be part of and that's a good thing. . . . You feel the progress, the energy in the streets, the kiosks, the active people, cars moving around, children are out in the street again. It's a measure of progress, the success taking place here.[27]

Once Rumsfeld had declared nationwide peace, his subordinates then announced the creation of " 'Joint Regional Teams' . . . eight to 10 relatively small regional bases across Afghanistan . . . [that] will include about 60 U.S. troops, as well as Special Forces civil affairs troops, U.S. AID officials, and diplomatic personnel." While recognizing the still-fragile security in some areas of the country, "senior defense officials" said that setting up these teams signaled "a transition from combat sweeps to 'stability' operations."[28] With brains still firmly rooted in the American, vice Afghan, experience, the Joint Regional Teams were out to bring good old American know-how to the Hindu Kush. "Though these teams will be armed with assault rifles," Christian Lowe wrote on *Weekly Standard.com*, "their most potent weapons will be their calculators, tape measures, and laptop computers. They will act as middle men—and women—to help get contractors in and construction projects going for local villages."[29] If only wishing made it so.

While former and serving U.S. officials could be expected to speak in accord with the administration's "party line," the analysis of private-sector commentators goes to show how far gone is America's case of imperial hubris. "[T]he first year of the present war has been a spectacular success—one rarely paralleled in military history," wrote the usually astute historian Victor Davis Hanson in the *Wall Street Journal*. "For all our worries about the fragility of the Karzai government and the continual terrorism in Kabul, the military phase of the Afghan theater is nearing an end. Pacification is increasingly turned over to security forces and international development officers." Davis optimistically concluded that U.S. "[c]ommandos and [air strikes] will win the Afghan phase of the war against terrorism. . . ."³⁰ Even the insightful historian Bernard Lewis had a bad day on Afghanistan. Arguing for Washington to quickly hand power to the Iraqis, Lewis pointed to the success U.S. officials had with such a process in Afghanistan. "Today with minimal help from the U.S.," Lewis wrote in the 29 August 2002 *Wall Street Journal*, "a central government [in Kabul] is gradually extending its political and financial control to the rest of the country and dealing more and more effectively with the maintenance of order."³¹

Even more inaccurate than the statements of Hanson and Lewis are a trio of essays—by Michael E. O'Hanlon, in *Foreign Affairs*; William R. Hawkins, in the Army War College's excellent journal *Parameters*; and Anthony Davis in *Jane's Intelligence Review*—that stun the reader with their resolute and absolute misreading of what had gone on in Afghanistan. O'Hanlon, Hawkins, and Davis offer what can only be called a unique take on the Afghan war.

O'Hanlon: What a difference a new century makes. Operation Enduring Freedom [in Afghanistan] has been, for the most part, a masterpiece of military creativity and finesse. . . . On the whole . . . [it] has been masterful in both design and execution. . . . More notably, the U.S. effort helped quickly galvanize Pashtun forces to organize and fight effectively against the Taleban in the south, which many analysts had considered a highly risky proposition and CENTCOM itself had considered far from certain. . . . Convincing the Pashtuns to change sides and fight against the Taleban required just the right mix of diplomacy, military momentum and finesse, and battlefield assistance from CIA and special operations teams.³²

Hawkins: U.S. forces could attack Afghanistan with impunity. The only real challenge was the remote geography and lack of existing agreements with neighboring countries regarding basing rights. The military victory over the Taleban rabble looked easy because it was. . . . The campaign in Afghanistan in contrast [to the U.S. campaign in Serbia] was an exercise in decisive warfare. . . . Winning decisively has been defined as the ability to march on an enemy capital, with the intent of overthrowing its regime.³³

Davis: Yet within a single week in early–mid November [2001], the U.S.A.'s coalition had all but won the war. . . . The totality of that defeat undercut any possibility of a Taleban reversion to organized guerrilla resistance in their southern heartland. . . . [T]here is no doubt that U.S. military planners were fully aware of the lessons of Russia's Afghan quagmire and concerned to avoid a protracted military engagement.[34]

These essays appear in what can be called "establishment" journals, ones written for and influenced by U.S. and Western political-military elites and that, in turn, are read by and influence the elites. They are, in essence, important inputs to U.S. policy and vital defenders of it and its consequences. They are shaped by what we want U.S. policy to accomplish in Afghanistan and by our assumptions about what should happen there. To some extent, therefore, they are immune to on-the-ground reality. The essays cast as victory an unmitigated defeat, one produced by the hubris of American leaders who assume the transplantation to Afghanistan of the U.S. lifestyle, capitalist economy, democratic system, dedication to human rights, inclusive politics, and reality-immune optimism is not only possible, but represents the most ardent desire of Afghans—and now of Iraqis. This hubris is now costing the United States slowly increasing amounts of blood and treasure and will continue to do so for the foreseeable future because it has locked America into a classic lose-lose situation. If America leaves Afghanistan, the Taleban and al Qaeda—with Pakistan's support—will resume control of much of the country, thereby restarting the civil war suspended in October 2001 against the Masood-less but still Iran-, India-, and Russia-backed Northern Alliance. This conflict, of course, will be lethally punctuated by both sides as they kill Afghans who assisted the U.S.-led occupation. If America stays, the Islamist insurgency will intensify, cost America more and more, and ultimately triumph whether or not the United States massively increases its occupying force and takes the war to the enemy as did the Russians. America's staying-on also all but ensures the unraveling of Pakistan and perhaps a civil war there.

None of this had to be; it results from our elites' ignorance of their own and world history, failure to appreciate the power of faith, and disdain for the views and analyses of idiosyncratic Americans and non-Westerners. "Afghanistan is our tar baby and we are stuck fast," Colonel David H. Hackworth wisely concluded. "Too bad the policy-makers who put our soldiers at risk didn't brush up on their Brit/Soviet/Afghan History 101 beforehand."[35] Hackworth also might have suggested a refresher in U.S. history to remind the same policy makers and elites of the unique, nontransferable nature of most of the American experience. "We have made a slogan of democracy abroad, imagining it is a practical means when it is in fact, the glorious end of a long and difficult road," Ralph Peters wrote in his invaluable book, *Beyond Terror: Strategy in a Changing World.* "Democracy must be earned and learned. It cannot be decreed from without. In a grim paradox, our insistence on instant democracy in shattered states . . . is our greatest contribution to global instability."[36] The acerbic Mr. Peters also assigns a superb moniker to advocates of instant overseas democracies—they are "the ass end of imperialism."[37]

Generals, G-Men, and Lawyers: The Architects of Non-War

The Generals

Never, the experts claim, has the United States had a better-educated, better-trained, and better-equipped military, and—person for person—a higher quality soldiery. Our military men and women from private to lieutenant colonel—which seems to be where truth-telling earns retirement—appear, as a group, to be people in whom those footing the bill can be confident. Indeed, when watching media coverage of the Iraq war and, now, the Iraq insurgency, one doubts if any country has produced such military professionals, men and women who move as warranted from warrior to policeman to humanitarian. Beyond lieutenant colonel, however, things look iffy, and at the rank of brigadier general and above we find a disaster manned by senior officers, mostly men, who tack as needed to protect their careers and their institution's insiders' club—retired U.S. Army Colonel David H. Hackworth calls it the "Liars' Club."[38] I said in *Through Our Enemies' Eyes* that my generation's risk aversion threatens the republic's survival, and that the bulk of U.S. intelligence officers are lions led by managers—usually men—who can barely be called donkeys.[39] Sadly, the U.S. military—excepting the Marine Corps—seems to have the same devastating dichotomy between leaders and led.

As noted in Chapter 2, the conduct of the Afghan war approaches perfection—in the sense of perfectly inept. But that war is only one example of the U.S. military hierarchy's failed leadership and moral cowardice; indeed, at this writing U.S. military leaders in Iraq are reaching for higher levels of failure. How so? We have declared victory in

Afghanistan and Iraq, some troops are home, and generals are planning parades and recommending each other for medals. What is so wrong, then, with the way U.S. generals conceive and wage war?

In many ways, the answer is there is nothing wrong with the way U.S. generals wage the wars they are tasked to fight. They follow their elected and appointed civilian leaders' orders, which in the past twenty years amount to a three-part directive: fight and win quickly; do not kill many of the enemy, destroy much of his property, or kill many of his civilians; and, above all, lose the barest minimum of U.S. soldiers because the soft American public will not tolerate high casualties. The trouble with this formula is not that the U.S. military executes it; that is their duty, their lawful, constitutional responsibility. No, the trouble is in the generals' acceptance of the order without telling their civilian leaders that it is a recipe for disaster, that it ignores the long, bloody history of warfare, and that it invariably leaves behind half-finished or, more accurately, half-started wars that will be refought later. The years since 1990 have seen a series of ill-conceived, half-started U.S. wars: the 1991 Iraq war, Somalia, Haiti, Serbia, Kosovo, Afghanistan, and Iraq again. Their remains litter the international landscape like huge land mines waiting to be detonated by an unanticipated pressure. All these wars satisfied the military's political masters—in itself, a scathing critique of U.S. politicians and their brainpower—and were, for the most part, dazzling displays of what America's high-tech-armed professional soldiers can do. They were, simultaneously, glaring examples of the careerism and moral cowardice that appear endemic in our general officer corps.

While U.S. general officers have resigned since 1990 for personal reasons, misbehavior, and—most often—lucrative defense-industry jobs, I recall no general resigning because he recognized the surefire failure, and ultimately larger body count, of trying to wage quick, casualty-free wars. Now, U.S. military academies are proud of the quality instruction in military history provided their students, and each service maintains a required-reading list for serving officers that is lengthy, covers military history from all eras, includes economic, social, and political history, and is updated with new works by leading military historians. We live, moreover, in something of a golden age of military history, with scholars like John Keegan, Victor H. Davis, Stephen W. Sears, Donald Kagan, Williamson Murray, Gordon Rhea, James M. MacPherson, Niall Ferguson, and others writing academic and popular military histories that are accessible to soldiers, academics, civil servants, politicians, and the reading public. If U.S. generals did their student reading, read their service's book list, and browsed Borders' shelves, they would not find serious studies arguing that quick, nearly bloodless wars can be planned and counted on to deliver total victory. Some wars turn out that way, but only a fool counts on achieving total victory in such a manner. Our military leaders know this, but the media do not tell of a U.S. general who resigned to publicly warn America that it has been engaged in a decade of military fecklessness, years that have left behind inevitable conflagrations that will consume more money and blood. If this is not evidence of widespread moral cowardice, I cannot imagine what it is.

Take just one aspect of the recent wars in Afghanistan and Iraq, that of speed. It is true that speed always has held a priority position in the American way of war. The concept of speed in the U.S. war-fighting canon long has involved maneuvering to hit enemy forces at points where U.S. forces could gain superiority, or to outflank the enemy and roll up his line, attack him from the rear, or drive him from a fixed position into the open to be defeated, or isolate him from his supply line and force surrender. Nathaniel Greene used rapid hit-and-run tactics during our revolution; Winfield Scott carefully chose his points of attack in the Mexican war; Jackson, Sherman, Lee, Bedford Forrest, and Grant all prized speed and maneuver in our civil war; and George Patton—perhaps America's master of speed in war-making—used speed and maneuver to the utmost in his slashing, destructive offensives in North Africa, Sicily, and Western Europe. Speed and maneuver in all these cases, however, was meant not only to end the war quickly, but as the means through which to wear out, kill, demoralize, and destroy the enemy's army, be that army British, Mexican, Yankee, Confederate, or German.

Each of these American soldiers knew—by training, intuition, or both—that war is a last resort and that once begun it is immoral and unnecessarily costly not to destroy the enemy and end the war as soon as possible. Damage is to be inflicted to the degree needed to ensure the enemy does not pose a military threat—this by measuring destruction on his order-of-battle—and that he no longer has the will, resources, or infrastructure to resist. Grant and Sherman, for example, would have recognized the uselessness of occupying Afghan cities without destroying the Taleban and al Qaeda, just as they knew victory was not won if Union armies occupied Richmond, Charleston, and Atlanta without destroying the rebel armies of Northern Virginia and Tennessee.

Although crude and surely abhorrent to our elites' politically correct ears, the words of Admiral William Halsey, USN, perhaps best depict the recipe for winning a war that has endured since antiquity and will endure until Gabriel's trumpet sounds. Charged with leading part of the 1941–1945 U.S. war against Imperial Japan, Halsey described the means to victory as the will to "kill Japs, kill Japs, kill more Japs" and to keep killing them until "Japanese is spoken only in hell."[40] Caesar, Alexander, Wellington, Lee, Grant, Rommel, Eisenhower, Patton and most of the West's great captains would have spoken with more style and sophistication, but the substance of their remarks would have been the same.

Speed for the sake of unambiguous victory has been America's way, not speed for the sake of a quick war that leaves the enemy unbeaten and low casualties on each side. This is a basic lesson of military history since Alexander, one, moreover, taught in our military academies, war colleges, and on staff rides that analyze the dazzling speed and maneuvering of Jackson's divisions in the Shenandoah Valley and at Chancellorsville. It is drummed into the heads of U.S. officers and becomes their default response when asked to define victory. For this reason, it is stunning that no U.S. general officer has had the moral courage to resign and speak publicly about the dangers accumulating from the type of war America has fought since the Iraq war of 1991. Our two current half-fought wars—Iraq and Afghanistan—are good examples of what happens when generals silently accept their civilian leaders' "political" requirements for war-fighting.

AFGHANISTAN

In a country surrounded by contiguous safe havens—Iran, Tajikistan, Turkmenistan, Pakistan, and Uzbekistan—the U.S. military closed no borders before starting the U.S.-led coalition's north-to-south offensive. As a result, the coalition's hammer had no anvil to strike. We pushed south and the enemy either went home to rural villages or crossed one of the open borders to safety. Only in mid-2003—twenty months late— did U.S. forces begin a modest effort to seal part of the Afghanistan–Pakistan border. Al Qaeda and the Taleban, moreover, were not decisively beaten and did not surrender; they merely dispersed to regroup and refit.

How much danger is in this failure? Well, the Taleban's order-of-battle was reported to have been near fifty thousand rifles on 1 October

2001.[41] If generous to the point of being unrealistic, we can assert that U.S.-led forces killed 20 percent of the total. Using this formula, forty thousand armed and often veteran Taleban insurgents were left to fight another day. Due to our obsession with a rapid start-to-finish war and unwillingness to kill or risk being killed, we closed no borders—an admittedly hard and bloody task—and let most Taleban fighters escape. Then, in that debacle's aftermath, we put a force in Kabul large enough—perhaps—to control the city but not a nation the size of Texas. We also cannot estimate al Qaeda's postwar manpower because the U.S. intelligence community did not keep a prewar order-of-battle for the group—another failure caused by the semantic confusion between "terrorist group" and "insurgent organization"—and so there is nothing against which to measure progress. A British study claims al Qaeda had about ten thousand fighters in Afghanistan at the start of the war, which means it might still field eight thousand fighters if we apply the same overly generous attrition rate used for the Taleban. [42] There is, of course, no way to count the volunteers who have joined the Taleban or al Qaeda since 2001; indeed, U.S. leaders detailing successes against the groups—x number of Taleban fighters killed; y number of al Qaeda chiefs captured—speak as if the groups are being reduced from a known and fixed base. In so speaking, they show little attention has been paid to the certainty that the U.S. invasions and occupations of Afghanistan and Iraq have prompted a steady flow of veteran fighters and untrained recruits to the groups. Ignoring reality, Secretary Rumsfeld—with the Taleban and al Qaeda intact, Karzai's writ fading, and guerrilla warfare flaring—went to Kabul in May, 2003 to declare victory. Mr. Rumsfeld, to be charitable, is ill-informed; America's Afghan war is still in its infancy.

IRAQ

With admirable speed, adoring media, and little killing, U.S. forces moved from Kuwait to Baghdad in less than a month. Soon after, on 9 April 2003, the president declared that the U.S. mission to liberate Iraq was complete. As in Afghanistan, however, there is more to the story, and the more again suggests U.S. generals are all too willing to silently obey their political masters' demand for fast, nearly bloodless war.

The media-academic consensus was that the Iraqi regime had about half a million men under arms when the war began.[43] As in Afghanistan, let us be too generous and assume the U.S.-led coalition killed 20 percent of the total. The resulting possibility is that there are still four-hundred-thousand trained or semi-trained Iraqis who went—really, were sent—home with their arms and no job, and are now waiting to see how events play out, perhaps ready to fight again in a religious or ethnic cause. And Iraq offers yet another example of the apparently insurmountable challenge posed to U.S. military leaders by the concept of borders. This time out, they failed to seal Iraq's borders with Iran, Syria, Jordan, Turkey, Kuwait, and Saudi Arabia. The issue here was not preventing egress from Iraq, but rather stopping the entry of jihadists from across the Muslim world bent on killing coalition soldiers and officials and those Iraqis collaborating with them. Notwithstanding claims of surprise by U.S. political and military leaders, the covey of frothing-at-the-mouth Iraq experts led by a former director of central intelligence, and some journalists, the surge of Islamist fighters into Iraq was easy to predict. The strength of Islam among Iraqi Shia and Sunnis was known—religion was a refuge from Saddam—and we were aware of fatwas ordering a defensive jihad against the U.S.-led invaders of Iraq that rivaled or exceeded in virulence those greeting the 1979 Soviet invasion of Afghanistan. In short, only a dunce or a man ready to be silent to protect his career could have failed to know the U.S.-led occupation of Iraq would create a "mujahideen magnet" more powerful than Moscow created in Afghanistan.

Having created the bloody and humiliating experience the world now watches on CNN, *Al-Jazirah*, and the BBC, one might think the point has been reached where at least one U.S. general would quit and speak out to say that the post-1991 U.S. way of war is a sham causing more instability than it prevents and costing more American lives than it saves. Not so. As I write, our generals have accepted their civilian leaders' decision to supply Mongolian troops in Iraq and to support their campaign to press India into contributing military units to help occupy Iraq. This thinking is inexplicable for any adult with a basic knowledge of Islam and world military history, and is even less possible to explain for, say, a West Pointer. Why would we seek Mongolian troops for occupation duty in Iraq? In Islamic history there are few more hated figures than the Mongol general Hulagu—Genghis Khan's grandson—who in 1258 sacked Baghdad, killed eight-hundred-thousand Muslims, and ended the city's status as the Arab world's largest urban center. On several occasions, bin Laden has described the United States as the "Hulagu" of the age, an allusion familiar to all his Muslim listeners.[44] Next, why would we think that sending polytheist Indian troops to Muslim Iraq—in Islam polytheism a worse offense to God than Christianity or Judaism—would increase security there? Is no one in U.S. officialdom aware of the Indian Army's decades-long record of savagery toward Muslims in Kashmir, or of the blind eye turned by Indian security forces to the early 2002 killing of almost two thousand Muslims by Hindu fundamentalists in Gujarat State? Are we seeking Indian help because they are experienced and reliable Muslim killers? That question is facetious, but the Islamists would portray Indian deployment in that way—and our leaders know they would. Not even in his most graphic visions and passionate prayers could bin Laden imagine his enemy trying to create such a situation. He must be eager for the chance to credibly reassert his claim that Christian and Hindu forces have joined in Iraq to suppress Islam, kill Muslims, and "establish a huge Jewish superstate (Greater Israel) that will include the whole of Palestine; parts of Iraq, Egypt, Syria, Lebanon, and Jordan; and a huge area from the land of the Two Holy Sanctuaries [Saudi Arabia]."[45] In Iraq, as in Afghanistan, our war is only beginning.

Now the question may, indeed must, arise as to whether U.S. general officers can be blamed for implementing their political masters' orders. The answer, of course, is no, they are legally obligated to obey. They can and must, however, be chastised for retaining their posts, supporting policies, and executing orders they know from several millennia of military history will produce more, not less, danger to their nation. "I was only following orders" is neither a good enough nor an honorable defense. It also is not good enough to keep inferring that only those who have been in the military can criticize military policy and operations, which now seems to be the default response to criticism by many in the Department of Defense. Even such a straight shooter as retired Lieutenant Colonel Ralph Peters has shown disregard for critics of the military who have "never laced up a combat boot" and behave as "the lions of the green room."[46] The inference has an obvious twofold purpose—to implicitly denigrate the questioner by impugning his or her bravery or patriotism, and to explicitly suggest that if the questioner has not served in the military, he or she has no experience on which to base pertinent questions. It is appalling to see how well this despicable tactic works to put questioners on the defensive. Those in the military who adopt this posture display, as in many other aspects of our fight against bin Laden, a profound ignorance of American history. For most of the nation's existence, there have been relatively few Americans who served in the country's military, both because America's standing professional army was minuscule until after World War II and because our Founding Fathers passed to us their belief that standing armies are a ruinous expense and a deadly threat to republican government. As Ralph Peters recalled for his countrymen, "The American tradition has been to despise and distrust the military. Our founding fathers debated and debated again the wisdom of maintaining a standing army of even a few battalions. . . . Soldiers were regarded as incapable do-nothings with their snouts in the national trough."[47] Only postwar conscription made "military experience" common for Americans and for some of today's U.S. politicians.

Because conscription ended in 1973, we now are approaching the last of the huge pool of Americans, and its subset of American politicians, who served in the military. As these men and women become less numerous, it will become ever easier for those veterans still in public life to use the facile dodge outlined above. The knowledge to ask pertinent questions of military leaders and militarily experienced politicians does require some reading and study, but it is not beyond the average citizen's ability to acquire and digest books, History Channel programs, university courses, and tours of our splendid national military parks. And it is worth remembering that for much of our history, America's survival depended on the conscripted citizen's ability to learn the military trade well and quickly enough to defeat the enemy. It was, after all, the decidedly unmilitary Abraham Lincoln who taught that eminent moral coward from West Point, George B. McClellan, that the path to victory lay in destroying the Army of Northern Virginia and not in capturing Richmond.

The questions to be asked of U.S. generals do not focus on their professional military skills or knowledge but on their integrity and moral courage. Today's U.S. general officers are the best-trained and -educated on earth; they know military history. And so they also know that the wars fought since 1991 have not been won. At best, they temporarily have suppressed problems that will rise again to cost America more blood and money. Bin Laden, because of the size, geographical reach, and lethality of his organization and its allies, may yet prompt at least one U.S. general to resign—if that occurs, my bet is the resignee will be a female U.S. Marine—and alert the citizenry that our war against the Islamists has been a shell game staged by those who think that by capturing al Qaeda leaders and hoping the 11 September attacks were one-off events, America will crush the Islamists' military capabilities and end their threat. Such a resignation would be the essential first step on the road to victory.

G-Men and Lawyers

Since 1945, America has come to view domestic and foreign affairs through a severely legalistic lens. And as American society becomes more litigious, we have in the last quarter century tried to inflict this probably fatal form of progressive sclerosis on the planet—apparently we are loath to suffer alone. Indeed, our ongoing conduct of a foreign policy meant to impose U.S. legal standards abroad—the FBI has forty-plus offices and training schools overseas—has become a new, more-oppressive-to-the-locals version of what Kipling called carrying the "white man's burden." In essence, America has created a twenty-first-century imperial fleet fueled by judicial decisions marking "unprecedented expansion of federal jurisdiction over crimes allegedly committed on foreign soil."[48] It is crewed by judges, prosecutors, and FBI officers who demand precise, legally untainted data before acting. When operating abroad, they resemble hectoring, white-skinned schoolmasters who have no respect for local law and are bent on teaching the world's legally unwashed how to live by the U.S. Code.

Instead of "painting the map red" as did Britain's imperial elite, America's elites use U.S. law—to paraphrase the inane Woodrow Wilson—to "teach the world to make good laws." A noted Harvard professor spoke for those eager to wage gavel-powered war, arguing that "[t]he most powerful weapon against terrorists is our commitment to the rule of law. We must use courts to make clear that terrorism is a criminal act, not jihad, not heroism, not holy war. And then we must not make martyrs of murderers."[49] The professor does not say who the courts would convince that jihad is a crime—Americans maybe, Muslims never—and also does not say how courts will stop attacks. Helpfully, however, a colleague of hers has said, "If alleged terrorists are planning future attacks, these attacks can be uncovered and thwarted while law enforcement officials gather evidence."[50] You see, there is nothing to it.

The legalistic lens America uses to deal with the world causes confusion about what we are doing, and what we need to do, against bin Laden: Are we waging war, or hot on the trail of Thelma and Louise? As I said, we are predisposed by two-plus centuries of history to look for law-enforcement solutions to problems. In bin Laden's case, this predisposition is encouraged by our leaders' insistence that bin Laden means to destroy our freedom, liberties, and democracy. If that is what bin Laden intends, it is only natural we seek protection from the FBI and the Justice Department. Here is more evidence of the danger that lies in our elites' inability or refusal to recognize bin Laden's goals and to respond effectively, rather than in ways they—and we—find intellectually comfortable. "Five years of investigation and trials and appeals, as after the first World Trade Center [attack in 1993], deter nobody," William Safire wrote on 12 September 2001[51], and yet the chase-and-arrest technique still holds sway, only now the world's most powerful military is packing the handcuffs.

The overseas role of the Department of Justice (DOJ) and the FBI in the war on bin Laden, as equal partners with U.S. intelligence and the U.S. military, has slowed the progress and dulled the edge of anti-al Qaeda efforts in several ways. First, the participation and prominence of the FBI paints America's counter–bin Laden campaign with too much law-enforcement color. This is natural enough. There is little more congenial to American thought than the Texas Rangers' formula of "chase 'em, catch 'em, and try, convict, and hang 'em." The FBI's high-profile role therefore feeds the legalistic predisposition of U.S. political leaders, civil servants, and citizens, and blurs the reality that the Islamists cannot be beaten by arresting one mujahid at a time. It is hard for Americans to think that jailing an enemy would weaken national security, but that is the case when we equate jailing with winning. It is always worth locking up a bad guy; the danger lies in believing that incarcerations are deathblows to al Qaeda in the way they are to criminal groups. For the U.S. military, moreover, the law-enforcement focus of U.S. policy makers has prevented killing enough of America's enemies, especially since 11 September. In early 2002, Professor R.K. Betts wrote a brilliant essay in the *Political Science Quarterly* decrying the threat to national security posed by the constraints of a too-legalistic foreign policy. "In recent decades," Betts warned, "the march of liberal legalism has delegitimized tactics and brutalities that once were accepted, but this delegitimization has occurred only in context of fundamental security and dominance of the Western powers, not in a situation where they felt under supreme threat. In a situation of that sort, it is foolhardy to assume that American strategy would never return to tactics like those used against Japanese and German civilians."[52] Notwithstanding Professor Betts's commonsense argument, however, the truth is that those who bet on what he called a "foolhardy" assumption would have won all the marbles, based on U.S. strategy against al Qaeda thus far.

U.S. law enforcement activity overseas also has dulled U.S. intelligence operations against al Qaeda, especially those of the CIA. For this there are two main reasons. First, the missions of the two organizations are fundamentally incompatible. At the most basic level, the FBI is meant to enforce U.S. law, and most of its work is done after the fact; that is, it solves crimes and brings criminals to justice. The CIA, on the other hand, is authorized to break foreign law to gather information that helps defend the United States. Both organizations gather data, but the FBI does so according to strict regulations that allow it to be used in court. CIA information, however, is best acquired clandestinely—by physical or electronic theft, or by persuading a foreigner to commit treason—and is most useful when the originating country or group does not know it has been collected. These are critical differences in statutory authority and mission, and they explain why the FBI is a domestic service and the CIA is foreign-focused and operates in the United States only in narrow, well-scrutinized parameters. This is as it should be.

There are areas where the two organizations can cooperate against al Qaeda, but they are at the margin and are, most often, instances where the CIA can supply actionable data, acquired abroad, on individuals entering or planning activities in the United States. This is not a criticism of the FBI; it is simply reality. At home, the FBI operates within U.S. law, and abroad within host-country law; the CIA follows U.S. law but is authorized to collect intelligence abroad in one way or another. While we want a world where sheep lay with wolves, such is not yet the case, and in most ways the FBI's *modus operandi* overseas is like a lamb politely asking for information from wolves. This dilemma is deepened by the FBI's naive faith that all law-enforcement officers belong to the same guild, one that crosses cultures, legal systems, and languages. "Once you get on the ground with a fellow law enforcement person," a senior FBI officer said while working on an al Qaeda attack overseas, "you may have a language barrier but you have the same purpose. It becomes a very positive and reciprocal experience as trust is gained on both sides."[53] This is not so. Frankly, America does not have many friends in its war on bin Laden, and none are willing to share all they hold on al Qaeda. This is another fact of life, and while U.S. officials can use the data acquired abroad by the FBI, the intelligence vital to national defense will not be given us in a liaison relationship with foreign intelligence or police services. That information must be stolen or acquired from a traitor by the CIA.

This said, I would add that cooperation among the FBI, DOJ, and CIA—when each operates in its area of responsibility—can contribute to the war on bin Laden, al Qaeda, and militant Islam. In the 1990s, for example, cooperation among this troika yielded substantive, often dramatic results and put several key bin Laden lieutenants, operatives, and supporters in prison for life. Among these figures are Ali Mohammed, Mamdouh Mahmoud Salim, Ramzi Ahmed Yousef, Wali Khan Amin Shah, and Wadih al-Hage. This is an impressive list, and it is essential to lock up every al Qaeda-related individual we can. These men ended up in U.S. prisons largely based on CIA-acquired intelligence that, in turn, FBI and DOJ used to develop cases that won guilty verdicts. The process of arrest and conviction is a superb tactical tool against al Qaeda, but not a war winner. It is on this point that U.S. policy has gone astray.

On too many occasions, U.S. officials and politicians—a few sincerely—have spoken as if al Qaeda can be beaten by law-enforcement activities. When the U.S. attorney for the Southern District of New York said in late 1998 that bin Laden's indictment "is an important step forward in our fight against terrorism. It sends a message that no terrorist can flout our laws and murder innocent civilians," and when the U.S. attorney general added that "those responsible for these brutal and cowardly acts . . . will be brought to justice," each reflected the skill and aggressiveness that characterize the handling of domestic criminals by the FBI and DOJ. Each also expressed this confidence because of the signal legal victories against al Qaeda scored by the courageous U.S. attorneys in the Southern District of New York. And when a senior State Department officer breathed easier after al Qaeda was banned under U.S. law because "now we have a legal basis to move against them," he gave a solid example of America's current "clear the decks, we're ready to indict" approach to national security.[54] So did Attorney General John Ashcroft when he cited the capture of two al Qaeda fighters as proof that, "[w]e are winning the war on terrorism."[55]

By making too much of law-enforcement successes, U.S. leaders obscure the fact that such successes do not alter the strategic balance in the U.S.–al Qaeda war and that they cannot be victory's engine. In most ways, as Steven Emerson and Daniel Pipes have written, trials do "almost nothing to enhance the safety of Americans" but blind them to threats by giving "an illusion of invulnerability . . . and a sense of protected isolation."[56] Hoorah-ing over court victories also confuses the U.S. policy debate on how to deal with al Qaeda; as Charles Krauthammer has said, "[O]ur addiction to trials infects and distorts our foreign policy."[57] This occurs at times due to good intentions and at others for ignoble reasons. Some policy makers, for example, genuinely believe the legal route is proper against bin Laden and therefore send unmerited funding into that area. For the less sincere, the legal track postpones admittedly hard decisions on anti-al Qaeda actions putting U.S. soldiers and prestige in harm's way. The aim of criminalizing terrorism and "making the Department of Justice and the FBI the lead counterterrorist agencies," R.M. Gerecht wrote in the *Weekly Standard*, was to secure "more foreign policy wiggle room: we can blink in the face of a foreign threat and pretend we didn't."[58] And, sadly, there are always senior executive-branch bureaucrats who favor the legal track because it gets them fifteen minutes on CNN.

Beyond misleading Americans and confusing U.S. foreign policy, Washington's obsession with overseas law-enforcement activity against al Qaeda weakens our enemies' perception of U.S. seriousness and the threat it poses to them. The conclusion Americans can bank on is that the bin Laden–incited jihad cannot be defeated, deterred, or worried—though it will be amused—by hearing Washington piously warn that the end of the jihad road is trial and prison. Notwithstanding the self-deluding assertion by a senior U.S. official that al Qaeda leaders are "worried stiff . . . that the little messenger on a mule is going to come over the hill at any moment and tell them another [al Qaeda] chapter has gone away," the threat of jail has no impact on the Islamists.[59] Indeed, al Qaeda documents and statements clearly tell the group's fighters that they have only two destinations: martyrdom or a U.S. prison, and each is equally pleasing to God. "In other words . . ." explained al Qaeda spokesman Abd-al-Rahman al-Rashid in 2002, "al Qaeda youths understand very well that either 'martyrdom' or captivity awaits them in their 'jihad.'"[60] Bin Laden and his men are motivated by religion, and the jailing of al Qaeda fighters under U.S. law will have the same impact on Islamism as did the resolute application of Roman law on the rise of Christianity—that is, to stimulate the flow of militant converts, contributions, and prayers to al Qaeda's banner.

Bin Laden's foes must always recall that he believes he is abiding by the spirit and letter of the law—as Anglo-Saxons might say—revealed by Allah and explained by His prophet. For Muslims, bin Laden said in 1999, "The only accused is he who disobeyed the command of Allah, has left the way of the Prophet, and has done away with the tenets of its [sic: "his"?] religion. . . . Law is not what man has made. Law is that which Allah has given."[61] In this era of Islamic history, bin Laden argues, each Muslim must fight the crusaders who are attacking his faith, brethren, and land. "In our religion," bin Laden says, "we believe that Allah created us to worship him. Allah is the one who created us and blessed us with His religion, and orders us to carry out the holy struggle 'jihad' to raise the word of Allah above the word of unbelievers."[62]

Bin Laden, then, is obeying God's law and abiding by the Prophet's warning that "people who see an unjust act and do nothing are about to be punished by God." It is thus most unlikely that bin Laden, al-Zawahiri, or their colleagues, as they sit near the hearth on wintry nights sipping tea and munching roast goat, will ponder whether to end the jihad because a few senior fighters have been killed or captured, or because they themselves are indicted in New York and, if caught, might only have public defenders. The prospect of a permanent cell in the Manhattan Metropolitan Correctional Center, Lewisburg, or a converted ICBM silo finds no space in eyes focused on winning eternal paradise. "As far as putting my name on the [FBI's] list of ten most wanted accused," bin Laden said, "I can only say that we should not be afraid of U.S. clutches but of the clutches of God. The United States is mortal and God is immortal. If we recognize the difference between mortal and immortal, it will not be difficult to succeed in the world hereafter."[63] If nothing else, bin Laden's words should make Americans heed Professor Ruth Wedgewood's advice. "We cannot effectively counter [bin Laden]," Wedgewood wrote, "if we limit ourselves to the tools of law enforcement. Americans have a deep faith in the power of the law. But the water's edge should mark the boundary of our legal romanticism."[64]

An apt question here is: if the missions of U.S. law enforcement and U.S. intelligence in the war on al Qaeda are compatible only at the margins, why do we insist on full cooperation between the two? The answer again is moral cowardice. By 1990, the concept contained in the phrase "intelligence community cooperation" had become a sacred mantra, not a difficult long-term goal. Like diversity and multiculturalism, "intelligence community cooperation" is an ideology; it also is the undefined, unquestioned watchword for Congress, the executive branch, and the civil service. The concept's forced implementation bred vast interagency acrimony—especially in the counterterrorism field— and less, not more, cooperation. Nonetheless, no agency would cite the refusal of others to cooperate, and all agreed that no such gripe reach Congress. Intelligence-community careers were made by ensuring Congress heard no evil and were ruined by citing the national security risks inherent in falsely claiming effective cooperation.

Thus, when the war on al Qaeda intensified in the 1990s, U.S. intelligence officials routinely misled congressional committees, staffers, and other U.S. officials whenever they said there was "seamless cooperation"—another deceptive IC buzzword—between the FBI and CIA. Leaving aside for now the question of ill intent, the oft-proclaimed CIA–FBI seamless cooperation was a lie because of a simple fact: The FBI, three decades into the computer age, did not—and does not—have computers that ensure quick, secure, and reliable communication inside the Bureau, let alone among the FBI, the CIA, and other agencies. In my own experience, there were scores of times my agency sent an electronic document to the FBI and immediately followed with a telephone call saying it was en route. Frequently, we would get a return call from the FBI saying our message could not be found and asking that we securely fax another copy. By the late 1990s, hard copies of documents were being hand-carried to the FBI because its message handling system was so unreliable. Needless to say, intelligence sent to the FBI via fax or courier never got into a retrievable electronic database, a fact that suggests where fault lies on the issue of watch-listing al Qaeda fighters before 11 September. And, on the flip side, the FBI's lack of a system to retrieve information for its own use, or to share with other agencies, suggests another fruitful area for post-11 September investigation.

The question of illl intent, unfortunately, must be addressed, and not only to find out why the FBI lacks a reliable computer system. More important, and based on my experience, I would say there was ill intent and negligence by senior FBI officers since major operations against bin Laden began in 1996.

The FBI effort against bin Laden that I saw daily from 1996 to 1999 focused on overseas, not U.S., operations. The FBI officers I worked with—some of whom I managed—were ordered by their superiors to stay side-by-side with my agency in its work abroad, this in line with FBI Director Freeh's passion to create FBI offices and academies overseas. Only one of these FBI officers—a very decent and courageous Irishman—did his best to run down U.S.–based al Qaeda leads provided by my service; the others were most interested in traveling with my officers, particularly on trips to Western Europe. And, on one occasion, a fine FBI analyst, after preparing for a year to exploit an overseas operation, was recalled to FBI headquarters days before its culmination so her expertise could be monopolized there. More important, few of my agency's requests for information were answered by the FBI—a fact easily documented—and, as we have learned, few of the domestic leads passed to the FBI's New York office, which ran FBI al Qaeda operations, were sent to other FBI offices for exploitation. Useless computers, obsessive focus on overseas operations, aggrandizement of self and institution, and disregard of al Qaeda leads in the United States—these failures must be attributed to deliberate decisions by senior FBI officers, living, retired, and dead. A more appalling case of negligence, however, lies in the moral cowardice of my own agency's leaders, men who were repeatedly briefed on the problems but did not try to correct them. They then compounded this dereliction by falsely assuring policy makers and congressional overseers that cooperation was "seamless." Of such things are made the events of 11 September 2001.

After punishing those who merit it, we must fix the problems and, I think, fix the lies in using common sense to decide what "intelligence community cooperation" will mean and in adopting reasonable expectations about what it can produce. As I said, there is room for cooperation among the FBI, DOJ, and U.S. intelligence, and such cooperation is essential to U.S. security. I would argue that the goal must be to make the FBI as effective as possible at destroying the U.S. presence of al Qaeda and its allies. We are years behind the curve on this and must get moving. I have seen the excellence of FBI officers when they work domestic issues and exploit long-standing cooperation with state and local law enforcement. It was said "Let Reagan be Reagan" when that great and good man was president, and the key here is to let the FBI and its police allies across America do things at which they excel and not insist they do things—especially, operations overseas—for which they are unsuited by mission, structure, training, and attitude. The FBI could make America safer by bringing home much of its overseas presence and stop dispatching scores of agents to overseas bombings. Even if Americans are killed abroad, and even if the FBI solves the case, U.S. domestic security is not improved. For America to be as safe as possible, the FBI must be freed of Judge Freeh's legacy of bloated overseas ambitions.

Leaks: Hubris or Treason?

Leaking classified intelligence to journalists, even the most highly classified, has long been common among senior U.S. government officials, politicians, civil servants, and senior military officers. From the vantage point of the author's career, there has been a marked acceleration in such leaking over the past decade, with the *Washington Times* being the leading acquirer of such data from its obviously high-level federal government contacts. That it does so whether the administration is Republican or Democratic, moreover, suggests it has strong ties to senior civil servants and military officers immune to electoral vagaries—and, apparently, the tug of conscience. Beyond the growing volume of leaks, there has been a sharp increase in leaking data that has no clear purpose in terms of shaping U.S. domestic or foreign policies but seems rather a form of bragging to the world and the enemy about what we know and how we know it.

Overall, there is an accelerating tendency to leak for leaking's sake, spurred by motives ranging from juvenile (officials currying favor with reporters), to ignorant (the post-11 September influx of federal, state, and local agencies unaccustomed to using classified data), to malicious (those outvoted in the cabinet, sub-cabinet, or National Security Council who decide to pursue a personal agenda and do not care about compromising sources and methods, thereby costing America intelligence vital to its defense and endangering the lives of the assets supplying the information). Too few leakers are mindful that by clandestinely providing privileged information to America, non-U.S. human sources are betraying their country or cause. While some do so just for money, others commit the life-risking act of treason because they believe America is, as Mr. Lincoln said, the last, best hope of man for self-government. Whatever the leaker's motivation, his or her resolve is strengthened by knowing that few, if any, senior U.S. officials are prosecuted or dismissed for the crime of leaking classified data. In twenty-plus years in the intelligence community, I have seen no senior official—appointee, civil servant, or military officer—cashiered for leaking secrets. Only junior officers and appointees without political clout are removed, and then but rarely. And this notwithstanding the fact that senior-level leakers are not too hard to identify; limited distribution of sensitive intelligence makes the pool of potential leakers relatively small.

Leaks are a major factor limiting the effectiveness of U.S. efforts to defeat Osama bin Laden, *et al.* The first serious leak about al Qaeda was in the *Washington Times* after the 20 August 1998 U.S. cruise missile attack on al Qaeda camps near Khowst, Afghanistan. The attack was in response to the bombing of our embassies in Kenya and Tanzania thirteen days earlier. In the 24 August *Times* article, "senior" U.S.

Department of Defense officials revealed that precise U.S. targeting of the camps was based on electronically intercepting bin Laden's conversations. "In the two weeks following the Aug. 7 attacks against the U.S. embassies in Kenya and Tanzania," Ernest Blazar wrote in his "Inside the Ring" column, "the United States reaped an intelligence bonanza from intercepted terrorists' radio and telephone calls." The senior leakers told Blazar they had not leaked sooner because "it was hoped that terrorists would again use their compromised networks to rally in the wake of the Tomahawk [cruise missile] attacks. Said one U.S. official: 'We want to see who is still using the same cell phone numbers.'"[65] Apparently these genius leakers had decided it was time to make sure the terrorists would not use the phone again. Well, as night follows day, the intelligence community lost this priceless advantage when bin Laden and his men stopped using the phones. A direct trail leads from the leak that caused the loss of access to bin Laden's planning conversations to the surprise attack on 11 September 2001. This leak, moreover, initiated a series of al Qaeda leaks that remains in full spate.

Because of such dastardly leaks, the United States cannot fully exploit its clandestine service's numerous, often astounding captures of senior al Qaeda fighters. From the capture of Abu Zubaydah in March 2002 to that of Khalid bin Attash in March 2003, word of the arrests has been leaked by senior U.S. officials within days, and often hours, of their occurrence. In part, the leaks are simply more evidence of the rivalry raging among the main components of the U.S. intelligence community, each trying to win the lead role in the anti-al Qaeda war and, with it, the largest cut of swag from the ever-growing terrorism budget. Based on my experience working against bin Laden for almost a decade, I can say with confidence that the most damaging leaks about al Qaeda come from the FBI, the Department of Defense, and the White House. A reliable rule of thumb for the reader is that the federal agencies who have done least to protect America from al Qaeda leak the most to take credit for others' work and disguise their years of failure. Indeed, when a history of the U.S. war with bin Laden is written, Americans will learn not only that their clandestine service scored all the major victories against al Qaeda, but that it did so in an environment where other intelligence-community agencies withheld support and were deliberately obstructive. The country-be-damned leaks by these agencies are meant to deny credit to the clandestine service, which neither defends itself nor notes its successes in public.

More dangerous than intra-bureaucracy war, however, is the

obtuseness of our elites. The greatest single motivation behind the flood of leaks, I would contend, is the inability of U.S. leaders—political, military, intelligence, and diplomatic—and much of the country's academic and media elites to give bin Laden's threat steady, serious attention. Yes, there have been huge increases in counterterrorism funding. Yes, there has been dramatic growth in technical and human collection against al Qaeda and its allies. Yes, the number of people working on terrorism has been greatly augmented, though the augmentees are inexperienced and will be of little use for years until they learn the issue from a small corps of nearly worn-out veterans. Yes, America's leaders talk stridently of fighting the "war on terrorism" and defeating the "devastating" threat al Qaeda poses to the "Homeland." Yes, the Department of Justice is taking protective domestic actions, ones that sadly appear to restrict some civil liberties in the name of national security.

The potential of the new resources, people, laws, and supportive rhetoric given to the intelligence community is, unfortunately, being sapped in a losing battle against Washington's corps of leakers. Notwithstanding improved intelligence and the clandestine service's heroics, the media landscape is still littered by classified disclosures. Senior U.S. officials, for example, tell *USA Today* that "intercepts by the National Security Agency" aided the capture of Khalid Shaykh Mohammed, planner of the 11 September attacks[66]; they tell the *Washington Post* that captured al Qaeda fighter and almost-suicide pilot Ramzi bin al-Shibh "is providing useful information" that will help capture others[67]; they tell the *New York Times* that the monitoring of telephone conversations helped to derail sabotage plans against ARAMCO facilities in Saudi Arabia[68]; they describe the contents of a "topsecret Memorandum of Notification" to the *New Yorker* [69]; and they tell the *Chicago Tribune* how intercepted communications allowed the CIA's armed-UAV—called "Predator"—to attack and kill six important al Qaeda members in Yemen.[70] These are just a few examples and not the most grievous. The list could go on and fill a chapter of its own. With each leak our post-11 September effort against al Qaeda is undercut, and the viability of the most lethal current threat to U.S. national security is prolonged.

Then there is Bob Woodward's book, *Bush at War*, which saps the faith of intelligence officers in the integrity of their leaders and institutions. A newly hired U.S. intelligence officer is inculcated with many beliefs peculiar to his trade. Prominent among them is one that identifies the media as the enemy, miscreants who ferret out and publish secrets, thereby compromising sources and methods and risking lives of assets. "[Journalists] are the world's gossips," General William T. Sherman wrote in 1875, "and gradually drift to the headquarters of some general who finds it easier to make a reputation at home than with his own corps or division. They are also tempted to prophesy events and state facts which, to an enemy, reveal a purpose in time to guard against it."[71] Sherman's view permeates the lesson taught to new intelligence officers, and in my case held sway until recently. For me, however, a steady erosion in this view began with the leak of the U.S. ability to intercept bin Laden's electronic communications. As similar leaks multiplied over the last years, I came to wonder who is the real culprit, the publisher of the secret or its leaker? While I still think editors of major U.S. publications ought to do more self-censoring in terms of publishing classified data, I am no longer undecided about the enemy. Mr. Woodward's book unarguably documents that the leaker, not the journalist, is the true enemy of U.S. security. Note, for example, his breezy description of the source base for his book, a statement so smoothly matter-of-fact that one tends to forget that those who gave him the information wantonly broke federal law and, to use old-fashioned terms, betrayed a trust and sullied their honor by endangering human and technical sources, the intelligence officers handling the assets, and America's security. "This is an account of President George W. Bush at war during the first 100 days after the September 11, 2001, terrorist attacks," Woodward explained.

> The information I obtained for this book includes contemporaneous notes taken during more than 50 National Security Council and other meetings where the most important decisions were discussed and made. Many direct quotations of the president and the war cabinet members come from these notes. Other personal notes, memos, calendars, written internal chronologies, transcripts and other documents also were the basis for direct quotations and other parts of this story. . . . In addition, I interviewed more than 100 people involved in the decision making and the execution of the war. . . . [72]

After reading Mr. Woodward's *Bush at War*, it seems to me that the U.S. officials who either approved or participated in passing the information—in documents or via interviews—that is the heart of Mr. Woodward's book gave an untold measure of aid and comfort to the enemy. The pages of *Bush at War* are larded with items that appear to be either classified intelligence information or the means of collecting the data, including, for starters, the following half-dozen:

> More recently, [DCI George] Tenet had worried that there would be attacks during the July 4, 2001 celebrations. Though he didn't disclose it to [former U.S. Senator David] Boren, there had been 34 specific communications intercepts among various bin Laden associates that summer making declarations such as "Zero hour is tomorrow" or "Something spectacular is coming."[73]

> One of the most guarded secrets in the CIA was the existence of 30 recruited Afghan agents, operating under the codeword GE/SEN-IORS, who had been paid to track bin Laden around Afghanistan for the last three years. . . . The CIA had daily secure communications with the "Seniors". . . . [74]

> Intelligence monitoring had overheard a number of known bin Laden operatives congratulating each other after the attacks.[75]

> In a private meeting with the emir of Qatar, Bush showed how much he was following the signals intelligence, especially on bin Laden. "We know Osama bin Laden called his mother," Bush told the emir. "One of these days, he'll make the mistake, and we'll get him."[76]

> The Top Secret/Codeword Threat matrix for Monday morning, October 29, was filled with dozens of threats, many new and credible, suggesting an attack in the next week. All kinds of signals intelligence, SIGINT, showed that many known al Qaeda lieutenants or operatives were saying that something big would happen soon.[77]

> Sensitive intelligence showed that the Iranian Revolutionary Guard, the radical element that held the real power [in Iran], was shipping weapons to the Taleban, and that it was reaching out to al Qaeda.[78]

Hubris, arrogance, and semantics are, I think, the reasons for these and most leaks about bin Laden and al Qaeda, although in *Bush at War,* at least one leaker traded classified data for the chance to have Mr. Woodward unwittingly rewrite the "facts" about the U.S. government's pre-11 September bin Laden–related activities. Hubris because U.S. officials appear to believe that America is so superior to our foes that leaking sensitive data and compromising sources and methods for political or other reasons will either escape the enemy's notice—fat chance—or that we will simply find a new way to acquire the data lost when leaks shut the tap. And because our elites are so full of themselves, they think America is invulnerable; cannot imagine the rest of the world does not want to be like us; and believe an American empire in the twenty-first century not only is our destiny, but our duty to mankind, especially to the unwashed, unlettered, undemocratic, unwhite, unshaved, and antifeminist Muslim masses. Arrogance (or is it racism?) because the elites cannot believe a polyglot bunch of Arabs wearing robes, sporting scraggily beards, and squatting around campfires in Afghan deserts and mountains could pose a mortal threat to the United States. The elites and other Americans, in the words of the *Economist*, "still seem to treat the [11 September] attacks as if they were a single, dreadful event, like a natural disaster, or a random crime committed against America. . . ."[79] While covering their behinds with warnings of worse al Qaeda attacks to come, their disbelief in the threat is marked by their readiness to take heroic-rhetoric-adorned military half-measures or less—in refusing, for example, to match their rhetoric with a remorselessly destructive war against al Qaeda—and their fatuous claims that better U.S. public diplomacy will dissuade Muslims from hating and attacking America.

Multiplying the negative impact of hubris and arrogance is a simply described semantic problem that is, at the same time, a complex obstacle to defeating our enemies and protecting America. The U.S. government assumes—I think incorrectly—that it knows what we are facing in al Qaeda and its allies: they are terrorists, roughly the same kind of state-supported terrorists we have faced since the 1970s, only there are more of them. This is not the assumption on which to operate. While it clearly is inaccurate to identify al Qaeda as a nation-state—mostly because it has no fixed address—it is a greater and more damaging error to describe them as terrorists. I have belabored this point before in *Through Our Enemies' Eyes* and earlier in this study, so I will not provide another exposition of the argument. I will say only that we will be defeated as long as we conceive and construct our anti-al Qaeda strategy using the terrorist paradigm. The use of this paradigm ensures a time-consuming, law-enforcement approach, one that focuses on dismantling the group one terrorist at a time, as if we were nicking away at the Mafia. This tack, in turn, leads to U.S. officials telling Americans that the one-capture-at-a-time process is making substantial progress, an assurance that graphically highlights official America's vast underestimate of al Qaeda's resourcefulness, popularity, manpower, durability, and lethality. Continued adherence to the terrorist paradigm will cause our ultimate defeat by bin Laden, and there is no more telling indictment of the intelligence-community's inadequate analysis of bin Laden and Islamist militancy generally than that U.S. policy makers are still using this paradigm. We must abandon this decades-old paradigm and accept the fact—yes, another checkable—that bin Laden and al Qaeda are leading a popular, worldwide, and increasingly powerful Islamic insurgency. An insurgency is fought in a different manner and on a larger scale than terrorism, and wars against a competently led insurgency—and bin Laden has proven himself far more than just competent—last longer, cost more money and lives, and are more steadily brutal than episodic confrontations with terrorists. In an extraordinarily insightful 2002 essay, Richard K. Betts pointed out,

> Apart from the victims of guerrillas, few still identify irregular paramilitary warfare with terrorism (because the latter is illegitimate), but the two activities do overlap a great deal in their operational characteristics. . . . The tactical logic of guerrilla operations resembles that in terrorist attacks: the weaker rebels use stealth and the cover of civilian society to concentrate their striking power against one among many of the stronger enemy's dispersed assets. . . . [80]

So, it may be that stepping back from the victim's perspective, accepting the need for this semantic change, and then making it, could ensure wide recognition that America is at war with a faith-driven force that dwarfs anything that can, with intellectual honesty, be called terrorism. In turn, the sobering impact of this realization might begin to slow the pace of leaks and the damage they cause to national security. The sooner this basically educational endeavor is accomplished, the sooner some of the hubris, arrogance, and institutional rivalries can be set aside to devise a strategy (not revise—current strategy is moribund) with which the United States can prevail. I have faith in this educational effort to reform leakers because there can be only two definitions of leakers. They are either loyal Americans who do not understand the threat the country faces—and so feel free to leak for petty personal or institutional reasons—or they are damnable traitors deliberately giving the enemy aid and comfort. The former are worth reforming, and the latter should be prosecuted to the extent the law allows. The definition of treason, you see, also is a checkable.

Democracy: America's Least Exportable Commodity

In early 1821, a time yet conversant with the Founders' ideas, fears, and principles, a District of Columbia citizens' committee asked the U.S. secretary of state to give a speech on Independence Day. On 4 July, Secretary of State John Quincy Adams stood in the well of the House of Representatives—then used for some public occasions—and made a speech understood to be his personal views, not those of the Monroe administration. As befits a man charged with running his country's foreign affairs, Adams used the speech to outline his ideas about America's proper role in the world. "America," Adams said on the forty-eighth anniversary of independence,

> does not go abroad in search of monsters to destroy. She is the well-wisher to the freedom and independence of all. She is the champion and vindicator only of her own. She will recommend the general cause by the countenance of her voice, and the benignant sympathy of her own example. She well knows that by once enlisting under banners other than her own, were they even the banners of foreign independence, she would involve herself beyond the power of extrication, in all the wars of interest and intrigue, of individual avarice, envy, ambition, which assumed the colors and usurped the standards of freedom. The fundamental maxims of her policy would insensibly change from liberty to force. . . . She might become the dictatress of the world. She would no longer be the ruler of her own spirit.[81]

As America today dwells on the issues of nation-building in Iraq and Afghanistan; regime change in Liberia, Burma, Haiti, and Zimbabwe; and westernizing and secularizing the most strongly held beliefs of the world's 1.3 billion Muslims—from their concept of war, to charitable giving, to school curricula—Secretary Adams's words, his warning really, seem more appropriate and needed in 2003 than they did in 1821. Their pertinence is especially striking amidst the clamor of calls by politicians, preachers, government officials, media experts, and political thinkers for the creation—or, some say, the formalization—of an American Empire, one that should include, a *Washington Post* writer argued, a cabinet-level "Department of Democratic Regime Change" to aid imperial administration.[82] The importance of Adams's words lies in that he was, at the State Department and later as president, one of our great empire builders, settling the nation's grip on much of today's continental United States. While focused on America, he was no isolationist, but a traditional, outward-looking New Englander. Adams believed that economic prosperity and all forms of knowledge were acquired by trading with the world and establishing an ongoing, catholic inter-course—commercial, diplomatic, intellectual, banking, etcetera—with foreign entities, governmental and private. Adams was at home in the world—he may have been our greatest diplomat—and was confident America must and could deal effectively with other nations. Neither was Adams a pacifist. He believed war to be an enduring if terrible fact of human life, and that every country, to survive, had to defend itself militarily when other means failed. He could not abide aggressive war, and in 1846, as a Massachusetts congressman, Adams was the most passionate and eloquent foe of the aggressive war James K. Polk's administration started with Mexico, which, until recently, surely was America's least morally justifiable war.

At this point, the reader may credibly ask what Mr. Adams's thoughts on U.S. foreign policy have to do with America's confronta-tion with Osama bin Laden and militant Islam. Well, I believe Mr. Adams points to two aspects of U.S. policy toward bin Laden that have not been thought through because of factors that again fall into the cat-egories of arrogance and hubris.

First, Adams's warning—that championing the cause of democracy for foreign peoples whose culture, politics, and society America does not understand would entrap the United States abroad "beyond the power of extrication"—ought to give Americans pause in this year of our Lord 2004. There is no more compelling example of Mr. Adams's chickens coming home to roost than the current situation in Afghani-stan, although Iraq will be a challenger. As I explained in Chapter 3, not only was Afghanistan about as non-American a milieu as is possible to conceive when we invaded, but there is little evidence—via our lead-ers' words and actions, or the war's results—that our elected, civil ser-vice, intelligence, diplomatic, or military officials spent any time reading and digesting what can be modestly described as the mass of "check-able" data about Afghanistan our official archives held before crossing the Oxus River from Central Asia.

In late 2001, we were out to kill what Adams called "monsters" abroad, and our leaders led us into that effort knowing nothing about Afghan history, culture, and society, but confident that after the slaying was done, we could rebuild the Afghan economy and infrastructure and install a Western-style democratic and secular political system to replace the Afghans' two-plus-millennia-old tribal traditions. U.S. leaders also expected to nudge aside six-century-old hardy and conservative Islamic faith, which had become more pervasive, militant, and Middle Eastern–like over nearly thirty years of the Afghans' continuous war against communists, atheists, foreign occupiers, and each other. In late 2003, as President Karzai's power constricted to little more than his palace's grounds, and as the Taleban and al Qaeda expand their anti-U.S. coalition to include the most militarily capable "old" mujahideen organizations—Hekmatyar, Khalis, Haqqani, et cetera—and attacks on U.S.-led forces increase, it is easy and proper to be haunted by Adams's belief that by "enlisting under banners other than her own . . . [America] would involve herself in all the wars of interest and intrigue, of individual avarice, envy, and ambition, which assumed the colors and usurped the standards of freedom." Is there anyone in high office in Washington who can explain to Americans what is going on in Afghanistan? Is there even anyone who understands what is going on, given official, palpably false declarations that the Afghan war is over and most of the country is stable? Does it not appear that what Adams called "wars of interest and intrigue" are today in Afghanistan not only beyond our leaders' understanding and control but also "beyond our power of extrication"? Is the only bright spot on the horizon the fact that while Afghanistan is a disaster for America, Iraq may surpass it because there were more checkables about Iraq to review that—like those about Afghanistan—were ignored or suppressed?

The U.S. approach to Afghanistan must be judged one that is suffused with arrogance. Knowing nothing of what we were getting into, we staged a mighty air attack followed by a dainty ground war that limited U.S. casualties but allowed most of the enemy to go home with their guns. We next installed a regime in Kabul with no credible members from the largest Afghan ethnic group—from which Afghan rulers historically come—and assigned it the task of pushing a Westernized political agenda unacceptable to the Afghans' tribal traditions and offensive to Islam. (This will sound familiar to those watching developments in Iraq.) In sum, our policies and actions in Afghanistan have marginally reduced the mobility there of al Qaeda and the Taleban, have reinvigorated a broad, popular, and predictable xenophobia toward foreign occupation—even among the late Masood's men, the bulk of Karzai's military, who will not trade Russian for U.S. masters—and have ensured the United States must soon decide whether to exponentially increase its military presence and wage a destructive nationwide war, or tuck its tail and skedaddle for home a la Vietnam and Somalia. As matters stand, bin Laden, Mullah Omar, and their Gulf benefactors need expend only patience and the modest costs of insurgency to make America pay the extraordinarily high price that, sadly, is the merited wages of arrogance and willful ignorance.

Arrogance is not the worst of it for America as she charges forward in the cause of instant democracy. That honor falls to the category of hubris, buttressed by ignorance. Since World War II, it seems, we have bred political, media, military, academic, and social elites who lead the country in a manner that shows little knowledge of, or respect for, American history. These ill-informed, mostly male leaders have made the United States into what the historian Niall Ferguson has described as a "colossus with an attention deficiency disorder."[83] When U.S. leaders speak blithely and *ad nauseam* of building a democracy like our own in Afghanistan or Iraq or Burma or Russia or Liberia or Saudi Arabia, saying that it can be done speedily and on the cheap, they betray ignorance of foreign lands, cultures, and histories as well as the creeds and ambitions of other peoples. Added to this is their vast ignorance of the bloody struggles and dearly bought accomplishments of American history. As I said above, this double-strength ignorance is likely to put us on the road to self-inflicted disaster. In August 2003, the historian Joshua Mitchell pointedly warned his countrymen about believing their leaders' glib assurances that democracy could be easily built abroad. Although few have listened to Mitchell, his brilliant appeal and prognosis deserve repetition, particularly because our failures as democracy builders become more apparent as each day passes.

> Nearly 250 years later [after U.S. independence], American foreign policy in Afghanistan and Iraq is driven by an idea so inscribed in the American psyche that it amounts to a syndrome: Cast off the tyrannical leaders, then citizens and leaders alike will band together to bring about that freedom a tyrant's presence precluded. It happened in America; surely it will happen elsewhere. Thus our war of liberation, to free Iraq of its King George III. . . .
>
> In both Afghanistan and Iraq we have won the war, but we stand in danger of losing what we won because our foreign policy suffers from the King George Syndrome. Freedom is neither a spontaneous nor a universal aspiration. Other goods captivate the minds of other people from other lands, order, honor, and tribal loyalties being the most obvious. And because these other goods orient these peoples no less powerfully than freedom orients us, we are apt to be sorely surprised when people who are liberated turn to new tyrants who can

assume order; to terrorists who die for the honor of their country or
Islam; and to tribal warlords whose winner-take-all mentality is corro-
sive to the pluralism and toleration that are the very hallmarks of
modern democracy. . . .

Our wars of liberation will breed illiberal aspirations, and rather
than standing back with incredulity when this happens, we had better
give plenty of thought beforehand to the fact that the tyrants we
depose will be preferable to the chaos a liberated people will initially
endure; that honor is still the currency of value in the Middle East,
more so than goods and services; and that affiliations of blood are
immensely more important than the sovereignty of the individual citizen.[84]

The tragedy-producing potential of this arrogance is increased
because it is wrapped in American hubris that has forgotten or—given
the education our youngest voters have received—never learned the
nature and length of the arduous and often bloody struggle Americans
have waged to get to their present stage of self-government. American
democracy began not in Jamestown in 1608, or at the Continental Congress in 1776 but—to pick a plausible date—in 1215 when the English
barons reduced King John's arbitrary powers at Runnymede. From that
medieval English glen to the American political system of 2003 is a
nearly eight-century journey tracing a gradual but not inevitable
advance of personal liberty, guaranteed civil rights, self-government, an
independent judiciary, and the separation of church and state. These are
unprecedented accomplishments, but the road traversed to attain them
has not been smooth; rather, it has been marked by brutal and bloody
events and personalities, as well as by civil war, protracted legal struggles, urban riots, noble lives sacrificed, voting fraud, lynchings, ethnic
and racial violence, labor–business clashes, and virtually every form of
hatred, prejudice, and bigotry. In defeating these obstacles Americans
have been helped—by great good luck or the kindness of Providence,
take your pick—by residing on a fertile, temperate, and resource-rich
continent tucked away from some of the most devastating events on the
road to where we stand today. How lucky we are, for example, to have
benefited from but not participated in the Reformation, the Counter-
Reformation, and the hundred years of religious wars they engendered,
thereby enabling us to become a nation where men have yet to kill each
other en masse over matters of faith.

The democratic system in America today did not magically appear,
nor was it wished into existence. Our forefathers first planted its seeds

in England and later in North America, and these heroic individuals span the eight centuries mentioned above and are not limited to the "greatest generation" of World War II that is so much, and too much, discussed in contemporary public discourse. While praise and thanks go to that generation, their effort pales in comparison to the efforts of those who set us solidly on the road to the present by defying Europe's absolutist kings and Catholic ultramontanes, as well as by defeating the British Empire against odds greater, to paraphrase Dr. Franklin, than a more generous God would have allowed. Perhaps our largest debt lies with those who stood and killed each other on half a thousand battle-fields between 1861 and 1865 to ensure that we, their descendants, would have a free and united nation to defend, protect, and cherish.

As a people, Americans have a heritage to be proud of and one that is worth defending with their children's lives. It is not, however, a heritage whose experiences, heroes, wars, scandals, sacrifices, victories, mistakes, and villains can be condensed, loaded on a CD-ROM, and given to non-Americans with an expectation that they will quickly, and at little expense, become just like us. This is a debilitating fantasy of how the rest of the world and its peoples live and work. Far worse, it shows a profound ignorance of America, one that mocks those who fought and died resisting tyrannical monarchies and churches, secession, foreign rule, slavery, segregation, discrimination, the union of church and state, and a thousand other issues for which blood was shed to fuel the incremental but still incomplete perfecting of American democracy.

Thus, as Americans today confront bin Laden and militant Islam, they must recognize that the solution to this conflict can never be a painless, quick transformation of the Muslim world to a Western-style democratic system. This is not to say that Muslims or any other people are incapable of democratic government, although there is a staggering incompatibility between American democracy in 2004 and contemporary Muslim society, between a world where Caesar and God each receive their due, and one where God and Caesar are the same. As Patrick J. Ryan concisely framed the problem in the journal *America*, "The Kingdom of Christ is not in this world," while "[c]reating in the concrete an ideal state lies at the heart of Islam. . . . Islam must work out, must succeed [on earth], in social and economic terms, or else its divine origins would appear in doubt."[85] Ryan's analysis was validated by Sayf al-Ansari writing in al Qaeda's *Al-Ansar* electronic journal. Jihad, al-Ansari explained, "is an unavoidable issue for the Muslim community when it moves seriously to establish this [Islamic] state. This state, without whose establishment the religion of Islam as revealed cannot be established, is the realization of the empowerment that God has promised to his believing friends."[86]

Whether or not an Islamic democracy is possible, we must recognize that our historical experience and the society it has produced are uniquely our own. While America can and should be, as Secretary Adams said in 1821, "the well-wisher to the freedom and independence of all," it should do so only so far as to "recommend the general case [of freedom] by the countenance of her voice, and the benignant sympathy of her example." To attempt more is to try to do the impossible and the unwanted, to ignore the hard, bloody road America has traveled, and to force upon other peoples a system of government and society there is little indication they want and every indication they will fight. Mighty though America is in military power, we have not the power to do as the bloody-handed fantasist Woodrow Wilson once suggested and make foreigners elect those America deems good men. Instead of founding and policing an empire with the arbitrary force and brutality used by the Roman Empire—a model much-loved by our elites, again showing their ignorance of how and why America came to be what it is—Americans should tread patiently, quietly, and, given our inheritance of freedom and plenty, with humility. We should be satisfied and honored to act as the "champion and vindicator" of our own freedom—to defeat bin Laden and the Islamic insurgency he leads, for starters—and not need to aspire to reform the world in democracy's name and in the guise of a hectoring, white-faced, pistol-packing, Wilsonian schoolmarm. Perhaps most of all, we must stop being the bulwark of overseas dictatorships and absolute monarchies—especially those in the Islamic world. Washington's half-century record of safeguarding tyrannies entirely discredits for Muslims any claim we make of intending to build democracies. The credibility issues that result from America's proven taste for any Muslim tyrant who maintains internal order and stability, peace with Israel, and low oil prices destroys what little democracy-building potential we may possess. When Secretary Adams warned against democracy-building adventures abroad, he surely never imagined that in 2004 the United States would be completely enmeshed in defending multiple foreign tyrannies against their citizens. "America thoughtlessly supports oppression because we find the lines of the map familiar and convenient," the always painfully honest Ralph Peters has written. "The ghosts of kaisers, kings, and czars must be howling with glee in hell. . . . We garner no respect, but are despised for our hypocrisy and fecklessness. We desecrate our heritage every day."[87]

Only when U.S. leaders stop believing and preaching that bin Laden and his allies are attacking us for what we are and what we think, and instead clearly state that they are attacking us for what we do, can we put aside our ill-advised and hallucinatory crusade for democracy—our current default response. At that point, Americans can begin to intelligently discuss how this national security threat is to be defeated or, more precisely, to decide if *status quo* U.S. foreign policies toward the Islamic world benefit America enough to offset increasing levels of human and economic loss that will be the cost of unchanged policies. Victory, I think, lies in a yet undetermined mix of stronger military actions and dramatic foreign policy change; neither will suffice alone. Defeat for America, I fear, lies in the military and foreign policy *status quo* and the belief that our Islamic foes will be talked out of hating us and disappear if only we can teach them voting procedures, political pluralism, feminism, and the separation of church and state. "Do not waste an inordinate amount of effort," Ralph Peters wisely advised in 1999, "to win unwinnable hearts and minds. Convince hostile populations through victory."[88] And, I would advise, by revising those foreign policies now endangering national security and leaving us with only the military option to pursue.

7

WHEN THE ENEMY SETS THE STAGE: HOW AMERICA'S STUBBORN OBTUSENESS AIDS ITS FOES

> A fatal mistake in war is to underrate the strength, feeling and resources of an enemy.
>
> General W.T. Sherman, 1861.[1]

> The better rule is to judge our adversaries from their standpoint, not from our own.
>
> Robert E. Lee, c. 1865.[2]

> Every attempt to make war easy and safe will result in humiliation and disaster.
>
> General W.T. Sherman, 1875.[3]

There are times when most cards you are dealt come up aces, when forces you cannot control—or even influence—combine to push you forward. Such a moment does not often last long, but Osama bin Laden and al Qaeda have enjoyed one since their smashing and still-reverberating victory on 11 September 2001. This serendipity seems appropriate, as the fate of bin Laden and his cause is not, after all, in his own hands alone. As he has said repeatedly since 1996, the survival of Islam and the Muslim world is, God willing, in the hands of every Muslim, and is the responsibility of each. Islam, bin Laden claims, is being attacked by

U.S.-led Christian Crusaders and Jews, and so each Muslim is bound by his faith to participate in a defensive jihad. Bin Laden has long said his main role in this jihad is as an inciter or instigator—via his words, those of his lieutenants, and al Qaeda's deeds—who motivates Muslims to do their duty as outlined by God in the Koran and by the Prophet in his words and actions.

Still bin Laden did prepare al Qaeda to take advantage of any opportunities that came along. He brilliantly focused his inciting rhetoric on the substantive international issues of most interest to Muslims, ones that play to his central goal of driving the United States from the Middle East and all of the Islamic world. Bin Laden's foreign policy goals, if they may be so termed, are six in number and easily stated. First, the end of all U.S. aid to Israel, the elimination of the Jewish state, and, in its stead, the creation of an Islamic Palestinian state. Second, the withdrawal of all U.S. and Western military forces from the Arabian Peninsula—a shift of most units from Saudi Arabia to Qatar fools no Muslims and will not cut the mustard—and all Muslim territory. Third, the end of all of U.S. involvement in Afghanistan and Iraq. Fourth, the end of U.S. support for, and acquiescence in, the oppression of Muslims by the Chinese, Russian, Indian, and other governments. Fifth, restoration of full Muslim control over the Islamic world's energy resources and a return to market prices, ending the impoverishment of Muslims caused by oil prices set by Arab regimes to placate the West. Sixth, the replacement of U.S.–protected Muslim regimes that do not govern according to Islam by regimes that do. For bin Laden, only Mullah Omar's Afghanistan met this criteria; other Muslim regimes are candidates for annihilation.

By setting these foreign policy priorities, bin Laden gave his followers and all Muslims tangible goals against which to measure progress and, as important, a contextual stage upon which U.S. policies toward the Muslim world are played out. He is not just asserting Islam's superiority and damning America and the West for decadence, debauchery, and secularism, as did Ayatollah Khomeini. Neither has he adopted the ambitious but daffy substitution goals—American-this for Islamic-that—of recent U.S. administrations. He has not, for example, demanded American school curricula be revised to Koranic standards, that charitable donations by Americans go only to al Qaeda-approved groups, or that church and state in the West be reunited. In short, bin Laden and his ilk do not demand Americans become Islamists.

Instead, bin Laden has reminded Muslims that God revealed Islam's superiority over all other religions, and he has focused Muslims on six specific aspects of the Crusaders' attack on their faith and on themselves as its adherents. While many Muslims agreed—and agree still—with Ayatollah Khomeini's claims about the West's moral and spiritual turpitude, few joined a jihad and gave their lives to stop Americans from brewing Budweiser, making X-rated movies, and buying Salman Rushdie's books. Khomeini's rhetoric was full of noise, hate, and fury, but, with minor exceptions, it motivated few battles to the death against the Great Satan. "Bin Laden has so far succeeded where Khomeini failed," journalist and author Geneive Abdo has written. "He has exported his revolutionary ideas across the Islamic world. While that was Khomeini's dream, his radical reading of the faith never penetrated much beyond southern Lebanon and other areas dominated by fellow members of his minority Shia sect."[4] And though I think Bernard Lewis is wrong to equate bin Laden's motivation and appeal with that of Khomeini—which he seems to do in a fine essay entitled "Targeted by a History of Hate"[5]—Lewis does provide an exact description of the difference I see between the two Islamic leaders, one which in large part accounts for bin Laden's success and Khomeini's failure. "A more important question, less frequently asked, is the reason for the contempt with which [the Islamists] regard us," Lewis wrote in the *Wall Street Journal* in September 2002.

> The basic reason for this contempt is what they perceive as the rampant immorality and degeneracy of the American way—contemptible but also dangerous, because of its influence on Muslim societies. What did the Ayatollah Khomeini mean when he repeatedly called America the "Great Satan"? The answer is clear. Satan is not an invader, an imperialist, an exploiter. He is a tempter, a seducer, who, in the words of the Koran, "Whispers in the hearts of men."[6]

Because bin Laden believes that the United States is "an invader, an imperialist, and exploiter" and has successfully portrayed it as such, his rhetoric has much greater anti-American impact than that of Khomeini. First, bin Laden is from the Muslim world's Sunni majority—and a Salafi, its fastest growing, most conservative, and most martially inclined sect—and not a minority Shia like Khomeini. Second, he has spurned the Ayatollah's wholesale condemnation of Western society and focused on six specific, bread-and-butter issues on which there is widespread agreement among Muslims, wherever they lie on the liberal-to-militant spectrum. Most Muslims would like to see the Prophet's land vacated by non-Muslims, the infidels whom, as Mohammed said on his deathbed, had no place on the Arab Peninsula. Likewise, many would relish the elimination of Israel and the creation of an Islamic Palestinian state. Large majorities also can be found in support of making a greater profit on the sale of Muslim-produced oil and natural gas to the rest of the world, and using the money to improve the quality of life for Muslims. Few Muslims, moreover, would oppose the destruction of a set of apostate governments that are among the planet's most brutal, repressive, corrupt, and hypocritical, family ruled regimes that have the profits from oil sales to fund their own debauchery and rent the loyalty of their bankers, businessmen, and academics. Finally, the oppression of Muslims outside the Arab heartland—in Kashmir, Chechnya, India, and Xinjiang—has become a gut issue for Muslims thanks to bin Laden's rhetoric and, even more, the pervasive presence of real-time, Muslim-owned satellite television. These six foreign policy goals are Mom-and-apple-pie for most Muslims, and bin Laden has tied them to the positive message that God promises Muslims victory if they take the path of jihad that He required and His Messenger explained and preached.

This chapter examines how U.S. assessments, decisions, and actions are redounding to bin Laden's advantage because of the context he has established for the Muslim world. The reader will see that while Washington narrowly focuses on destroying bin Laden and al Qaeda via "the global war on terrorism," the U.S. policies pertinent to bin Laden's foreign policy goals are, in effect, doing much of his work for him. As noted earlier, bin Laden aspires to be the Muslim world's premier inspirer of jihad. This is a tall assignment, even for a man of the Shaykh's height, but *status quo* U.S. policies on these six issues give bin Laden steady and invaluable aid in trying to instigate a worldwide defensive jihad against the United States.

Iraq: The Hoped for but Never Expected Gift

Time for a question in the field of cross-cultural analysis: Why is today's Iraq like a Christmas present you long for but never expected to receive? Give up? Well, there is nothing bin Laden could have hoped for more than the American invasion and occupation of Iraq. The U.S. invasion of Iraq is Osama bin Laden's gift from America, one he has long and ardently desired, but never realistically expected. Think of it: Iraq is the second holiest land in Islam; a place where Islam had been long suppressed by Saddam; where the Sunni minority long dominated and brutalized the Shia majority; where order was kept only by the Baathist barbarity that prevented a long overdue civil war; and where, in the wake of Saddam's fall, the regional powers Iran and Saudi Arabia would intervene, at least clandestinely, to stop the creation of, respectively, a Sunni or Shia successor state. In short, Iraq without Saddam would obviously become what political scientists call a "failed state," a place bedeviled by its neighbors and—as is Afghanistan—a land where al Qaeda or al Qaeda-like organizations would thrive. Surely, thought bin Laden, the Americans would not want to create this kind of situation. It would be, if you will, like deliberately shooting yourself in the foot.

While still hoping against hope, bin Laden would then have thought that the United States must know that it is hated by many millions of Muslims for enforcing sanctions that reportedly starved to death a million and more Iraqis. In this context, an invasion would sharply deepen anti-American sentiment in the Muslim world, a hatred that would only worsen as Muslims watched the U.S. military's televised and inevitable thrashing of Saddam's badly led and hopelessly decrepit armed forces. And then, dreamed bin Laden wildly, things would get bad for the Americans. They would stay too long in Iraq, insist on installing a democracy that would subordinate the long-dominant Sunnis, vigorously limit Islam's role in government, and act in ways that spotlighted their interest in Iraq's massive oil reserves. All Muslims would see each day on television that the United States was occupying a Muslim country, insisting that made-man laws replace God's revealed word, stealing Iraqi oil, and paving the way for the creation of a "Greater Israel." The clerics and scholars would call for a defensive jihad against the United States, young Muslim males would rush from across the Islamic world to fight U.S. troops, and there—in Islam's second holiest land—would erupt a second Afghanistan, a self-perpetuating holy war that would endure whether or not al Qaeda survived. Then bin Laden awoke and knew it was only a dream. It was, even for one of Allah's most devout, too much to hope for.

But in March 2003 bin Laden—to his astonishment—got his longed-for gift, complements of America, when the United States invaded Iraq. The fatwas that greeted the invasion essentially validated all bin Laden has said in arguing for a defensive jihad against the United

States. Even leaving aside the fatwas issued by pro-bin Laden clerics, the virulence of the remaining fatwas is clear in those published by such notable scholars as Shaykh Sayyid Tantawi, Shaykh Yusuf Qaradawi, and Shaykh Salman al-Awdah, all of whom "are not voices in the wilderness, but [are] rather the core of the Sunni Muslim establishment," according to Professor Daniel Byman.[7] "Once an enemy lands in Muslim territory," Shaykh Tantawi, head of al-Azhar University, declared in March 2003, "jihad becomes the individual duty of every Muslim man and woman. Because our Arab and Muslim nation will be faced with a new crusade that targets land, honor, creed, and homeland, scholars ruled that jihad against U.S. forces has become the duty of every Muslim man and woman."[8] In the end, something much like Christmas had come for bin Laden, and the gift he received from Washington will haunt, hurt, and hound Americans for years to come.

Semantic Suicide: Fighting Terrorists When Faced by Insurgents

In the aftermath of the 11 September attacks, it was impossible to imagine how a war waged against al Qaeda could fail to benefit the United States. While neither our European allies nor our reputed Muslim friends—some of whom, as Michael Ignatieff said, "whispered America had it coming"[9]—were eager for the United States to use its overwhelming military power, they dared not protest while CNN was still showing Americans jumping to their death from the World Trade Center. So America sallied forth and waged an ineffective war in Afghanistan (see Chapter 2) and, while senior Department of Defense officials were distracted by their pining for a chance to throttle Saddam, proceeded to expand its halfhearted war on terrorism to such countries as Yemen, Georgia, Somalia, Iraq, and the Philippines. More than two years later, the war on terrorism perks along and has grown to dimensions that far exceed destroying al Qaeda for the 11 September attacks—which, of course, we have not yet done. We still have a small force engaged in Afghanistan, though it now fights defensively, not offensively; the troubles we defined as "terrorism" in the just-noted countries are growing; and we have waged a second ineffective war against Iraq that has inaugurated an intensifying Islamist insurgency. What began as a war almost no one opposed is now a military campaign that is undefined, open-ended, and failing. It is, moreover, perceived by many to be based on the idea that any anti-U.S. action or rhetoric constitutes "terrorism," and it has become a war that attracts only feeble support outside the English-speaking world. "Usama Bin Ladin in his wildest dreams could hardly have hoped for this," Richard Dawkins accurately wrote in *The Guardian* in early 2003. "A mere 18 months after he boosted the United States to the peak of worldwide sympathy unprecedented since Pearl Harbor, that international goodwill has been squandered to near zero."[10] At this writing, the war on terrorism has failed to defeat the main enemy, lost focus on national interests in favor of a Quixotic attempt to democratize and secularize Islam, and is generating enemies and animosities faster than we can kill or quell them.

For reasons perfectly in line with the tenets of late-twentieth-century U.S. foreign policy, we delayed acting against Osama bin Laden's al Qaeda and Mullah Omar's Taleban until each had grown—the former in international reach and presence, the latter in terms of a consolidated regime—to the point where a single, intensive application of U.S. military power could not destroy them. We dithered fatally because our leaders and their analysts wrongly assessed the nature of the threat and refused to accept the shift in the terrorism problem from one of state sponsors and their surrogates to one of Islamist insurgents. Indeed, I would argue that we have not thought through this shift—from lethal nuisance to national-security threat—because we were transfixed by the spectacular terrorist attacks that appeared on television at irregular intervals, attacks that caused relatively little human or property loss but embarrassed governments, yielded media-attractive stories of individual loss, and prompted spasms of short-duration moral outrage. We were exclusively focused, if you will, on the flashbulb's brief, intense heat and light. We never stuck around to study more than a single print from a thirty-six-exposure roll, study that would have shown, as U.S. military instructors are now concluding, that the regimen in the so-called terrorist training camps was geared more toward combat.

Between 1975 and 2001, most U.S. administrations—save on occasion that of President Reagan and his CIA director, William J. Casey, peace be upon them—blustered loudly about fighting terrorism when attacks occurred but fell silent and inactive when the pain of the moment and the media's focus had passed. Near the period's end, the president even appointed a terrorism czar—a sort of "blusterer-in-chief"—to deflect the media from the president and give a postattack impression that Washington had an effective counterterrorism policy. This incident-driven approach led neither to a steady flow of resources nor a steady application of thought. More than that, the terrorist attacks were sporadic, and so it seemed we were never ready to respond with anything save a solemn administration-of-the-day promise that the FBI would bring the perpetrators to justice, as if the attacks were a challenge to our domestic legal system.

Also constraining our counterterrorism measures (and I say this with extensive firsthand knowledge) is the tragic reality that American lives mean little when weighed against U.S. officialdom's concerns for the opinions and reactions of foreign, especially European, governments and international institutions, or for what intelligence community leaders call the *"Washington Post* Giggle Test"—the measure of stark fear that seizes senior U.S. officials when a major decision looms that could go awry, earn scorn from the *Post* or another media giant, and delay the next step up the career ladder. In seventeen years of work on Islamist terrorism and insurgency, and after attending scores of meetings with senior members of the U.S. government, I never heard a senior official ask which action, from a list of options, would best protect Americans, or what bad things might happen to Americans if we did not act. I have even seen actions delayed against WMD-related threats aimed at Americans in order to curry favor with the Europeans. In all such sessions, the question most heard is: What will Congress—or the *Post*, CBS, Oprah, the *New York Times*, Ted Koppel, Jay Leno, or fill-in-the-blank—say if the action we take fails or gets someone killed? Driving the U.S. failure vis-à-vis bin Laden, then, is not only a refusal to recognize and accept that Islamist terrorism has become Islamist insurgency, and to recognize the accompanying shift from lethal nuisance to national security threat, but the dependable moral cowardice of my generation, which staffed much of the senior bureaucracy in the period.

While there are many examples of events, trends, and personalities that should have caused U.S. officials to detect the terrorism-to-insurgency paradigm shift and begin framing an appropriate response, the one that stands in sharpest relief, at least to my eye, is the issue of "terrorist" training camps. Since the mid-1990s, the United States and the West have claimed that the "terrorist" training camps in Afghanistan are proof that al Qaeda is a terrorist group, and also proof of Taleban complicity—that government provided the land for the camps and took no step to halt their operations. That training occurred in al Qaeda's Afghan camps is indisputable. The question is, rather, whether Washington's operative assessment was correct. Was the training regimen meant to produce the kind of terrorists the West defines as the greatest threat—suicide bombers, hijackers, kidnappers, and assassins? The answer clearly is no. A "camp" is not necessary to teach the skills needed for such operations. That kind of training can be done inside houses, in basements, in mosques, in forest glens and public parks, in a rented garage, at a legitimate martial arts school, just about anywhere. It is, moreover, the type of training that sensible terrorist chiefs—as Robert E. Lee said, we ought "to assume the enemy shall do what he should do"—would try not to expose to other camp attendees, to local authorities, or to Uncle Sam's satellites.

The foregoing is not to say al Qaeda's Afghan camps did not produce these types of terrorists; captured documents, firsthand accounts, and the history of the group's attacks show that they did. The point is that the Afghan camps were not built primarily to produce terrorists, nor were al-Qaeda camps in Sudan, Yemen, the Philippines, Chechnya, or Saudi Arabia, or those that surely have been built elsewhere in the world after Afghanistan became problematic for the type of training that requires camps. The main function of the camps was and is to provide quality and uniform religious and paramilitary—or insurgent—training to young Muslims; after inspecting the Afghan sites and reviewing training curricula, U.S. military instructors have said that the camps taught "a deep skill set over a narrow range," one that produced a "complete grunt"—or, in al Qaeda's case, an insurgent.[11] Since the mid-1980s, the camps have produced large numbers of skilled fighters—who then return home to fight and train others—not swarms of terrorists. The terrorists trained in the camps are more accurately viewed as al Qaeda's urban warfare arm, or special forces. The camps' dual-production capability has been obvious for nearly thirty years, but this was little noticed in a West fixated on the small number of terrorists the camps produced. That the camps were producing far larger numbers of well-trained insurgents did not receive a serious think-through—and still has not—and, meanwhile, the trainees learned, according to documents captured in Afghanistan, how to use: AK-47s, Stinger missiles, GPS systems, advanced land navigation, RPGs, map reading, demolition techniques, celestial navigation, hand-to-hand combat techniques, trench digging, weapons deployments, escape and evasion techniques, first aid, scientific calculations to plot artillery fire, first aid, secure communications, et cetera, et cetera.

While we obsessed over the camps producing assassins and suicide bombers—and did nothing about that—al Qaeda's Afghan camps systematically trained an army of non-Afghan Muslims and many hundreds of competent paramilitary trainers. It also appears that the camps housed WMD experts who were building weapons and training others to do so or to use them. The documents and debriefings acquired during the U.S.–Afghan war clearly show al Qaeda and other Islamist groups worked to fix the problems caused by patchwork training during the anti-Soviet jihad. In that jihad, a U.S. official has recalled, "When you went to one valley, they fought one way. When you went to the next they fought another."[12] After al Qaeda was formed in the late 1980s, its military leaders began "developing martial curriculums" and "were cunningly resourceful in amassing knowledge," much of it from U.S. and Western sources.[13] In one of the most important—and, sadly, most ignored—articles ever written about al Qaeda's military capabilities, C.J. Chivers and David Rohde explained that "American tactics and training became integral parts of the [al Qaeda] schools," that instruction was standardized so "courses taught in different languages and hundreds of miles apart . . . were identical," and that the curriculum was "'modular,' meaning self-contained. Lesson A need not be completed to successfully learn Lesson B."[14] Chivers and Rohde assessed that al Qaeda's efforts produced camps that offered

> a uniform training program that assimilated recruits with different cultures and skills. . . . "The classes have the same prearranged instruction scripts, because you see the exact same classes being given in different years, different regions, different languages," said an American tactics instructor. . . . Another added: "This is why you can take so many different ethnic groups . . . and you can put them together, and they can fight together. They all have the same basic skills. . . . [Al Qaeda trainers] are leaving the bureaucracy out, and teaching them a couple of basic things very, very well," one [U.S.] instructor said. "It is a classic saying; become brilliant at the basics. If you take care of those, when the time comes for combat, you'll do better than okay."[15]

This also was true of camps run for Afghan trainees by the Taleban, the Northern Alliance, and the major Afghan resistance groups who had formerly fought the Soviets. In addition, these Afghan-run camps trained non-Afghan Muslims. Hizbi Islami-Khalis commander Haqqani, for example, welcomed Kashmiris, Arabs, and Asians to his camps and received funds from Gulf donors to cover costs. And the late Ahmed Shah Masood and Abdul Rasul Sayyaf trained Muslims from Central Asia, western China, Turkey, the Persian Gulf, and elsewhere.

Completing the picture, we have learned since the U.S. invaded Afghanistan that camps also were dedicated to training Tajiks, Uzbeks, Chechens, and Uighurs. In Afghanistan, then, camps training Islamist insurgents numbered many more than those belonging to al Qaeda and the Taleban, and together they built a store of trouble for the United States and the West by preparing men to fight in current insurgencies and ones not yet begun. Many observers, however, still have trouble absorbing the fact that there is a huge cadre of camp-trained Islamist insurgents available around the world—a veteran force in being, if you will, ready to deploy whenever and wherever the opportunity arises. In March 2003, for example, a *Wall Street Journal* writer claimed that Islamist fighters entering Iraq posed little danger. "These groups," concluded Yaroslav Trofimov, inexplicably ignoring the Afghan camps' production, "pose almost no immediate threat to the U.S.-led war effort because of their poor-training, small numbers and lack of local knowledge."[16]

Now, let us gaze outward from Afghanistan at a wider world of Islamist training camps and facilities not directly associated with al Qaeda. Since the 1980s, the United States and its allies have known, studied, and protested the fact that various Sunni Islamist groups have been running training camps in, conservatively, Yemen, Pakistan, Kashmir, Sudan, and the Philippines. More recently, say, since 1990, Somalia, Uzbekistan, Montenegro, Eritrea, western China, Chechnya, Algeria, Tajikistan, Lebanon, Bosnia, northern Iraq, and Albania can be added to the list. And, currently, we are training at Guantanamo Bay a brigade of Muslim insurgents who will be among the most dedicated and mentally tough cadre available to Sunni Islam. These fighters will have iconic status when they return to the combat arena, and, ironically, they are likely to be the healthiest guerrillas in the field thanks to the balanced diet and medical care they received from U.S. military doctors at U.S. taxpayer expense.

To cap this lethal litany, and as noted in Chapter 3, the World Wide Web is facilitating 24/7 instruction for any would-be mujahideen around the world who can use a computer, cell phone, or satellite phone to access the Internet. Again, Chivers and Rohde documented how al Qaeda "aggressively cribbed publicly available information from the U.S. military and paramilitary press."[17] This reality relieves the aspiring but often dirt-poor jihadi of the expensive and insecure necessity of traveling to a foreign training camp. The sum of all this is that while the West was bore-sighted on car bombers, assassins, and kidnappers, the

Sunni Islamists produced well-trained and now veteran insurgents who currently are challenging the United States and other legitimate governments—often U.S. allies—in the Middle East, the Pacific Region, South and Southeast Asia, the Persian Gulf, northern and eastern Africa, and the former Soviet Union. Terrorists alone cannot threaten national security; terrorists who are a complementary subset of a larger international Sunni Islamist insurgency surely can.

And while we blithely ignored the Sunni training camps' core purpose, we likewise willfully ignored the main function of camps run by Hizballah, the Shia insurgent organization in Lebanon. Since its inception in 1982, Hizballah has run training camps in Lebanon, including the famous Bekaa Valley facilities. For twenty-plus years the camps—like those of the Sunni Islamists in other countries—have turned out scores of suicide bombers, assassins, and kidnappers, but also thousands of well-trained guerrilla fighters. While the Bekaa Valley camps initially trained Hizballah fighters, class lists over the years expanded to include Shias from abroad and gradually growing numbers of Sunni trainees from such places as Syria, Sudan, Egypt, Jordan, and Palestine. Paramilitary training in the Bekaa camps was taught not only by veteran Hizballah cadre, but by instructors from Iran's Islamic Revolutionary Guard Corps (IRGC); the IRGC also ran training camps in Iran for Shia and Sunni fighters and sent trainers to Afghanistan, Sudan, Bosnia, and Central Asia. It is also fair, I think, to speculate that Bekaa-trained Sunni fighters may have gotten some combat experience during the years Hizballah waged an ultimately successful guerrilla war against Israel's occupation of southern Lebanon.

While the West focused on Hizballah's kidnapping of Westerners, sporadic aircraft hijackings, and a few spectacular but militarily inconsequential suicide car-bomb attacks—three in Beirut against U.S. and French interests in 1983, and two against Israeli interests in Buenos Aires in 1992 and 1994—the group's Bekaa Valley camps produced increasing numbers of competent insurgents for Hizballah and for Islamist organizations elsewhere. And, as with the Sunni camps already discussed, the foreigners trained in the Bekaa Valley returned home not only to fight their governments but to train their colleagues, thereby becoming force multipliers. Overall, the West's main concern with Hizballah—as with al Qaeda and other Sunni groups—was misplaced in its focus on the terrorist, or, more appropriately, the organization's special forces arm. The most dangerous thing about Hizballah was and is its insurgent capabilities. The group's prowess and durability as insurgents finally drove the Israeli Defense Forces out of Lebanon, something car-bomb attacks on Israeli interests outside Israel would never have accomplished. Likewise, America may soon find that the Hizballah insurgents sent to fight and train others to fight U.S. forces in Iraq—either on their own or with IRGC units—are more dangerous than the Hizballah suicide bombers who killed more than three hundred Americans in Beirut in summer 1983.

And so we are bedeviled again, as noted elsewhere herein, by what too many individuals more intelligent and influential than I consider an inconsequential semantical difference between the terms "terrorist" and "insurgent." And, again, the question must be asked: does it matter if we describe camps as "terrorist" or "insurgent"? The answer, I think, is yes, it emphatically matters when you are drafting a strategy to deal with the threat the camps produce. The right term is pivotal to correctly deciding how to fight bin Laden, al Qaeda, and other Sunni and Shia organizations. If camps remain "terrorist training camps" for U.S. policy makers, we will stay bound to an approach strongly favoring the use of law-enforcement agencies, military special forces, and the clandestine service in what is, in essence, an attempt to meld these organizations into a sort of international Royal Canadian Mounted Police. I suppose its motto would be: "We always get our Islamist." This is the approach we took and clung to for six years before 11 September 2001, and it has failed miserably. It also is the tack we have followed since that sad day—with an add-on air offensive that destroyed piles of ancient, inoperative Soviet-era military junk, broke up some rocks, but did little else—and it is the reason we are losing in Afghanistan. The small U.S. force there, and its reliance on Afghan surrogates, might make sense if the camps produced a finite number of terrorists and we knew the number. It makes no sense if the camps produced an unknown but probably massive numbers of insurgents—which they did.

The U.S. president, vice president, secretaries of state, justice, defense, and homeland security, the attorney general, the FBI director, the director of central intelligence, and endless numbers of experts, reporters, and pundits continue telling Americans and the world that the United States is beating bin Laden by dismantling al Qaeda one man at a time; in the president's words: "One by one, the terrorists are learning the meaning of American justice."[18] Indeed, so ingrained in the American mind and experience is this paradigm of fighting terrorism—which amounts to police work abroad—that we seem stuck in a time warp. Even in the 2003 war against Iraq's half-million-man military—

most of whom survived and went home armed—we came up with the now-famous "deck" of fifty-five cards depicting the "most wanted" members of Saddam's regime, suggesting to Americans that the problems in Iraq will be licked when the fifty-five fugitives are captured and an "X" is drawn through the face on each card. As they did in Afghanistan, al Qaeda insurgents will help many others to prove the paradigm wrong in Iraq.

What must be done, I think, is that which is most difficult. We must soon abandon a long-standing mind-set that is comfortable and makes sense to us when imposed on a chaotic and often—in our terms—unintelligible world. And we must do it in trying circumstances: when we are being attacked and our citizens are dying, an environment not conducive to calm reflection. The training camps that have scared us for so long are and always have been insurgent, vice terrorist, camps, and though they turned out a few thousand terrorists, they turned out a hundred thousand or more insurgents. The graduates, in turn, trained tens of thousands more insurgents after returning home. A simple application of logic leads to numbers so large that a hundred or more Guantanamo Bay–like Camp Deltas would be filled if you could catch them all—which you cannot. The brutal reality we face—because of the reality we willfully ignored for a quarter-century—is that we must kill many thousands of these fighters in what is a barely started war that will be unimaginably costly to each side. This judgment, I believe, is harsh but accurate. It will remain so as long as unchanged U.S. policies motivate Muslims to become insurgents. The butcher's bill will only increase if we keep bucking reality.

When Coalition-Building Is Embracing Tyranny

That America had to try and destroy the Taleban and al Qaeda by military means after the 11 September attacks is a truism. We had a brief chance to do that, but—as noted in Chapter 2—we failed utterly, and both organizations are now regrouped, re-equipped, and on the offensive. Part of this failure lies in our knee-jerk reaction to the attacks: create an international coalition to support, succor, and applaud the U.S. military in Afghanistan. Except for blind support for Israel, there has been nothing harder to oppose in the last decades of U.S. foreign policy-making than the rock-solid belief in the absolute need to form a multinational coalition before tackling a "crisis" that has popped up. U.S.

presidents in the past quarter-century often have resembled nothing so much as teenage girls who cannot possibly go to the restroom in a public venue without the accompaniment of their closest girlfriends. In some cases, it is indeed true that such a coalition is the best way to resolve a crisis. This is especially true of catastrophic physical disasters, such as earthquakes, hurricanes, floods, and droughts, as well as in such humanitarian cases as famine and disease. Coalitions also can be effective in situations where there is a multinational consensus that favors military intervention to stop the potential for slaughter in countries where we have no earthly interest, such as Liberia in 2003 and Haiti in early 2004. In cases where our national interests are at risk, or, at least, where we believe them at risk, coalition-building delays action, ties our policy and goals to those of tyrants, and limits options, all of which undercut the optimal protection of our national security. Notwithstanding the droning, oracular, and on-demand op-ed piece from Henry Kissinger urging coalition-building in every crisis, speed and preserving the widest range of options are, at times, the better way to ensure U.S. goals are accomplished.

In Afghanistan, coalition-making brought delay, good-guy and barbarous allies, and constricted options. The 11 September attacks were not apocalyptic onslaughts on Western civilization. They were country-specific attacks meant to inflict substantial, visible, and quantifiable human and economic destruction on America. The attacks also were meant to inflict psychological damage on Americans. The attacks were acts of war and had limited goals, which were achieved; intellectual honesty forbids describing them as efforts to destroy such unquantifiable things as our freedom or a way of life. If anything, bin Laden crafted the attacks with an eye toward isolating the United States. He meant the strikes to fix the United States in the spotlight of all Islamist militants, while implying to the Europeans—through the very specificity of the attacks—that he currently had no axe to grind with them unless they joined the U.S. attack on al Qaeda. And, as is evident, post-11 September European support has been light in substance, heavy in rhetoric, and has faded as time passed, al Qaeda warning attacks on European intersts occurred, and the United States invaded Iraq.

Al Qaeda's act of war—not terror—against the United States merited an unambiguously savage military response against the organization and its Taleban hosts. Because we already had military bases in the Persian Gulf, we needed only to secure minimal cooperation from Pakistan and the use of military bases and airfields in Uzbekistan, Tajikistan, and

Kyrgyzstan. "Pakistan's help is welcome, indeed essential," historian John Keegan advised in the 20 September 2001 *Daily Telegraph*, but "[m]ore promising as a base area is ex-Soviet central Asia, much of it subject to Moscow's authority. The populations are small and the leaders anti-Islamic. Several states have large military installations constructed by the old Soviet Union for its Afghan war. As America may, and should plan to mount only punitive operations, central Asia promises to be the best basing area available."[19] This minimalist approach would have supplied sufficient support in a short period of time, although—on the downside—all our allies would have been dictatorships, most anti-Muslim. Washington quickly made the Keegan-suggested arrangements, but then, as if a Pavlovian automaton, refused to leave well enough alone and again returned to the big-tent approach to war-making, expending time, energy, and cash to recruit as many coalition partners as possible, whether or not they brought anything we needed to the table. Indeed, so eager were we for coalition partners that we invited and accepted those who amounted to net losses to our cause—Russia and India, for example.

Overall, the time taken to build the coalition probably had little impact on the result in Afghanistan; as noted in Chapter 2, we were caught unprepared and then fought a tardy, ill-informed, and ineffective war that our coalition made only marginally less effective. The price America has paid for this coalition since the U.S. military's large-scale offensive operations ended in Afghanistan—say, 1 April 2002—has been exorbitant in terms of the aid and comfort it has afforded bin Laden and militant Islam in the Muslim world. This particularly is the case in two areas: the limits imposed by our Western allies' concerns and U.S. officialdom's terror of media criticism on America's ability to use its military power as it sees fit, and the tainting of America's actions and goals as a result of its cheek-by-jowl alliance with what the Muslim world regards as murderous tyrannies, such as Russia and Israel.

Because the U.S. military failed to ready a devastating response to an al Qaeda attack in the United States—which U.S. officialdom now says was inevitable—America, as noted in Chapter 2, missed a one-time chance to blow al Qaeda and the Taleban to the Stone Age. The rapid post-11 September dispersal of both entities moved U.S. targeting efforts from difficult to impossible, eroding the U.S. advantage of concentrated firepower. Worse yet, when the United States attacked on 7 October 2001 it was encumbered by the U.S. media, the forces and media of the NATO countries, Australia, and New Zealand, and by the pre-positioned reporters and camera crews from the Arabic satellite television channels. By that time, U.S. leaders also had framed the war as a black-and-white contest between "good and evil" or between "Western civilization and armed anarchy." From the first, the cost of coalition for the United States was that its allies and their media would make sure U.S. forces conducted a "civilized war," refraining from actions that would produce large civilian casualties—this in a war where the enemy wore no uniforms, lived among civilians, and never heard of the Geneva Convention. In turn, the real-time war coverage by Arab satellite television forced the media-fearing U.S.-led coalition to be even more dainty in its use of military force. In essence, the Arab media, the U.S. and Western media, and the political leaders of the coalition's non-U.S. forces all shared the common goal of making sure the U.S. application military power was "civilized." In this case, the coalition's good-guy members severely limited the thoroughness and savagery the U.S. military could have used to destroy large numbers of al Qaeda and Taleban fighters.

In return for acquiescing in the U.S invasion of Afghanistan, our more unsavory coalition "partners" expected and, unfortunately, received Washington's formal backing for their own wars against "terrorism." The most senior U.S. government leaders, for example, have endorsed Russian president Putin's war against Chechnya's Islamist separatists, notwithstanding the prolonged barbarity of Russian security and military forces against Chechen civilians. Beijing, too, won official U.S. endorsement for its decades-old campaign to annihilate not only Uighur separatism in western China, but the Uighur ethnic group itself. The Chinese government is waging the same deliberate genocide by inundation in Xinjiang Province—moving in vast numbers of Han Chinese to change forever its demography, making the Uighurs a minority in a land they had dominated—that they have conducted for decades in Tibet, and to which we and our allies vigorously have objected. In South Asia, Washington has taken measures to enhance its ties to India and simultaneously to coerce Pakistan to halt aid for Muslim Kashmiri insurgents, thereby giving *de facto* sanction to India's sorry record of abusing its Kashmiri Muslim citizens, as well as its Israel-like refusal to obey long-standing UN resolutions on Kashmir. Similarly, Washington has supported and armed the Indonesian military's efforts to smash Islamist separatists in Aceh, advised and participated in Manila's attacks on Moro Islamist groups in Mindanao, and backed the Yemeni regime's drive to keep local Islamists at bay.

The point here is not to question whether the governments above are entitled to handle domestic "terrorism" as they see fit—they are—but to ask if the United States is wise to ally itself with regimes whose barbarism has long earned the Muslim world's hatred. This is a particularly important question given the U.S. administration's decision to identify America's motivations for battling al Qaeda as identical to those of Russia, China, and India for fighting Chechens, Uighurs, and Kashmiris. Does this stance advance the U.S. war on bin Laden? From any perspective, I believe, the U.S. decision to associate its war against al Qaeda with this malodorous trio—plus Israel—can only be judged counterproductive. It is America that is on bin Laden's bull's-eye; at this time, Russia, China, and India are not. Our decision to identify with and support the wars these three states are waging on domestic Muslim opponents legitimizes their activities—from mass murder in Chechnya, to extra-judicial killings in Kashmir, to the silent genocide of a people in Xinjiang—and earns America only inconsistent rhetorical support from the thugs in Moscow and Beijing and India's Hindu fundamentalists, none of whom bring tangible benefits. We are in a fight to the death with al Qaeda whether or not these states approve, and our support for them makes the fight harder because it again validates bin Laden's contention that the United States is attacking Islam and supports any country willing to kill or persecute Muslims.

Overall, Washington's Pavlovian eagerness to form a coalition to fight bin Laden was not a military necessity, and it clearly was not wise or in U.S. interests to further stoke Muslim hatred. A coalition that includes Russia, China, India, the Philippines, Indonesia, and Yemen; the dictators of Saudi Arabia, Jordan, the UAE, Kuwait, and Egypt; the titans of nineteenth-century colonialism in the Middle East, Britain, and France; and the state of Israel makes bin Laden look like a prophet of old, as his supporters or sympathizers believe they see the truth of his argument that America wants allies only among those willing to oppress Muslims and eliminate Islam.

The Burden of an Eternal Dependent

Israel. There is certainly not a more difficult or dangerous issue to debate in the field of postwar U.S. foreign policy. The American political and social landscape is littered with the battered individuals—most recently the president of the United States—who dared to criticize

Israel, or, even more heretically, to question the value to U.S. national interests of the country's overwhelmingly one-way alliance with Israel. Almost every such speaker is immediately branded anti-Semitic and consigned to the netherworld of American politics, as if concerns about U.S. national security are prima facie void if they involve any questioning of the U.S.–Israel status quo. Surely there can be no other historical example of a faraway, theocracy-in-all-but-name of only about six million people that ultimately controls the extent and even the occurrence of an important portion of political discourse and national security debate in a country of 270-plus million people that prides itself on religious toleration, separation of church and state, and freedom of speech. In a nation that long ago rejected an established church as inimical to democratic society, Washington yearly pumps more than three billion taxpayer dollars into a nation that defiantly proclaims itself "the Jewish state" and a democracy—claims hard to reconcile with its treatment of Muslims in Israel, its limitations on political choice for those in the occupied territories, and the eternal exile it has enforced on those camped in the refugee diaspora across the Levant. At the UN and other international fora, the U.S. government stands four-square, and often alone, with Israel to free it from obeying UN resolutions and nonproliferation treaties; with U.S. backing, Israel has developed and deployed weapons of mass destruction at the pace it desires. Objectively, al Qaeda does not seem too far off the mark when it describes the U.S.–Israel relationship as a detriment to America.

> The close link between America and the Zionist entity is in itself a curse for America. In addition to the high cost incurred by the U.S. Treasury as a result of this alliance, the strategic cost is also exorbitant because this close link has turned the attack against America into an attack against the Zionist entity and vice versa. This contributes to bringing the Islamic nation together and pushing it strongly to rally around the jihad enterprise.[20]

One can only react to this stunning reality by giving all praise to Israel's diplomats, politicians, intelligence services, U.S.–citizen spies, and the retired senior U.S. officials and wealthy Jewish-American organizations who lobby an always amenable Congress on Israel's behalf. In an astounding and historically unprecedented manner, the Israelis have succeeded in lacing tight the ropes binding the American Gulliver to the tiny Jewish state and its policies; as Anatol Lieven has written, the Israelis have been so successful that Israeli nationalism "for many Americans has become deeply entwined with their American nationalism."[21]

There perhaps was a time in the late 1970s and 1980s when America could afford today's relationship with Israel, one that drains resources, earns Muslim hatred, and serves no vital U.S. national interest. For much of the period, the "Arab–Israeli peace process"—as it was then known—was a hothouse plant, an issue of intense interest to and constant cultivation by a small coterie of experts steeped in its arcane history, parlance, and mechanics. While this coterie lived only to push the "peace process" ahead, the rest of the world mostly took a pass, unless Palestinian, and later Hizballah, fighters struck, or the two sides edged too close to a conventional war. As in the realm of U.S.–Soviet arms control talks, most of the world—Muslim and Western—was satisfied if the sides kept talking to each other through peace-process specialists; substantive progress was nice to see but not needed as long as the "process" crawled along and talking continued.

Today, things are different. "The United States often treats the Israeli–Palestinian dispute as a local conflict that can be contained," Clyde Prestowitz wrote in the *Washington Post*, "but it is spilling over. It is radicalizing attitudes in such countries as Indonesia and Malaysia."[22] Prestowitz's "spillover" is hard to date with precision, but it was certainly pushed along by the late-1987 founding of the Islamist Palestinian resistance group, Hamas, and the activities of its insurgent wing with that of the older Palestinian Islamic Jihad (PIJ). The groups brought a new and more often lethal dimension to the Israeli–Palestinian war, and their blatant Islamism won greater interest and sympathy in the Muslim world than did earlier, more secular Palestinian groups, such as Sabri al-Banna's Abu Nidal Organization, Yasser Arafat's PLO, and Ahmed Jibril's Popular Front for the Liberation of Palestine-General Command. The ground for Hamas and PIJ had been prepared by the Ayatollah Khomeini–led Islamic revolution in Shia Iran and its ignition of an international "Islamic awakening," which added a sense of ferociousness, confidence, assertiveness, and optimism to contemporary Islam that startled Westerners as well as many Muslims. Almost simultaneously, the jihad of Afghanistan's Sunni mujahideen began turning the tide of war against the Red Army and Afghan communists, providing a real-world example of the glorious goals militant Muslims could accomplish through warfare waged in God's name and with His help.

These events, moreover, were tied together and given a sense of steady progress by the growth in real-time global satellite television coverage. Thus the bloody battles between Israel's military and PIJ and Hamas were broadcast—at times live—to a worldwide Muslim audience that was participating vicariously in the mujahideen's fight for Allah in the Hindu Kush, as well as personally in the Khomeini-guided reinvigoration of Islam, which instructed each believer to be aware of and support all Muslims. Thus, at the start of the second Intifadah in 1999, the increasingly Islamist nature of Palestinian resistance, the worldwide Islamic awakening, the Afghans' victorious jihad, and the daily coverage of all three by satellite television channels that now included the Arabic outlet *Al-Jazirah*, had combined to internationalize a conflict that long was a vital issue for a few insiders but never before an impassioned, life-and-death issue for all.

Enter Osama bin Laden. In regard to Palestine, everyone from Yasser Arafat to dozens of Western and Muslim officials and commentators have declared bin Laden an Osama-come-lately, one who is cynically using the Palestinian cause to advance his jihad. As I described in *Through Our Enemies' Eyes*, bin Laden has been focused on the Israeli–Palestinian conflict since the end of the Afghan jihad and probably before.[23] He and other al Qaeda leaders have stated the organization's desire to attack inside Israel, while noting such attacks have been all but impossible for al Qaeda due to the refusal of Jordan, Syria, Lebanon, and Egypt—to please Washington and Israel—to provide the group a contiguous safe haven. "If the [Arab] rulers are serious about finding a solution for this problem [of Palestine]," al Qaeda spokesman Sulayman Abu Gayeth said in July 2002, "then they must open their borders . . ."[24] This is the same factor bin Laden says stymied al Qaeda from placing a significant insurgent force in Bosnia during the Balkans wars of the 1990s. Still, the October 2002 attacks on an Israeli hotel and charter airliner in Mombasa, Kenya, and the November 2003 attacks on two synagogues in Turkey put al Qaeda squarely and energetically into the anti-Israel war. "In this blessed month [of Ramadan]," said al Qaeda's postattack Internet statement claiming responsibility for the 2002 attacks, "We deliberately delayed extending these [Ramadan] greetings to coincide with the two Mombasa operations in Kenya against Israeli interests so they would have meaning in the conditions facing the nation at the hands of its crusader and Jewish enemies."[25] Al Qaeda's apparent expansion into Lebanon, noted in Chapter 3, also strongly suggests bin Laden is devoting thought, money, and cadre to position al Qaeda to attack inside Israel. Given bin Laden's tradition of extracting an eye for an eye, Israel's apparent March 2003 murder of Abd al-Sattar al-Masri, al Qaeda's commander in Lebanon, probably will spur efforts to build an effective combat presence there.

While bin Laden and al Qaeda are not yet major military actors in the Israel–Palestine war, they do play a role in further internationalizing the issue. The group, for example, pays much attention to the war on the popular, al Qaeda-associated Internet websites *Al-Neda* and *Al-Ansar*.[26] More important in fixing Muslims on Palestine, however, is bin Laden's international stature. Whether or not bin Laden focuses his words or al Qaeda's attacks and propaganda on Israel, he has created an environment in which Western and Muslim media provide consistent, priority coverage to virtually all locales where Muslim fighters are struggling. In terms of Muslim leaders, as noted earlier, bin Laden stands alone; no one else is close. Because of his larger-than-life status, where he often is portrayed as directing all Islamist groups, journalists covering Sunni attacks anywhere in the world inevitably refer to al Qaeda or bin Laden as the attacker's manager, ally, financier, or inspirer. Because of this reality, most Sunni militant groups have won a higher profile and are more media worthy than they would be minus bin Laden's international standing. That Hamas, PIJ, and, most recently, Fatah's al-Aqsa Brigades benefit from increased publicity is due not just to their attacks, but also to the intense media focus on Sunni militancy writ large, which is a derivative of bin Laden's personal example, rhetoric, and al Qaeda's attacks. "Symbols have not lost their value," Abu-Ubayd al-Qurashi wrote in *Al-Ansar* in early 2002. "This Shaykh Usama has become a symbol of the oppressed east and west, even for non-Muslims." A symbol, one might add, whose luster is only enhanced by the arrogant racism symbolized by the wall Israel is building to separate Jews from Muslims, and our own obtuseness in seeing the wall as a means of Israeli self-protection and not, as Muslims see it, as further persecution of the Palestinians twined with yet another Israeli land grab.[27]

Even When Right, the Price Is Hatred and Mockery

A price America pays as the world's great power, and for being home to its most powerful media organizations, is that it lives under a microscope the rest of the world peers through. And some peer with maliciousness, or at least a readiness to recast legitimate actions in a malignant manner. There is neither use nor dignity in whining about this. It is a fact of life, and one that should always be held in mind when drafting and executing foreign policy. Several post-11 September U.S. government actions to improve domestic security, for example, have increased the hatred of Muslims toward America, whether or not they support al Qaeda. This is not to say Washington should have refrained from acting. It is to say, however, that in gauging the mind-set and intentions of our Islamist foes it is well to be aware of as many as possible of the things that can fire their hatred and energize their military activities. Following, therefore, for the sake of America's awareness and not the Islamists' hurt feelings, is a discussion of some measures, most necessary, that have furthered our enemies' goal of causing Muslims to take up arms against us.

To set the scene, we must recall al Qaeda's description of the U.S.-led West as the eternal enemy of Muslims that will go to any length to humiliate, impoverish, and, in the end, destroy any Muslim unwilling to abandon his faith and obey the Christian West and its Jewish allies. We cannot forget, al-Zawahiri said in October 2002, that "Muslims have suffered the worst and most serious disasters, for more than a century. Their lands are occupied either by foreign forces, or through political influence. Their resources are deemed lawful and plundered. They are deprived of free will. Their rights are thrown away and stolen. Their sanctuaries are surrounded and taken over."[28] In the context of al Qaeda's words on this theme—which Westerners often hear but do not digest—it is clear that U.S. military attacks and economic embargos on Muslim states; the clandestine chase, capture, and jailing of mujahideen; and the invasion and occupation of Muslim lands are events that validate and sharpen the rapacious image of America that bin Laden and other Islamists have created. Not as clear, I believe, is the fact that other U.S. government actions that Americans and many Westerners see as mundane, commonsensical, or educational are seen by Muslims as more proof of bin Laden's claim that America is malignantly inclined toward Islam.

Tighter Immigration Rules or "No Muslims Need Apply"?

The need to reform U.S. immigration rules and enforce regulations already in place made good sense both before and after the 11 September attacks. Within American society, the Congress's postattack tightening of immigration policy was mostly taken in stride, although some civil-liberties concerns remain. Most Americans agreed that after 11 September it was time to find out how many foreigners were in the country illegally; indeed, it is dangerous and dismaying that Washington did not finish the job by finding all illegals and either legalize their status or send them home. For many Muslims and their governments, however, the new regulations were blatant discrimination, meant to humiliate Muslims and make them appear evil. Pakistani foreign minister K. M. Kasuri, for example, urged Washington to ease the rules because they were strengthening anti-U.S. sentiment in Pakistan, while in the Cairo daily *Al-Sah'b*, commentator Mohammed A. A. Salih recommended that "Egypt request the Americans [in Egypt] be finger-printed, register their names with competent authorities and [be] questioned about their connections with Israel and the CIA."[29]

While bin Laden's rhetoric did not cause this reaction, his consistent theme calling attention to the West's deliberate post-World War I policy of humiliating Islam ensured that U.S. actions were perceived in the worst possible way. That the World Trade Center and Pentagon attackers were Muslims who died waging a war on America declared by the Muslim Osama bin Laden matters not to bin Laden's audience, be they supporters or just listeners. When Muslims are delayed by airport police for secondary security examinations, and when only citizens from twenty-four Muslim countries must regularly report to U.S. immigration during U.S. visits—a rule imposed otherwise only on North Koreans—they do not see tighter domestic security measures but rules meant to harass, discriminate against, and humiliate Muslims. "The U.S., which considers itself a 'republic of immigrants,'" Abd al-Bari Atwan wrote in *The Observer*, "has turned against all its values and principles, detaining thousands of its Arab and Muslim citizens."[30] The universally negative interpretation by Muslims also is seen in the strong May–June 2002 public denunciations of the regulations by media and governments in Yemen, Egypt, Pakistan, Qatar, Jordan, and Saudi Arabia. "Clearly, the latest measures . . . will exacerbate the general paranoia that already exists in America against the Islamic world," claimed the pro-government *Saudi Gazette* in June 2002[31], while the pro-regime Qatari paper *Al-Watan* decried the "racist and unprecedented" U.S. actions that make Muslims "targets for revenge, regards them as suspects, and isolates them. . . . We would have liked the United States to have remembered some of Abraham Lincoln's policies."[32] In Pakistan, the respected daily *Nawa-i-Waqt* damned the new rules as a mockery of U.S. "teaching[s] of civilization and culture to the world" and warned that this "offense against a universal religion like Islam and a Muslim peace-loving nation would not be fruitful for the United States. The U.S. government, nation, and Congress should give it thought."[33] The new immigration laws make the United States more secure and should be kept, but they clearly increase for Muslims the salience of bin Laden's claim that U.S. policies are anti-Islamic and that Muslim regimes—like those damning the measures without effect—are powerless to protect their citizens against the United States, thus leaving the task to al Qaeda and its ilk. As the *Nawa-i-Waqt* editors said, "The Muslim community lacks the courage, will and capability" to challenge the United States on the immigration regulations.[34]

War Measures or Racism?

Bin Laden always is explicit in arguing Washington is hypocritical in its claim that all people have the right to the liberties and personal freedoms enshrined in American law, saying that the U.S. government will ensure such rights are extended only to Christians and whites. These rights would be given to Muslims, bin Laden says, only if they abandon Islam and obey America. In this context, bin Laden's audience is likely to see some legitimate U.S. war measures as proof of his claims of American hypocrisy and racism. For example, U.S. efforts to disrupt al Qaeda's electronic communications—by attacking the *Al-Neda* and *Al-Ansar* websites and pressing *Al-Jazirah* not to air al Qaeda videos—are basic security measures. Allowing the enemy free communication in wartime would be as criminally negligent as not being ready to respond militarily to the 11 September attacks. That said, these U.S. actions appear to validate bin Laden's claims of hypocrisy and racism by showing that freedom of speech is not allowed to Muslims. As al-Zawahiri has said, U.S. actions show the hypocrisy of American claims of " 'freedom of thought,' 'freedom of speech,' human rights, justice, and equality. . . ."[35]

Bin Laden's point was driven home for him by two U.S. actions. The first was in the contradiction between U.S. pressure on *Al-Jazirah* to censor or refuse to broadcast tapes from bin Laden and his lieutenants, and the secretary of state's February 2003 rush to publish a not-yet aired bin Laden tape so it would "prove" to the UN Security Council the reality of al Qaeda–Iraq cooperation. "[T]he administration pounced on the [bin Laden] tape," Maureen Dowd wrote in the *New York Times*. "In the past, [U.S. National Security Adviser] Condi Rice has implored the networks not to broadcast the tapes outright, fearing

he might be activating sleeper cells in code. . . . But this time the administration flacked the tape. . . . So the Bushies no longer care if Osama
sends a coded message to his thugs as along as he stays on message [re:
al Qaeda–Iraq cooperation] for the White House?"[36] The second U.S.
action that drove home bin Laden's point was Washington's decision to
jail Islamist prisoners in Guantanamo Bay camps and not afford them
legal representation, an action thus far upheld in U.S. courts. This is
seen across the Muslim world as validation of bin Laden. The existence
of Camp Delta, for bin Laden, shows U.S. civil liberties are not for
Muslims, and that humiliation—orange jump suits, shackles, blind-
folds, and cyclone-fenced cages—will be their lot if they stand by their
faith. The gloss on this point provided by U.S. military personnel working in Iraqi prisons needs no comment.

U.S. Military Briefings: Precision Warfare or Shooting Muslims in a Barrel?

Since the 1991 Gulf War, U.S. military officers—usually from CENT-
COM—have given daily televised briefings about U.S. operations in—
usually Islamic—war zones. By now, Americans anticipate and enjoy
these briefings and appear to believe they are the right of U.S. citizens;
the briefings have become part of the open, transparent government of
which Americans are proud. The briefings begin with an introduction
by the general officer/star performer of the day, followed by video of
U.S. aerial attacks on enemy military positions, industrial facilities, and
infrastructure targets. Each clip is roughly similar: The viewer sees a
target in the pilot's crosshairs and remains fixed on that aiming point
until a tremendous but always silent explosion occurs. The clips end
without coverage of what the postattack damage looks like or the number of casualties inflicted, perhaps validating Chris Hedges's judgment
in *War Is a Force that Gives Us Meaning*: "The generals, who are no
more interested in candor than they were in Vietnam, have at least per-
fected the appearance of candor."[37] These videotapes, I have always
supposed, are meant to display the proficiency of our pilots and their
equipment, cause fear among enemy units not yet attacked, demonstrate to Americans that their taxes are well spent, and to reassure the
world that America is waging war with care and precision to limit the
casualties we inflict.

These goals make solid sense to Western audiences, among which
there has been amazing growth in what Robert D. Kaplan has called the
imprudent "myth" that war can be waged with few casualties on either

side.[38] For Muslim audiences, however, the video clips are counterproductive because, paradoxically, they portray both violence against Muslims and not enough violence against Muslims. In the first instance, no matter how precise the weapon dropped or fired by a U.S. aircraft, it still kills the Muslim or Muslims on the receiving end. Crusaders kill Muslims in these clips, and the reality is worsened by our officials' public claims that most young Afghans and Iraqis serving in the armies of Mullah Omar and Saddam were conscripts who had been forced to choose between becoming soldiers or risking their lives and the lives of their families at the hands of the state. In the second instance, Islamists and many other Muslims in the Islamic world—where violence, at times indiscriminate, is often the *lingua franca*—see America's precise and intentionally casualty-limiting attacks as a lack of bloody-mindedness of the type in which, ironically enough, Ulysses S. Grant and Robert E. Lee first tutored the world in 1864's Overland Campaign. Dainty U.S. military attacks convince our Muslim friends and foes that America lacks the military savagery to either protect its allies or destroy its enemies, and that, despite massive U.S. military power, the Islamists can absorb U.S. attacks and fight again. "Warriors will interpret such an aversion to violence as a weakness, emboldening their cause," Robert D. Kaplan argues in *Warrior Politics*. "For such adversaries, our moral values—our fear of collateral damage—represent our worst vulnerabilities."[39] Both these reactions make bin Laden's points for him in large-font, boldface type: The Americans are perfectly willing to kill innocent Muslims—in this case conscripts—but not willing to risk their own soldiers' lives and the wrath of world opinion inherent in the thorough annihilation of their foe.

Change the Script

As we continue to tread the stage of our own creation in the Islamic world, we are locked in a downward spiral by the policy script from which we read our lines. Steps we take to protect ourselves and save the lives of others—immigration measures and precision bombing—are seen by our Muslim foes as evidence of racism, hypocrisy, and a lack of courage to risk U.S. lives. The measures we take in self-defense or to protect others unfailingly empower our Muslim enemies to hate us all the more, and to attack us with greater impunity. America's stubborn obtuseness in failing to see the counterproductive nature of its policies toward the Muslim world is a powerful force-multiplier for bin Laden and those he leads and inspires, and one to which U.S. leaders and elites are all but blind.

8

THE WAY AHEAD: A FEW
SUGGESTIONS FOR DEBATE

After it is all over, as stupid a fellow as I am can see that mistakes were made. I notice, however, that my mistakes are never told me until it is too late.

Robert E. Lee, 1863.[1]

The difference between Mr. Lincoln's moral conclusion and the moral arguments usually made during wartime is that he did not identify the enemy alone as evil.

Kent Gramm, 1994.[2]

There is no lack of bravery in our armed forces, but bureaucratic cowardice rules in our intelligence establishment (as well as at the highest levels of military command).

Ralph Peters, 1999.[3]

From their first workday, intelligence officers are told never to suggest policy. They are not policy makers and policy is not their concern, so goes the indoctrination. This is not to say intelligence officers have no policy views—they all do. That said, all are made to understand their job is to present the best intelligence in a clear, concise, and unbiased manner. For the most part, intelligence officers present the facts and hold their comments from the start of their careers through mid-level managership. It is when they enter the ranks of almost-senior managers—a purgatory forcing the officer to prove he or she is a "team" player who will tow the party line—and then go to senior ranks that that first-day lesson fades. Senior officers still hold their comments, but their willingness to present the facts complete and unslanted decreases. It is at this point that, as Ralph Peters has written, officers learn to "make far too much of loyalty, and far too little of integrity . . ." meaning, I presume, loyalty to their institution at the cost of personal and professional integrity. And, I think, that is why we often end up, as Lee did at Gettysburg, surveying the wreckage of a plan, policy, or attack that would have benefited from prior complete information and frank comments by those knowledgeable about the issue at hand.[4]

In the risk-averse air of the executive floors of intelligence-community (IC) buildings—seventh floors suffer particularly heavy concentrations—senior intelligence officers remain clear, concise, and unbiased but become more selective when deciding what to tell policy makers, including the president. This selectivity includes substantive issues—al Qaeda, North Korea, China, et cetera.—and information about the status of IC cooperation, areas of acute concern for policy makers. Substantive selectivity can exclude subjects in which policy makers are uninterested or those that will stir anger, such as intelligence showing a specific U.S. policy is cocked up. This process also yields the deselection of data that would spur policy-maker requests for action that, if taken, might yield an IC failure—and so criticism from Congress, policy makers, or the media—or expose the IC's unaddressed systemic failures. Regarding the bin Laden threat, for example, Francis Fukuyama could not have been more wrong when he argued that U.S. intelligence in the 1990s "was biased toward overestimation of threats."[5] The truth, from my seat at the theater, was exactly the opposite; the 1990s intelligence process deliberately downplayed the al Qaeda menace. In *The Age of Sacred Terror*, Steven Simon and Daniel Benjamin—two men who saw the show firsthand and daily—truthfully wrote that "CIA counterterrorism officials . . . took calming down the White House as one of their core tasks. . . ." The reason for soft-pedaling the threat was fear that the White House would order risky—and career-ending if botched—preemptive actions if the threat was presented honestly.[6]

Part I: Guidelines for Consideration

And so, to stop being a subordinate of the type that earned and merited Marse Robert's scorn, it is my turn. After twenty-plus years of not recommending policy, I will try my hand at suggesting not policy but guidelines America can consider using in efforts to defeat bin Laden and militant Islam. At day's end, the guidelines are one guy's ideas, and they come from one who knows that many men and women are smarter than he on the issues. Still, there is, at least, solace in knowing the guidelines offered cannot be worse for America than those our leaders have been advised to follow to date.

Relax, It's Only a War, Unique Like All Others

For better and worse, America has fought wars big and little, local and global, since Mr. Winthrop governed the Massachusetts Bay Colony. Since 11 September 2001, however, we collectively have behaved as if this war is our first. We have spent the past couple years making unmanageable federal government departments into gigantic unmanageable federal departments; embarrassing ourselves with threat-warning levels delineated in color on an indoor traffic signal unaccompanied by advice on defensive steps to take; and endless, almost-daily cabinet-level statements that simultaneously exalt the great progress being made against al Qaeda and warn the group is more of a threat than on 11 September.

It has been a dizzying, confusing, and, at times, a profoundly sophomoric performance. The conduct of war is never sedate, orderly, and silent, but it need not produce a cacophony of voices overstating small victories and downplaying a threat not yet grasped. Always tougher than their elites and never more so than now, workaday Americans do not need constant hand-holding and daily briefings from their leaders. They need quiet, confident performance that produces measurable progress and is reported without drama and hyperbole when leaders have something to say. Frenetic activity, ceaseless chatter, and loud voices usually signal confusion, and nowhere more than in Washington. Let us get on with the war and recall the power of silence. After all, bin Laden has us scared to death, and we have heard little from him since 2001.

Stop Celebrating Death and Defeat

Since the 11 September attacks, many Americans have engaged in an almost nonstop celebration of the massive U.S. defeat suffered that day. Purportedly sorrowful commemorations of the dead, these endless, well-planned and -scripted effusions of grief, international contests for memorial designs, and, most of all, rivers of stilted, never-forget oratory serve no purpose save to recall our utter defeat and allow us to wallow in dread of the pain to come. In my own organization in 2003, we celebrated "Family Day" by treating visiting relatives to this sort of celebration of defeat. In the main corridor stood a shrine erected to the debacle of 11 September. Beautifully matted photos of the twin towers burning and collapsing, framed artist renderings of architects' plans for memorials to the dead, photos of pseudo-Diana flower piles placed in front of U.S. embassies abroad, and—the macabre centerpiece—a glass display case holding metallic and concrete shards from the World Trade Center. All these are, to use an old-fashioned phrase, unmanly. Americans are made of sterner stuff—or, at least, better be, for, as Robert D. Kaplan wrote about our current foes in the *Atlantic Monthly*, "In a world of tribes and thugs manliness goes a long way."[7]

Generations of our forefathers marked America's defeats and casualties in quiet, unadorned, once-a-year observances; celebrations were kept for victories marked by the enemy's annihilation and war's end. Would that we relearn to mourn with quiet dignity and to celebrate only when the cause of mourning is eradicated. Our response to attacks should be to bury our dead while confirming our resolve to destroy their killers by reciting graveside verses from the 144th Psalm: "Blessed be the Lord my strength, which teaches my hands to war and my fingers to fight. . . . Bow thy heavens, O Lord, and come down: touch the mountains and they shall smoke. Cast forth lightning, and scatter them: shoot out thine arrows and destroy them. . . ."

Accept that We Are Hated, Not Misunderstood

The United States is hated across the Islamic world because of specific U.S. government policies and actions. That hatred is concrete not abstract, martial not intellectual, and it will grow for the foreseeable future. While important voices in the United States claim the intent of U.S. policy is misunderstood by Muslims, that Arabic satellite television channels deliberately distort the policy, and that better public diplomacy is the remedy, they are wrong. America is hated and attacked because Muslims believe they know precisely what the United States is doing in the Islamic world. They know partly because of bin Laden's words, partly because of satellite television, but mostly because of the tangible reality of U.S. policy. We are at war with an al Qaeda-led, worldwide Islamist insurgency because of and to defend those policies, and not, as President Bush mistakenly has said, "to defend freedom and all that is good and just in the world."[8]

To recognize the validity of this point, always keep in mind how easy it is for Muslims to see, hear, experience, and hate the six U.S. policies bin Laden repeatedly refers to as anti-Muslim:

- U.S. support for Israel that keeps Palestinians in the Israelis' thrall.
- U.S. and other Western troops on the Arabian Peninsula.
- U.S. occupation of Iraq and Afghanistan.
- U.S. support for Russia, India, and China against their Muslim militants.
- U.S. pressure on Arab energy producers to keep oil prices low.
- U.S. support for apostate, corrupt, and tyrannical Muslim governments.

Get Used to and Good at Killing

This guideline follows the last because unchanged U.S. policies toward the Muslim world leave America only a military option for defending itself. And it is not the option of daintily applying military power as we have since 1991. "U.S. soldiers are unprepared for the absolute mercilessness of which modern warriors are capable," Ralph Peters correctly said in *Fighting for the Future: Will America Triumph?*, "and they are discouraged or prohibited by their civilian masters and their own customs from taking the kind of measures that might be effective against members of the warrior class."[9] To secure as much of our way of life as possible, we will have to use military force in the way Americans used it on the fields of Virginia and Georgia, in France and on Pacific islands, and from skies over Tokyo and Dresden. Progress will be measured by the pace of killing and, yes, by body counts. Not the fatuous body counts of Vietnam, but precise counts that will run to extremely large numbers. The piles of dead will include as many or more civilians as combatants because our enemies wear no uniforms.

Killing in large numbers is not enough to defeat our Muslim foes. With killing must come a Sherman-like razing of infrastructure. Roads and irrigation systems; bridges, power plants, and crops in the field; fertilizer plants and grain mills—all these and more will need to be destroyed to deny the enemy its support base. Land mines, moreover, will be massively reintroduced to seal borders and mountain passes too long, high, or numerous to close with U.S. soldiers. As noted, such actions will yield large civilian casualties, displaced populations, and refugee flows. Again, this sort of bloody-mindedness is neither admirable nor desirable, but it will remain America's only option so long as she stands by her failed policies toward the Muslim world.

Cant Will Kill Us

"Our principles stop us from fighting bin Laden as he fights us." "We must fix the sources of al Qaeda's support—poverty, illiteracy, and hopelessness." "Bin Laden is attacking the civilized world; we must work with others and respond in a manner in line with international law." "Islam has nothing to do with this war; only maniacal Muslims support al Qaeda." Cant, all cant—the obfuscating and ahistorical language of cowardice and defeat. "Never listen," Ralph Peters has advised his countrymen, "to those who warn that ferocity on our part reduces us to the level of terrorists. . . . Historically we have proven time after time that we can do a tough, dirty job for our country without any damage to our nation's moral fibre."[10]

America is in a war for survival. Not survival in terms of protecting territory, but in terms of keeping the ability to live as we want, not as we must. Already, constrictions have occurred in civil liberties and societal openness; perhaps they are not permanent. As bin Laden and his like attack, we shun the offensive, speak with smug moral superiority, and respond in a limited, defensive manner that is changing society— the ease of travel, the way police view citizens, the difficulty of using public buildings and museums, the way we treat foreign visitors and nonnative U.S. citizens, the pathetic under-siege look of the White House. There are two choices. We can continue using and believing the cant cited above, or we can act to preserve our way of life—what Mr. Lincoln said is man's last best hope for self-government—by engaging in whatever martial behavior is needed. We owe this to ourselves, our heritage, and our posterity. We protect none of these by cloaking cowardice with canting words about international comity, civilized norms, and high moral standards. Such words are proper only in a suicide note for the nation.

Professional Soldiers Are Paid to Die

Because Americans are not used to a professional military fighting their wars, they are too worried by casualties—though not as worried as their elites believe. No soldier's life can be wasted, but America should not be less than optimally defended for fear of losing military lives. Gone, for now, are the days of valorous volunteers and eager draftees flocking to the colors in a national emergency. The U.S. military's men and women are professionals; they are soldiers by choice; it is their chosen career. For whatever reason they joined—love of country, money for college, avoiding jail, a taste for violence, a desire to travel, shelter from the competitive economy, or a hundred other reasons—the contract is as it was in ancient times: In return for getting what you sought by enlisting, the nation sends you where you are needed and you die if necessary. Only the U.S. Marines always recall this truism and go quietly and efficiently about the business of killing.

This is a harsh statement, but no less true for being harsh. The sooner our leaders start speaking of the cruel reality of professional soldiering, the sooner Americans will stop knee-jerk yellow ribboning—itself a constant reminder of our defeat by Iran's Islamists—and calling to "bring the troops home" almost before they deploy to the war zone. Common sense and the extraordinary expense of a professional military demand that U.S. leaders spend the capital accumulated between wars—trained, professional soldiers—as needed when the nation is at war. Today's U.S. military is, more than at any time in our history, a professional killing machine. The decision of when and how to use it must not be made in the nostalgic fog wrought by the unending deification of World War II's fuzzy-cheeked draftees, but rather in the clear-eyed recognition that each U.S. soldier put in harm's way goes there not just for country, but for pay and other recompense.

Others Will Not Do Our Dirty Work

Most of us learn this lesson early in life. America, too, learned it early, but seems to have forgotten. UN mandates, coalition-building, and multinational forces are contemporary concepts meant to limit the U.S. expenditure of blood and money. When such efforts are made on issues peripheral to U.S. national interests, such as the 2003 Liberia intervention, they are tolerable. But for defending core U.S. national interests they usually yield delay, limits on U.S. military power due to squeamish allies, and problems half-solved or wars half-fought. The lesson is not only that others will not do our dirty work, but that others will stop us from doing our dirty work as completely as possible.

So committed are we to finding others to do hard and bloody things for us that we misread reality and enlist allies who cannot or will not do the job. The Afghan war provides good examples of both. In late 2001, our Afghan proxies let bin Laden, Mullah Omar, and most of their soldiers escape because we foolishly trusted them so we could avoid deploying—and thereby risking—enough U.S. troops to ensure victory. Tribal customs and law, Islamic tenets, and the xenophobia of Afghans acted as brakes on our allies; we knew this—or should have—going into the war, but we ignored reality and tasked and paid them to do what they would not do. Afterwards, we enlisted Pakistan and its military to do our dirty work in the Afghanistan–Pakistan border area where our foes found refuge. Our ardor to avoid casualties, in this case, pushed us into a delusion. Islamabad's writ does extend to the Pashtun-dominated border, and Pakistani military action there would anger powerful, well-armed tribes that tolerate the central government only because they receive tribute and are otherwise left alone. The sum here is that effective Pakistani military action on the border could prompt a civil war, which, in turn, would drastically weaken Pakistan vis-à-vis India. Thus, we have fooled ourselves and done nothing to defeat our enemies. Pakistan will say the right words, take our arms and money, stage minor actions and take casualties to defuse U.S. frustration, but will not risk its fifty-year *modus vivendi* with the tribes. Effective action would risk life-and-death national interests, threatening Pakistan's survival as a nation via civil war, an opportunistic Indian first strike, or both. By seeking others to do our Afghan dirty work, U.S. national security has been hurt. This probably is a lesson that is globally applicable.

Do the Checkables and Demand Expertise

With a military, intelligence agencies, and civil service better educated ever before, we cocked up the Afghan and Iraq wars because we did not exploit knowledge we had. In Afghanistan, we ran a campaign that showed no sign of having learned anything from the 1979–1992 U.S. experience there. As a result, we ignored the relatively young leaders of the anti-Soviet jihad who, in American terms, held the swing vote. They are now allied with the Taleban and al Qaeda against the Afghan Transitional Administration (ATA). We named as ATA president a smart, decent, but follower-less man who is alive because he is "the West's kind of Afghan" and attracts foreign aid. We did not seal the Afghan borders—thereby allowing the enemy to exit and reenter—and for unknown reasons said Afghanistan's neighbors share our goal of a secular, stable, and pro-Western Kabul regime. In Iraq, we missed that the country is—after the Arab Peninsula—Islam's second holiest land, and that a U.S. invasion and occupation would be bin Laden's dream fulfilled, drawing large numbers of anti-U.S. fighters from the Muslim world, all enjoined by multiple, theologically valid fatwas to wage jihad. We also missed that none of Iraq's neighbors shared our goal of a secular, democratic Iraq, and that Saddam's end inevitably would spur a sectarian struggle pitting Iraqi Shias and Iran against Iraqi Sunnis and the regional Sunni states, and all of them against us. And we failed to close Iraq's borders.

We ignored realities because—in general—U.S. government foreign-policy agencies hold expertise and experience in low esteem, perhaps even contempt. Beyond technical subjects like ballistic missiles, weapons design, and satellite imagery, prolonged work on a single issue (say, Islam), a single region (say, South Asia), or a single problem (say, insurgency) classifies officers as having no management potential. Expertise is a career killer, especially in the intelligence community. Most prized is the "generalist," the officer who changes jobs every two years, flitting from Europe to East Asia to arms control to narcotics. Conversant in many topics, expert in none, these usually male officers are fast-tracked for senior management. In command, the glib but clueless appoint clones, building an impermeable, self-perpetuating wall between officers who, in the generalist's eyes, "waste" their careers developing expertise, and elected officials who annually allocate huge sums to develop the expertise America needs. For their money, elected leaders get access to well-dressed, articulate, and politically sensitive dilettantes, and hear nothing from idiosyncratic, intuitive, and reality-prone experts. And so, we have disasters in Iraq and Afghanistan. For those who doubt the foregoing, review Bob Woodward's portrait of the cabinet's relentlessly banal decision-making sessions before the Afghan war. In *Bush at War*, there is no discussion or debate about the influence of Islam on the motivation, ideology, war aims, or strategy of bin Laden and the Taleban; indeed, the index has entries only for "Islamabad" and "Islamic fundamentalists" and "Islamic Movement of Uzbekistan." There are, on the other hand, fifteen citations on delaying the attack—thereby letting al Qaeda disperse—until all search-and-rescue aircraft were in place. Woodward, unwittingly I think, shows that those who loosed the flood of damaging leaks that made his book possible did not serve the president well.

Do Not Deal with bin Laden as a Terrorist

This advice most Americans will choke on, object to, or revile, but it must be accepted. Al Qaeda attacks are terrifying, but acts of war are like that. Bin Laden is leading and inspiring a worldwide anti-U.S. insurgency; he is waging war while we fight him with counterterrorism policies dominated by law-enforcement tactics and procedures. It has not and will not work. America fought terror from 1975 to 1995 mainly with its intelligence services. We have done the same with al Qaeda, with America's clandestine service inflicting damage magnitudes beyond anything we ever did to a "terrorist group," but al Qaeda can still use weapons of mass destruction in the United States. The battle with al Qaeda is a plain old war, not an intelligence service–led counterterror campaign. We will not defeat bin Laden, al Qaeda, and their allies unless our strategy melds all U.S. war-fighting capabilities— military, intelligence, political, diplomatic, and economic—in a substantive manner, not in the rhetorical manner in use since 1995. We face a foe more dangerous than a traditional nation-state because it has a nation-state's goals and resources, draws manpower from a 1.3 billion-person pool, has no fixed address to attack, and fights for a cause in which death while killing enemies earns paradise.

The persistent misidentification of bin Laden and al Qaeda as "terrorists" is sponsored by the well-entrenched, well-funded, and sclerotic U.S. counterterrorism (CT) community. This entity was created to combat state sponsors of terrorism and their surrogate terrorist groups— Iran, Iraq, Syria, Libya, and groups like Lebanese Hizballah. It has largely and expensively failed but trundles along absorbing massive funding and many people to fight lethal nuisances, not national-security threats. Politicians and bureaucrats built the CT community to avoid militarily attacking a state staging such acts of war as downing commercial airliners (Libya) or destroying a U.S. embassy (Iran and Hizballah). Instead of the U.S. military smashing the miscreants and being done with them—easy, we know where each lives—Washington used a gun loaded with standard, dud CT bullets: endless diplomatic demarches; threats of pursuit, trial, and jail; life-risking intelligence collection; and a near complete cancellation rate for CT operations involving the slightest risk. As practiced by the United States, counterterrorism is appeasement; it lets the enemy attack and survive, keeps allies sweet by staying the hand of the U.S. military forces they hate, and ignores the true terrorist states in the Sunni Persian Gulf because they own much of the world's oil. The bloated, risk-averse, and lawyer-palsied CT community ensured state sponsors and their proxies survived, and now it blocks the counterinsurgency strategy needed to beat al Qaeda.

Demand Energy Self-Sufficiency

After thirty years' delay, we and our allies must move to energy self-sufficiency by exploiting domestic oil fields and, as important, by accelerating the development and use of alternative energy sources. Environmental, botanical, economic, or zoological concerns must, for the moment, be back-burnered. We must act because this is a dire national-security need, not a hedge against theoretical supply disruptions. With self-sufficiency, the United States can disengage from the Persian Gulf regimes—especially Saudi Arabia—which are among the earth's most corrupt, dictatorial, and oppressive. They rule peoples eager to be free of their yoke and who think their torturers survive because of U.S. protection. We have nothing in common with the regimes; the tie is based overwhelmingly on the West's obsession with cheap oil. Break the link and we are free of associations that earn us only hatred and violence in the Muslim world. Bin Laden and his like would have one less anti-U.S. grudge and over time would dispatch the medieval, authoritarian regimes the United States and the West have kept in power.

Such action would not only end U.S. energy dependence and political ties that mock our heritage and mar our democratic example, but it would promote the end of governments anti-American to their core. Saudi Arabia and the other Gulf states—not bin Laden—are what historian Malise Ruthven and others describe as the real imperial Islamic expansionists, seeking to spread fundamentalist Islam from Madrid to Manila and beyond.[11] For decades, these regimes, with Riyadh in the van, have "tutored generation after generation [of their subjects] in what amounts to jihadist incitement against non-Muslims."[12] They also have systematically funded and staffed organizations that foster an intensely anti-American brand of Islam around the world and in the United States. While bin Laden fights to defend Islam against U.S. attacks, the Saudi, Kuwaiti, Emirati, and other Gulf rulers hate us because we are not Muslims and because they fear that our example of representative government—again, Mr. Lincoln's last, best hope—will inspire their people to rebel, thereby threatening their autocratic rule and unfettered access to oil wealth. It is the Gulf royals—not Osama bin Laden—who hate us for what we are, not what we do. Shedding dependence on Gulf oil by the means noted above, Washington and its allies can deal properly with the Gulf states—that is, as regimes hostile to America's interests and survival.

End the Fifth Column of Senior Military and Intelligence Retirees

As noted earlier, senior military and intelligence officers seem unwilling to disagree with, much less condemn, their political leaders' plans, even when they know them to be potentially harmful to the country. Their acceptance and propagation of the idea that near-casualty-free wars can be decisive is surely the best example of their high tolerance for egregious stupidity. Again, I do not say these officers should criticize policy decisions publicly while serving; neither the constitution nor our political tradition can abide that. And yet, after working with generals and senior intelligence officers, I have found that few strongly oppose sure-to-fail polices during in-house discussions, and none have resigned to oppose what has become a standard set of policies that weaken America abroad, cause discord at home, and ultimately cost us far more lives, respect, and money than necessary.

Self-interest, I think, causes senior officers to acquiesce in counterproductive policies. In my career, the most-heard preretirement refrain has gone from "Now I'll be able to relax and do as I please" to "Now I can go and make some real money." The relatively young retirement age for generals and senior intelligence officers leads to day-after-retirement private-sector jobs with large pay hikes, shorter hours, and perks not given civil servants. The bag of gold at the end of public service is now visible early in a career and, I believe, persuades generals and senior intelligence officers not to vigorously challenge policy lest long memories deny them postretirement jobs in firms dependent on government contracts. Thus, general officers retire directly to well-appointed defense industry offices from where they deal with serving cronies and sell them everything from rifles to uniforms to F-16s. Or they join firms lobbying for the defense industry or Israel, or receive lucrative Pentagon consulting contracts. "Self-serving, supersmooth MBA types," Colonel Hackworth has described them, "looking to make the move from the Pentagon to plummy destinies with America's major companies. . . . We lost in Vietnam because management types finally outnumbered warriors, and since then it has only gotten worse thanks to the cancerous system that consistently promotes Hollywood-handsome careerists—who in turn pick equally corrupt clones as the next generation of generals."[13] Senior intelligence officers also wallow in the money trough offered by corporations that rent expensive contract help to the depressingly people-poor intelligence community. Most appalling are the retired senior intelligence officers working for Congress's oversight committees—making a lucrative salary and ensuring problems created or prolonged on their watch stay buried—and those who surface as high-paid "advisers" to foreign regimes, especially for our "friends" in Sudan and Saudi Arabia.

The smooth path from public service to private-sector jobs that offer "real money" all but ensures unwise, uninformed policies will prevail. Perhaps it is time to give senior military and intelligence officers a chance to speak their minds while in government and after retirement by banning many postretirement jobs in exchange for a full-salary annuity after thirty years. While costly, any consequent willingness by these officers to challenge feckless policies during or after public service would compensate Americans for the increased expense. Without such a scheme, America will remain without those Colonel Hackworth calls "truth-tellers," men and women—Hackworth is speaking of the military but his words are just as important for the intelligence services—

> who stand tall and stick to their guns with any and all civilians, from the president on down, over what our forces are capable of doing, the probable consequences of jumping into places like Afghanistan and Iraq, and how running-sore commitments like these degrade their outfit's ability to defend America from international terrorism.[14]

Islam Is at War with America

While U.S. leaders will not say America is at war with Islam, some of Islam is waging war on the United States, and more is edging closer to that status. "The war is fundamentally religious," bin Laden said in late 2001. "Under no circumstances should we forget this enmity between us and the infidels. For, the enmity is based on creed."[15] The war is being waged against us for specific, quantifiable reasons—which have been delineated in this study—and not as our leaders claim because a few Muslim fanatics hate democracy and freedom. This claim belittles the Muslims opposing us—reducing them to madmen throwing bombs at liberty—and thereby weakens America's ability to resist by underestimating the brains, patience, and religion-based fortitude of our foes.

The one thing accomplished by refusing to admit a war exists with an enemy of immense durability, manpower, and resources is to delay design of a strategy for victory. Only in today's America could the simple statement of fact that much of Islam is fighting us, and more is leaning that way, be labeled discriminatory or racist, a label that kills thought, debate, and, ultimately, Americans. But such is the case, and so U.S. leaders prepare for and fight the enemy they want to see, not the one standing on the battlefield.

What does it mean to be at war with Islam? It means deadly, matter-of-survival business that must be taken more seriously than it has been to date. War is being waged on us because of what we, as a nation, are doing in the Islamic world. Bin Laden's September 1996 declaration of war specifies U.S. actions causing him to incite war. His declaration is a neutral, factual statement, parts of it like Thomas Jefferson's Declaration of Independence. As a sovereign state, the United States is free to decide and implement its policies and actions in the Muslim world. They have been designed by elected leaders to meet national interests, approved and funded by elected representatives, and validated repeatedly in presidential and congressional elections. To say America is responsible for the polices against which Islam is waging war is a truism, as it is to say that those policies have propelled us into a religious war. So, what does it mean to be at war with Islam? First, it means we must accept this reality and act accordingly. Second, it means a U.S. policy *status quo* in the Muslim world ensures a gradually intensifying war for the foreseeable future, one that will be far more costly than we now imagine. Third, it means we will have to publicly address issues—support for Israel, energy self-sufficiency, and the worldwide applicability of our democracy—long neglected and certain to raise bitter, acrimonious debates that will decide whether the American way of life survives or shrinks to a crabbed, fearful, and barely recognizable form.

A Time for Discriminate International Involvement

George Washington's warning about the dangers of "entangling alliance," and John Quincy Adams's caution to Americans not to go abroad to slay dragons they do not understand in the name of spreading democracy are generally treated as the core of one of postwar America's most-despised "isms"—isolationism. As such, they are misunderstood. Now, Washington and Adams were sophisticated, thoughtful men, and each saw that America's economic growth depended not just on domestic industry and agriculture, but on trading with the world. Neither gentlemen argued for nonintercourse—that nonsense was fathered by Jefferson—but both did warn against unnecessary commitments and actions. Each advocated U.S. activity abroad in business, diplomacy, trade, education, science, finance, and other realms. What Washington and Adams argued was that U.S. involvement overseas should be of net benefit, and, being hardheaded, practical, and pessimistic men, they defined benefit in material and political terms, not in terms of self-satisfaction derived from being the deliverer of democracy to the oppressed. Life was a zero-sum affair for the Founders—even for the often egregious Jefferson—and the position of Washington and Adams was simply that America should not enter unprofitable arrangements, situations she did not understand, and, most of all, other peoples' wars. They argued for America first, not America alone, and sought to spread the democracy that was their pride by example, not coercive foreign action. The lessons of Washington and Adams guided Americans until the postwar era, when our elites slowly came to believe and teach that America owes more to others than to itself. More, they came to preach that guilt and shame are attached to wanting to care first for America, that somehow it is nobler to force-feed foreigners democracy than to expend time and resources to perfect our democracy.

Perhaps the best book I read while writing this study was Ralph Peters's *Fighting for the Future: Will America Triumph?* In it, Peters makes a suggestion that still stuns, haunts, and encourages me. "We Americans must avoid fantastic schemes to rescue those for whom we bear no responsibility," Peters said. "In dealing with nationalism and fundamentalism we must be willing to let the flames burn themselves out whenever we are not in danger of catching fire ourselves. If we want to avoid the needless, thankless deaths of our own countrymen, we must learn to watch others die with equanimity."[16] Peters is right, brutally updating the guidance of Washington and Adams. Can any U.S. official, academic, politician, or pundit credibly claim to know what is going on in Iraq's sectarian and tribal politics, Afghanistan's tribal and ethnic rivalries, or the tribal-religious-ethnic politics of the Balkans, Rwanda, Liberia, or Congo? Can anyone honestly believe the claim that Washington will broker a "just peace" between Israel and Palestine is anything other than a thirty-year-old, mindlessly repeated mantra? Can anyone even describe the basic elements of the Islamic faith and their impact on world affairs? More to the point, can it be proven that it would make a substantive—vice emotional—difference to U.S. security if every Hutu killed every Tutsi, or vice versa; every Palestinian killed every Israeli, or vice versa; or if Serbs, Croats, and Bosnians exterminated each other to the last person? The brutal but correct answers are: we do not understand these conflicts, and none of them, regardless of who wins, endanger U.S. interests. All evoke empathy and stir emotion, but it is, as always, a cruel world, and each nation's one mandatory duty is to care for and defend itself.

For our own welfare and survival, we must "watch others die with equanimity" and help after "the flames burn themselves out" by focusing our overseas intercourse on trade, sharing knowledge, and donating food and medicine. America must not commit abroad unless genuine national interests are at risk, and she must go to war only for survival and then act to annihilate the enemy. We must let our efforts to perfect self-government and ensure equality for all at home be the example that spurs democracy abroad. We must unflinchingly let foreign dragons devour each other without expending American lives, treasure, and self-respect on an endless series of fool's errands.

Part II: The Need to Debate the Guidelines Now

The guidelines need to be debated now because, in most ways, America is in a position not much different from that on which it stood on 10 September 2001. If the media are correct, the leaders of the U.S. intelligence community were warning Congress and the White House for months prior to that date that a major al Qaeda attack was coming. When it came, we did not stop it—an impossible task that gets too much focus—and were utterly unprepared to respond, an as yet unnoted scandal. The latter, moreover, is a blistering indictment of our governing, foreign policy, academic, and media elites who, for all their militant words about al Qaeda after the East Africa bombings and the attack on the *Cole,* never really took the bin Laden threat seriously.

In the period since 11 September, the United States has dealt lethal blows to al Qaeda's leadership and—if official claims are true—have captured three thousand al Qaeda foot soldiers. We have waged two failed half-wars and, in doing so, left Afghanistan and Iraq seething with anti-U.S. sentiment, fertile grounds for the expansion of al Qaeda and kindred groups. We have sent U.S. forces to Yemen, East Africa, the Philippines, and the Caucasus, forces small enough to have little or no impact on the Islamist insurgencies there but large and attention-getting enough to convince more of the Islamic world that Washington will use its military wherever Muslims fight what they see as tyranny. Worse, we have officially backed Russia, China, and India in their wars on "terrorism" in, respectively, Chechnya, Xinjiang, and Kashmir. In each case, God help us, America stands by governments determined to exterminate Islamist fighters struggling not just for independence but against institutionalized barbarism. These dilemmas exist for America because our elites obsessively insist that violence by Muslims is terrorism and that none of those Muslims could possibly be freedom fighters. We are, overall, in a hell of a fix.

And yet, amidst this self-inflicted disaster, there is a golden opportunity, one unlikely to come again in this generation's lifetime. For the first time since the Cold War's end—perhaps since 1945—Americans must make a definitive choice about U.S. relations with the Muslim world. If bin Laden has done us any favors, beyond underscoring the power of words and ideas, it surely is that he has driven us to this point. And, in a fine example of strategic savvy, he has created a situation whereby not choosing—by keeping a policy *status quo*—America chooses prolonged war. We can either reaffirm current policies, thereby denying their role in creating the hatred bin Laden personifies, or we can examine and debate the reality we face, the threat we must defeat, and then—if deemed necessary—devise policies that better serve U.S. interests.

Let me stress that we are not choosing between war and peace. America has a war it cannot avoid and, at least for now, one that will grow more savage no matter what we do. The choice we have is between keeping current policies, which will produce an escalating expenditure of American treasure and blood, or devising new policies, which may, over time, reduce the expenditure of both. We cannot talk or negotiate our way out of this mess; the enemy has listened for thirty years and believes U.S. promises of fairness for Muslims have been lies. Simply put, the enemy wants war and is not listening; he has no reason to listen, he is winning. We have no choice but to fight; it is the decision about policy that will determine the fight's length and cost.

So far in this book, I have hewed closely to topics on which I have some knowledge and experience: bin Laden, Islam, Islamic insurgencies, and Afghanistan. In this chapter, I will continue on this course, but, with the reader's indulgence, I will add comments about U.S. policies and actions that strike me, as an intelligence officer and a student of history, as radically out of touch with the American experience and with traditional U.S. interests. I found the courage—or perhaps, in my case, foolishness—to overstep the comfort zone of professional and educational experience after reading a number of books and articles I found provocative in their ability to inspire reflection on America's role in the world, its purported responsibilities to the so-called international community, and, most important, its responsibilities to itself. Among the works I would cite and recommend to readers of this book are Robert D. Kaplan's *Warrior Politics: Why Leadership Requires a Pagan Ethos* (2002); Kent Gramm's *Gettysburg: A Meditation on War and Values*; Ralph Peters's *Fighting for the Future: Will America Triumph?* (1999) and *Beyond Terror: Strategy in a Changing World* (2002); Bernard Lewis's *The Crisis of Islam: Holy War and Unholy Terror* (2003); retired U.S. colonel David H. Hackworth's media commentary; Richard Betts's brilliant essay in the spring 2002 *Political Science Quarterly*, "The Soft Underbelly of American Primacy: Tactical Advantages of Terror"; the books and journalism of Geneive Abdo; and Stephen Biddle's monograph that spoke truth to power (or is it hubristic arrogance?), *Afghanistan and the Future of Warfare: Implications for Army and Defense Policy* (2002). I do not agree with all these individuals have written; they will not agree with all I write here. Their analysis, however, is compelling, and their ability to draw on thinkers from centuries past and couple that legacy with their own experience and incisiveness produces a rare and valuable commodity: an intellectual stimulus that enthralls a reader, steels him to do some thinking of his own, and risk exposing the result to the criticism of others. What follows, then, is an aspiring minor leaguer's attempt to pursue the examples set by the major leaguers just noted.

Short and Sweet: Bin Laden Is as He Seems

Enough. Let us talk no more of Osama bin Laden the gangster, mass murderer, sexual deviant, psychopath, tool of others, or dilettante terrorist spendthrift. Let us surely keep our eyes open for credible information pointing in one or more of these directions, but until that first piece of corroborated data appears, let us agree that America is facing a talented, sturdy, charismatic, and determined enemy, one whose example and leadership is producing a growing threat to U.S. security from much of the Muslim world and not just from its lunatic fringe. With this judgment, we can behave and debate like responsible adults, accurately gauge the threat we face, and stop believing the 11 September attacks were one-off events. At that point, we can at last make a rational decision about whether we want to live with or destroy the threat bin Laden personifies. Until we reach a valid conclusion about the nature of our foe, feel able to publicly state and debate that view, and then are ready to act on it, we will continue losing ground to the Islamists, as we have since 11 September. "You cannot lead a nation to war if you dare not recognize the enemy," Mark Helprin argued in the *Wall Street Journal*. "The Islamic world, no stranger to war for the faith, has tentatively renewed its energy of expansion and given rise to those within it who have begun to rekindle its ancient conflict with the West."[17] Though Mr. Helprin is wrong about bin Laden-led Islamic expansionism, the al Qaeda chief clearly is one of "those within it" who is leading a defensive war against us. Let us accept, until proven otherwise, that bin Laden is what he seems—a worthy and dangerous foe—and agree with what Mr. Holmes told Dr. Watson, that after eliminating all other options, "Whatever remains however improbable must be the truth."

Thought Police Be Damned: Nothing Is Too Dangerous to Talk About

America's problem vis-à-vis al Qaeda is not limited in a way that allows it to truthfully be described as the "bin Laden problem." Honesty demands that it must be described as a Muslim or an Islamic problem. To say this is simply to accept reality. The statement has no connotations—explicit or implicit—of denigrating one of the world's great religions. Indeed, there was a time in Western history when Christians were ready to fight, die, and even burn at the stake rather than renounce or abandon their faith. "Christian history," Kenneth Minogue reminded the readers of *National Interest*, "is testimony to the ferocity which lovers of peace can respond to what they conceive to be a challenge."[18] In the Catholic tradition, which is my own, some of those who today are worshipped as saints won their status as fighters in Rome's version of jihad, the series of crusades launched by Pope Urban II. In the Catholic military order of the Knights Templar, for example, James Reston Jr. has written that the order "drew its inspiration from St. Bernard of Clairvaux who declared that 'killing for Christ' was 'malecide not homicide' and 'to kill a pagan is to win glory, for it gives glory to Christ.'"[19] The simple reality is that Muslims believe what Muslims believe, and today tens of millions of Muslims—beyond bin Laden, al Qaeda, the Taleban, and like-minded Islamists—believe their faith is being attacked by the U.S.-led Western Crusaders and that Islam will be changed beyond recognition, if not eradicated, if each Muslim does not step forth to defend it with his life, as has been prescribed by Allah and His prophet.

If any doubt this claim, they can read the fatwas issued by leading Muslim clerics and jurists—liberal, conservative, and radical—at the start of the second U.S.-led war against Iraq. The fatwas unanimously call for a defensive jihad against the United States for attacking Iraq and its people. Without mentioning bin Laden, the fatwas mirror the religious arguments for an anti-U.S. defensive jihad bin Laden has expounded since 1996; in many ways, they validate the theological accuracy of bin Laden's fatwas. The Iraq-war fatwas also describe as "apostates"—deserving death—any Muslim individual, organization, or government that in word or deed helps the United States attack the Iraqi people and occupy their country. "[I]t is not permissible for [a Muslim] individual, or a group, or a country," warned the eminent Saudi Shaykh Salman al-Awdah, "to assist by word, deed, sign, or supply any attack that would destroy the country and kill the people of Iraq."[20] Again, such words precisely mirror bin Laden's judgments.

Leaving aside political-correctness concerns will allow us to recognize and candidly discuss the genuine and growing substantive, not just visceral, hatred for America among the world's 1.3 billion Muslims. Because Muslim leaders—with bin Laden in the van—repeatedly have told us that they hate Americans for what we do and not for what we think, look like, or talk about, there can be no valid charge of racism or Islamophobia in such a discussion. "We regret to tell you that you are the worst civilization in the history of mankind," bin Laden explained in his October 2002 letter to Americans. "You ransack our lands, stealing our treasures and oil. . . . Your forces occupy our land. . . . You have starved the Muslims of Iraq. . . . So what is left on the list of the most heinous, evil and unjust acts that you have not done?"[21] Reality for America is simply a matter of saying that there is a large and growing number of Muslims who hate our policies and actions toward the Islamic world, many of whom have or will take up arms against us as a result. Accepting this reality, we would at long last be ready to publicly debate and decide what we, the American people, are going to do to defeat the threat to our country's security and way of life. Such a debate would begin a process toward something America has lacked since the end of the Cold War: a clear definition of the national interest. "No clear national interest has emerged. No clear conversation about the national interest has emerged," Michael Ignatieff wrote in 2003 in the *New York Times Magazine*. "Policy . . . has seemed to be mostly the prisoner of international lobbies with access to the indignation machines of the modern media. . . . At the moment the United States is fighting two wars with no clear policy of intervention, no clear end in sight, and no clear understanding among Americans of what their nation has gotten itself into."[22]

Having gotten this far, the start of frank debate will become infinitely harder because, to be effective, it will need to dissect policies about which Americans seldom question their government for fear of getting sideways with political correctness police, those Ralph Peters correctly calls "mortal enemies" of democracy practicing "the tyranny of often-arcane minorities."[23] Ironically, if we find the guts to debate, we will find the issues to be debated are at the core of bin Laden's foreign policy. The questions needing debate include the following:

- Does unvarying military, economic, and political support for Israel serve substantive—vice emotional—U.S. interests, those that, by definition, affect America's survival? Do we totally support Israel because it is essential to our security, or because of habit, the prowess of Israel's American lobbyists and spies, the half-true mantra that Israel is a democracy, the fear of having no control over a state we allowed to become armed with WMD, the bewildering pro-Israel alliance of liberal Democrats and Christian fundamentalists, and a misplaced sense of guilt over the Holocaust? Like America or any state, Israel has a right to exist if it can defend itself or live peacefully with its neighbors; that is not the question. The question is whether U.S. interests require Americans to be Israel's protectors and endure the endless blood-and-treasure costs of that role. Status quo U.S. policy toward Israel will result in unending war with Islam.
- The question of Israel leads to a much more important question for Americans: that is, in Michael Ignatieff's words, "the difficult questions . . . of whether their own freedom entails a duty to defend the freedom of others beyond their borders."[24] There is no greater duty today's Americans can perform for their nation and posterity than to finally abandon the sordid legacy of Woodrow Wilson's internationalism—which soaked the twentieth century in as much or more blood as any other "ism"—and recall and institutionalize John Quincy Adams's advice that the United States must be "the well-wisher to the freedom

and independence of all . . . [but] the champion and vindicator only of her own."[25]

- Beyond below-market oil prices, what do we gain from backing Muslim regimes that are corrupt, repressive tyrannies—be they monarchical, military, or family-run—and that use control of oil pricing to extort U.S. protection while using their U.S.- and Western-armed militaries to suppress and persecute their own people?

- Have we the moral courage to defy the alliance of oil companies, hardline environmentalists, and the political backers of each and install an energy policy leading to self-sufficiency? Today's wars show the direct tie between the West's dependence on Persian Gulf oil and the loss of U.S. lives: the more dependence, the more deaths. In a region where we have no national interest save oil, the question is: How many lives are we willing to pay per thousand barrels of oil?

- Do we need military and naval bases on the Arabian Peninsula, and do we need to continue occupying Muslim lands? Is there a security threat to America sufficient to justify these things, when each strengthens bin Laden's appeal among Muslims? If there is such a threat, will we be able, as Ralph Peters asked, "to engage and sustain the level of sheer violence it can take to eradicate this kind of threat?"[26] Indeed, while preaching the equality of all cultures, can we even admit that such a level of violence against another culture might be needed to ensure our survival?

- Does U.S. security require, and have we the moral right, to aggressively try to install secular, democratic systems in countries that give no hint of wanting them? Is our nation more likely to perish if the rest of the world is not just like us, or if our democracy-making crusade destabilizes much of the world?

As the reader can imagine, such questions, if honestly examined, would spur passionate, far-reaching debate, not to mention much mudslinging and charges of racism, anti-Semitism, Islamophobia, isolationism, nationalism, and—specifically for the author—simpleton-ism. Several generations of America's elites—who have long accepted as axiomatic our support of Israel, iron ties to Arab tyrants, the sanctity of inviolate homes for caribou and Arctic hare, and a duty to make all nations democratic and secular—would rise up in righteous indignation. Some will do so from genuine faith in these axioms. More will rise due to the bountiful honoraria they draw from Saudi and other Gulf royals, the political and philanthropic funds they derive from U.S. energy and arms companies, and an inability induced by lobbyists and U.S. electoral politics to realize the term "U.S. national interest" is not interchangeable with "Israeli national interest."

These men and women will argue that the policies listed above are beyond debate, that they are sacrosanct, universally accepted by Americans, and require no more thought, analysis, or discussion. Behind the elites' claims on these issues, I think, lurks fear that the consensus they assert is neither broad nor durable. The suspicion may be taking root among our elites that most working Americans see no gain in alienating a billion-plus Muslims; that Washington's talk of democracy-spreading while practicing tyranny-protecting is an embarrassing, shameful hypocrisy; that the time for an energy policy that values tundra, reindeer, and lichens over U.S. soldiers and civilians has past; and that perfecting America—in terms of democracy, education, and economics—is overwhelmingly more important than financing quixotic, hate-earning campaigns to democratize countries and peoples who do not want to be like us and are not essential to our nation's survival.

The rhetorical fireworks and public acrimony from such a debate would greatly stimulate thoughtful policy reevaluation by Americans, especially those outside academe, the Washington–Boston corridor, and Hollywood. Perhaps Americans would find that, after a long hiatus, they can still think for themselves, define what is in their interest and that of their country, and decide that the elites' foreign policy mantras need not only review but silencing. But, with this said, no one can predict the outcome of such a debate. It may be bin Laden is correct, that the *status quo* in U.S. policies toward the Muslim world will be reaffirmed. Although I, for one, hope this is not the debate's result, if it is, so be it—as always, the majority must rule. Whatever the decision, as I said earlier, America's military confrontation with Islam will continue. An honest debate will, however, allow Americans to know what they are signing up for: a policy *status quo* that will guarantee broadening conflict with escalating human and economic expense, or new policies that have potential, over time, for a less confrontational and bloody relationship with Islam. Whatever the choice, it must be made by all Americans after all options are presented and debated, and not solely by their elites with the guidance, lobbying, money, and machinations of oil companies, weapons makers, evangelical preachers, and Israel and its acolytes.

Epilogue: No Basis for Optimism

☪

> I have no word of encouragement to give! . . . [T]he people have not yet made up their minds that we are at war with the South. They have not buckled down to the determination to fight this war through; for they have got the idea into their heads that we are going to get out of this fix somehow by strategy! . . . General McClellan thinks he is going to whip the rebels by strategy; and the army has got the same notion. . . . The people have not yet made up their minds we're at war I tell you! They think there is a royal road to peace, and that General McClellan is to find it. The army has not settled down into the conviction that we are in a terrible war that has got to be fought out—no; and the officers have not either.
>
> Abraham Lincoln, 1862.[1]

Mr. Lincoln's disgust at McClellan's failure to destroy Lee's Army of Northern Virginia at Antietam should be felt by Americans today because of their leaders' misperceptions and operational failures against bin Laden and the cause he personifies. This point I have made often and shall not belabor here. It is sufficient, I think, to note that, in the quote above, Mr. Lincoln was making the point that after seventeen months of war, most Americans—leaders and led—had yet to understand the reality of our civil war. The same problem—that today's Americans also "just don't get it"—was apparent when I began writing this book in January 2003 and remains as I conclude in May 2004, thirty-plus months after we invaded Afghanistan. We still see the war through the eyes of McClellan, not Lincoln, and we recognize neither the size and nature of the bin Laden threat, nor that we have not yet begun to fight the kind of war needed to defeat the forces he leads and inspires.

And this may be because, in one crucially important sense, it is a war unlike any other America has fought. In our struggle with bin Laden we have encountered but not yet accepted a counterintuitive reality. Trained to look for what Clausewitz called the enemy's "center of gravity"—attacks on which will ultimately defeat him—U.S. leaders are assaulting bin Laden's safe havens, finances, leadership cadre, allied groups, and even the charitable donations and educational curricula believed to support him. For nearly three years, these attacks have been under way, have scored the successes noted in Chapter 3, and yet in a late-February 2004 worldwide threat briefing, the director of central intelligence told the Senate Select Committee that the threat from bin Laden was growing.

> So far we have made notable strides [against al Qaeda]. But do not misunderstand me. I am not suggesting al Qaeda is defeated. It is not. We are still at war. [Al Qaeda] is a learning organization that remains committed to attacking the United States, its friends and allies. . . .
>
> So far I have been talking only about al Qaeda. But al Qaeda is not the limit of [the] terrorist threat worldwide. Al Qaeda has infected others with its ideology, which depicts the United States as Islam's greatest foe. Mr. Chairman, what I want to say to you now may be the most important thing I tell you today.
>
> The steady growth of Usama Bin Ladin's anti-U.S. sentiment throughout the wider Sunni extremist movement and the broad dissemination of al Qaeda's destructive expertise ensure that a serious threat will remain for the foreseeable future—with or without al Qaeda in the picture.[2]

The director's courageous words—starkly at odds with those of other senior U.S. officials regarding the al Qaeda war—were heard but not understood by his audience and the media. The statement said, in essence, that while America has scored major tactical victories against al Qaeda, it is losing the strategic war because bin Laden's "anti-U.S. sentiments" have spread across the worldwide Sunni extremist movement. Exactly. But why? The DCI [director of central intelligence] fought shy of candor here, adopting the virus analogy favored by those who do not know or do not want to accept reality. Bin Laden, the DCI said, has "infected" others with al Qaeda's ideology.[3]

The director's statement that bin Laden is winning is the clearest we have had from our leaders. Bin Laden, however, has inspired and instigated other Sunnis; he has not infected them. The Islamists in al

Qaeda, in other similar groups, and ordinary Muslims worldwide have been infected by hatred for U.S. policies toward the Muslim world. America's support for Israel, Russia, China, India, Algeria, Uzbekistan, and others against Islamists; its protection of multiple Muslim tyrannies; its efforts to control oil policy and pricing; and its military activities in Afghanistan, Iraq, the Arabian Peninsula, and elsewhere—these are the sources of the infection of hatred spreading in the Islamic world. Bin Laden has astutely taken advantage of this U.S.–induced illness, and, by reminding Muslims of their history and religious duty and by attacking America, has emerged as the leader of what the DCI accurately described as "a serious threat [that] will remain for the foreseeable future."[4]

Bin Laden, at day's end, has turned Clausewitz on his head. Indeed, bin Laden has no center of gravity in the traditional sense—no economy, no cities, no homeland, no power grids, no regular military, et cetera Bin Laden's center of gravity, rather, lies in the list of current U.S. policies toward the Muslim world because that status quo enrages Muslims around the globe—no matter their view of al Qaeda's martial actions—and gives bin Laden's efforts to instigate a worldwide anti-U.S. defensive jihad virtually unlimited room for growth. So long as this fact is unrecognized by Americans and their leaders, bin Laden will keep winning the strategic war, notwithstanding continuing tactical losses. Until those policies change, the United States has no option but an increasingly fierce military response to the forces marshaled by bin Laden, an option that will prolong America's survival but at as yet undreamed of costs in blood, money, and civil liberties. "All war is based on deception," the Chinese philosopher Sun Tzu wrote long ago. To date, America's war against bin Laden and al Qaeda has deceived only the American public.

Notes

The most frequently cited journals, magazines, newspapers, and media services are referred to by the following abbreviations after their first citation.

Agence-France Presse—AFP
Al-Hayat—AH
Al-Jazirah Space Channel Television—AJSCT
Al-Quds Al-Arabi—AQAA
Al-Sharq Al-Awsat—ASAA
Chicago Tribune—CT
Christian Science Monitor—CSM
Foreign Affairs—FA
Jane's Intelligence Review—JIR
Long Island Newsday—LIN
Los Angeles Times—LAT
National Interest—NI
National Journal—NJ
New York Times—NYT
New York Times Magazine—NYTM
Philadelphia Enquirer—PI
USA Today—USAT
U.S. News and World Report—USNWR
Wall Street Journal—WSJ
Washington Post—WP
Washington Times—WT

Preface

1. Quoted in Peter G. Tsouras (ed.), *Civil War Quotations: In the Words of the Commanders*. New York: Sterling Publishing Co., Inc., 1998, p. 88.
2. Robert Baer. *See No Evil: The True Story of a Ground Soldier in the CIA's War on Terrorism*. New York: Three Rivers Press, 2002, p. xvii.
3. *Ibid.*, p. 205.

4. Ralph Peters. *Beyond Terror: Strategy in a Changing World*. Mechanicsburg, PA: Stackpole Books, 2002, pp. 195, 197.

5. Kent Gramm. *Gettysburg: A Meditation on War and Values*. Bloomington, IN: University of Indiana Press, 1994, p. 107.

Introduction: "Hubris Followed by Defeat"

1. Michael Ignatieff, "The American Empire (Get Used to It)," *New York Times Magazine*, 5 January 2003.

2. Nicholas D. Kristof, "Cassandra Speaks," *New York Times*, 18 March 2003.

3. Stanley Kurtz, "The Future of 'History': Francis Fukyama vs. Samuel P. Huntington," *Policy Review*, (June–July 2002), p. 43.

4. Andrew J. Bacevich, "The Nation at War," *Los Angeles Times*, 20 March 2003.

5. For a recent look at Seward's war gambit and Lincoln's reaction to it, see Dean Mahin. *One War At a Time: The International Dimensions of the American Civil War*. Washington, D.C.: Brassey's Inc., 1999, x and 343p.

6. Miller is quoted in Alan Taylor's review of Edmond S. Morgan's biography of Benjamin Franklin in *New Republic*, 13 January 2003, p. 29.

7. Bernard Lewis. *The Crisis of Islam: Holy War and Unholy Terror*. New York: The Modern Library, 2003, p. 17.

8. Robert Fisk, "He Is Alive. There Can Be No Doubt about It. But the Questions Remain: Where on Earth Is He, and Why Has He Resurfaced Now?" *Independent*, 14 November 2002.

9. Robert D. Kaplan. *Warrior Politics: Why Leadership Requires a Pagan Ethos*. New York: Vintage Books, 2002, p. 5.

10. Ralph Peters. *Fighting for the Future: Will America Triumph?* Mechanicsburg, PA: Stackpole Books, 1999, p. 117.

11. "Recorded Audio Message by Ayman Zawahiri," *Al-Jazirah Satellite Channel Television*, 10 September 2003.

Chapter 1: Some Thoughts on the Power of Focused, Principled Hatred

1. Bernard Lewis, *Crisis of Islam*, pp. 22–23.

2. Ralph Peters, *Fighting for the Future: Will America Triumph?*, p. 13.

3. "Azzam Exclusive: Letter from Usamah Bin Mohammad Bin Ladin to the American People," *Waaqiah.com* (Internet), 26 October 2002.

4. Bernard Lewis. *What Went Wrong? Western Impact and Middle East Response*. New York: Oxford University Press, 2002, p. 100.

5. Dana Millbank, "Conservatives Dispute Bush's Portrayal of Islam as Peaceful," *Washington Post*, 30 November 2002, p. 4.

6. *Ibid.*

7. Atif Adwan, "Why Iraq?: The Religious Dimensions of a Campaign Against Islam," *Al-Sha'b* (Internet version), 22 March 2003.

8. Mark O'Keefe, "Plans Under Way for Christianizing the Enemy," *Newhouse.com* (Internet), 26 May 2003.

9. Muhamad Wahbi, "Bush Only Distanced His Administration from the Vile Campaign in the U.S. against Islam," *Al-Musawwar*, 22 November 2002, pp. 18–20.

10. "Is it Not High Time Bush Reined in the Priests of Hatred?," *Al-Jazirah* (Internet version), 16 November 2002.

11. Atif Adwan, *Al-Sha'b*, 22 March 2003, *op. cit.*

12. Anthony Sahdid, *Legacy of the Prophet: Despots, Democrats, and the New Politics of Islam*. Boulder, CO: Westview Press, 2001, p. 12.

13. Daniel Pipes, "Jihad and the Professors," *Commentary* (November 2002), p. 19.

14. Bernard Lewis, *Crisis of Islam*, pp. 29, 31–32, and Daniel Pipes, *Commentary* (November 2002), p. 20.

15. James Turner Johnson, "Jihad and Just War," *First Things: A Journal of Religion and Public Life*, June–July 2002, p. 12.

16. *Ibid.*

17. Ronald Spiers, "Try Clearer Thinking About Terrorists," *International Herald Tribune*, 14 January 2003.

18. Dr. Mohammed Abd-al-Halim Umar [Head, Center for Economic Studies, Al-Azhar], "The United States Has Begun Its War Against Islam," *Lailatalqadr* (Internet version), 21 March 2002.

19. Malise Ruthven. *A Fury for God: The Islamist Attack on America*. London: Granta Books, 2002, p. 246.

20. "Life and Religion," *AJSCT*, 14 October 2001.

21. Iqbal al-Siba'i, "Interview with Al-Azhar Grand Imam Shaykh Mohammad Sayyid Tantawi," *Rose al-Yusuf*, 5 January 2001, pp. 26–27.

22. Daniel Byman, "Scoring the War on Terrorism, *National Interest*, no. 72 (Summer 2002), pp. 82–83.

23. Bernard Lewis, "Time for Toppling," *Wall Street Journal*, 27 September 2002.

24. M. Karwash, "Reconstruction or Destruction," Al-Arab Al-Yawm, 13 November 2003, p. 32.

25. Abu-Ubayd al-Qurashi, "The Autumn of Iraqi Fury," *Al-Ansar* (Internet), 24 August 2002.

26. "Statement of Abu Hafs al-Masri Brigades, 19 August 2003," *Quds Press* (Internet version), 25 August 2003.

27. "Now the War Has Begun," *Al-Ansar* (Internet), 17 April 2003, p. 3.

28. Shaykh S. al-Awdah, "Youth . . . and Youth!," *Al-Jazirah* (Internet version), 20 July 2003.

29. Chris Hedges. *War Is a Force that Gives Us Meaning.* New York: Anchor Books, 2002, p. 77.

30. Dr. Ahmad al-Khatib, "We Should Utilize Al-Azhar's Fatwas," *Al-Sh'ab* (Internet version), 14 April 2003.

31. Genieve Abdo, "Some Moderate Islamic Clerics Take a New Hard Line Against U.S.," *Boston Globe*, 16 March 2003, p. 20.

32. Stephen F. Hayes, "Uncle Sam's Makeover," *Weekly Standard*, 3 June 2003.

33. *Ibid.*

34. Shibley Telhami, "Understanding the Challenge," *The Middle East Journal*, vol. 56, no. 1 (winter 2002), p. 9.

35. Abu-Ubayd al-Qurashi, "Why Did Baghdad Fall?" *Al-Ansar*, 17 April 2003.

36. Ralph Peters, *Beyond Terror: Strategy in a Changing World*, p. 21.

37. "Statement by Usama Bin Ladin," *AJSCT*, 6 October 2002.

38. Kent Gramm, *Gettysburg. A Meditation on War and Values*, p. 252.

Chapter 2: An Unprepared and Ignorant Lunge to Defeat—The United States in Afghanistan

1. P. G. Tsouras (ed.). *Civil War Quotations*, p. 39.

2. "Message from Mullah Omar to the Islamic Nation," *Jihad Online News Network* (Internet), 13 September 2002.

3. John Keegan, "How America Can Wreak Vengeance," *The Daily Telegraph* (Internet version), 14 September 2001.

4. Sayf-al-Din al-Ansari, "They Will Not Cease to Fight with You," *Al-Ansar* (Internet), 15 January 2002.

5. Malise Ruthven, *A Fury for God: The Islamist Attack on America*, op. cit. p. 31.

6. Don Chipman, "Air Power and the Battle for Mazar-e Sharif," *Air Power History*, vol. 50, no. 1 (spring 2003), p. 34.

7. Jonathan Calvert, "Bin Ladin Family Sells London Offices," *Sunday Times*, 8 December 2002, and Frank Rich, "Pearl Harbor Day, 2002," *NYT* (op-ed), 7 December 2002.

8. Frederick Kagan, "Did We Fail in Afghanistan?" *Commentary*, (March 2003).

9. B.M. Jenkins, "This Time It Is Different," *San Diego Union-Tribune*, 16 September 2001.

10. Bob Woodward. *Bush at War.* New York: Simon & Schuster, 2002, p. 25.

11. Colin Machines, "A Different Kind of War? September 11 and the United States War," *Review of International Studies*, vol. 29, no. 2 (April 2003), p. 175.

12. Richard K. Betts, "The Soft Underbelly of American Primacy: Tactical Advantages of Terror," *Political Science Quarterly*, vol. 117, no. 1 (spring 2002), p. 19.

13. "Interview with Arab Afghan 'Military Field Commander' Abd-al-Had al-Iraqi," *Al-Neda* (Internet), 28 July 2002.

14. Graham Allison, "Could Worse Be Yet to Come?" *The Economist*, 3–9 November 2001.

15. Jonathan Stevenson, "Lessons From Kenya: Al Qaeda's Threat Is Now Truly Global," *WSJ*, 2 December 2002. See also David Cook, "The Recovery of Radical Islam in the Wake of the Defeat of the Taleban," *Terrorism and Political Violence*, vol. 15, no. 1 (spring 2003), p. 53.

16. Quoted in Christopher Lowe, "What Not to Do: The Soviets' Afghanistan War," *Defense Week*, 1 October 2001, p. 1.

17. Bob Woodward, *Bush at War*, p. 51.

18. D. J. Schemo, "U.S. Finds Itself Lacking Experts on Afghanistan," *NYT*, 11 October 2001.

19. George Crile. *Charlie Wilson's War: The Extraordinary Story of the Largest Covert Operation in History.* New York: The Atlantic Monthly Press, 2003, 560p.

20. L.A. Grau and M. A. Gress, (eds./trans.). *The Soviet-Afghan War: How a Superpower Fought and Lost.* Lawrence, KS: University of Kansas Press, 2002, xxvii and 364p.

21. Bob Woodward, *Bush at War*, p. 103.

22. L.A. Grau and M.A. Gress, *The Soviet-Afghan War: How a Superpower Fought and Lost*, pp. 304–305.

23. *Ibid.*, p. 310.

24. Frederick W. Kagan, "Did We Fail in Afghanistan?" *Commentary*, (March 2003).

25. John Lee Anderson, "Letter From Kabul: The Assassins," *New Yorker*, 10 June 2002, p. 72.

26. Michael Doran, "The Pragmatic Fanaticism of al Qaeda: An Anatomy of Extremism in Middle Eastern Politics," *Political Science Quarterly*, vol. 117, no. 2 (2002), p. 188.

27. Michael Massing, "Losing the Peace," *The Nation*, 13 May 2002, p. 11.

28. Frederick W. Kagan, *Commentary* (March 2003)

29. *Ibid.*

30. Ralph Peters, *Fighting for the Future: Will America Triumph?*, p. 108.

31. Bob Woodward, *Bush at War*, pp. xix and 382.

32. Ralph Peters, *Fighting for the Future: Will America Triumph?*, p. 66.

33. Michael Massing, *The Nation*, 13 May 2002.

34. Bob Woodward, *Bush at War*, p. 313.

35. Michael Isikoff, "Getting Warmer," *Newsweek*, 12 May 2003, p. 8.

36. Max Boot, "Forget Vietnam—History Deflates Guerrilla Mystique," *LAT*, 6 April 2002.

37. Daniel Benjamin and Steven Simon, "The Worst Defense," *NYT*, 20 February 2003.

38. Scott Baldauf, "Taleban Appears to Be Regrouped and Well-Funded," *Christian Science Monitor*, 8 May 2003, p. 1.

39. Walter Pincus, "Attacks in Afghanistan Are on the Rise," *WP*, 15 November 2003, p. A-16.

40. Steven Simon and Daniel Benjamin. *The Age of Sacred Terror*. New York: Random House, 2002, p. 101.

41. "Influential Afghan Jihad Leader Condemns Any Attack of Aggression," *Afghan Islamic Press*, 21 September 2001.

42. Siavosh Ghazi, "Defend Afghanistan: Interview with Gulbuddin Hekmatyar," *Le Soir*, 2 October 2001, p. 6.

43. See "Chapter 11: Bin Laden Returns to Afghanistan: Getting Settled and Politicking," in Anonymous. *Through Our Enemies' Eyes: Osama bin Laden, Radical Islam, and the Future of America*. Washington, D.C.: Brassey's, Inc., 2001, pp. 151–67.

44. John Lee Anderson, *New Yorker*, 10 June 2002.

45. Rahimullah Yusufzai, "Khalis Declares Jihad against U.S.," *The News* (Internet version), 29 October 2003; *Ibid.*, "Khalis Goes into Hiding after Calling for Jihad," *The News* (Internet version), 30 October 2003, pp. 1, 8; and "Statement by Yunis Khalis," *Afghan Islamic Press*, 29 October 2003.

46. "Mujahedin Volunteers in Afghan Army Behind Attacks, Assassination Attempts; Appeal for Muslim Support," *Al-Neda* (Internet), 30 September 2003.

47. Quoted in Ralph Joseph, "Taleban Fighters Blend into Afghan Population, Regroup," *WT*, 2 October 2002, p. 11.

48. Gulbuddin Hekmatyar, "An Open Letter to the Leader of the Democratic Party of the United States and Members of His Party in Congress," *Afghan Islamic Press*, 7 October 2002.

49. John Tierney, "Even for $25 Million, Still No Osama Bin Laden," *NYT*, 1 December 2002.

50. Bob Woodward, *Bush at War*, p. 143.

51. *Ibid.*, p. 360.

52. D. Bergner, "Where the Enemy Is Everywhere and Nowhere," *NYTM*, 20 July 2003, p. 38.

53. Abu-Ubayd al-Qurashi, "The Moscow Theater Operation," *Al-Ansar* (Internet), 6 November 2002.

54. Abu-Ubayd al-Qurashi, "The Illusions of America," *Al-Ansar* (Internet), 22 September 2002.

55. Bob Woodward, *Bush at War*, p. 321, and Charles Santos, "Myth of 'One Afghanistan,'" *LAT*, 25 May 2003.

56. Ahmed Rashid, "The Other Front (Cont.)," *WSJ*, 24 March 2003, and David Rohde, "An Anti-U.S. Safehaven for al Qaeda," *NYT*, 26 December 2002.

57. Fahni Huwaydi, "Interview with Afghan Leader Abd-Rab-al-Rasul Sayyaf," *Al-Sharq Al-Awsat*, 10 February 2002, p. 6.

58. "[Report on Afghan Taleban Radio]," *Voice of Shariah*, 28 September 2001.

59. Aleksey Markov, "Interview with Taleban Spiritual Leader Mullah Omar," *Argumenty I Fakty*, 11 June 2002, p. 8, and Moshin Iqbal, "Interview with Taleban Supreme Leader Mullah Mohammad Omar," *Pakistan*, 29 April 2002, p. 9.

Chapter 3: Not Down, Not Out: Al Qaeda's Resiliency, Expansion, and Momentum

1. P. G. Tsouras (ed.), *Civil War Quotations*, p. 17.

2. *Ibid.*, p. 18.

3. Sayf al-Adil, "A Message to Our Kinfolk in Iraq and the Gulf, in Particular, and Our Islamic Nation, in General. The Islamic Resistance against the American Invasion of Kandahar and the Lessons Learned from It," *alfjr.com* (Internet), 5 March 2003.

4. George F. Tenet, "The Worldwide Threat 2004: Challenges in a Changing Global Context," Statement to the Senate Select Committee on Intelligence, 24 February 2004, *www.cia.gov.*

5. *Ibid.*

6. Stephen Biddle. *Afghanistan and the Future of Warfare: Implications for Army and Defense Policy.* Carlisle, PA: Strategic Studies Institute, U.S. Army War College, 2002, p. 22.

7. "Taleban Withdrawal Was Strategy, Not Rout," *Stratfor.com*, 13 November 2001.

8. C.J. Chivers and David Rohde, "Turning Out Guerrillas and Terrorists to Wage Holy War," *NYT*, 18 March 2002, p. A-1.

9. Mahmud Khalil, "Interview with Al-Qaida Spokesman Abd-al-Rahman al-Rashid," *Al-Majallah*, 13–19 October 2002, pp. 30–32.

10. "Interview with Arab Afghan 'Military Commander' Abd al Hadi from Iraq," *Al-Neda* (Internet), 28 July 2002; Bob Woodward, *Bush at War*, p. 298; and James Risen and Dexter Filkins, "Al Qaeda Fighters Said to Return to Afghanistan," *NYT*, 10 September 2002, p. 1.

11. Asif Shahzad, "Outlawed Groups Help al Qaeda Suspects," *Dawn* (Internet version), 20 April 2002.

12. "Statement from Qaida al-Jihad," *Al-Neda* (Internet), 27 April 2002.

13. Stephen Biddle, *Afghanistan and the Future of Warfare: Implications for Army and Defense Policy*, p. viii.

14. Mark Steyn, "A Bombing Pause—For 12 Months?" *National Post* (Internet version), 21 November 2002.

15. D. Zucchino, "Afghanistan's Toughest Battle Lies Ahead," *LAT*, 13 December 2001, p. 1.

16. *Through Our Enemies' Eyes*, pp. 142–43; 211–221.

17. Daniel Byman, "Scoring the War on Terrorism," *NI*, no. 72 (summer 2003), p. 76.

18. "Part 3: Al Qaeda One Year Later," *Stratfor.com*, 10 September 2003, and Andrew J. Bacevich, "The Long Battle Ahead," *LAT*, 21 July 2003.

19. Sayf al-Adil, "Under the Shadows of the Spears," *Al-Neda* (Internet), 10 March 2003.

20. *Al-Neda* (Internet), 27 April 2002.

21. David E. Kaplan, "Playing Offense," *U.S. News and World Report*, 2 June 2003.

22. "Transnational Terrorism after the Iraq War," *Strategic Comments*, vol. 9, no. 4/*International Institute of Strategic Studies* (Internet), 1 July 2003.

23. David Charter, "Al Qaeda's 17,000 Troops 'Still a Threat to Britons,'" *London Times,* 1 August 2003.

24. Phillippe Grangereau, "Al-Qaida Is Seeking to Attack," *Liberation* (Internet version), 7 August 2003.

25. Abu-Ubaydah al-Qurashi, "Al-Qaida and the Art of War," *Al-Neda* (Internet), 13 June 2002.

26. Abu-Ubayd Al-Hilali, "Mombasa and the Fulfillment of the Promises," *Al-Ansar* (Internet), 5 December 2002.

27. "The U.S. Deception," *Al-Ansar* (Internet), 12 June 2002, p. 3.

28. Peter H. Stone, "Can We Fight Iraq and Hunt al-Qaida," *National Journal*, 22 February 2003, p. 579.

29. Ralph Peters, *Fighting for the Future. Will America Triumph?* p. 111.

30. Sanjoy Anand, "Osama Bides His Time," *The Spectator*, 21 June 2003, p. 16.

31. Edward Luttwack, "The Head of the al Qaeda Snake," *LAT.com*, 11 September 2003.

32. Daniel Benjamin and S. Simon, "The Next Debate: Al Qaeda Link," *NYT*, 20 July 2003.

33. Jason Burke. *Al Qaeda: Casting a Shadow of Terror*. London and New York: I.B. Tauris and Co., Ltd., 2003, vii and 292p., and Rohan Gunaratna. *Inside al Qaeda: Global Network of Terror*. New York: Columbia University Press, 2002, xiii and 272p.

34. "Transnational Terrorism after the Iraq War," *Strategic Comments*, vol. 9, no. 4/*International Institute of Strategic Studies* (Internet), 1 July 2003.

35. "Al-Quds Opinion: The Gulf and the American Watchdog," *AQAA*, 10–11 August 2002, p. 19.

36. Adam Garfinckle, "Weak Realpolitik: The Vicissitudes of Saudi Bashing," *NI*, No. 67 (spring 2002), p. 145.

37. Faiza Saleh Ambah, "Wide Al Qaeda Presence Conceded," *Chicago Tribune*, 30 July 2002.

38. A. Cullison and A. Higgins, "One Acolyte of Many Vows to Die for the Al Qaeda," *WSJ*, 30 December 2002, p. 1.

39. Mohammed Kurayshan, "Interview with Sa'd al-Faqih," *AJSCT*, 18 June 2002.

40. Rohan Gunaratna, *Inside al Qaeda: Global Network of Terror*, p. 76.

41. Faiza Saleh Ambah, *CT*, 30 July 2002.

42. Michael Isikoff and Mark Hosenball, "Waiting for Another Strike," *Newsweek* (Web Exclusive), 12 November 2003.

43. Abd-al-Bari Atwan, "A Recipe for Spreading Extremism," *AQAA*, 21 October 2002, p. 1.

44. Mahmud Khalil, "Following the Uncovering of the Terrorist Cell in Saudi Arabia, al-Qaida: 'We Will Strike the U.S. Army Rear,'" *Al-Majallah*, 18–24 May 2003.

45. C.J. Chivers, "Instruction and Methods from al Qaeda Took Root in Iraq with Islamic Fighters," *NYT*, 27 April 2003.

46. C.J. Chivers, *NYT*, 27 April 2003.

47. Quoted in Malise Ruthven, *A Fury for God. The Islamist Attack on America*, p. 204.

48. T. Zakaria, "U.S. Senator Says Hizballah 'A-Team of Terrorists,'" *Reuters*, 9 July 2002, and Ralph de Toledano, "Hezbollah Emerging as Terrorist A-Team," *Insight Magazine*, 16 March 2004.

49. Jessica Stern, "The Protean Enemy," *FA*, vol. 82, no. 4 (July–August 2003), p. 27.

50. Ralph de Toledano, "Hezbollah Emerging as Terrorist A-Team," *Insight Magazine*, 16 March 2004.

51. Abu-Ubayd al-Qurashi, "The al-Aqsa Intifadah: A Fruitful Jihad and Continued Dedication," *Al-Ansar* (Internet), 8 October 2002.

52. "Al-Qaida Elements Reportedly Present in Ayn al-Hulwah Refugee Camp in Lebanon," *Al-Majallah*, 9–15 February 2003, p. 27.

53. *Ibid.*

54. Peter L. Bergen, "Al Qaeda's New Tactics," *NYT*, 15 November 2002.

55. Robert Fisk, "With Runners and Whispers, al Qaeda Outfoxes U.S. Foxes," *Independent* (Internet version), 6 December 2002.

56. Paul Eedle, "Al Qaeda Takes Fight for 'Hearts and Minds' to Web," *JIR*, vol. 14, no. 8 (August 2002).

57. "Interview with Abu-al-Layth al-Libi, al-Qaida 'Field Commander' in Afghanistan," *Islamic Jihad On Line* (Internet), 10 July 2002.

58. Paul Eedle, *JIR*, vol. 14, no. 8 (August 2002).

59. Mohammed Salah, "Al-Qaida Organization Regains 'Electronic' Health, Returns to Internet with Zawahiri's Book," *AH*, 19 January 2003, pp. 1, 6.

60. "Statement by the Center for Islamic Studies and Research," *Al-Neda* (Internet), 3 October 2002.

61. Paul Eedle, *JIR*, vol. 14 , no. 8 (August 2002).

62. Re'uven Paz, "Global Jihad and the United States: Interpretation of the New World Order of Usama Bin Ladin," *http://gloria.idc.ac.il* (Internet), 6 March 2003.

63. David Martin Jones, "Out of Bali: Cybercaliphate Rising," *NI*, no. 71 (spring 2003), p. 83.

64. "The Crusaders Translate Their Failure to Blackout al-Jihad Web Sites Using Stupid Tools," *Al-Neda* (Internet), 20 July 2002.

65. Jonathan Stevenson, *WSJ*, 2 December 2002.

66. David H. Hackworth, "The Bigger Threat: Osama or Saddam?" *DefenseWatch* (Internet), 18 December 2003.

67. "MIRA Bulletin No. 317," *Movement for Islamic Reform in Arabia* (Internet), 3 June 2002.

68. "An Appeal to Our Brother Workers in the Airbases, Airports, Naval Bases, Seaports, and Others," *http://www.alrakiza.com* (Internet), 19 November 2002.

69. Abu Ubayd al-Qurashi, "America's Nightmares," *Al-Ansar* (Internet), 13 February 2002.

70. Mark Helprin, "Failing the Test of September 11," *WSJ*, 16 September 2002.

71. Quoted in William Russell Meade. *Special Providence: American Foreign Policy and How It Changed the World*. New York: Routledge, 2002, p. 253.

72. Ayman Zawahiri. *Loyalty and Enmity: An Inherited Doctrine and a Lost Reality*. London: No Publisher, December 2002, n.p.

73. "Militant Killed by Police Had Bin Ladin Letter," *Arab News* (Internet version), 4 June 2003.

74. Anonymous, *Through Our Enemies' Eyes*, pp. 138–141, 198–204.

75. "Message to Our Brothers in Iraq by Usama Bin Ladin, Leader of [the] al-Qaida Organization," *AJSCT*, 11 February 2003.

76. "Statement from Qaeda al-Jihad," *Al-Neda* (Internet), 27 April 2002.

77. "You Fight Fire with Fire," *Al-Ansar* (Internet), 14 May 2002.

78. Abu-Ubayd al-Qurashi, "America's Nightmares," *Al-Ansar* (Internet), 13 February 2002; and Salim al-Makki, "Believers Exact Sweet Revenge in Mukalla, Faylaka, and Bali," *Al-Neda* (Internet), 14 October 2002.

79. "Statement of al-Qaida Organization on the Faylaka Operation," *al-Qal'ah* (Internet), 18 October 2002.

80. "Bali Bombing Suspect Proud of Attack," *WT*, 13 June 2003, p. 19.

81. Abu-Ubayd al-Qurashi, "The Moscow Theater Operation," *Al-Ansar* (Internet), 6 November 2002; and Fred Weir, "Shifting Tactics in Chechnya," *Christian Science Monitor*, 30 December 2002, p. 1.

82. "U.S. President Says Chechnya 'Internal Affair,'" *Interfax*, 21 November 2002; "A Separate War," *New Republic*, 2 December 2002, p. 7; and Abu-Ubayd al-Qurashi, *Al-Ansar* (Internet), 6 November 2002.

83. M. Zaatari, "No Leads Yet in Probe of Murder in Sidon; American Woman Had Been Warned to Stop Proselytizing," *The Daily Star* (Internet version), 25 November 2002.

84. Abu-Ubayd al-Hilali, "Mombasa and the Fulfillment of the Promise," *Al-Ansar* (Internet), 5 December 2002.

85. Ian Fisher, "Recent Attacks in Yemen Seen as Sign of Large Terror Cell," *NYT*, 3 January 2003; and Faysal Mukarram, "Sanaa: More Signs of Two Killers' Links to al Qaeda . . ." *AH*, 3 January 2003, pp. 1, 6.

86. "Deputy Amir of Al-Jawf Province in Northern Saudi Arabia Assassinated," *Ilaf* (Internet), 17 February 2003.

87. "Cyanide Sent to Three Missions in New Zealand," *Radio Australia*, 25 February 2003, and "New Zealand Police Release Text of Cyanide Threat Letter," *AFP*, 26 February 2003.

88. Erik Eckholm, "Pakistani Guards Shot Dead at U.S. Office," *NYT*, 1 March 2003, and Ashraf Khan, "Gunman Kills 2 Police Guards Outside U.S. Consulate in Pakistan," *AFP*, 28 February 2003.

89. Fawaz Gerges, "Muslims Called to Jihad," *LAT*, 26 March 2003; and Abu-Ayman al-Hilali, "The Fall of the Iraqi Regime and the Beginning of the Nation's Rise, Part 1," *Al-Ansar* (Internet), 17 April 2003.

90. Christine T. Tjandraningsih and Rudy Madanir, "Jakarta Blast Was against U.S.: Bali Bombing Suspect," *Kyodo World Service*, 6 August 2003.

91. "Statement of the Abu Hafs al-Masri Brigades," *Quds Press* (Internet version), 25 August 2003.

92. Victor Hanson Davis, "Hoping We Fail," *National Review Online*, 28 August 2003.

93. "Audio Recording of Ayman al-Zawahiri," *Al-Arabiyah Television*, 28 September 2003.

94. Ahmed Rafat, "The Spanish Will Not Be Safe Even in Their Homes," *Tiempo de Hoy*, 24 March 2003.

95. Al-Qurashi, Abu-Ubayd, "A Lesson in War," *Al-Ansar* (Internet), 19 December 2002.

96. *Ibid.*

97. *Ibid.*

98. *Ibid.*

99. *Ibid.*

Chapter 4: The World's View of Bin Laden: A Muslim Leader and Hero Coming into Focus?

1. J. Reston Jr., *Warriors of God: Richard the Lion Heart and Saladin in the Third Crusade*, New York: Anchor Books, 2001, p. xiv.

2. Sun Tzu. *The Art of War* (translated by Samuel B. Griffith). London: Oxford University Press, 1963, p. 148.

3. Andrew J. Bacevich and Sebastian Mallaby, "New Rome, New Jerusalem," *Wilson Quarterly*, vol. 26, issue 3 (summer 2002), p. 50.

4. Bruce Hoffman, "Rethinking Terrorism and Counterterrorism since 9/11," *Studies in Conflict and Terrorism*, vol. 25 (2002).

5. D. Bergner, "Where the Enemy Is Everywhere and Nowhere," *NYTM*, 20 July 2003, p. 38.

6. J. Kitfield, "Breaking al Qaeda Means Getting Bin Laden," *NJ*, 23 November 2002, p. 3496.

7. Simon Jenkins, "Bin Ladin's Laughter Echoes across the West," *LondonTimes* (Internet version), 19 March 2003; William R. Hawkins, "What Not to Learn from Afghanistan," *Parameters*, vol. 33, no. 2 (summer 2002); Kevin Whitelaw and Mark Mazetti, "War in the Shadows," *USNWR*, 3 September 2002, p. 51; "From National Conflict to Holy War," *The Economist*, 7 December 2002, p. 16; and David Remnick and H. Hertzberg, "A Year After," *New Yorker*, 16 September 2002.

8. Mona Charen, "Let's Show Bin Laden We're Not Frightened," *Baltimore Sun*, 17 February 2003.

9. Don. D. Chipman, "Osama Bin Laden and Guerrilla War," *Studies in Conflict and Terrorism*, vol. 26, no. 3 (2003).

10. Fareed Zakaria, "How to Fight the Fanatics," *Newsweek*, 9 December 2002.

11. "Remarks by Deputy Director of Operations James L. Pavitt at the American Bar Association Standing Committee on Law and National Security Breakfast Program," 23 January 2002, *www.cia.gov*.

12. L. Harris, "Al Qaeda's Fantasy Ideology," *Policy Review* (August/September 2002), p. 35.

13. Jessica Stern, "The Protean Enemy," *FA*, vol. 82, no. 4 (July/August 2003), p. 27.

14. James Traub, "Osama, Dead or Alive," *NYTM*, 29 December 2002, p. 7.

15. Gerald F. Seib, "What Bin Laden Is Doing and Why It Matters," *WSJ*, 19 February 2003.

16. Rohan Gunaratna, *Inside Al Qaeda: Global Network of Terror*, pp. 27, 41.

17. Mansur Ibrahim Nuqaydan, "An Analysis of Bin Ladin's Recent State-

ment: The Abatement of Support after the Praise of Those Who Carried Out the Bombings in America for the Defeated Language in the Recent Statement," *Al-Watan* (Internet version), 5 November 2001.

18. Victor Hanson Davis. *Autumn of War*, p. 174.

19. Jane Mayer, "The House of Bin Laden," *New Yorker*, 12 November 2001.

20. Neil MacFarquhar, "Bin Laden's Wildfire Threatens Saudi Rulers," *NYT*, 6 November 2001.

21. Patrick Bishop, "A Cowboy Fan Who Grew Up to Hate America," *Daily Telegraph* (Internet version), 11 September 2002.

22. Catherine Taylor, "Former Bin Ladin Friend Denies Terror Ties," *CSM*, 21 January 2003; Matthew Carney, "Osama's Best Friend," *Australian Special Broadcast Service Website*, 15 January 2003; and Cecilia Zecchinelli, "Usama and I, Struggle Companions, Then Rift Over Afghanistan," *Corriere della Serra* (Internet version) 20 April 2003, p. 7.

23. Muhammed Najib Sa'd, "Interview with Former Saudi Director General of the Ministry of Finance, Dr. Abdullah al-Mu'ayyad," *AH*, 14 December 2001, p. 5.

24. Patrick Bishop, *Daily Telegraph* (Internet version), 11 September 2002.

25. Cecilia Zecchinelli, *Corriere della Serra* (Internet version) 20 April 2003, p. 7.

26. Daniel Benjamin and Steven Simon, *The Age of Sacred Terror*, p. 151.

27. Rohan Gunaratna, *Inside Al Qaeda: Global Network of Terror*, pp. 25–26.

28. Ralph Peters, *Beyond Terror: Strategy in a Changing World*, p. 46.

29. Mavise Ruthven, *Fury for God: The Islamist Attack on America*, p.116.

30. Victor Hanson Davis, "Hoping We Fail," *National Review Online*, 28 August 2003.

31. Bernard Lewis, *Western Impact and Middle East Response*, p. 159.

32. James Klurfield, "Bin Laden Is No Match for the Modern World," *LIN*, 11 July 2002.

33. Bernard Lewis, *The Crisis of Islam: Holy War and Unholy Terror*, pp. 162–163.

34. Ralph Peters, "The Plague of Ideas," *Parameters*, vol. 30, no. 4 (winter 2000).

35. P. G. Tsouras (ed.), *Civil War Quotations*, p. 105, and Ralph Peters, *Beyond Terror: Strategy in a Changing World*, pp. 51–52.

36. *Ibid.*, "Rolling Back Radical Islam," *Parameters*, vol. 32, no. 3 (autumn 2002).

37. "Exposing the New Crusader War—Usama Bin Ladin—February 2003," *Waaqiah* (Internet), 14 February 2003.

38. Ellen Laipson, "While America Slept (Book Review)," *FA,* vol. 82, no. 1 (January/February 2003), p. 142.

39. *Ibid.*

40. Thomas Friedman, "No Mere Terrorist," *NYT,* 24 March 2002.

41. Bruce Hoffman, *Studies in Conflict and Terrorism,* vol. 25 (2002).

42. Brian M. Jenkins quoted in *The Economist,* 8 March 2003.

43. Christopher Bellamy, "He May Look Medieval, but Bin Ladin is Modern Tactician of Real Genius . . ." *The Independent* (Internet version), 24 September 2001.

44. Larry Seaquist, "Bin Laden's Innovations," *CSM,* 8 August 2002, p. 9.

45. Bruce Hoffman, "The Leadership Secrets of Osama Bin Laden: The Terrorist as CEO," *Atlantic Monthly* (April 2002).

46. Bernard Lewis, "Deconstructing Osama and His Evil Appeal," *WSJ,* 23 August 2002.

47. Genieve Abdo. *No God But God: Egypt and the Triumph of Islam.* New York: Oxford University Press, 2000, xi and 223p.

48. *Ibid.,* "Spiritual Voice. Embodiment of Evil. Osama Bin Laden," *CT,* 14 September 2003.

49. Bernard Lewis, *WSJ,* 23 August 2002.

50. *Ibid.*

51. "Bin Ladin Begins the Struggle," *Al-Sha'b* (Internet version), 15 September 2001.

52. "Brother-in-Law: Osama 'a Nice Guy,'" *CNN.com,* 15 January 2003.

53. Bernard Lewis, *WSJ,* 23 August 2002.

54. M. Fahd al-Harithi, "King Faysal Practiced Guidance by Action, Not Words," *Al-Rajul,* 1 February 2002.

55. Mohammed Kurayshan, "A Day that Shook the World," *AJSCT,* 10 September 2002.

56. Jamil Azar, "Interview with Hani al-Saba'i," *AJSCT,* 12 November 2002.

57. Ahmed Hazim, "Interview with Hamid Mir," *Al-Sinnarah,* 9 November 2001, p. 12.

58. Mohammed al-Shafi'i, "Interview with Issam Darraz," *ASAA,* 17 January 2003, p. 3.

59. Anthony Lloyd, "Fear, Vendetta and Treachery: How We Let Bin Ladin Get Away," London *Times* (Internet version), 3 December 2002.

60. Ahmad Mansur, "Without Borders," *AJSCT,* 10 July 2002.

61. "Part one of a series of reports on Bin Ladin's life in Sudan . . ." *AQAA* (Internet version), 24 November 2001, p. 13.

62. Anthony Lloyd, London *Times* (Internet version), 3 December 2002.

63. K. Kokita and Yuji Moronaga, "Terrorist Asks Writer to Compile a Biography—Testimony of Pakistanis Who Have Met with Bin Laden," *AERA Magazine,* 8 October 2001, pp. 18–20.

64. "Interview with Ibn Khattab," *Al-Sha'b* (Internet version), 2 November 2001.

65. Larry Seaquist, *CSM*, 8 August 2002, p. 9.

66. *The Economist*, 8 March 2003.

67. *AJSCT*, 10 September 2002.

68. *Waaqiah* (Internet), 14 February 2003.

69. "Transcript of Usama Bin Laden Videotape," *CNN.com*, 13 December 2001.

70. Aijaz Mangi, "Usama Is Not Caught Despite Exhaustive Efforts," *Ibrat*, 10 March 2003, p. 4.

71. Maulvi Abdul Ghafoor, "Usama: Name Is Enough," *Islam*, 29 March 2002, p. 2.

72. Moshin Iqbal, "Exclusive Interview with Taleban Supreme Leader Mullah Mohammad Omar," *Pakistan*, 29 April 2002, p. 9.

73. Kent Gramm, *Gettysburg. A Meditation on War and Values*, pp. 184 and 76.

74. *Ibid.*, p. 22.

Chapter 5: Bin Laden Views the World: Some Old, Some New, and a Twist

1. Kent Gramm, *Gettysburg: A Meditation on War and Values*, p. 159.

2. Bruce Hoffman, *Studies in Conflict and Terrorism*, vol. 25 (2002).

3. "Azzam Exclusive: Letter from Usamah Bin Mohammad Bin Ladin to the American People," *Waaqiah.com* (Internet), 26 October 2002; Hamid Mir, "U.S. Using Chemical Weapons—Usama Bin Ladin," *Ausaf*, 10 November 2001, pp. 1, 7; and "About the Heroes' Will and the Legitimacy of the New York and Washington Operations," *Al-Neda* (Internet), 24 April 2002.

4. Bernard Lewis, *The Crisis of Islam: Western Impact and Middle East Response*, p. 143.

5. J.T. Johnson, "Two Worlds," *Humanities*, vol. 21, no. 6 (November/December 2000), p. 39.

6. *Waaqiah.com* (Internet), 26 October 2002.

7. "Recorded Audio Message by Ayman al-Zawahiri," *AJSCT*, 10 September 2003, and Abu-Ubayd al-Qurashi, "A Lesson in War," *Al-Ansar* (Internet), 19 December 2002.

8. "Exclusive Transcript of Previously Unaired Interview with Usama Bin Ladin," *Qoqaz* (Internet), 23 May 2002.

9. "Exposing the New Crusader War—Usama Bin Ladin—February 2003," *Waaqiah* (Internet), 14 February 2003.

10. "Interview with Usama Bin Ladin," *Ummat*, 28 September 2001, pp. 1, 7.

11. "Message from Usama Bin Ladin to the Youth of the Muslim Ummah," *Markaz al-Dawa* (Internet), 13 December 2001.

12. *Ibid.*

13. *Al-Qal'ah* (Internet), 14 October 2002.

14. *Ibid.*

15. *Waaqiah* (Internet), 14 Feberuary 2003.

16. "A New Bin Laden Speech," Middle East Media Research Institute/ MEMRI (Internet), no. 539, 18 July 2002.

17. Abu-Ayman al-Hilali, "Highlights of the Political Thinking of Imam Bin Ladin in Light of His Latest Speech (3)," *Al-Ansar* (Internet), 15 March 2002.

18. *Al-Qal'ah* (Internet), 14 October 2002.

19. *Ibid.*

20. *Ibid.*

21. *Waaqiah* (Internet), 14 February 2003.

22. *Markaz al-Dawa* (Internet), 13 December 2001, and Bin Laden quoted in, Zuhayr al-Nakhah, "Islamic Studies and Research Center Slaps at Al-Majallah Magazine and Its Mercenaries: We Subjected the Alleged Will to an Examination that Shows It to Be the Will of Al-Majallah Magazine, Not of [the] Shaykh," *Al-Qal'ah* (Internet), 30 October 2002.

23. *Markaz al-Dawa* (Internet), 13 December 2001.

24. "Transcript of Usama Bin Ladin Videotape," *CNN.com*, 13 December 2001.

25. "A Day that Shocked the World," *AJSCT*, 10 September 2002.

26. *Al-Qal'ah* (Internet), 14 October 2002.

27. "Statement by Shaykh Usama Bin Ladin, May God Protect Him, and [the] al-Qaida Organization," *Al-Qal'ah* (Internet), 14 October 2002.

28. *MEMRI* (Internet), no. 539, 18 July 2002.

29. "Statement by Usama Bin Ladin," *AJSCT*, 3 November 2001.

30. *Al-Qal'ah* (Internet), 14 October 2002.

31. "Poems by Usamah and Hamzah Bin Ladin," *arabforum.net* (Internet), 30 June 2002.

32. David Rohde, "Verses from Bin Ladin's War: Wielding the Pen as a Sword of Jihad," *NYT*, 7 April 2002, p. 20.

33. Daniel Benjamin and Steven Simon, *The Age of Sacred Terror*, p. 119.

34. "Interview with Dr. Abdullah al-Nafisi," *AJSCT*, 13 February 2002.

35. James P. Pinkerton, "War of Ideas May Be Toughest U.S. Faces," *LIN*, 2 January 2003.

36. DeWayne Wickham, "Even If USA Won't Say It, Terrorists Want Religous War," *USAT*, 30 October 2002, p. 11.

37. Susan Page, "Foreign Distrust of U.S. Increases," *USAT*, 4 June 2003, p. 1; "Global Backlash," *Financial Times*, 4 June 2003; and "Muslims and the U.S.," *CSM*, 4 June 2003.

38. *Al-Qal'ah* (Internet), 14 October 2002.

39. Hamid Mir, *Ausaf*, 10 November 2001.

40. *Ibid.*

41. Daniel Benjamin and Steven Simon, *The Age of Sacred Terror*, p. 134.

42. Dennis Mullins, "Call It By Any Other Name, It Still Adds Up to a Crusade," *NYT*, 5 January 2003.

43. "Statement by British Foreign Secretary Jack Straw in Istanbul," *NTV*, 20 November 2003.

44. M. Ruthven. *A Fury for God: The Islamist Attack on America*, p. 87, and S. P. Huntington. *The Clash of Civilizations and the Remaking of World Order*. New York: Touchstone, 1997, p. 156.

45. *Ibid.*, pp. 264–265.

46. "Address from the Shaykh: Hammoud bin Uqla al-Shuaibi, Ali al-Khudayr, and Sulaiman al-Awan to the Commander of the Believers: Muhammad Umar and Those Mujahedin with Him, May Allah Grant Them Victory," *Qoqaz* (Internet), 22 January 2002.

47. Stephen Schwartz. *The Two Faces of Islam: The House of Sa'ud from Tradition to Terror*. New York: Doubleday, 2002, p. 28.

48. R. Gunaratna, "Confronting the West: al Qaeda's Strategy after 11 Sept.," *JIR*, vol. 14, no. 7 (July 2002).

49. "Statement by Usama Bin Ladin," *AJSCT*, 3 November 2001.

50. "Letter to the Afghan People," *IslamOnline.net* (Internet), 25 August 2002.

51. Abu-Ayman al-Hilali, *Al-Ansar* (Internet), 15 March 2002.

52. *Qoqaz* (Internet), 23 May 2002.

53. "Al-Qaida Statement Congratulates Yemenis on the Bombing for the French Tanker off Yemen's Coast," *AQAA*, 16 October 2002, p. 2.

54. *Ibid.*

55. M. Ignatieff, "Why Are We in Iraq? (And Liberia? And Afghanistan?)," *NYTM*, 7 September 2003.

56. *Waaqiah* (Internet),14 February 2003.

57. Sayf al-Ansari, "And Fight the Unbelievers Totally," *Al-Ansar* (Internet), 27 February 2002.

58. *Ummat*, 28 September 2001, pp. 1, 7.

59. "A Day that Shocked the World," *AJSCT*, 10 September 2002.

60. "Statement from Abdallah Usama Bin Ladin to the Peoples of the Countries Allied to the Tyrannical U.S. Government," *Al-Neda* (Internet), 21 November 2002.

61. "A Statement by Usama Bin Ladin Entitled: 'Abdallah's Initiative . . . The Great Treason,'" *www.cybcity.com/mnzmas/osam.htm*, 1 March 2003.

62. *Waaqiah* (Internet), 14 February 2003.

63. *www.cybcity.com/mnzmas/osam.htm*, 1 March 2003.

64. *Waaqiah* (Internet), 14 February 2003.

65. *Al-Qaal'ah* (Internet), 14 February 2002.

66. *Ibid.*

67. "The Day that Shocked the World," *AJSCT*, 10 September 2002.

68. *MEMRI* (Internet), no. 539, 18 July 2003.

69. *Ibid.*

70. *Ibid.*

71. Hamid Mir, *Ausaf*, 10 November 2001.

72. *Al-Neda* (Internet), 21 November 2002.

73. *Ibid.*

74. *Qoqaz* (Internet), 23 May 2002, and *Al-Qal'ah* (Internet), 14 October 2002.

75. John Kelsay, "Religion, Morality, and the Governance of War: The Case of Classical Islam," *Journal of Religious Ethics*, vol. 18, no. 2 (fall 1990), p. 125.

76. James Turner Johnson and John Kelsay. *The Holy War in Western and Islamic Traditions*. University Park, PA: Pennsylvania State University Press, 1997, p. 122.

77. John Kelsay, "*Journal of Religious Ethics*, vol. 18, no. 2 (fall 1990), p. 125.

78. "Statement by Usama Bin Ladin," *AJSCT*, and *Waqiaah* (Internet), 26 October 2002.

79. Shaykh Nasir bin-Hamid al-Fahd, "A Treatise on the Legal Status of Using Weapons of Mass Destruction against Infidels," *www.al-fhd.com* (Internet), 1 May 2003. (Hereafter al-Fahd, *Treatise*, 1 May 2003.)

80. *Ibid.*

81. *Ibid.*

82. *Ibid.*

83. *Ibid.*

84. *Ibid.*

85. *Ibid.*

86. *Ibid.*

87. Hamid Mir, *Ausaf*, 10 November 2001, pp. 1, 7.

88. *Ummat*, 28 September 2001, pp. 1, 7.

89. *Waaqiah* (Internet), 26 October 2002.

90. Hamid Mir, *Ausaf*, 10 November 2001, pp. 1, 7.

91. Al-Fahd, *Treatise*, 1 May 2003.

92. Malise Ruthven, *Fury for God: The Islamist Attack on America*, p. 30.

93. *Ummat*, 28 September 2001, pp. 1, 7.

94. *Qoqaz* (Internet), 23 May 2002.

95. Nicolo Machiavelli, *The Prince*, pp. 14–15 and 21.

Chapter 6: Blinding Hubris Abounding: Inflicting Defeat on Ourselves—Non-War, Leaks, and Missionary Democracy

1. P. G. Tsouras (ed.), *Civil War Quotations*, p. 106.
2. *Ibid.*, pp. 67–68.
3. Andrew Greeley, "Victory Doesn't Justify War," *CT*, 18 April 2003.
4. David M. Halbfinger and Timothy Egan, "Terror Warning Responses Range from Fear to Fatalism," *NYT*, 13 February 2003, and Eli J. Lake, "Noise Pollution: Al Qaeda's Misinformation War," *New Republic Online* (Internet), 4 November 2002.
5. Anonymous, *Through Our Enemies' Eyes*, pp. 24–28.
6. Lee Harris, *Policy Review* (August/September 2002), p. 35.
7. Victor Davis Hanson, *Autumn of War*, p. 15.
8. Steven Simon, "The New Terrorism: Securing the Nation against a Messianic Foe," *Brookings Review*, vol. 21, no. 1 (winter 2003) p. 18.
9. Susan Page, "Foreign Distrust of U.S. Increases," *USAT*, 4 June 2003, p. 1; "Global Backlash," *Financial Times*, 4 June 2003; and "Muslims and the U.S.," *CSM*, 4 June 2003.
10. *Ummat*, 28 September 2001, pp. 1, 7; "Message to Our Iraqi Brothers from Usama Bin Ladin, Leader of [the] Al-Qaida Organization," *AJSCT*, 11 February 2003; and *Al-Neda* (Internet), 21 November 2002.
11. *AJSCT*, 1 February 2003.
12. "Statement of Usama Bin Ladin to Iraqis and Americans," *AJSCT*, 18 October 2003.
13. "Recorded Audio Message of Ayman al-Zawahiri," *AJSCT*, 10 September 2003.
14. Ahmad Muwaffaq Zaydan, "Al-Zawahiri in New Article: The Awakening Is Frightening the Enemies of Islam," *AH*, 18 February 2003, pp. 1, 6, and "Statement by Ayman al-Zawahiri," *AJSCT*, 21 May 2003.
15. Abu-Ubayd al-Hilali, "Mombasa and the Fulfillment of a Promise," *Al-Ansar* (Internet), 5 December 2002.
16. Quoted in Craig L. Symonds. *Joseph E. Johnston: A Civil War Biography.* New York: W.W. Norton and Company, 1992, pp. 272, 284, and P.G. Tsouras (ed.), *Civil War Quotations*, p. 167.
17. Tod Lindberg, "Deterrence and Prevention," *Weekly Standard*, 3 February 2003.
18. Peter G. Tsouras (ed.), *Civil War Quotations*, p. 235.
19. Scott Baldauf, "Taliban Sympathies High in Border Towns," *CSM*, 19 September 2002.
20. Rahimullah Yusufzai, "Taleban Volunteers Joining Resistance," *The News* (Internet version), 4 February 2003.

21. Muzzafar Iqbal, "Thank You, Mr. Bush," *The News* (Internet version), 6 December 2002.

22. John Keegan, "If America Decides to Take on the Afghans, This Is How to Do It," *Daily Telegraph* (Internet version), 20 September 2001.

23. Ilene Prusher, "A Year after the Taleban, Little Change," *CSM*, 19 November 2002, p. 1.

24. Robert Oakley, "The New Afghanistan: Year 2," *WP*, 3 January 2003, p. 19.

25. Peter Smolowitz, "Franks: Afghan Model Could Work to Build Iraq," *Miami Herald*, 12 January 2003.

26. Rowan Scarborough, "War on Terrorism in 'Cleanup' Phase," *WT*, 2 May 2003.

27. Chris Kraul, "Rumsfeld Declares a Shift in Mission," *LAT*, 2 May 2003.

28. Vernon Loeb, "U.S. Hopeful on Afghan Security," *WP*, 23 December 2002, p. 14.

29. Christian Lowe, "Nation Building," *Weekly Standard.com* (Internet), 6 February 2003.

30. Victor Davis Hanson, "Finish the War," *WSJ*, 17 September 2002, and Victor Davis Hanson, *Autumn of War: What America Learned from September 11th and the War on Terrorism*, p. 70.

31. Bernard Lewis, "Put the Iraqis in Charge," *WSJ*, 29 August 2003.

32. Michael E. O'Hanlon, "A Flawed Masterpiece: Assessing the Afghan Campaign," *FA*, vol. 81, no. 3 (May/June 2002).

33. William R. Hawkins, "What Not to Learn from Afghanistan," *Parameters*, vol. 32, no. 2 (summer 2002).

34. Anthony Davis, *JIR*, vol. 14, no. 2 (February 2002).

35. David H. Hackworth, "No Light in the Afghan Tunnel," *DefenseWatch/sftt.org* (Internet), 13 May 2003.

36. Ralph Peters. *Beyond Terror: Strategy in a Changing World*, pp. 179–181.

37. *Ibid.*, *Fighting for the Future: Will America Triumph*, p. 30.

38. David H. Hackworth, "Bad Call on Iraq," *DefenseWatch* (sftt.org/Internet), 5 August 2003.

39. Anonymous, *Through Our Enemies' Eyes*, p. xiv.

40. Adm. Halsey: http://www.battle-of-leyte-gulf.com/Leaders/Americans/Halsey/halsey.html, and *http://www.angelfire.com/la/raeder/Unitedstates.html*.

41. William R. Hawkins, *Parameters*, vol. 33, no. 2 (summer 2002).

42. Daniel Bergner, *New York Times Magazine*, 20 July 2003, p. 38.

43. Of many, see "Key Components of the Iraqi Ground Forces," *http://www.rjlee.org/iraq2002-1.htm*, and Juan O. Yamayo, "Iraqi Forces Cut in Half, Weapons Outdated," The State.com (*http://www.thestate.com/mld/thestate/5194150.htm*), 16 February 2003.

44. James Brooks, "Mongolians Return to Baghdad, This Time as Peace Keepers," *NYT*, 25 September 2003, and Stephen. Schwartz. *The Two Faces of Islam: The House of Sa'ud from Tradition to Terror*, p. 54.

45. *Waaqiah* (Internet), 14 February 2003.

46. Ralph Peters, "The New Warrior Class Revisited," *Small Wars and Insurgencies*, vol. 13, no. 2 (summer 2002), p. 16.

47. *Ibid.*, *Beyond Terrorism: Strategy in a Changing World*, p. 136.

48. David A. Vise, "A New Global Role Puts the FBI in Unsavory Company," *WP*, 29 October 2000, p. A-1.

49. Jessica Stern, "Execute Terrorists at Our Own Risk," *NYT*, 28 February 2001.

50. J. Lobel, "The Use of Force to Respond to Terrorist Attacks: The Bombing of Afghanistan and Sudan," *Yale Journal of International Law*, vol. 24, no. 2 (summer 1999), p. 522.

51. William Safire, "New Day of Infamy," *NYT*, 12 September 2001.

52. Richard K. Betts, *Political Science Quarterly*, vol. 117, no. 1 (spring 2002), p. 19.

53. D. A. Vise and Dan Egan, "FBI Widens Cole Probe as Yemen Cooperates," *WP*, 27 January 2001, p. A-14, and Lally Weymouth, "Pieces of the Puzzle," *Newsweek*, 18 December 2000, p. 48.

54. J.J. Goldman and R.J. Ostrow, "U.S. Indicts Terror Suspect Bin Laden," *LAT*, 5 November 1998, p. A-1.

55. Quoted in Daniel Byman, *NI*, no. 72 (summer 2003), p. 75.

56. Steven Emerson and Daniel Pipes, "Terrorism on Trial," *WSJ*, 31 May 2001.

57. Charles Krauthamer, "The Trouble with Trials," *WP*, 9 March 2001, p. 27.

58. Reuel March Gerecht, "G-Men East of Suez," *Weekly Standard*, 30 October 2000.

59. Vernon Loeb, "Planned Jan. 2000 Attacks Failed or Were Thwarted," *WP*, 24 December 2000, p. A-2.

60. Mahmud Khalil, "Interview with Al-Qaida Spokesman Abd-al-Rahman al-Rashid," *Al-Majallah*, 13–19 October 2002, pp. 30–32.

61. "Usama Interview: Not Up to Him to Call a Holy War," *Takbeer*, 5–12 August 1999, p. 22.

62. John Miller, "An Exclusive Interview with Usama Bin Ladin: Talking to Terrorism's Banker," *ABCNEWS.com* (Internet), 28 May 1998.

63. *Takbeer*, 5–12 August 1999, p. 22.

64. Ruth Wedgewood, "Cause for Alarm," *WP*, 3 June 2001, p. B-1.

65. Ernest Blazar, "Inside the Ring," *WT*, 24 August 1998, p. A-8.

66. Kevin Johnson *et al.*, "Arrest of 9/11 Suspect Yields 'Lots of Information,'" *USAT*, 3 March 2003, p. 1.

67. W. Pincus, "Bin al-Shibh Said to Provide 'Useful Information,'" *WP*, 4 October 2002, p. 17.

68. Jeff Gerth, "Pro-al Qaeda Workers a Sabotage Threat for Saudis," *NYT*, 13 February 2003.

69. Jane Mayer, "The Search for Osama," *New Yorker*, 4 August 2003.

70. Howard Witt, "US: Killing of al Qaeda Suspects Was 'Legal,'" *CT*, 24 November 2002, p. 1.

71. Peter G. Tsouras (ed.), *Civil War Quotations*, p. 185.

72. Bob Woodward, *Bush at War*, p. xi.

73. *Ibid.*, p. 4.

74. *Ibid.*, p. 6.

75. *Ibid.*, p. 27.

76. *Ibid.*, p. 196.

77. *Ibid.*, p. 269.

78. *Ibid.*, p. 298.

79. "A Ghastly Probability," *Economist*, 14 September 2002.

80. Richard K. Betts, *Political Science Quarterly*, vol. 117, no. 1 (spring 2002), p. 19.

81. Quoted at hhtp://www.thisnation.cm/library/jqadams.html.

82. Michael McFaul, "Wrong Time to 'Stay the Course,'" *WP*, 24 August 2003.

83. Niall Ferguson, "The 'E' Word," *WSJ*, 6 June 2003.

84. Joshua Mitchell, "Not All Yearn to Be Free," *WP*, 10 August 2003, p. B-7.

85. Patrick J. Ryan, "The Roots of Muslim Anger: The Religious and Political Background of Worldwide Islamic Militancy Today," *America*, vol. 185, no. 17 (26 November 2001), p. 8.

86. Sayf al-Ansari, "Fight the Friends of Satan," *Al-Ansar* (Internet), 28 January 2002.

87. Ralph Peters. *Beyond Terror: Strategy in a Changing World*, pp. 107, 111.

88. *Ibid.*, p. 59.

Chapter 7: When the Enemy Sets the Stage: How America's Stubborn Obtuseness Aids Its Foes

1. Peter G. Tsouras (ed.), *Civil War Quotations*, p. 89.

2. *Ibid.*, p. 90.

3. *Ibid.*, p. 176.

4. G. Abdo, "Spiritual Voice. Embodiment of Evil. Osama Bin Laden," *CT*, 14 September 2003.

5. Bernard Lewis, "Targeted By a History of Hatred," *WP*, 10 September 2002, p. 15.

6. *Ibid.*

7. Daniel Byman, *NI*, no. 72 (summer 2003), p. 83.

8. "Clerics Underline 'Jihad' Against 'Enemy'; Writer Urges Donations," *Al-Ahram Al-Arabi*,
   22 March 2003.

9. Michael Ignatieff, *NYTM*, 7 September 2003.

10. Richard Dawkins, "Bin Ladin's Victory," *The Guardian* (Internet version), 22 March 2003.

11. C.J. Chivers and David Rohde, "Turning out Guerrillas and Terrorists to Wage Holy War," *NYT*, 18 March 2002, p. A-1.

12. *Ibid.*

13. *Ibid.*

14. *Ibid.*

15. *Ibid*

16. Yaroslav Trofimov, "Iraq Resistance Strikes a Chord with Locals on Mideast Street," *WSJ*, 26 March 2003, p. 1.

17. C.J. Chivers and David Rohde, *NYT*, 18 March 2002.

18. Quoted in Daniel Byman, *NI*, no. 72 (summer 2003), p. 75.

19. John Keegan, *Daily Telegraph* (Internet version), 20 September 2001.

20. "The U.S. Deception," *Al-Ansar* (Internet), 12 June 02.

21. Anatol Lieven, "The Empire Strikes Back," *The Nation*, 7 July 2003, p. 26.

22. Clyde Prestowitz, "Why Don't We Listen Anymore?" *WP*, 7 July 2002, p. B-1.

23. Anonymous, *Through Our Enemies' Eyes: Osama Bin Laden, Radical Islam, and the Future of America*, pp. 82, 87, 252.

24. "Interview with Sulayman Abu-Gayth: 'We Will Launch New Attacks against U.S. Interests,'" *El Youm* (Internet version), 9 July 2002, pp. 1, 5.

25. "Statement from the al-Qaida Organization on the Two Mombasa Operations against the Jews," *http://www.mojahedoon.net* (Internet), 2 December 2002.

26. For example, Abu-Ayman al-Hilali, "Bin Ladin and the Palestinian Cause," *Al-Ansar* (Internet), 15 January 2002; "A Statement from Qaida-al-Jihad to the Muslim Nation and the Heroic Palestinian People," *Al-Neda* (Internet), 10 April 2002; Abu-Ubayd al-Qurashi, "Janinograd," *Al-Ansar* (Internet), 14 April 2002; and Abu-Ayman al-Hilali, "Arafat and the High Treason," *Al-Ansar* (Internet), 28 May 2002.

27. Abu-Ubayd al-Qurashi, "From Munich to New York," *Al-Ansar* (Internet), 22 February 2002.

28. "Interview with Dr. Ayman al-Zawahiri," *Qoqaz* (Internet), 11 October 2002.

29. James Dao, "Pakistan Asks U.S. to Reduce Restrictions on Its Citizens," *NYT*, 30 January 2003, and Mahmud Abbas Ahmad Salih, "Why Does Not Egypt Reply to the United States in Kind," *Al-Sha'b* (Internet version), 31 January 2003.

30. Abd-al-Bari Atwan, "The Arab View—Americans Are Masters of Destruction; The U.S. Is Driving the Muslim World to Hatred," *The Observer* (Internet version), 10 March 2002.

31. "Arabs Not Welcome," *Saudi Gazette* (Internet version), 9 June 2002.

32. Bassam Daw, "The United States' 'Racism,' " *Al-Watan*, 6 May 2002.

33. "Insulting U.S. Immigration Laws," *Nawa-i-Waqt*, 7 June 2002, p. 2.

34. *Ibid.*

35. *Qoqaz* (Internet), 11 October 2002.

36. Maureen Dowd, "Pass the Duct Tape," *NYT*, 12 February 2003, p. A-25.

37. Chris Hedges. *War Is a Force That Gives Us Meaning*, p. 54.

38. Robert D. Kaplan. *Warrior Politics: Why Leadership Demands a Pagan Ethos*. New York: Viking Books, 2002, p. 127.

39. *Ibid.*, p. 128.

Chapter 8: The Way Ahead: A Few Suggestions for Debate

1. Randall Bedwell. *May I Quote You General Lee?* New York: Gramercy Books, 2002, p. 63.

2. Kent Gramm, *Gettysburg: A Mediation on War and Values*, p. 22.

3. Ralph Peters, *Beyond Terrorism: Strategy in a Changing World*, p. 196.

4. *Ibid.*, p. 204.

5. Francis Fukuyama, "The Real Intelligence Failure?" *WSJ*, 5 August 2003.

6. Daniel Benjamin and Steven Simon, *The Age of Sacred Terror*, p. 243.

7. Robert D. Kaplan, "Supremacy by Stealth," *Atlantic Monthly* (July–August 2003), p. 69.

8. Quoted in Chris Hedges, *War Is a Force That Gives Us Meaning*, p. 4.

9. Ralph Peters, *Beyond Terror: Strategy in a Changing World*, p. 39.

10. *Ibid.*, p. 61.

11. M. Ruthven, *A Fury for God: The Islamist Attack on America*, p. 173; R. Peters, "The Saudi Threat," *WSJ*, 4 January 2002; S. Schmidt, "Spreading Saudi Fundamentalism in U.S.," *WP*, 2 October 2003, p. 1; and S. Schwartz, *The Two Faces of Islam: The House of Sa'ud from Tradition to Terror*.

12. Adam Garfinckle, *NI*, No. 67 (spring 2002), p. 145.

13. David H. Hackworth, "Fire the Losers before the Army Goes Down," *Orlando Sun-Sentinel*, 14 August 2003, p. 21.

14. David H. Hackworth, "Try a Little Decent Leadership," *Defense-Watch* (sftt.org/Internet), 22 July 2003.

15. "Statement by Usama Bin Ladin," *AJSCT*, 3 November 2001.

16. Ralph Peters, *Fighting for the Future: Will America Triumph?* p. 132.

17. Mark Helprin, "Failing the Test of September 11," *WSJ*, 16 September 2002.

18. Kenneth Minogue, "Religion, Reason, and Conflict in the 21st Century (Book Review)," *NI*, no. 72 (summer 2003), p. 129.

19. J. Reston Jr., *Warriors of God: Richard the Lion Heart and Saladin in the Third Crusade*, p. 12.

20. "Prominent Saudi Cleric Issues Anti-War Fatwa," *islamtoday.net* (Internet), 4 March 2003.

21. *Waaqiah* (Internet), 26 October 2002.

22. Michael Ignatieff, *NYTM*, 7 September 2003.

23. Ralph Peters, *Beyond Terror: Strategy in a Changing World*, pp. 220–221.

24. Michael Ignatieff, "The American Empire (Get Used to It)," *NYTM*, 5 January 2003.

25. Quoted at hhtp://www.thisnation.cm/library/jqadams.html.

26. Ralph Peters, *Fighting for the Future: Will America Triumph?* p. 46.

27. *Ibid.*, *Beyond Terror: Strategy in a Changing World*, p. 337.

Epilogue: No Basis for Optimism

1. Peter G. Tsouras (ed.), *Civil War Quotations*, p. 104.

2. George F. Tenet, "The Worldwide Threat 2004: Challenges in a Changing Global Context," Statement to the Senate Select Committee on Intelligence, 24 February 2004, *www.cia.gov.*

3. *Ibid.*

4. *Ibid.*

Select Bibliography

☪

NOTE: A comprehensive bibliography can be found and downloaded at www.brasseysinc.com.

Bin Laden Statements, Interviews, and Letters (Chronologically)

Miller, John. "An Exclusive Interview with Usama Bin Ladin: Talking to Terrorism's Banker," *ABCNEWS.com* (Internet), 28 May 1998.

"Usama Interview: Not Up to Him to Call a Holy War," *Takbeer*, 5–12 August 1999, p. 22.

"Interview with Usama Bin Ladin," *Ummat*, 28 September 2001, pp. 1, 7.

"Statement by Usama Bin Ladin," *Al-Jazirah Satellite Channel Television*, 3 November 2001.

Mir, Hamid. "U.S. Using Chemical Weapons—Usama Bin Ladin," *Ausaf*, 10 November 2001, pp. 1, 7.

"Message from Usama Bin Ladin to the Youth of the Muslim Ummah," *Markaz al-Dawa* (Internet), 13 December 2001.

"Transcript of Usama Bin Laden Videotape," *CNN.com*, 13 December 2001.

"Statement by Al-Qaida Leader Usama Bin Ladin," *Al-Jazirah Satellite Channel Television*, 27 December 2001.

"About the Heroes' Will and the Legitimacy of the New York and Washington Operations," *Al-Neda* (Internet), 24 April 2002.

"Exclusive Transcript of Previously Unaired Interview with Usama Bin Ladin," *Qoqaz* (Internet), 23 May 2002.

"Poems by Usamah and Hamzah Bin Ladin," *arabforum.net* (Internet), 30 June 2002.

"A New Bin Ladin Speech," *Middle East Media Research Institute/MEMRI* (Internet), no. 539, 18 July 2002.

"Letter to the Afghan People," *IslamOnline.net* (Internet), 25 August 2002.

291

"A Day That Shocked the World," *Al-Jazirah Satellite Channel Television*, 10 September 2002.

"Statement by Usama Bin Ladin," *Al-Jazirah Satellite Channel Television*, 6 October 2002.

"Statement by Shaykh Usama Bin Ladin, May God Protect Him, and [the] al-Qaida Organization," *Al-Qal'ah* (Internet), 14 October 2002.

—"Azzam Exclusive: Letter from Usamah Bin Mohammad Bin Ladin to the American People," *Waaqiah.com* (Internet), 26 October 2002.

al-Nakhah, Zuhayr, "Islamic Studies and Research Center Slaps at Al-Majallah Magazine and Its Mercenaries: We Subjected the Alleged Will to an Examination That Shows It to Be the Will of Al-Majallah Magazine, Not of [the] Shaykh," *Al-Qal'ah* (Internet), 30 October 2002.

"Statement from Abdallah Usama Bin Ladin to the Peoples of the Countries Allied to the Tyrannical U.S. Government," *Al-Neda* (Internet), 21 November 2002.

"Bin Ladin in a Special Message to the 'People of the Peninsula': Take Up Arms to Defend Your Honor. Warns of 'Critical Days and All-Out War," *Al-Quds Al-Arabi*, 28 November 2002, p. 1.

"Message to Our Brothers in Iraq by Usama Bin Ladin, Leader of [the] al-Qaida Organization," *Al-Jazirah Satellite Channel Television*, 11 February 2003.

"Exposing the New Crusader War—Usama Bin Ladin—February 2003," *Waaqiah* (Internet), 14 February 2003.

"A Statement by Usama Bin Ladin entitled: 'Abdallah's initiative . . . The Great Treason,'" *www.cybcity.com/mnzmas/osam.htm*, 1 March 2003.

"Statement of Usama Bin Ladin to Iraqis and Americans," *Al-Jazirah Satellite Channel Television*, 18 October 2003.

Books

Abdo, Genieve. *No God But God: Egypt and the Triumph of Islam*. New York: Oxford University Press, 2000, xi and 223 p.

Anonymous. *Through Our Enemies' Eyes: Osama bin Laden, Radical Islam, and the Future of America*. Washington, D.C.: Brassey's, Inc., 2001, xix and 394p.

Baer, Robert. *See No Evil: The True Story of a Ground Soldier in the CIA's War on Terrorism*. New York: Three Rivers Press, 2002, xix and 292p.

Benjamin, Daniel, and Steven Simon. *The Age of Sacred Terror*. New York: Random House, 2002, xiii and 490p.

Biddle, Stephen. *Afghanistan and the Future of Warfare: Implications for Army and Defense Policy*. Carlisle, PA: Strategic Studies Institute, U.S. Army War College, 2002, ix and 58p.

Burke, Jason. *Al Qaeda: Casting a Shadow of Terror.* London and New York: I.B. Tauris and Co., Ltd., 2003, vii and 292p.

Crile, George. *Charlie Wilson's War: The Extraordinary Story of the Largest Covert Operation in History.* New York: The Atlantic Monthly Press, 2003, 560p.

Emerson, Steven. *American Jihad: The Terrorists Living Among Us.* New York: The Free Press, 2003, p. 177.

Ewans, Martin. *Afghanistan: A Short History of Its People and Politics.* New York: HarperCollins, 2002, ix and 244p.

Al-Fahd, Shaykh Nasir bin-Hamid al-Fahd, *A Treatise on the Legal Status of Using Weapons of Mass Destruction Against Infidels, www.al-fhd.com* (Internet), 1 May 2003.

Grau, Lester A., and Michael A. Gress (eds. and translators). *The Soviet-Afghan War: How a Superpower Fought and Lost.* Lawrence, KS: University of Kansas Press, 2002, xxvii and 364p.

Gunaratna, Rohan. *Inside al Qaeda: Global Network of Terror.* New York: Columbia University Press, 2002, xiii and 272p.

Hanson, Victor Davis. *Autumn of War: What America Learned from September 11th and the War on Terrorism.* New York: Anchor Books, 2002, xx and 218p.

Hedges, Chris. *War Is a Force That Gives Us Meaning.* New York: Anchor Books, 2002, 211p.

Huntington, Samuel P. *The Clash of Civilizations and the Remaking of World Order.* New York: Touchstone, 1997, 367p.

Johnson, James Turner, and John Kelsay. *The Holy War in Western and Islamic Traditions.* University Park, PA: Pennsylvania State University Press, 1997, ix and 185p.

Kaplan, Robert D. *Warrior Politics: Why Leadership Requires a Pagan Ethos.* New York: Vintage Books, 2002, xxii and 198p.

———. *Soldiers of God: With Islamic Warriors in Afghanistan and Pakistan.* New York: Vintage Books, 2001, xxi and 278p.

Lewis, Bernard. *The Crisis of Islam: Holy War and Unholy Terror.* New York: The Modern Library, 2003, xxxii and 184p.

———. *What Went Wrong? Western Impact and Middle East Response.* New York: Oxford University Press, 2002, vii and 180p.

Machiavelli, Nicolo. *The Prince* (translated by N.H. Thomson). New York: Barnes and Noble Books, 1994, 92p.

Magnus, Ralph H., and Eden Naby. *Afghanistan: Mullah, Marx, and Mujahid.* Boulder, CO: Westview Press, 2002, xiv and 289p.

Meade, William Russell. *Special Providence: American Foreign Policy and How It Changed the World.* New York: Routledge, 2002, xviii and 378p.

Peters, Ralph. *Beyond Terror: Strategy in a Changing World.* Mechanicsburg, PA: Stackpole Books, 2002, xii and 353p.

────. *Fighting for the Future: Will America Triumph?* Mechanicsburg, PA: Stackpole Books, 1999, xii and 210p.

Reston Jr., James. *Warriors of God: Richard the Lion Heart and Saladin in the Third Crusade.* New York: Anchor Books, 2001, xxi and 410p.

Ruthven, Malise. *A Fury for God: The Islamist Attack on America.* London: Granta Books, 2002, xxii and 324p.

Schwartz, Stephen. *The Two Faces of Islam: The House of Sa'ud from Tradition to Terror.* New York: Doubleday, 2002, xxii and 312p.

Shadid, Anthony. *Legacy of the Prophet: Despots, Democrats, and the New Politics of Islam.* Boulder, CO: Westview Press, 2001, xi and 340p.

Tsouras, Peter G. (ed.). *Civil War Quotations: In the Words of the Commanders.* New York: Sterling Publishing Co., Inc., 1998, 288 p.

Woodward, Bob. *Bush at War.* New York: Simon & Schuster, 2002, xix and 382p.

Zawahiri, Ayman. *Loyalty and Enmity: An Inherited Doctrine and a Lost Reality.* London: No Publisher, December, 2002, n.p.

Articles

Ajami, Fouad, "Hail the American Imperium," *U.S. News and World Report,* 11 November 2002, p. 16.

Allison, Graham, "Could Worse Be Yet to Come?" *The Economist,* 3–9 November 2001.

al-Ansari, Sayf, "And Fight the Unbelievers Totally," *Al-Ansar* (Internet), 27 February 2002.

────. "Fight the Friends of Satan," *Al-Ansar* (Internet), 28 January 2002.

al-Ansari, Sayf al-Din, "They Will Not Cease to Fight with You," *Al-Ansar* (Internet), 15 January 2002.

Atwan, Abd-al-Bari, "A Recipe for Spreading Extremism," *Al-Quds Al-Arabi,* 21 October 2002, p. 1.

────. "The Arab View—Americans Are Masters of Destruction: The U.S. Is Driving the Muslim World to Hatred," *The Observer* (Internet version), 10 March 2002.

Bacevich, Andrew J., "The Nation at War," *Los Angeles Times,* 20 March 2003.

────. "The Long Battle Ahead," *Los Angeles Times,* 21 July 2003.

────. and Sebastian Mallaby, "New Rome, New Jerusalem," *Wilson Quarterly,* vol. 26, issue 3 (summer 2002), p. 50.

Baldauf, Scott, "Portrait of an al Qaeda Camp," *Christian Science Monitor,* 17 January 2003, p. 1.

Bellamy, Christopher, "He May Look Medieval, but Bin Ladin is Modern Tactician of Real Genius . . ." *The Independent* (Internet version), 24 September 2001.

Benjamin, Daniel, and Steven Simon, "The Worst Defense," *New York Times*, 20 February 2003.

———. "The Next Debate: Al Qaeda Link," *New York Times*, 20 July 2003.

Bergen, Peter L., "Al Qaeda's New Tactics," *New York Times*, 15 November 2002.

Bergner, Daniel, "Where the Enemy Is Everywhere and Nowhere," *New York Times Magazine*, 20 July 2003, p. 38.

Betts, Richard K., "The Soft Underbelly of American Primacy: Tactical Advantages of Terror," *Political Science Quarterly*, vol. 117, no. 1 (spring 2002), p. 19.

Boot, Max, "Forget Vietnam—History Deflates Guerrilla Mystique," *Los Angeles Times*, 6 April 2002.

Byman, Daniel, "Scoring the War on Terrorism, *National Interest*, no. 72 (summer 2002), pp. 75–84.

Chipman, Don, "Air Power and the Battle for Mazar-e Sharif," *Air Power History*, Vol. 50, No. 1, (Spring 2003), p. 34.

———. "Osama Bin Laden and Guerrilla War," *Studies in Conflict and Terrorism*, vol. 26, no. 3 (2003), pp. 163–170.

Chivers, C.J., "Instruction and Methods from al Qaeda Took Root in Iraq with Islamic Fighters," *New York Times*, 27 April 2003.

———. and David Rohde, "Turning Out Guerrillas and Terrorists to Wage Holy War," *New York Times*, 18 March 2002, p. A-1.

Cook, David, "The Recovery of Radical Islam in the Wake of the Defeat of the Taleban," *Terrorism and Political Violence*, vol. 15, no. 1 (spring 2003), pp. 31–56.

———. "How the Afghan War Was Won," *Jane's Intelligence Review*, vol. 14, no. 2, (February 2002).

Daw, Bassam, "The United States' 'Racism,'" *Al-Watan*, 6 May 2002.

Doran, Michael, "The Pragmatic Fanaticism of al Qaeda: An Anatomy of Extremism in Middle Eastern Politics," *Political Science Quarterly*, vol. 117, no. 2 (summer 2002), pp. 177–190.

———. "Palestine, Iraq, and American Strategy," *Foreign Affairs*, vol. 82, no. 1 (January/February 2003), p. 19.

Eedle, Paul, "Al Qaeda Takes Fight for 'Hearts and Minds' to Web," *Jane's Intelligence Review*, vol. 14, no. 8 (August 2002).

Friedman, Thomas, "No Mere Terrorist," *New York Times*, 24 March 2002.

Fukuyama, Francis, "The Real Intelligence Failure?" *Wall Street Journal*, 5 August 2003.

Ghazi, Siavosh, "Defend Afghanistan: Interview with Gulbuddin Hekmatyar," *Le Soir*, 2 October 2001, p. 6.

Gunaratna, Rohan, "Confronting the West: Al Qaeda's Strategy after 11 September," *Jane's Intelligence Review*, vol. 14, no. 7 (July 2002).

Harris, Lee, "Al Qaeda's Fantasy Ideology," *Policy Review* (August/September 2002), pp. 19–36.

Hawkins, William R., "What Not to Learn from Afghanistan," *Parameters*, vol. 33, no. 2 (summer 2002).

Hayes, Stephen F., "Uncle Sam's Makeover," *Weekly Standard*, 3 June 2003.

Hekmatyar, Gulbuddin, "An Open Letter to the Leader of the Democratic Party of the United States and Members of His Party in Congress," *Afghan Islamic Press*, 7 October 2002.

Helprin, Mark, "Failing the Test of September 11," *Wall Street Journal*, 16 September 2002.

Hoffman, Bruce, "Rethinking Terrorism and Counterterrorism Since 9/11," *Studies in Conflict and Terrorism*, vol. 25 (2002), pp. 303–316.

———. "The Leadership Secrets of Osama Bin Laden: The Terrorist as CEO," *Atlantic Monthly* (April 2002), pp. 26–27.

Huwaydi, Fahni, "Interview with Afghan Leader Abd-Rab-al-Rasul Sayyaf," *Al-Sharq Al-Awsat*, 10 February 2002, p 6.

Ignatieff, Michael, "The American Empire (Get Used to It)," *New York Times Magazine*, 5 January 2003.

———. "Why Are We in Iraq? (And Liberia? And Afghanistan?)," *New York Times Magazine*, 7 September 2003.

Iqbal, Moshin, "Interview with Taleban Supreme Leader Mullah Mohammad Omar," *Pakistan*, 29 April 2002, p. 9.

Jenkins, Brian M., "This Time It Is Different," *San Diego Union-Tribune*, 16 September 2001.

Johnson, James Turner, "Jihad and Just War," *First Things: A Journal of Religion and Public Life* (June–July 2002), p. 12.

Jones, Martin Jones, "Out of Bali: Cybercaliphate Rising," *National Interest*, no. 71 (spring 2003), pp. 75–85.

Robert D. Kaplan, "Supremacy by Stealth," *Atlantic Monthly* (July–August 2003), pp. 65–83.

Kokita, Kiyohito, and Yuji Moronaga, "Terrorist Asks Writer to Compile a Biography—Testimony of Pakistanis Who Have Met with Bin Laden," *AERA Magazine*, 8 October 2001, pp. 18–20.

Kurtz, Stanley, "The Future of 'History': Francis Fukuyama vs. Samuel P. Huntington," *Policy Review* (June–July 2002), p. 43.

Lake, Eli J., "Noise Pollution: Al Qaeda's Misinformation War," *New Republic Online* (Internet), 4 November 2002.

Lewis, Bernard, "Time for Toppling," *Wall Street Journal*, 27 September 2002.

———. "Deconstructing Osama and His Evil Appeal," *Wall Street Journal*, 23 August 2002.

Lieven, Anatol, "The Empire Strikes Back," *The Nation*, 7 July 2003, pp. 25–30.

Lindberg, Tod, "Deterrence and Prevention," *Weekly Standard*, 3 February 2003.

Lobel, Jules, "The Use of Force to Respond to Terrorist Attacks: The Bombing of Afghanistan and Sudan," *Yale Journal of International Law*, vol. 24, no. 2 (summer 1999), p. 522.

Lowe, Christian, "Nation Building," *Weekly Standard.com* (Internet), 6 February 2003.

Lowe, Christopher, "What Not to Do: The Soviets' Afghanistan War," *Defense Week*, 1 October 2001, p. 1.

Massing, Michael, "Losing the Peace," *The Nation*, 13 May 2002, p. 11.

Mayer, Jane, "The House of Bin Laden," *New Yorker*, 12 November 2001.

——. "The Search for Osama," *New Yorker*, 4 August 2003.

Mullins, Dennis, "Call It By Any Other Name, It Still Adds Up to a Crusade," *New York Times*, 5 January 2003.

O'Hanlon, Michael, "A Flawed Masterpiece: Assessing the Afghan Campaign," *Foreign Affairs*, vol. 81, no. 3 (May/June 2003).

Paz, Re'uven, "Global Jihad and the United States: Interpretation of the New World Order of Usama Bin Ladin," *http://gloria.idc.ac.il* (Internet), 6 March 2003.

Peters, Ralph, "The New Warrior Class Revisited," *Small Wars and Insurgencies*, vol. 13, no. 2 (summer 2002), p. 16.

——. "The Plague of Ideas," *Parameters*, vol. 30, no. 4 (winter 2000).

——. "Rolling Back Radical Islam," *Parameters*, vol. 32, no. 3 (autumn 2002).

——. "The Saudi Threat," *Wall Street Journal*, 4 January 2002.

Pipes, Daniel, "Jihad and the Professors," *Commentary* (November 2002), pp. 17–21.

al-Qurashi, Abu-Ubayd, "The Autumn of Iraqi Fury," *Al-Ansar* (Internet), 24 August 2002.

——. "The Illusions of America," *Al-Ansar* (Internet), 22 September 2002.

——. "Al-Qaida and the Art of War," *Al-Neda* (Internet), 13 June 2002.

——. "The al-Aqsa Intifadah: a Fruitful Jihad and Continued Dedication," *Al-Ansar* (Internet), 8 October 2002.

——. "America's Nightmares," *Al-Ansar* (Internet), 13 February 2002.

——. "Why Did Baghdad Fall?" *Al-Ansar* (Internet), 17 April 2003.

——. "A Lesson in War," *Al-Ansar* (Internet), 19 December 2002.

Rashid, Ahmed, "The Other Front," *Wall Street Journal*, 11 February 2003.

——. "The Other Front (Cont.)," *Wall Street Journal*, 24 March 2003.

——. "Dangerous Neighbors," *Far Eastern Economic Review*, 19 January 2003.

——. "Taking the Initiative, Karzai Seeks to Extend Kabul's Writ," *Wall Street Journal*, 3 January 2003.

——. "The Net Tightens on Al Qaeda Cells," *Far Eastern Economic Review*, 13 March 2003.

Rohde, David, "Verses from Bin Ladin's War: Wielding the Pen as a Sword of Jihad," *New York Times*, 7 April 2002, p. 20.

Rubin, Barnett R., and Andrea Armstrong, "Regional Issues in the Reconstruction of Afghanistan," *World Policy Journal*, vol. 20, no. 1 (spring 2003).

Seaquist, Larry, "Bin Laden's Innovations," *Christian Science Monitor*, 8 August 2002, p. 9.

Seib, Gerald F., "What Bin Laden Is Doing and Why It Matters," *Wall Street Journal*, 19 February 2003.

Simon, Steven, "The New Terrorism: Securing the Nation against a Messianic Foe," *Brookings Review*, vol. 21, no. 1 (winter 2003) p. 18.

Stern, Jessica, "The Protean Enemy," *Foreign Affairs*, vol. 82, no. 4 (July–August 2003), p. 27.

Stone, Peter H., "Can We Fight Iraq and Hunt al-Qaida," *National Journal*, 22 February 2003, p. 579.

Traub, James, "Osama, Dead or Alive," *New York Times Magazine*, 29 December 2002, p. 7.

Weir, Fred, "Shifting Tactics in Chechnya," *Christian Science Monitor*, 30 December 2002, p. 1.

Zakaria, Fareed, "How to Fight the Fanatics," *Newsweek*, 9 December 2002.

———. "Don't Feed the Fundamentalists," *Newsweek*, 28 October 2002.

Index

The Author

☪

"Anonymous" is a senior U.S. intelligence official with nearly two decades of experience in national security issues related to Afghanistan and South Asia. Anonymous previously authored *Through Our Enemies' Eyes: Osama bin Laden, Radical Islam, and the Future of America.* As in that book, the author remains anonymous as the condition for securing his employer's permission to publish *Imperial Hubris.*

309